The Puzzle of Exi

MW00574915

This groundbreaking volume investigates the most fundamental question of all: Why is there something rather than nothing? The question is explored from diverse and radical perspectives: religious, naturalistic, platonistic, and skeptical. Does science answer the question? Or does theology? Does everything need an explanation? Or can there be brute, inexplicable facts? Could there have been nothing whatsoever? Or is there any being that could not have failed to exist? Is the question meaningful after all? The volume advances cutting-edge debates in metaphysics, philosophy of cosmology, and philosophy of religion and will intrigue and challenge readers interested in any of these subjects.

Tyron Goldschmidt is a lecturer in philosophy at the University of Wisconsin at Stevens Point, USA.

Routledge Studies in Metaphysics

The Puzzle of Existence

Why Is There Something Rather Than Nothing?

Edited by Tyron Goldschmidt

Routledge
Taylor & Francis Group

NEW YORK AND LONDON

First published 2013
by Routledge
711 Third Avenue, New York, NY 10017

Simultaneously published in the UK
by Routledge
2 Park Square, Milton Park, Abingdon, Oxfordshire OX14 4RN

First issued in paperback 2014

*Routledge is an imprint of the Taylor & Francis Group,
an informa business*

Library of Congress Cataloging-in-Publication Data
The puzzle of existence : why is there something rather than nothing? /
    edited by Tyron Goldschmidt. — 1 [edition].
        pages cm. — (Routledge studies in metaphysics ; 6)
    Includes bibliographical references and index.
    1. Ontology.   I. Goldschmidt, Tyron, 1982– editor of compilation.
    BD311.P89 2013
    111—dc23
    2012049727

ISBN 13: 978-0-415-62465-7 (hbk)
ISBN 13: 978-1-138-82344-0 (pbk)

Typeset in Sabon
by Apex CoVantage, LLC

For Yael and Hannah Tehillah

Contents

viii   *Contents*

1   Introduction
Understanding the Question

Tyron Goldschmidt

Why is there something rather than nothing? The question encapsulates the puzzle of existence. This chapter introduces the puzzle and the rest of the volume. After some terminological preliminaries in Section 1, Section 2 explains the puzzle by identifying and distinguishing more particular questions. Section 3 surveys the main answers that have been put forward and outlines the chapters in the rest of the volume, identifying their bearing on the different questions and on each other. There are a couple of original and pertinent points too.

1   PRELIMINARIES

A few philosophical notions are helpful in formulating the questions and are at work in the chapters that follow. Particularly prevalent are the pairs of notions of *concreteness* and *abstractness*, and *contingency* and *necessity*, and then, the trickiest of all, the notion of *possible worlds*.

Concreteness and Abstractness

The distinction between concrete and abstract beings has been drawn in various ways but usually by using spatiotemporal and causal criteria. On the spatiotemporal criterion, concrete beings are spatiotemporal: concrete beings are in space or time, whereas abstract beings are spaceless and time-less. On the causal criterion, concrete beings are causal in nature: concrete beings have causal powers, whereas abstract beings are powerless. There are then the tasks of providing more precise criteria for spatiotemporality and causal powers in turn. In any case, concrete beings are typically thicker and heavier, abstract beings thinner and wispier, and the categories mutually exclusive and exhaustive.

The spatiotemporal and causal criteria have similar extensions: planets and plants count as concrete on either, while numbers and propositions, as conceived by platonists, count as abstract on either. But they might not overlap entirely. On the one hand, there are candidates for spatiotemporal beings that are not causal: for example, spatiotemporal points. On the other hand, there are candidates for causal beings that are not spatiotemporal: for example, God. But these are controversial exceptions, both as to whether they exist and as to whether they are exceptions: some ascribe powers to spatiotemporal points, and spatiotemporality (or at least temporality) to God.

I take the criteria to be stipulative definitions; *concrete* and *abstract* are terms of art. When philosophers disagree about them they disagree only about how to use the terms, and not about the nature of things. Thus, we do not have to decide which is correct; we have only to decide how to use our terms.[1]

Contingency and Necessity

Contingent beings are things that both could exist and also could fail to exist, whereas necessary beings are things that could not fail to exist. Necessary beings have a stronger grip on reality than do contingent beings. Planets and plants are contingent beings. If the boundary conditions of the universe or natural laws were ever so slightly different, no planets would have formed, and even with the boundary conditions and natural laws there are, if the planet were ever so slightly nearer to or further from the sun, plants would not have evolved.

God, as traditionally conceived, would be a necessary being. God would not just *happen* to exist; if God exists at all, then God is the sort of being that could not have failed to exist. Other candidates for necessary beings are numbers and propositions (once again, as conceived by platonists), though these are controversial candidates, both as to their necessity and as to their very existence, which is at least as controversial as the existence of God.

The examples show that the categories of concrete and abstract, on the one hand, and contingent and necessary, on the other, could cut across each other. While most readily available examples of concrete beings are also contingent (thus plants and planets), there could be exceptions: for example, God would be concrete but necessary. Then there are abstract beings that are necessary (thus numbers and propositions), but there are also contingent abstract beings: for example, sets are abstract beings, but sets whose members are contingent—such as {Aristotle, the Eiffel Tower}—would themselves be contingent.

Possible Worlds

A possible world is a comprehensive way things could have been. The world could have contained many more planets than it does, and it could have

---

1. Peter van Inwagen (2007: 200) demurs, positing an essence of concreteness captured by none of our criteria but allowing that we don't need to know it to recognize the distinction between concrete and abstract beings or to identify instances of either.

contained fewer planets. There is thus a possible world containing more planets than does our world, and there is a possible world containing fewer planets. In contrast, there could never have been a square circle. There is thus no possible world containing a square circle. The actual world, the way things actually are, is a possible world because the way things are is a way things could have been.

Possible worlds have been said to *contain* beings, or (what is the same) beings have been said to exist in worlds. Possible worlds can also be said to *obtain* or *not to obtain*, or (what is the same) to be *actualized* or to be *unactualized*. The actual world is the possible world that obtains, whereas all other worlds are *merely* possible worlds. If a world contains a being or a being exists in a world, then if the world obtains, the being exists. Thus the actual world contains plants and planets, but only some merely possible world contains a unicorn.

The notion of possible worlds can help to explicate, or at least to make vivid, the notions of contingency and necessity just outlined. A contingent being, like a planet, is a being that exists in some possible worlds but not in all, while a necessary being, like God, is a being that exists in all possible worlds. One reason for believing in possible worlds is that they are useful in making sense of such and various other philosophical notions. The notion of possible worlds will be helpful in framing and distinguishing our questions, and some of the contributions also employ it.[2]

However, what exactly the notion amounts to—what the real nature of the worlds is, if it is anything at all—is the subject of extensive dispute, as are the notions of a world's obtaining or containing other beings. Some take worlds to be spatiotemporally discrete universes no less real than our own (and thus to be concrete), whereas others take them to be spaceless and timeless sets of propositions about how things could be (and thus to be abstract). Some take them to be merely a sort of useful fiction or heuristic (and thus to be nothing much at all), whereas others take them to be not-so-useful fictions (contrast Lewis 1986; Plantinga 1974; Rosen 1990; and Heil, this volume). As we will see, the debate bears crucially on the puzzle of existence.

2   THE QUESTIONS

The puzzle of existence can now be framed in terms of the notions introduced. More particularly, various fundamental questions about the world and the universe can be distinguished; one or more of these questions has been

---

2. Leibniz was the first to employ the notion of possible worlds and to frame the question "*why is there something rather than nothing?*" (see Leibniz 1989/1714: 210, italics in original; also see Leibniz 1989/1697). But he had something slightly smaller in mind by a possible world: what he meant was a possible divine creation. Thus on Leibniz's understanding God stands outside the system of possible worlds and could not coherently be said to exist in a world.

intended by the question "Why is there something rather than nothing?" The most frequently intended are the following.

Why Are There Any Beings at All?

This question asks why a world containing any beings obtains. This is the broadest question of all. The question would remain had any other world, no matter how radically different from our own, obtained; it would remain in a world containing only abstract beings, though of course there would be no one in such a world to ask it. The question amounts to a question about why any world obtains. After all, worlds are ways things could be, and without any ways or things—*beings* broadly construed—there can be no world. (The question should thus not be construed as a question about why a possible world containing some being obtains rather than a world containing no beings at all. The notion of such a perfectly empty world is incoherent.[3])

Why Are There Any Concrete Beings?

This question differs depending on the criterion of concreteness employed. On the spatiotemporal criterion, the question asks why a possible world containing beings in space or time obtains rather than a world containing no beings in space or time. On the causal criterion, it asks why a world containing beings with causal powers obtains. We could frame yet other criteria of concreteness, and thus other questions: for example, we could combine both criteria to ask why a world containing any spatiotemporal *or* causal beings obtains. The questions would remain in worlds containing spatiotemporal or causal beings—and even in a world containing only a particle, though there would then be no intelligent beings to ask it.

Why Are There Any Contingent Beings?

This question asks why a possible world containing any contingent being obtains. Assuming there are contingent beings, the question can be asked in our world and in worlds containing other contingent beings. When *beings* is construed so broadly as to cover contingent things of any kind (substances, events, sets, facts, etc.), perhaps every world will contain some contingent being—perhaps even a world containing no contingent substances or events would have to contain the very negative but contingent fact of there being no such beings. But *beings* can be construed more narrowly to mean substances

---

3. Or is my framing of the notion of a world as a *way things* could be not impartial enough? The notion of a world as a *comprehensive possibility* does not so immediately rule out a perfectly empty world. For my part, I don't really get the notion of such a bare possibility as there being nothing at all; compare Heil (this volume: 174–6).

(like planets or plants) or events (like battles or big bangs). The question would then ask why a world containing any such thing as a planet or a big bang obtains rather than a world containing no such beings, even should that world contain the contingent fact of there being no such beings. Yet another question combines the questions about concrete and contingent beings to ask why there are any beings that are *both* concrete and contingent.

Why Are There the Concrete/Contingent Beings There Are?

Besides the questions about why there are *any* concrete beings and *any* contingent beings, there are questions about why there are precisely the concrete and contingent beings there are. There is the question about why the particular collection or sum of concrete beings there are exists. This question would remain only in worlds containing all the concrete beings of our world. It is at least close to the question of why the universe exists, since *the universe* could mean the sum of all spatiotemporal things related to us or, alternatively, the sum of all things causally related to us. But there might be concrete beings beyond our universe—there might be multiple other universes of concrete beings, a multiverse. The question about why *any* universe exists could coincide with the question about why any concrete being exists.

The question about why the particular contingent beings there are exist would differ depending on the meaning of *beings*—again, whether this covers any kind of contingent being or only substances and events. On the broadest interpretation of *beings*, possible worlds are distinguished by the contingent beings they contain. The question would then ask why our particular world obtains rather than some other possible world. This question is less general than the previous ones in the sense that it can't be asked in any other world. Of course, the inhabitants of some other world can ask why their world obtains; if theirs were actualized, then that would be a fair enough question, at least as fair as the question about why the actual world obtains.[4] But their question is not why *this*—our—world obtains. In contrast, the previous questions can be asked in other worlds. The first question would remain in any world whatsoever, the second in any world containing concrete beings, and the third in any world containing contingent beings.

---

4. Might philosophical inhabitants of other worlds realize that our world, and not theirs, is actualized and ask why that is so? Or perhaps ours is the world that is merely possible; after all, there are far more merely possible worlds than the one actualized world. This teasing thought harbors some mistake about the nature of worlds (see Armstrong 1989: 14)—or else we think too much of ourselves. On Lewis's view of possible worlds as concrete universes of a kind with our own (see Lewis 1986), we do not think too much of ourselves so much as not enough of the inhabitants of other worlds.

Why Do Concrete/Contingent Beings Exist *Now*?

Less frequently asked, but worth distinguishing from the previous questions, are questions about why there exist concrete beings *now*, and why there *now* are the contingent beings there are. These questions differ from the previous ones. We could imagine worlds identical to our own up until, but not including, the present moment, when the beings then pop out of existence. Such worlds would still contain concrete beings, and if they obtained the question about why there are such beings would remain. But the questions about why the beings exist *now* can't be properly asked since they don't—at least on criteria of concreteness that do not count the present moment as concrete, for otherwise there could be no *now* without concrete beings. Similarly, the worlds could contain all the contingent substances there are, albeit with gappy or truncated lives, and if they obtained the question about why these beings exist would remain, though not the question about why they exist now.

There are yet other questions about why things continue to exist, perdure, or endure, over other times: Where do things find their continuing source of ontological fuel? What grounds their existential inertia? Doubtless the inhabitants of worlds where things don't run so smoothly would face their own pressing questions.

Why Is There Not a Void?

Another question that is less frequently asked but worth distinguishing is about why a world containing only a void does not obtain, where a void would be something like an empty space-time, a totally dark and vast abyss. When addressing the questions about why there are concrete or contingent beings, there's a tendency to try to represent the alternative as a void. So long as the void is itself concrete or contingent this is a misrepresentation. For example, if the question is about why any world containing concrete beings obtains, and a void counts as concrete (since spatiotemporal), then the alternative is not accurately represented by a void; when asking, "Why is there something rather than nothing?" the "nothing" is not a name for a void, an especially thin being but concrete nonetheless.

Once again, there are yet other cosmological questions about the void or at least void-like states of affairs. These are motivated by contemporary scientific proposals that the universe arose from a quantum vacuum. How did the universe arise from a quantum vacuum? Why was the quantum vacuum on the scene in the first place? The first question is close to one about why the universe exists if *the universe* is taken to cover only states of affairs subsequent to the quantum vacuum; the second question is closer if *the universe* covers everything spatiotemporal or causal and the quantum vacuum counts as spatiotemporal or causal.

These are enough questions for now; we turn to canvassing a few answers. The projects of understanding a question and of answering it are related in both directions: while there is no prospect of answering a question without some understanding of what is being asked, understanding what would count as an answer also helps in understanding the question.

3 THE ANSWERS

All the above questions are *why-questions*, and the answers to such are *explanations*. There are other kinds of responses to the questions—responses denying that there is any explanation to be had or contending that the questions are somehow nonsensical or ill-formed. Many answers have been proposed for the many questions posed, more even than can be covered in our wide-ranging volume. However, the answers to a few of the questions are typically of a few kinds. We can now trace the most popular of these (*popularity* being a very relative matter among philosophers), along with the questions they promise to answer and those they hold no promise for. We'll also outline the chapters that follow and explore how they bear on traditional answers and on each other.

Necessary Being

By far the most traditional answer is in terms of God, conceived of as a necessary being. Indeed, the most traditional argument for the existence of God is just that God's existence would answer one or more of our questions—including the questions about why concrete beings exist, why contingent beings exist, and why all these continue to exist. Hence, the various versions of the cosmological argument.

The question about why concrete beings exist (on either the causal or the spatiotemporal criterion) would be answered in terms of the existence of God. God would count as concrete on the causal criterion, and indeed as necessarily concrete—since God, being essentially omnipotent, could not fail to have causal power. There would thus be a necessary and necessarily concrete being. This would mean that there being a concrete being is necessary; in terms of possible worlds, that all possible worlds contain a concrete being. One way of explaining why a kind of being exists is by showing that it had to exist, and so the existence of concrete beings would be explained.

Assuming that God is not spatial or temporal, God would not count as concrete on the spatiotemporal criterion. However, the existence of God still provides the resources for explaining why there are any spatiotemporal beings: so long as God has power enough to bring about such spatiotemporal beings, these beings could be explained in terms of God exercising this power. The explanation would be a causal explanation, rather than the kind of necessitarian explanation proffered for the existence of any beings with causal powers. That question can have no causal explanation, since such an explanation postulates yet another being with causal powers. But there is no such trouble in a causal explanation of why there are any spatiotemporal beings. Thus, while the answers to each question are in terms of the existence of God, they invoke diverse attributes: necessity and power respectively.

Since spatiotemporal beings compose the universe, an explanation of why there are any spatiotemporal beings would begin to explain why there is a universe. Furthermore, since spatiotemporal beings are typically taken to be contingent, the answer begins to address the questions about why there are contingent beings—because God brings them about.

However, at this point the explanation becomes especially problematic. The divine causation would itself be either necessary or contingent. If it were necessary, then there would be no contingency after all, since what is necessarily caused by a necessary being is itself necessary. If it were contingent, then it would either be unexplained or have an explanation. If it were unexplained, then there would be no ultimate explanation of all contingency after all. If it were explained, then the explanatory factor would either be necessary or contingent. Once again, a necessary explanatory factor threatens contingency, whereas a contingent explanatory factor threatens the prospects for an ultimate explanation of all contingency—or an infinite regress or an explanatory circle (for example, in a self-explanatory contingent being).

There have been various reactions to the above explanatory predicament. Pressed towards ultimate explanation, some philosophers prefer to relinquish all contingency. Spatiotemporal beings would then be necessary—they might even be identical to or necessary emanations of God. There would thus be an explanation of the existence of spatiotemporal beings in terms of necessity or necessary emanation rather than contingent causation. Balking at such consequences, other philosophers relinquish any hope for an ultimate explanation and settle for an inexplicable, brute fact—in the realm of spatiotemporal things or beyond. Yet others countenance ultimate yet contingent explanations, especially a self-explanatory contingent being or a necessary being whose *contingent causing* of other beings is self-explanatory (compare, for example, Della Rocca 2010 and Pruss 2006).

In Chapter 2 of this volume, Timothy O'Connor defends the prospects of an ultimate explanation of all contingent beings in terms of a necessary, transcendent being—so long as the explanation does not require *contrastive* explanation in every case. There will sometimes be no explanation for why a certain being exists *rather than* some other, but O'Connor shows how there being no such explanation can itself be explicable and unproblematic, before addressing various objections against the model of explanation he advances and against the project of pursuing an ultimate explanation altogether.

In Chapter 3, Graham Oppy argues that ultimate explanation is more likely naturalistic than transcendent, whether or not the terminus of explanation is in a necessary being or a contingent being, and indeed whether or not there is a terminus of explanation altogether. Oppy focuses on explanations of causal beings, and thus on the question of why there is anything concrete on the causal criterion. Neither O'Connor nor Oppy promises a definitive demonstration of their respective views, and both emphasize that their arguments rest on diverse and disputed philosophical theories, particularly about modality, causation, and explanation—but that's hardly a special problem for either position since *all* substantive philosophical views rest on contentious theories.

Chapter 4 by Shieva Kleinschmidt and Chapter 5 by Jacob Ross explore how far and deep explanation can go. They focus on the Principle of Sufficient Reason (PSR), which states that every truth, or at least every *contingent* truth, has an explanation. The PSR is at the heart of the traditional cosmological argument from contingency, and it is also thought to motivate the question of why there are contingent beings: if the PSR is true, then there must be some explanation of the fact that there are any contingent beings (and presumably an explanation invoking something outside the realm of contingent beings, namely, a necessary being); if there is no explanation, then there will be some brute, inexplicable contingency, and the pursuit of an ultimate explanation is in vain.

Kleinschmidt and Ross respectively respond to the most influential arguments for and against the PSR. Kleinschmidt contends that the argument *for* the PSR fails but that an alternative explanatory principle that the argument points towards is perfectly consistent with there being an explanation for why there are any contingent beings. Ross contends that the argument *against* the PSR fails but that the reason why it fails itself threatens the traditional cosmological argument: once saved from the objection, the PSR no longer implies the existence of a necessary being.

Chapter 6 by Christopher Hughes is a close study of another kind of cosmological argument for a necessary being. Besides (something very close to) the PSR, such arguments advert to a controversial premise about how contingent beings compose a whole. Hughes explores the metaphysics of composition and pluralities, supporting the premise and showing how the argument doesn't require it anyhow—all the while leaving open the possibility of diverse reactions to the argument, from rational acceptance to rational skepticism.

Aside from the cosmological argument, there is another traditional argument for a necessary divine being—the ontological argument. The argument introduces the being not to explain why there is something rather than nothing, but via the concept of a-being-than-which-no-greater-can-be-conceived. Such a being would have to be all-powerful (and so concrete on the causal criterion) and thus capable of bringing about contingent and spatiotemporal beings. Pure reflection on the concept of a-being-than-which-no-greater-can-be-conceived is supposed to reveal that the being exists: indeed, it cannot even be conceived not to exist, since otherwise we could conceive of an even greater being—one that could *not* be conceived not to exist—but we cannot conceive of a being greater than the being than which no greater is conceivable.

Such a line of reasoning strikes many as sheer philosophical mischief. Yet traditional objections fail to identify where exactly it goes wrong or are avoided by slight improvements to the argument—the argument as well as the objections have undergone various epicycles. Most recently, Peter Millican (2004) has framed an objection identifying how exactly the ontological argument falters. In Chapter 7, Earl Conee discovers some defects in this treatment and carefully formulates improved versions of both the ontological argument and the objection. This proposes an insurmountable critique that won't be overcome by subsequent reformulations of the ontological argument—an-objection-than-which-no-greater-can-be-conceived.

Goodness Gracious

Another kind of answer is given in extreme axiarchism, the view that ethical requirements are creatively effective: the universe exists simply because its existence would be good, without any intermediate mechanism bringing it about because it is good, without an intermediate God bringing it about for a good purpose. The ethical requirements have been taken to be necessary beings and necessarily creatively effective. The alternative of taking the ethical requirements to be contingent or contingently creatively effective would allow for the possibility of there being nothing but would leave the existence and creative efficacy of the ethical requirements unexplained.

Extreme axiarchism can be framed as a form of Spinozism, with necessary ethical requirements necessitating our particular universe and all its features—with whatever costs accrue to the denial of the contingency of and in our universe. The view can also be framed theologically, with the ethical requirements being responsible for the existence of a divine being or even identified with God, albeit conceived of a little more abstractly than usual (see Rice 2000).[5] Extreme axiarchism will then face some of the same criticisms as other theological answers, particularly those invoking divine goodness in explaining why there is anything at all. Most salient is the problem of evil: Why would a perfectly good God permit the existence of evil? Why would creatively effective ethical requirements? But then the same kind of response is available in each case: for example, there might be reasons in higher-order goods that cannot be had without the existence of evil, though on extreme axiarchism they cannot be the reasons *of* any being.

The most frequent objection raised against extreme axiarchism is that the explanatory relation between ethical requirements and the universe is mysterious: what is it for such abstract beings to bring anything about? The appeal of axiarchic explanations might trade on the plausibility of purposive explanations in terms of agents recognizing and acting on ethical

---

5. According to Rescher (2000: 157–8), such principles can be *self-explanatory*: efficacious ethical requirements exist because *that* is good.

requirements—but once stripped of purpose and agent, explanation in terms of such requirements alone becomes less intelligible.

This objection is hardly a decisive advantage for traditional purposive explanations of our universe—for how any transcendent being brings about all of space and time will be mysterious to beings so conditioned to think about *bringing about* in terms of their own acts within space and time. And that is not a decisive advantage for other explanations in turn. After all, causation within space and time is a conundrum, deepened by the very weird interactions discovered by science. No surprise then that the transcendent and original source of the universe—whether a traditional divine being or a more abstract ethical requirement—will be puzzling. Compare Derek Parfit in this connection: "If there is some explanation of the whole of reality, we shouldn't expect this explanation to fit neatly into some familiar category. This extraordinary question may have an extraordinary answer" (2011: 633; compare Nozick 1981: 116).

In Chapter 8, John Leslie defends extreme axiarchism, particularly in comparison with other answers to the question of why the universe exists and against various objections. With an elegant, sweeping review of the Platonic tradition, Leslie develops extreme axiarchism into a radical Spinozism (*radical* even by the standards of Spinozism) on which our universe and universes beyond are necessary and divine, the thoughts of infinitely many infinite minds. Even without such pantheistic and polytheistic embellishments, such extreme axiarchism is not a traditional kind of theism, but Leslie contends it is nevertheless worthy of the term.

If the ethical requirements emanate our particular concrete universe, so that the universe turns out to be a necessary being, extreme axiarchism comports with answers in terms of necessary being. But extreme axiarchism need not entail that the ethical requirements emanate our universe. They might instead have to emanate some concrete universe or other, but not necessarily *our* universe. In that case, extreme axiarchism would comport with the next kind of answer.

Being Necessarily

There are other answers to the question about why there are concrete beings—causal or spatiotemporal—in terms of the necessity of there being concrete beings or a universe but without invoking any necessary concrete beings: there had to be some or other concrete beings but without any particular one being necessary; in terms of possible worlds, every world contains some concrete beings, but no concrete being need exist in all possible worlds. If a universe is just a sum of concrete beings, then this would also answer the question about why a universe exists.

There are a few arguments for this kind of answer, and a few of these arguments draw from the metaphysics of modality: very general theories of the nature of possibility and possible worlds. Two of the most prominent theories of the nature of possible worlds entail that every world contains some concrete being or other.

The first is David Lewis's modal realism: possible worlds are causally and spatiotemporally isolated sums of spatiotemporally related beings—nothing very different *fundamentally* from our own universe, though quite a few contain talking giraffes, and such like. Every world contains some spatio-temporal being, and thus some concrete being, at least on the spatiotem-poral criterion (see Lewis 1986). Lewis accepted this consequence but then rejected its relevance for explaining why there is something rather than noth-ing on the grounds that explanation must be in terms of causes whereas the explanation here is not (see Lewis 1986: 73–4). However, these are strange grounds since not every explanation need be causal; there are other kinds of explanation—explanations in fields as diverse as mathematics and moral-ity do not typically take a causal form. I should think that solving another philosophical puzzle counts in favor of Lewis's theory.

The second relevant metaphysics of modality is David Armstrong's com-binatorial theory: possible worlds are diverse combinations of the particu-lars and properties of our own world. Thus there are worlds containing talking giraffes, constructed out of the camelopardalic particulars and lo-quacious properties of our own world. There is also the possibility of barer landscapes, contracted worlds containing fewer things than our world does; even though other worlds must be constructed only from the ingredients of our world, they need not contain all of these ingredients. However, there is no perfectly empty world. All worlds, however contracted they may be, are constructions, even if of only a single particular and a simple property. Furthermore, on Armstrong's naturalism, all the particulars and properties of our world are spatiotemporal, and thus every world would contain some concrete being (see Armstrong 1989).

Unlike Lewis's worlds, Armstrong's are not just as real as our own; merely possible worlds are mere fictions. On Lewis's view, talking giraffes exist as much as do the more reserved kind, even if nowhere near us; on Armstrong's view, talking giraffes exist merely in fictions, if that is even so much as ex-istence. Similarly, other modal theories make for a deep divide between the actual world and what it contains and other possible worlds and what they contain—the merely possible beings they contain would exist if the world were actualized, but they don't exist and the worlds aren't actualized. There is the question about why our world has this special ontological distinc-tion. In contrast, Lewis views actuality as perfectly indexical; being actual is being a part of the world we inhabit and confers no ontological distinction.

Unlike Armstrong's theory, Lewis's would explain not only why there are any concrete beings but also why there are the contingent beings there are. On Lewis's view, beings are contingent insofar as they not do not exist in every world—but not insofar as they could have failed to exist altogether. For the worlds themselves could not have failed to exist. After all, they are supposed to provide the ontological applications for modal discourse that is necessarily true; the worlds are supposed to be possibilities, and what is possible is necessarily possible (at least in some cases, and in all if S5 captures the logic of modality). Even though giraffes do not exist in every world, those worlds in which they do exist are just as real as our own and could not have failed to exist, so that ultimately the giraffes could not have failed to exist.

However, these consequences are problematic. The original meaning of "a contingent being"—a being that could have failed to exist altogether—is distorted (compare the criticism in van Inwagen 1986), and the theory fails to secure the existence of such beings. Meanwhile, concrete worlds themselves *appear* to be contingent, whereas they would have to exist necessarily. Contrast rival modal theories that introduce abstract worlds: the kinds of entities the worlds are typically reduced to, e.g. sets of propositions, do not appear contingent.

Answers depending on Lewis's modal theory inherit these and other problems. Answers depending on Armstrong's theory inherit the problems facing that theory. One serious problem is that the theory fails to accommodate the possibility of certain beings that could have existed but do not, alien particulars and properties (see Schneider 2002). For example, fundamental physical properties unlike those of our world appear possible; the possibility is supported by considering contracted worlds where there are only the fundamental properties there are in ours but not all of them—if alien properties are possible relative to those worlds, then why not relative to ours? However, such properties cannot be constructed from recombinations of properties in our world, and so their possibility is excluded by Armstrong's theory.

David Efird and Tom Stoneham have contributed widely to the debate about whether there could have been nothing concrete, and have contended that modal realism and combinatorialism can and should be reworked in ways that permit that possibility: modal realism can be extended to permit a world constituted by abstract beings, and combinatorialism to permit a world constructed out of no particulars and properties (see Efird and Stoneham 2005a, 2006). Chapter 9 by Efird and Stoneham is a methodological exposition on how to deal with conflicts between particular views about what is possible and more general modal theories about what possibility is, especially in the context of the debate over the possibility of there being nothing concrete.

Chapter 10 by John Heil explores how philosophical thinking about possibility and necessity is conditioned by problematic, if sometimes imperceptible, assumptions. Quite at odds with Efird and Stoneham, Heil is suspicious about the prospects of even framing such far-fetched possibilities as there being nothing whatsoever or there being nothing concrete. He proposes an alternative view on which there had to have been concrete beings, and a universe like ours in particular, while allowing for some contingency arising out of its indeterministic functioning. Heil's guiding principle is that there is no presumption in favor of every or any thing being contingent—proposals about contingency require as much support as do those about necessity.

There remain other arguments, arguments not appealing to any modal theory, for the conclusion that there had to be some concrete beings or other but without any particular one being necessary. E.J. Lowe (1996, 1998) proposes an argument appealing to the nature of abstract beings—particularly that

(1) some abstract beings necessarily exist;
(2) the only possible kinds of abstract beings are sets and universals;
(3) sets depend upon non-sets (their members); and
(4) universals depend on non-universals (their instances).

Premise (1) is grounded on numbers being the truthmakers for the necessary truths of mathematics, and (2) on considerations of parsimony. Premise (3) is grounded in the rejection of the empty set and, what is a consequence, any pure set, and (4) on an immanent realism requiring that every universal have a particular instantiation. With premises (1) to (4) in place, the argument proceeds simply: if there could be only sets and universals, then the sets would have to depend on the universals, and the universals would depend on the sets in turn, which is a vicious circle of dependence. Thus there could not only be sets and universals. Thus, since sets and universals are the only possible kinds of abstract beings, there could not only be abstract beings; abstract beings depend on concreta. Therefore, since necessarily some abstract beings exist, necessarily some concrete beings exist.

In Chapter 11, Lowe updates his argument and answers various objections leveled against his views about abstract beings and the relations between abstract and concrete beings. Most saliently, he explains how the necessary existence of abstract beings—what I've listed as premise (1)—is not required for the original dialectical context of the argument. Even leaving open the possibility that there could have been no abstract beings, and that there could have been neither abstract beings nor concrete beings, the argument would show that there could not have been *only* abstract beings, which was what the argument was originally supposed to show to be impossible anyhow.

The Possibility of Nothing

We've seen a few answers appealing to the necessity of there being something (or other) concrete or, what is the same, the impossibility of there being nothing concrete. They are thus threatened by arguments for metaphysical nihilism, the thesis that there being nothing concrete is possible. The most significant of these is the subtraction argument, which has attracted considerable recent debate (see Coggins 2010).

Thomas Baldwin introduced the argument as follows:

(A1) There might be a world with a finite domain of "concrete" objects.

(A2) These concrete objects are, each of them, things which might not exist.
(A3) The nonexistence of any one of these things does not necessitate the existence of any other such thing. (1996: 232)

By (A1), there could have been finitely many concrete beings—ten, say, including $b10$, $b9$, $b8$, and so on. By (A2), all these beings could exist minus poor little $b10$. By (A3), no other being would need to take its place. So there could have been fewer finitely many concrete beings, nine in our case. Wash, rinse, and repeat—until you recognize that there could have been only one concrete being, little $b1$. By (A2), $b1$ could have failed to exist, and by (A3) no other being would need to have taken its stead—that is, there could have been no concrete beings whatsoever.

Those proposing the answers outlined above will dispute the premises of this argument. Proponents of a necessary concrete being will deny that all concrete beings are contingent, contrary to premise (A2). Proponents of the view that there had to be something or other will insist that, were there only one concrete being, its nonexistence would require another concrete being in its place, contrary to (A3). Whether these are plausible moves depends on whether the premises they start from—for example, the existence of a necessary being, or modal realism—are more plausible than those of the subtraction argument.

However, much of the criticism of the subtraction argument focuses on premise (A1). There are problems in securing a finite number of concrete beings. For example, if unit sets of concrete beings are themselves concrete, then, for any concrete being, there will in turn be the concrete unit set of that being, and the concrete unit set of that concrete unit set, and so on *ad infinitum*. Then there are problems arising from the infinite number of space-time parts and overlapping regions contained in regions of space-time, and problems arising from the infinite number of arbitrary undetached parts of concrete beings, each occupying one of the infinitely many regions occupied by the beings—for example, the top half of little $b1$, the top half minus a particular point, the top half minus another point, and so on.

These problems have been avoided in two ways: first, by denying that there need be infinitely many unit sets of concrete beings, infinitely many space-time points or regions, or infinitely many arbitrary undetached parts of concrete beings; and, second, by framing criteria of concreteness that don't count the infinitely many beings as concrete. For example, a spatio-temporal criterion restricting concreteness to beings existing "in" space and time, but not the space-time points or regions themselves, would not recognize an infinite number of such points or regions as concrete (see Gonzalo Rodriguez-Pereyra 1997; Lowe 2002).

A few of the criteria of concreteness employed in versions of the subtraction argument are a little different from those introduced above. For example, on Baldwin's criterion concrete beings are those not obeying the identity of indiscernibles, where a being obeys the identity of indiscernibles just in case no other being could share its intrinsic properties. These criteria of concreteness allow for framing yet further questions about why there are any concrete beings in terms employing the criteria.

However, with so many criteria there's risk of the subtraction argument losing its sting. If the argument shows only that there could have been no concrete beings on a certain criterion, but not that there could have been none on another criterion, then the argument does not threaten the view that the existence of concrete beings on the other criterion is necessary—and the question about why such beings exist might be more pressing for us. For example, if the subtraction argument successfully shows only that there could have been no beings "in" space and time, it won't eliminate answers in terms of a necessary being for questions employing a broader criterion of concreteness.

Chapter 12 by Gonzalo Rodriguez-Pereyra develops his version of the subtraction argument. The argument avoids the problem of infinitely many concrete beings by employing the trickier notion of a *concrete** being. However, Rodriguez-Pereyra shows how the possibility of there being nothing concrete* entails the possibility of there being nothing concrete on a broader spatiotemporal criterion. He then tries to show how his version of the subtraction argument is superior to a version formulated by Efird and Stoneham (2005b).

Even if the subtraction argument demonstrated the possibility of there being nothing concrete on every criterion of concreteness, that would not destroy the prospects of answering the question about why there are any concrete beings at all. There are answers that countenance the possibility of there being none whatsoever.

The Probability of Something

Robert Nozick (1981) and Peter van Inwagen (1996) put forward an answer to our question in terms of the probability of concrete beings, rather than their necessity. The answer thus countenances the possibility of there being nothing concrete and avoids the threat of the subtraction argument. The line of reasoning supporting this answer can be summarized as follows:

(1) There are more possible worlds containing concrete beings than possible worlds containing no concrete beings.
(2) All possible worlds have an equal intrinsic probability of obtaining.
(3) Therefore, a possible world containing concrete beings has a higher intrinsic probability of obtaining.

Indeed, van Inwagen proposes that the probability of a possible world containing concrete beings is as high as can be—since there are infinitely many such worlds whereas there is at most one world containing no concrete beings. But perhaps there could be many such worlds—differing in terms of the abstract beings they contain, e.g. transcendent universals or contingent counterfactuals. In any case, there would remain a greater proportion of worlds containing concrete beings.

More pressing is an objection rejecting premise (2) for a principle assigning simpler possibilities higher probabilities—indeed, Leibniz originally pressed our question on the presumption that the simplest and most probable state of affairs is there being nothing: "the first question we have the right to ask will be, *why is there something rather than nothing?* For nothing is simpler and easier than something?" (1989/1714: 210, italics in original).[6]

Van Inwagen supports his assignment of probabilities via various analogies: for example, a computer spontaneously generated out of an evaporating black hole would as likely contain a novel written in French as English as German. However, the analogies might trade on the wrong kinds of probability—for example, physical probability, which would measure how near or far a state of affairs (the computer containing an English novel) is from being determined by prior states of affair (the evaporating black hole). That kind of probability cannot be at work in the argument; there is no question of the physical probability of any world obtaining since there is no prior state of affairs.[7] The probability involved in the argument is instead of an intrinsic, and rather recondite, kind.

While the probabilistic answer addresses the question about why there are any concrete beings, it does not answer our other question about why the contingent beings there are exist. Indeed, it deepens this puzzles since the probability of our contingent order obtaining—given all the infinite number of alternatives—would be very low. But the argument might hold some promise for another question not raised above: why does such a complex universe exist? After all, there are more ways there could be complexity than simplicity: with more beings comes more possible arrangements. Like the others, the probabilistic answer would have costs as well as benefits.

In Chapter 13, Matthew Kotzen addresses the probabilistic argument as it bears both on the question of why there are any concrete beings, and also on the more particular question of why there are material beings. He illustrates further cases where possibilities are properly assigned equal probabilities as well as cases where such an assignment would be crazy—including cases where the possibilities are isolated and maximal, such as possible worlds are. Consideration of such scenarios shows when exactly we are

---

6. If simpler states have higher intrinsic probabilities of obtaining, then could the simple original conditions (e.g. of the universe or of a divine being) have been less probable than there being nothing concrete, but nevertheless not very improbable—so that there remains a puzzle of why there are concrete beings rather than none, but the puzzle is a little reduced? Compare Swinburne (1991: 288–9).

7. Neither does epistemic probability play any role. That would measure the extent to which a hypothesis is supported by evidence. We hardly need point out that the epistemic probability that the empty world obtains is 0.

justified in assigning equal probabilities to possibilities—when we have *a posteriori* grounds, which we do not have in the case of possible worlds. Kotzen concludes that the probabilistic answer fails.

Down to Earth and Up Again

Perhaps the answers to our questions are not to be had in these or any philosophical speculations, but in the domain of science. Recent popular science literature points to speculation about how our complex universe emerged from very simple original conditions: since simple states in nature tend to be unstable and give rise to more complex states, the very simple original conditions would likely give rise to a more complex state, such as a universe (see Wilczek 1989; Stenger 2007: 135). The original conditions are so simple—empty of space, time, mass, and energy—that the theories are then advertised as explaining how something comes from "nothing" (see Krauss 2012; Hawking and Mlodinow 2010).

These theories promise answers to some of our questions, e.g. about why the universe exists (so long as *the universe* is taken to mean only what is subsequent to the simple original conditions) and about why there are any concrete beings (so long as by *concrete* we mean such spatiotemporal beings as those constituting the universe). But there remain questions about why the original conditions existed and were governed by such natural laws as to give rise to the universe. Until these are answered, science has not explained why there are any contingent beings rather than none at all.

Science has also not explained why there are any concrete beings on the causal criterion of concreteness. For the original conditions have causal powers—the disposition or tendency to give rise to a more complicated state of affairs—and would themselves count as concrete. Indeed, science *in principle* cannot explain why there are any causal beings if it is the very nature of scientific explanations to invoke causes. Some give up hope of science ever resolving our deepest questions (see Parfit 2011: 623; Swinburne 1998: 428).

There might yet be prospects of a scientific explanation if such explanation extends beyond causal explanation. Chapter 14 by Marc Lange outlines a noncausal scientific explanation of why there are any contingent beings. The explanation invokes laws of nature: natural laws could necessitate (without causing) there being some contingent beings. The laws would themselves appear to demand explanation, especially if they too are contingent. But Lange considers laws not to be the kind of *thing* the question is about—indeed, not to be "things" at all so much as "facts". Contingent things could then be explained in terms of contingent laws, without requiring an explanation of the laws in turn. In our terminology, the answer explains why there are contingent, concrete beings by invoking laws that, while contingent, are not the kind of concrete being the question is about. Natural laws are contingent, abstract beings.

The answer then depends on a conception of natural laws as abstract beings that are metaphysically prior to, and so can explain the existence of, concrete beings. Alternative views have natural laws as the conjunctions of concrete events (the Humean view; see Lewis 1994 for a contemporary variation) or the shared disposition of concrete substances (the essentialist view; see Bird 2007). If such views are correct, then concrete beings are metaphysically prior to natural laws, and the answer fails. However, the explanatory power of the view of natural laws might be a reason for accepting it. Lange's view has yet another advantage: by taking natural laws to be contingent, abstract beings, we can allow for the possibility of there being no laws, and hence no laws necessitating concrete beings—and hence the possibility of there being nothing concrete, the possibility supported by the subtraction argument. Even if the probabilistic answer fails, Lange provides the resources for explaining why there are concrete beings without ruling out the possibility of there being none.

Challenging the Question

Lange sketches how a scientific answer in terms of natural laws might go but leaves it to future science to discover what exactly the relevant natural laws and beings they necessitate are. That requires nothing less than our discovering the fundamental structure of the universe. In Chapter 15, Stephen Maitzen advances an easier empirical answer, no more requiring a final physics or cosmology than a superficial zoology: there are contingent, concrete beings because penguins exist. Since penguins are essentially contingent, concrete beings, the existence of penguins entails the existence of concrete, contingent beings. The entailment of one fact by another is often enough for an explanation, and is so in this case, but we even have a pretty good explanation of why penguins exist in turn.

The explanation appears not so much as a bad answer to our deepest questions as not an answer at all—the explanation appears to fail altogether at addressing the question of why there is that sum of contingent/concrete beings of which penguins are a mere part, or why there are any of the kind of contingent/concrete beings of which penguins are mere instances. Maitzen replies that insofar as our questions cannot be answered in terms of the existence of penguins, this is not because they are deep but because they are ill-formed: the questions don't so much as make sense. Those that make sense are superficial and solved perfectly in terms of penguins. All other questions are to be *dissolved*.

Chapter 16 by Kris McDaniel challenges the significance of the question of why there is something rather than nothing in another way. He contends that, as sometimes posed, the question very well might have a quite teenagerish answer: there is something rather than nothing because had there been nothing, the absence of beings would exist, and so there'd be something after all, even if only an absence. That shows that the question is shallow. The question about why there are any concrete beings is shallow, too: neither the something/nothing nor the concrete/abstract distinctions are metaphysically fundamental—neither carve reality at the joints—and McDaniel contends that deep questions must employ distinctions that are fundamental.

McDaniel draws on the view that things can exist in fundamentally different ways and to different degrees in order to frame different questions: Why are there any things with such-and-such a way of being rather than no such things? Why are there any beings with such-and-such a degree of being? Framing the question in terms of distinctions between fundamental modes of being that carve reality at the joints might prove more promising. Ultimately, however, McDaniel thinks that the prospects of a deep question are at best unclear.

Perhaps, by this stage, we've been too taken in by the questions for them to lose their grip on us. But if the proposed answers we've considered still seem to be getting at (perhaps even answering) deep questions that "because there are penguins" doesn't, then we're at least left with the challenge of figuring out what exactly those questions are.

4   CONCLUSION

The puzzle of existence has received less attention than other fundamental questions; at least, the literature devoted *directly* to it is much sparser than that devoted to, say, the problem of universals, the problem of free will or the problem of consciousness. But the puzzle bears as much on our deepest commitments (at least if it is meaningful, and the question of its meaningfulness deserves consideration for that reason). It bears on various topics in metaphysics, philosophy more generally, and beyond. This volume brings together exciting new work in metaphysics, philosophy of religion, and philosophy of science and hopefully will bring the puzzle a little more of the attention it deserves.[8]

REFERENCES

Armstrong, D.M. (1989). *A Combinatorial Theory of Possibility*. Cambridge: Cambridge University Press.

Baldwin, T. (1996). 'There Might Be Nothing', *Analysis*, 56, 231–8.

Bird, A. (2007). *Nature's Metaphysics: Laws and Properties*. Oxford: Oxford University Press.

Coggins, G. (2010). *Could There Have Been Nothing? Against Metaphysical Nihilism*. New York: Palgrave-Macmillan.

Della Rocca, M. (2010). 'PSR', *Philosophers' Imprint*, 10:7, 1–13.

Efird, D. and Stoneham, T. (2005a). 'Genuine Modal Realism and the Empty World', *European Journal of Analytic Philosophy*, 1:1, 21–38.

———. (2005b). 'The Subtraction Argument for Metaphysical Nihilism', *Journal of Philosophy*, 102:6, 269–80.

---

8. Thanks to Thomas Flint for comments and discussion.

———. (2006). 'Combinatorialism and the Possibility of Nothing', *Australasian Journal of Philosophy*, 84:2, 269–80.

Hawking, S.W. and Mlodinow, L. (2010). *The Grand Design*. New York: Random House.

Krauss, L.M. (2012). A Universe from Nothing: Why There Is Something Rather Than Nothing. New York: Free Press.

Leibniz, G.W. (1989/1697). 'On the Ultimate Origination of Things', in *Philosophical Essays*. Trans. Ariel, R. and Garber, D. Indianapolis: Hackett Publishing Company, 149–55.

———. (1989/1714). 'Principles of Nature and Grace, Based Upon Reason', in *Philosophical Essays*. Trans. Ariel, R. and Garber, D. Indianapolis: Hackett Publishing Company, 206–13.

Lewis, D.K. (1986). *On the Plurality of Worlds*. Oxford: Blackwell.

———. (1994). 'Humean Supervenience Debugged', *Mind*, 103:412, 473–90.

Lowe, E.J. (1996). 'Why Is There Anything at All?', *Proceedings of the Aristotelian Society*, supp. vol. 70, 111–20.

———. (1998). *The Possibility of Metaphysics: Substance Identity, and Time*. Oxford: Oxford University Press.

———. (2002). 'Metaphysical Nihilism and the Subtraction Argument', *Analysis*, 62, 62–73.

Millican, P. (2004). 'The One Fatal Flaw in Anselm's Argument', *Mind*, 113:451, 437–76.

Nozick, R. (1981). *Philosophical Explanations*. Cambridge, Mass.: Harvard University Press.

Parfit, D. (2011). 'Why Anything? Why This?', in *On What Matters*, Vol. 2. Oxford: Oxford University Press, 623–48.

Plantinga, A. (1974). *The Nature of Necessity*. Oxford: Oxford University Press.

Pruss, A. (2006). *The Principle of Sufficient Reason: A Reassessment*. Cambridge: Cambridge University Press.

Rescher, N. (2000). *Nature and Understanding: The Metaphysics and Methods of Science*. Oxford: Oxford University Press.

Rice, H. (2000). *God and Goodness*. Oxford: Oxford University Press.

Rodriguez-Pereyra, G. (1997). 'There Might Be Nothing: The Subtraction Argument Improved', *Analysis*, 57, 159–66.

Rosen, G. (1990). 'Modal Fictionalism', *Mind*, 99:395, 327–54.

Schneider, S. (2002). 'Alien Individuals, Alien Universals, and Armstrong's Combinatorial Theory of Possibility', *Southern Journal of Philosophy*, 39:4, 575–93.

Stenger, V.J. (2007). *God: The Failed Hypothesis—How Science Shows That God Does Not Exist*. Amherst, Mass.: Prometheus Books.

Swinburne, R. (1991). *The Existence of God* (revised ed). Oxford: Oxford University Press.

———. (1998). 'Response to Derek Parfit', in van Inwagen, P. and Zimmerman, D. (eds.) *Metaphysics: The Big Questions*. Oxford: Blackwell, 427–9.

Van Inwagen, P. (1986). 'Two Concepts of Possible Worlds', *Midwest Studies in Philosophy*, 11, 185–213.

———. (1996). 'Why Is There Anything at All?', *Proceedings of the Aristotelian Society*, supp. vol. 70, 95–110.

———. (2007). 'A Materialist Ontology of Human Persons' in van Inwagen, P. & Zimmerman, D. (eds.) *Persons: Human and Divine*. Oxford: Oxford University Press, 199–215.

Wilczek, F. (1989). 'The Cosmic Asymmetry Between Matter and Antimatter', in Carrigan, R.J. and Trower, W.P. (eds.) *Particle Physics and the Cosmos: Readings From American Scientific Magazine*. New York: W.H. Freeman, 164–77.

2 Could There Be a Complete Explanation of *Everything*?

Timothy O'Connor

> One need only shut oneself in a closet and begin to think of the
> fact of one's being there, of one's queer bodily shape in the dark-
> ness . . . of one's fantastic character and all, to have the wonder
> steal over the detail as much as over the general fact of being, and
> to see that it is only familiarity that blunts it. Not only that *anything*
> should be, but that *this* very thing should be, is mysterious!
>
> —W. James, *Some Problems of Philosophy* (1911)

The world is a complicated place. The naked human eye reveals many kinds
of things, animate and inanimate. Natural science, and especially fundamental science, brings some unity to the blooming and buzzing confusion of
ordinary observation. But it still involves a lot of particular detail—the specific mass and charge of electrons, for example, the number of them, and the
size and structure of spacetime and lots of other things. Whichever way you
look at it, it doesn't seem to be *necessary* that things be this way. I might have
been a roofer like my father instead of a philosopher, and there might have
been 'schmectrons' instead of electrons as among the basic building blocks
of physical reality. There seems to be no end to the ways things might have
been, as opposed to the one complete way that things are (including the past
and future). Philosophers express this by saying that most things about the
world seem *contingent*—such that they might have been otherwise—rather
than *necessary*—such that things *had* to be that way. Science is about the
business of trying to explain how things actually are, at a deep level, and
how they behave: that is, it proposes and ever refines accounts of the world's
structure and dynamics. However, there can seem to be something necessarily left over, something left unaccounted for, in principle, by our best theories: the fact that things *in general* are as they are: that there happens to be
a world of the sort that we find and that science aims to better understand.

Is contingent existence a proper target for explanation? If so, what kind
of constraints might there be on an acceptable explanation? There undeniably is a powerful impetus in us to ask the question 'Why is there *this*—why,

indeed, is there anything at all?' Yet a little reflection shows that a satisfactory answer to this question would require an altogether different kind of explanation from familiar sorts. Would *any* sort manage to do? If so, would more than one?

Long dismissed by philosophers in the grip of various empiricist doctrines concerning meaning or explanation, these questions have begun to attract renewed attention, and I hope in what follows to advance this recent discussion.[1] My aims are modest. I begin by reminding most of us (and perhaps informing a few of us) of the simple and compelling reasons for thinking that an explanation of contingent existence itself is something that empirical science cannot aspire to. I will then bring out some key assumptions concerning modal truth (and knowledge) and causation that underlie either the question concerning the explanation of contingent existence or certain attempts to provide a constructive response to it, and I will situate these assumptions in the context of recent philosophical developments. I find these assumptions to be plausible, but here I will only be able to gesture at the reasons I have for accepting them. That any interesting metaphysical thesis will require contentious assumptions should go without saying. However, discussions with many philosophers have made me aware that some are prone to applying a double standard when it comes to this topic, given its deep roots within the history of natural theology. Many past thinkers have made inflated claims to offer 'proofs' of this or that constructive natural theological thesis. Nearly all contemporary philosophers rightly deny that 'proof' or 'certainty' can be attained for such claims. Yet some appear to believe that this fact shows that constructive projects in this area—or at least nonnaturalistic constructive projects—cannot be profitably pursued. Where this skepticism is applied across the board to all claims or theories in metaphysics generally, it at least has the virtue of consistency. I shall offer no general defense of metaphysics here, though I note that in recent decades it has been a thriving area of philosophical inquiry. In any case, the reader is encouraged to apply appropriate epistemic standards to the present inquiry, just as I take care to note my contentious assumptions and be careful in the conclusions that I draw from them. With my assumptions spelled out, I turn to my central argumentative burden: rebutting a common objection to the enterprise of seeking an explanation of contingent reality, viz., that the enterprise is bankrupt since contingent reality, by definition as it were, precludes the possibility of

---

1. Excellent contributions include Leslie (1979, 2001), Parfit (1998), Koons (1997, 2001, 2008), Oppy (1999, 2000, 2004, 2009), Pruss and Gale (1999), Pruss (1998, 2006), and Della Rocca (2010). O'Connor (2008) is my own prior contribution to this discussion. The present paper is a sequel of sorts to that book, occasioned by discussion with several philosophers and reviews of the book (Forrest 2009, Koons 2009, Mawson 2009, Newlands 2010, Oppy 2008, and the 2010 symposium in *Philosophia Christi*). I want to clarify and develop some key stage-setting claims and arguments that I make there.

complete explanation. I also respond to the typical fallback objection that the enterprise is animated by an implausibly strong form of rationalism.

My goal, then, is to help get the question of existence itself back on the table of serious philosophical discussion, by showing how it falls naturally out of an attractive (if, inevitably, contentious) metaphysical orientation, making plausible that its resolution must be nonnaturalistic, and arguing that the choice between a thoroughgoing necessitarian picture and one involving 'brutely' inexplicable facts is a false one: we can have both contingency and complete explanation. I argue this last point through reflection on a broadly theistic metaphysics. If my contention is correct, it is worth considering what other metaphysical schemes might likewise be consistent with complete explanation of contingency. I argued in O'Connor (2008) that a theistic form of such explanation is to be preferred to alternatives that I can presently envision, but I neither assume nor conclude that here. I will be delighted, in fact, if the present modest contribution to the growing body of serious reflection on the question of contingent existence occasioned further development and more powerful defense of nontheistic theories of the *fons et origo* of existence, unshackled from empiricist handcuffs. The possibilities for explaining contingent existence have been underexplored in contemporary metaphysics. This was inevitable, as real progress has required development on a number of ancillary fronts. The time is now ripe.

1 COMPLETE EXPLANATION IS NOT TO BE FOUND IN EMPIRICAL SCIENCE

Complete explanation of contingent reality—the sum total of all the existing objects and their histories that might not have been—would be explanation that involves no brute givens and leaves no explanatory loose ends whatsoever. It would be such that one could not intelligibly ask for anything more. All true, more limited explanations would rest on something that not only *has* no further explanation but *can have* no further explanation. I will argue that no foundational physical theory could aspire to explanation of this sort by considering in broad outline three main ways that one might try to pull it off, showing why those ways cannot succeed, and suggesting that the lesson generalizes.

Consider first the *Way of Eternity*: the attempt to provide an adequate theory on which physical reality had no beginning (whether of finite or infinite temporal measure); every temporal stage is fixed by what has gone before; and the totality of physical reality is just the sum of the stages. The Way of Eternity is instantiated by a generalized Newtonian theory of infinite space and time, by contemporary physicist John Wheeler's theory of oscillating universes, or by any theory on which our universe is generated by a primordial 'universe generator', itself eternal or spawned by a sequence of structures that has no beginning.

Second, there is the *Way of Unification*: the attempt successively to reduce physical theory's number of fundamental properties and property bearers, and the laws governing their co-evolution through spacetime. This way's theoretical limit is a single simple equation governing the distribution of a single fundamental entity—realizing physicist Steven Weinberg's dream of an equation that our descendants might display on their T-shirts. With maximal unification, it suggests, comes maximal explicability.

Finally, the *Way of Plenitude*: the attempt to provide complete explanation not by burrowing down to simple foundations or pushing back in beginningless time but by spreading out. Satisfyingly complete explanation may be achieved, it is claimed, through the devising of an elegant and empirically adequate theory that locates our universe within a vast structure of totalities that exhibits completely nonarbitrary properties. This might be a plenum of disjoint island universes or of causally noninteracting, n-dimensional spacetimes embedded within a single hyperspace of $n + 1$ dimensions. This way's limit case involves the existence of all mathematically consistent totalities: all possible universes, including every hyperspace configuration, as Massachusetts Institute of Technology physicist (and closet metaphysician) Max Tegmark (2008) proposes.

One might go further and combine *Eternity* and *Unification*, though neither seems to square with *Plenitude*, as universes that have a beginning or are less than ideally unified would seem to be part of any robust plenitude.

Suppose first that some version of the *Way of Eternity* were correct. Some have thought that, if this were so, there would be nothing left unexplained (that is, unexplain*able* in principle). David Hume, for example, in his *Dialogues Concerning Natural Religion*, contends that a beginningless sequence of events may admit of a complete, purely internal explanation—even if each of its constituent objects is a contingent being, such that it might not have existed. All that is needed is that each stage of the sequence has a causal explanation in terms of what preceded it.

That there can be immanent, stepwise explanations for particular events in terms of prior causes is hardly news. The crucial claim here is that the aggregation of explanations of this kind can be *complete*, leaving nothing further to be explained. This claim is plainly mistaken. A complete explanation would be *unconditional*—it would not appeal to factors that are themselves left unexplained. This requirement evidently is not met for local, sequential explanations where one event is explained in terms of another *that itself is an unexplained given* in terms of the explanation at hand. (This is not to say that there is anything wrong with conditional scientific explanations. I am merely pointing out that such explanations do not *aspire* to what would be required for Hume's contention to go through.) The point generalizes to other forms of scientific explanation familiar from contemporary theorizing. Explanations of the unfolding of cosmic history that point to the universe's earliest conditions plus its fundamental dynamical patterns treat these latter facts as simply given. Explanations cannot be unconditional if the terms are themselves all contingent, such that they might have not occurred.

Alex Pruss (2006: 44) gives the following nice example that illustrates the essential explanatory incompleteness of simply noting the stepwise dependence within a beginningless sequence of events. Suppose a cannon is fired at time t_0 and the cannonball lands at t_1. Now consider the infinite sequence of momentary events spanning all times between the two events, excluding t_0 and including t_1. There is no first event in this sequence, as there is no first temporal instant after t_0. (Time, we assume, is continuous like the real numbers, rather than discrete like the integers.) Thus, though the entire sequence has a finite duration, it still meets Hume's envisioned scenario of a beginningless infinite sequence of events, each causally dependent on events that precede it. Hume should conclude that this series is explanatorily complete, but this is evidently false: the entire sequence of events has a partial explanation in terms of an event external to it—the firing of the cannon at t_0.

One might object that in the scenario Hume envisions, in which the infinite sequence constituting the universe's history *also* has infinite temporal duration, there is reason to think that explanation is complete: unlike in the temporally finite sequence involving the cannonball, there could not be an event temporally prior to the temporally infinite sequence that might play an explanatory role in relation to it. This in turn suggests that there is no room for an explanation of it, which is a pretty good reason to conclude that it is explanatorily complete.[2] However, this response makes a big assumption that is unmotivated, viz., that there cannot be either atemporal or synchronic causal explanations. It seems possible that there is a causal agent or condition outside the infinite sequence but not temporally anterior to it that is either always or timelessly giving being to the series.

There is reason, then, to suppose that further explanation is possible even in the case of a universe of infinite temporal duration. If so, and if our universe truly is contingent, the obtaining of some fundamental facts or other will be unexplained within empirical theory, whatever the topological structure of contingent reality. An infinite regress of beings in or outside the spatiotemporal universe cannot forestall such a result.

We might hope to be able to conjoin *Eternity* with the *Way of Unification*. But, even supposing an eternal physical reality that is maximally simple at the fundamental level in terms of its ontology, dynamics, and topological structure, complete explanation would still elude our grasp. A cooperatively simple world reduces the *number* of contingent facts needing *independent* explanation. But in the end, what we get is conditional in character. The most fundamental fact of existence itself is left unexplained.

---

2. Oppy (2011).

The same basic problem confronts the *Way of Plenitude*. There undeniably *is* an elegance, a lack of arbitrariness, in the hypothesis that every 'consistent' universe exists. It's a beautiful idea that readily appeals to the foundational theorist, whether physical or metaphysical. But if it is a fact, and our reasons for embracing it are wholly *empirical*, then we must suppose that fact to be contingent: just the way things happened to be, among the ever so many less elegant alternatives. There might have been no 'multiverse', or a less complete multiverse, or a single universe of any arbitrary type. That the plenitudinous multiverse exists at all will not, then, have an unconditional explanation.

If we seek a complete explanation of existence, we must pass from physics to metaphysics. More specifically, many philosophers have pretty widely agreed (though see below on one alternative), if there is to be complete explanation at all, we must suppose that there can be a kind of *necessary existence*—existence having the same necessity as the truths of pure mathematics—whether had by physical reality itself, à la Spinoza, or by some kind of maximally unified, transcendent cause of physical reality. Necessary existence could have no direct role within empirical theory, though it is open to a scientist of a philosophical bent to suppose that it has application to physical reality (as Einstein, following Spinoza, seems to have done). On a view that accepts the legitimacy of appealing to this feature, *necessary existence* is claimed to be a substantial, distinctive property, involving a superior mode of existing. The natures of other things (whether instanced or not) will include the property of *being a contingent being*—that is, existing contingently, if at all. And the difference between these two classes of things is intrinsic and fundamental. The one class will include natures that are self-existing, whereas those in the other class are ontologically and explanatorily incomplete in themselves, existing, if at all, in dependency on other things, and ultimately on a necessary being.

2   THE 'OPACITY' OF NECESSITY AND ITS ROLE IN THEORETICAL EXPLANATIONS

My remarks concerning the distinction between contingent and necessary beings draw on the first of two important assumptions (or assumption clusters) that are needed to motivate the question of existence and to develop constructive proposals in response to it, or at least the kind of proposals I find plausible. Much traditional criticism stemming from Hume of philosophical attempts at complete explanation rests on the belief that the notion of necessary *existence* is radically defective. According to these critics, the interdefinable modal notions of *necessity* and *possibility* can be given only a 'thin' or 'empty' understanding; they concern (in Hume's words) mere 'relations of ideas', formal entailment between concepts, or something supposed to be similarly 'thin'. While the broad spirit of Hume's view has been very common in the empiricist tradition, the many empiricist attempts to excise or deflate any lurking appeal to more-than-verbal necessity in empirical explanations have failed, I think it's fair to say, and resoundingly enough as to suggest that the attempt is futile. Philosophical and empirical explanations alike often (and legitimately) depend on reality's being characterizable by a rich structure of truths taken as necessary. We might call such truths 'opaque necessities': propositions that we accept for explanatory reasons, not because they are 'transparent' or self-evident in the way that basic logical axioms allegedly are. Indeed, it can plausibly be argued that opaque necessities are implicit in logic and mathematics themselves, in the forms of essentialist commitments concerning propositional entities (see O'Connor [2008: ch. 1]). More readily apparent is that there are opaque necessities concerning causation, natural kinds, and basic normative claims concerning what may constitute objective evidence for what. (Consider the vicious circle one would find oneself in if one supposed that the canons of inductive reasoning were not necessary but contingent, and so themselves stand in need of empirical support.)[3]

More needs to be said than can be said here to develop a general modal epistemology that doesn't rely on the hyperrationalist notion of 'directly seeing' the truth of certain basic modal claims. Consistent with a number of recent thinkers, I believe that we should think instead in terms of a fallibilist procedure that seeks to bring into reflective equilibrium the results of our continuously developing formal disciplines and the considered modal commitments that arise out of scientific and metaphysical theories.[4]

That the metaphysician likewise appeals to this primitive feature of necessity in attempting to provide a form of explanation of that most general fact of existence itself, then, should not be ruled out of bounds absent some compelling, specific reason to think that necessity cannot characterize any existing entity. And note that necessary mathematical truths are often taken to be entities—propositions—that exist of necessity with the property of truth. (We might follow Leibniz and streamline our ontology by taking them instead to be necessary divine ideas, but that route is obviously of no help to the would-be deflater of necessary existence.)

I noted above that there is one prominent, constructive response to the question of contingent existence that does not (or at least need not) posit the existence of a necessarily existing being. According to John Leslie, the world

---

3. For development of this point, see Wright (1986 and 1980: 415–20). Famously, Quine (1961) argued for epistemological holism on which even logical and basic epistemic norms are subject to the 'tribunal of experience'. But as Quine recognized, the choice of whether and how to modify such commitments to 'accommodate recalcitrant data' will inevitably be pragmatic, rather than epistemically objective. I assume that most of my readers will agree with me that there lies shipwreck.

4. In O'Connor (2008: ch. 2), I try to sketch out an account along these lines. See also Koons (2000: ch. 15), Plantinga (1993: 110–3), and Goldman (1999).

exists *because it should.*[5] There are Platonic facts about the existence of some things and the absence of others being ethically required. These facts, says Leslie, are not existing things such as agents, but they are *realities*. The existence of our world is objectively better than nothing, and also better than many on-the-whole-bad worlds. Leslie posits that facts about what is ethically required can be creative without any agent, arguing that only in this way can the contingent-existence question be adequately answered.

Derek Parfit (1998) accepts the formal adequacy of Leslie's approach but holds that there are still other possibilities (although he refrains from endorsing any particular one). Here are some important 'global possibilities': this universe alone exists; every conceivable universe exists; no universe exists; the best possible universe exists; all universes above some threshold of overall goodness exist. Each of these possibilities, he claims, *could* obtain for no reason. It could be just a coincidence, for example, that the best possible universe alone exists. So the Random Hypothesis is that whatever global possibility obtains, even if an 'interesting' one, its obtaining has no explanation. Nonrandom Hypotheses, by contrast, claim that there is a Selector, a feature had by the actual global possibility, such that its obtaining is no coincidence—it is explained by some true principle. So, for example, if the best global possibility is one having our universe alone, and that is what obtains, the hypothesis will be that this possibility obtains *because* it is best. (Or it might be that the best possibility has all universes that are on-balance good, and *that* is what obtains.) While it could have obtained for no reason, it is more plausible to suppose that it obtains just because it is best. Supposing this to be a coincidence, says our hypothesizer, would be unreasonable.

Here I can only confess that I am not able to make sense of the form of explanation considered by Leslie and Parfit. What sort of 'because' is involved in asserting that a global possibility obtains because *P*, for some nonagential principle *P*? Evidently, it is not causal in the efficient-causal sense. (If it were, we should go on to ask about the nature of this peculiar causal entity. In particular, we can ask whether it is a necessary being and whether its causality is structurally analogous to nonpersonal causal agents in the universe. It will not do to ward off further inquiries by saying it is an 'abstract' entity.[6]) But if the explanation is not causal, we are left with a truth without an ontological foundation—and not just any old truth but the most fundamental truth of all. That does not seem like an illuminating explanation at all.

That said, I am not claiming here to have conclusively rebutted the principle-based approach, just indicating the kind of reason that I judge to be compelling and that warrants discussion by its proponents. In Parfit's

---

5. See his 1979 and 2001 books and the concise statement of his position in Leslie (1997).
6. Cf. Lewis's quip in another connection (1986a: 111): 'Could "abstract" just mean "don't worry"?'

case, at least, it is pretty clear that he prefers the principle-based approach to one that appeals to necessary being because he embraces a view of absolute possibility as encompassing whatever is 'fully conceivable', or perhaps ideally conceivable. (Since it is fully conceivable in the intended sense that there is no necessary being, alleged opaque necessities get us nowhere, as any such truth will itself be a brute contingency from a higher vantage point.) As I have taken pains to emphasize, I am here assuming that this contention is false. If one accepts this assumption, one may have to work a little harder to motivate the principle-based approach than its recent defenders have done.

3   THE IRREDUCIBILITY OF CAUSATION AND THE NATURE OF INDETERMINISTIC PROPENSITIES

Explanations of the most fundamental sort are often causal, and one sort of causal explanation will feature prominently in the discussion to follow. As with modality, the nature of causation is itself a large and much disputed topic. Here I will have to assume the truth of a general approach to the nature of causation (which I discussed in O'Connor [2008] and elsewhere). I maintain that reductionist accounts of causation, including variants on the influential neo-Humean counterfactual theory proposed by David Lewis, are one and all untenable, for quite general reasons. Reductionist theories purport to analyze causal facts entirely in terms of the noncausal facts, so that causation is not a metaphysically basic feature of the world but instead is wholly derivative.[7] Though popular throughout the metaphysics-disparaging twentieth century, the reductionist program has consisted in the advancement of one implausible and extensionally inadequate proposal after another. It's time to call it quits.[8] The alternative that I favor is (loosely speaking) neo-Aristotelian. The details of differing versions of this approach are not important in what follows. All I will assume is the ecumenical core, on which fundamental intrinsic properties

---

7. As Lewis thinks of it, causal facts and the laws of nature are reducible to facts concerning the global spatiotemporal arrangement of fundamental natural properties, which we allegedly may conceive in nondispositional terms. Roughly, the laws are the best system of generalizations over such natural facts, where bestness is determined by the optimal balance of simplicity and strength (or explanatory power). Causation in turn consists in a restricted kind of counterfactual dependence of one event on another, where the counterfactuals are grounded in cross-world similarities. See the Introduction to Lewis (1986b).
8. I also deem inadequate the novel nonreductionist account developed by David Armstrong (1997) and Michael Tooley (1987), on which causation is a specific higher-order relation among universals. To my mind, this view is neo-Humeanism in disguise, one that simply adds ornamental second-order structure to a cause-less manifold, gaining nothing in explanatory power. (For discussion, see O'Connor [2008: ch. 2], itself building on criticisms by Lewis [1986b] and van Fraassen [1988].)

of objects are by nature tendencies to contribute toward specific effects. The dispositional does not reduce to the nondispositional, and the manifestations of a disposition consist in the instantiation of a real relation—the relation of causation—that is ontologically basic.[9] These dispositions may be deterministic or probabilistic, relative to a specific type of circumstance, or perhaps even be an indeterministic tendency that is not probabilistically structured.

Within this account of causation, it is natural to understand 'probabilistic causation' not (with some reductionists) as the *causation of probability*—the inducement or alteration of an objective probability of various outcomes, giving formal structure to the context of what is a 'chance' occurrence—but instead as the *probability of causation*: the probability measures the objective likelihood that a given set of causal factors will bring about a potential effect. They are *propensities* toward a plurality of possible effects. They are sufficient for each of them only in the sense that they are all that is needed, not in the sense that they are a causally sufficient condition. Every indeterministic event is produced, though none is necessitated.

Some of what I say below crucially depends on the possibility of there being a transcendent cause of the universe as a whole, which causation would be a real relation that does not supervene on any set of nondispositional facts and the patterns therein. One might embrace a mixed view—some variety of deflationary neo-Humeanism about causation within the universe, which in turn has a neo-Aristotelian cause—as Thomas Reid (1788) did (though he grouped human causes with the divine cause, rather than Humean mechanistic causes). I take such a mixed ontology of causation to be implausible, although by my lights it is preferable to a strict Humeanism that denies the possibility of a neo-Aristotelian cause of contingent existence.

The neo-Aristotelian theory of causation is naturally associated with a broader ontology of the physical world whose elements are basic individuals and a sparse set of natural properties and relations. This ontology, in turn, has implications for the theory of explanation, as we will see below. However, while I shall develop my preferred account of causal explanation, or of a fundamental form of causal explanation, in terms of this sparse ontology of concreta, my position will not essentially depend on it, as the fundamental point I will make can be motivated independently of it.

4   EXPLANATIONS AND EXPLANATION SCHEMAS

If the two sets of assumptions concerning the legitimate role of 'opaque' necessities in some forms of explanation and the irreducible, productive character of causation are granted, how should one proceed in constructing and evaluating possible answers to the 'existence question'? A good place

---

9. A number of recent authors have defended versions of this general approach. See, for example, Ellis (2001), Molnar (2003), Bird (2007), and Jacobs (2011).

to start is to distinguish between explanations, properly speaking, and explanation *schemas* that specify a mere broad outline of the causally relevant features of a putative cause and its manner of operation. The distinction drawn, we should recognize that we could have reason to endorse an explanation schema even in the absence of an explanation that fills in the missing details if the schema seems to provide the only, or the best, form of answer, as measured by material adequacy and other standards of theory comparison. (Note that evolutionary theory offers, for many historical events, only an explanatory schema—though a quite rich one, to be sure. It entails that there are true, detailed explanations of a certain type for ever so many specific facts about biological history, most of which are unavailable to us in any detail.)

Consider the hypothesis that the totality that is the physical universe is metaphysically contingent while being a timeless causal product of a being that exists of absolute necessity. This is not much of a possible explanation of the universe, since it tells us nothing about the manner by which and the circumstances in which the necessary being gave rise to it. We might give the claim a little more specificity: the necessary being blindly and inevitably 'emanated' the universe of necessity (in which case the universe itself turns out to be derivatively necessary, though not necessary *from itself*). Alternatively, we could suppose that the necessary being generated the universe through an internal, indeterministic mechanism, capable of generating any of a vast array of possibilities. As it happened, it gave rise to this one, but it needn't have done so. Third, we might say instead that the necessary being is a personal agent whose actions are guided by purposes. It caused the universe in accordance with some goal or set of goals. This option subdivides into two possibilities: on the first, the totality of its goals and beliefs rendered it inevitable that it would give rise to a universe of just this sort, which perfectly reflects those goals (so thought Leibniz). On the second, the reasons were resistible. It might have chosen a different sort of universe, holding fixed its actual goals and beliefs. (This accords with the more common theistic view.) While these explanatory schema are more informative than the initial barebones thesis, they are still far from full explanations. They tell us very little about the nature of the necessary being or its manner of activity. And there are other, similarly sketchy possibilities besides. We could, e.g., try to follow Einstein and his hero Spinoza in thinking that, appearances to the contrary, the universe itself is a self-contained wholly necessary being, down to the last, most contingent-seeming fact. (As Spinoza would say, the appearance of contingency here is a result of our ignorance of the totality of causes.) Or we might enrich the *Way of Plenitude* with the metaphysical (not empirical) thesis that the existence of the multiverse is itself necessary.[10]

---

10. We must distinguish this proposal—on which there are an infinite number of *universes*, each of which exists necessarily in virtue of having a primitive property of necessity—from David Lewis's (1986a) notorious *reduction* of modality to nonmodal facts concerning concrete 'possible worlds'. I have

Though all these hypotheses are only schematic, we might have reason to embrace a particular one of them even if precious few additional details are forthcoming. We would have such reason if (i) one of them seemed to 'work' on reflection and to not generate insoluble puzzles of its own, (ii) we had weighty reasons to think that each of the alternatives we could envision either implode on examination (best case) or face grave problems for which there are no clear remedies (less decisive), and (iii) there is reason to think that the range of alternatives we had considered are exhaustive. Even absent (iii), we would have some reason to adopt the favored view, albeit with less confidence.

We might think of this class of possible explanations this way. Explanations, especially the very general sorts of explanations offered in philosophy, logic, mathematics, and physics, often posit possibility-constraining structures of various kinds. For example, physics posits spatiotemporal structure and the causal-similarity structure induced by the fundamental properties and relations of matter and by natural kinds, such as *electron*. The philosopher who tentatively endorses one of the existence-explaining schema I mentioned is positing an additional kind of structure to reality: a necessary *ontic* dependency of contingent physical things on a necessary being. Like pure mathematical structure and unlike spatiotemporal structure in physics, it is conceived to be a structure that would obtain for any possible reality.[11]

5   COMPLETE EXPLANATION AND INDETERMINISM: MODAL COLLAPSE OR BRUTE FACTS?

Perhaps the fundamental objection to the project of seeking a satisfactory explanation schema for contingent existence takes the form of a dilemma: either we (implausibly) embrace 'modal collapse' and suppose that, in the final analysis, nothing is contingent and 'all is necessity'; or we concede the existence of 'brute', wholly inexplicable contingency somewhere or other and so give up on the possibility of *complete* or ultimate explanation. The objectors reason as follows: if there truly is a sufficient reason for every truth, a reason why it is so *and not otherwise*, then every truth will be a necessary truth, because a direct consequence of the fully explicable (and hence necessary) activity or choice of a necessary being. If not, if there is at some point a merely contingent link between necessary being and contingent being, so that this contingent world might not have existed, even given the existence and nature of a necessary being, then we've after all conceded that some contingent truths are 'brute facts', lacking complete explanation.

here assumed that all varieties of modal reductionism are false. For my assessment of Lewis's account, see O'Connor (2008: ch. 1). Lewis professed to be 'inured to brute contingency' and recognized that given his metaphysics, explanation 'inevitably terminate[s] in brute matter of fact' (1986a: 129).
11. For an engrossing discussion of structure in metaphysics, see Sider (2011).

(And if we have some brute facts, why not let existence itself be one such fact?)[12]

This sort of objection is apt, I believe, when directed at philosophers such as Leibniz who maintain the *Principle of Sufficient Reason* (PSR), strongly construed. However, it shares with defenders of that principle the false assumption that any *complete* explanation of some state of affairs is necessarily and fully *contrastive*, in the following sense: it explains (explicitly or implicitly) why that state of affairs obtains rather than any seemingly possible contrast whose occurrence is consistent with all the available mechanisms and the circumstances in which they operated.

Note that causal explanations can be targeted at a variety of explananda: events, objects, processes, or facts, with these being more or less finely individuated. I noted above that on an attractive ontology I favor, concrete reality consists in basic individuals and their histories, the latter understood as the instancing by one or more such individuals of one or more causally efficacious natural properties and relations. If this is correct, then plausibly there is a basic, or minimum-grade, form of causal explanation that targets concrete entities (occurrences or the existence of objects) rather than one of the abundant, more fine-grained facts *about* those entities, and such explanation consists in giving information concerning the causal/dispositional profile of the entity or entities that produced the explanandum, whether proximately or remotely. As noted previously, that profile may involve deterministic or probabilistic tendencies, relative to a specific type of circumstance, or perhaps even an indeterministic tendency that is not probabilistically structured. Thus, when we seek an explanation of the existence of the universe as a whole, minimum-grade causal explanation is a permissible form. Of course, we might also seek explanations of more fine-grained truths concerning the universe, such as the fact that this reality obtains rather than a particular alternative. But it should not be assumed that potential explanations of these fine-grained contrastive facts will simply fall out of a viable explanation of the more basic kind, which is the explanation of the concrete actual reality itself.[13]

Within this framework, we may advance the following explanatory principle:

---

12. Peter van Inwagen (1996: 97–9) and William Rowe (1984) have formulated versions of this objection.
13. As Peter Lipton (1990) made clear, a request for a contrastive explanation ('Why P rather than Q?') presumes that there is an explanatory relationship between fact (P) and 'foil' (*not-Q*); it presumes that the occurrence of P and the nonoccurrence of Q can be given a unifying explanation. But this assumption plainly will not hold for every such pairing even in a deterministic world—as when the occurrence of P and the absence of Q are completely unrelated matters. In an indeterministic world, contrastive explanation will also fail (plausibly) wherever P and Q are mutually exclusive and each had a significant, nonzero chance of occurring.

Principle of Contingent Explanation (PCE) I

The existence of every contingent basic individual (and arbitrary collections thereof) and the occurrence of every concrete event in or among such individuals have true minimum-grade causal explanations, ones that cite the activation of a dispositional tendency (possibly indeterministic) in a distinct entity or entities.

One *example* of a metaphysics that is consistent with the principle in its full generality without entailing modal collapse is classical theism. Theism yields the following schematic explanation of the entire realm of contingently existing entities: (i) the totality of such entities and the events that they undergo are the causal product of a divine act of will or choice that is guided by some goal or reason; and (ii) this totality was chosen despite God's having either competing reasons to will a different outcome or attractive, alternative ways of achieving the very same goals that guided what was in fact willed.[14]

If this explanation were correct, the existence of every natural particular and the events in which they participate admit, in principle, of a fully adequate explanation in terms ultimately involving their causal dependency on a necessary being, whose activity was guided but not determined by some goal(s) that the actual order of things were seen to satisfy. Which is to say, there is an account of why there is anything at all and why the natural order has the character it has.[15] And note further that by understanding schematically the purposive and free nature and characteristic activity of the being on whom all possibilities and actualities ultimately depend, we might see, too, why these

---

14. Objection: In that case, whatever aspect of the divine nature explains the actual outcome must be brutely contingent. Game over. Reply: Not so. A necessarily existing divine being would *necessarily* have a range of creative motivations or goals that point toward different options. For simplicity, say there are two options A and B, such that A is motivated by the state of God's having reason R_A and B is motivated by God's having reason R_B. In the actual world, God chooses A. This is explained by R_A, a necessary part of the divine nature. Similarly, had God chosen B, it would have been explained by God's having R_B, a state that God also has necessarily. The fact that one or the other of these states is explanatory of the divine action only contingently (since the action itself might not have occurred) does not imply that the *existence* of these states is contingent.

15. As Eleonore Stump has reminded me, the ultimacy of explanation on this metaphysics requires the (standard) assumption that the divine being is constituted by a nature all of whose features are essentially interdependent. If this assumption were not made, then there would be an unexplainable and brute fact that this being's nature was contingently constituted by this particular set of properties. Famously, this sort of consideration led many medieval philosophical theologians to embrace a very strong doctrine of divine simplicity. I believe that this stronger assumption is resistible, but we need not consider this matter here. (See O'Connor [2008: ch. 6].)

dependent entities exist *only* contingently. (We would see, that is, that it is the very nature of a freely choosing agent, whether human or divine, to bring about effects that are not necessitated, and hence which are contingent.)

We would need to say more about this model of purposive agency in order to adequately defend its coherence. Here I will instead note that the more general point—there can be explanations that are not contrastive and do not entail the existence of contrastive explanations for their explananda—is a familiar fact outside the contentious matter of how to understand the will, whether divine or human: it is assumed in our best-confirmed scientific explanations, those given by quantum mechanics (at least on most interpretations). There, it is common to explain a phenomenon such as radioactive decay in terms of mechanisms that are presumed to operate indeterministically. The phenomenon is adequately explained by describing a mechanism that had a nonzero probability of producing that result in the circumstances and that did in fact produce it. This is so even though there is no explanation of why *this* result was produced rather than *that* one, whose probability of occurring was likewise nonzero. Here, too, we have an explanation of why there *cannot be* a correct contrastive explanation of the outcome, for every possible contrast. The very nature of an indeterministic causal agent precludes such explanations.

The contrast between a wholly uncaused ('brute') event and one that is indeterministically caused to occur is no less stark than that between a wholly uncaused event and a deterministically caused one. Indeterministic causal explanations are not an altogether different kettle of fish from deterministic explanations, as the mechanisms to which both sorts appeal are not deeply different in kind. Indeed, deterministic mechanisms are simply the limit cases of analogous probabilistic mechanisms arranged on a continuum ordered by the strength of their antecedent probability to cause the actual outcome. To put it in other terms, there is nothing *partial* or otherwise defective about indeterministic, noncontrastive explanations in stochastic physical theories—or, for that matter, in accounts of freely willed choices. Nothing pertaining to the target phenomena is left out of the explanatory picture: which events actually occur, how they actually are locally produced, and whether and why specific types of alternative events were possible, given the prior circumstances. Things don't go all mysterious just because some of our world's causes operate indeterministically.

In the envisioned theistic framework, which aspires to maximal comprehensiveness in our explanatory project, there are no *brute* contingencies—no unexplained or incompletely explained events—whatsoever. True, where contingency is preserved through the nonnecessitation of outcomes, there will be abstract, contrastive facts *about* those events that are not explicable. But this is just to say that the fully explicable events were not causally/metaphysically determined to occur. It is fully explicable why those contrastive facts do not admit specific explanation: the events they concern are the product of a causal agent or agents that operate indeterministically, an agent or agents whose existence admits of complete explanation. I submit that there is no explanatory surd in this scenario, nothing that seems to cry out for some kind or other of explanation where there is none—as would be the case on the naturalist-empiricist view that physical reality is ultimate but without explanation of *any* sort.

The plausibility of the above explanatory principle rests on an ontology that draws a sharp distinction between concrete contingent events, consisting in one or more individuals instantiating one or more basic properties and relations, and the uncountable abundance of contingent facts those events make true. However, we may make the required distinction between brute and nonbrute truths without this particular ontology, while continuing to avoid modal collapse. It is embodied in the following alternative principle, implicit in some of my above remarks:

Principle of Contingent Explanation (PCE) II

For *every* contingent event or truth, either there is a true explanation of it or there is a nonvacuous true explanation why the event or truth has no true explanation.

Where an event is caused but not determined by a prior factor, there is no true explanation why that event occurred rather than some causally possible alternative (at least where the probability of the alternative is significant). That this is so, however, is not mysteriously brute. It is fully explained by the indeterministic nature of the causal factor in question. This shows that seeking an explanation for contingent existence itself need be neither quixotic nor arbitrary. If contingent reality is causally grounded in a necessary being operating indeterministically, the PCE II will be satisfied. By contrast, were the totality of contingent existence to lack explanation altogether, as contemporary naturalists suppose, it will not be satisfied. There would be not only no explanation for this totality but also no substantial explanation that enabled us to see why it has no explanation: it would be objectionably brute.[16]

---

16. And thus my reply to Newlands's insistence that 'in the absence of the general justification which the PSR so wonderfully provides, O'Connor must show why we should favour metaphysical outlooks which provide meaningful answers to the "Why anything contingent at all?" question in preference to those which answer with nothing but iterated bruteness' (2010: 439). The generality of PCE I and II also undercuts Della Rocca's (2010) argument that non-arbitrary commitment to popular and more limited explicability arguments requires acceptance of PSR.

6 NATURALISM, TRANSCENDENT NECESSARY BEING EXPLANATIONS, SIMPLICITY, AND ECONOMY

In its barest form, the theistic explanatory schema for existence is this: the reason that any contingent thing exists at all (and, in particular, the world of which we are part) is that it is a contingent, causal, and intended consequence of an absolutely necessary being. Absent a powerful case for supposing that explanatory appeal to necessary being is illusory, it seems unreasonable, at least on the face of it, to allow that the question *Why this?* is a perfectly coherent one and that it correctly presupposes that the universe and everything therein need not have existed—that is to say, its existence is entirely contingent—and nonetheless hold that there is no answer to it: hold that the universe's existence is simply a brute, unexplain*able* fact. In practice, we would not countenance local contingent facts entirely lacking in causal antecedents, regardless of the length and thoroughness of failed attempts to generate plausible hypotheses. A difference of attitude when it comes to the most general of contingent facts seems arbitrary. It seems even more unreasonable to deny that, other things being fairly equal, given two metaphysics such that one of them is consistent with there being an ultimate, nonarbitrary explanation of existence while the other precludes such explanation, we should prefer the one that answers it on account of its greater explanatory power.

Tom Senor suggests that this stance begs the question against theism's chief rival—'brute naturalism', on which the existence of the universe is a brute fact.[17] Explanatory power is a theoretical virtue only when dealing with a phenomenon that clearly *has* some explanation. But the bare existence of the universe just isn't one of those facts that *cry out for explanation* (even if, as Senor himself supposes, it in fact has an explanation).

In reply, I don't see how we might make a principled, let alone plausible, distinction between facts that do and facts that don't cry out for explanation of any sort whatsoever. I don't see this distinction at work in any ordinary explanatory context, steering us away from so much as contemplating the possibility of explanations for certain facts among others (the explanation-worthy ones) within a domain. Certainly, all manner of practical considerations partly determine which facts a theorist might sensibly hope to explain at a given stage of inquiry. And fruitful theories frame inquiry in ways that place certain kinds of facts front and center while folding others into the theoretical superstructure, rendering them impervious to substantive explanation from within the theory. In practice, there will always be limits of these kinds to human inquiry. But Senor, I take it, wants to claim something much stronger: certain contingent facts just are such *in and of themselves* as not to require causal explanation of any kind whatsoever (purposive or mechanistic,

---

17. See Senor's contribution to a symposium on O'Connor (2008) in *Philosophia Christi* (2010). Some of my remarks to follow in the text are taken from my response to Senor in that volume.

deterministic or merely probabilistic, or even a nontrivial explanation of why they have no explanation). What does it take to be a fact like that? Time has not dealt kindly with Enlightenment suggestions on this score: modern cosmology is rife with attempted explanations of the universe we inhabit and facts concerning the nature of time and space. One suspects that the only way for a philosopher to delineate in advance the fact or facts that *cry out to be ignored* is this: whatever turn out to be the most basic facts of natural reality. That kind of special pleading is quite a comedown for the heirs of Hume and Kant.

It's important to see my appeal to greater explanatory power in setting aside brute naturalism in context. As noted earlier, Hume, Kant, and others have tried to argue that the idea of necessary (concrete) existence is incoherent and/or 'empty' (and so explanatorily useless), or that appeal to necessary existence to explain contingency leads to 'modal collapse', such that all is necessity. If either of these familiar contentions were correct, then we would indeed have a principled reason for thinking that explanation cannot be pushed through entirely, so that there must be brute (inexplicable) contingency somewhere or other. In the present discussion, I have assumed the falsity of the first of these contentions and argued against the second. If—but only if—my positions on these matters are well founded, and an explanation for contingent existence itself is a coherent theoretical possibility, then it does seem proper to prefer a metaphysics on which it is explain*able* (in principle, even if we will never be in a position to fill out the explanation in detail) to one on which it is not, *other things being equal*.

Graham Oppy (2011) urges that it is inevitable that other things will *not* be roughly equal in this context. We need to weigh explanatory scope against other desiderata for theories, such as simplicity and ontological economy. And he contends that when we do take these into account, it is not at all obvious that *Naturalism* (as a metaphysical doctrine) will not come out ahead of *Theism*, all things considered. As he notes, accepting the theistic explanatory framework commits one to a new kind of entity having new kinds of properties and new theoretical problems (reconciling human freedom and divine conservation, etc.).

In reply, we should observe first of all that not all explanations of existence that posit the existence of a necessary being are theistic. An initial advantage of a broadly 'Spinozistic' ontology is precisely that it involves no new entities (at least, no new and wholly independent entities).

But suppose that there were powerful reasons to prefer a theistic construal of necessary being to other accounts. Then we should observe, second, that (contingentist) Naturalism simply is not a rival *explanatory* scheme for existence to Theism. Naturalism accepts as brute what Theism seeks to explain. Further, if we let *naturalism* (small *n*) denote the full, structured set of true empirical explanations supposed to exist by philosophical *Naturalism* (big *N*), *minus* any claim of explanatory comprehensiveness, then the theistic explanatory schema can (and ought) to *absorb* small-*n* naturalism. For an unconditional explanation of existence need not in any way compete with conditional, empirical explanations of the sort that comprise the explanatory nuts and bolts of the naturalist scheme. Indeed, it is natural to suppose that empirical explanations will be subsumed within the larger structure of the complete explanation, consistent with the plausible, deep assumption that reality is unified.

Now, Oppy is correct to insist on the relevance of the fact that a naturalist might judge the internal conceptual problems facing Theism to be intractable. Conditional on this judgment, would it not be rationally preferable to forgo the possibility of explaining existence? I don't believe so. For if one does make this judgment, there is a better fallback option: a construal of necessary being as an *impersonal* transcendent and indeterministic cause of contingent existence. Such a view likely doesn't face whatever problems Oppy or other naturalists might judge to afflict Theism. It would require giving implausibly decisive weighting to economy of ontological commitment to judge that it is better to forgo explanation altogether than to accept the existence of an unobserved necessary being.

That said, I would make one modest concession to Oppy on this matter. Since, as a practical matter, we are at best in a position to give reasons in favor of this or that explanatory *schema*, epistemic modesty is in order. We must always allow for the *epistemic* possibility that a favored, or indeed any, explanatory schema cannot be fully and consistently developed. If we knew this to be so, we would after all have reason to reject our principles of explanation on the excellent grounds that they cannot possibly be satisfied. But this concession does not invite skepticism about the project any more than the possibility of overlooked difficulties with complex physical theories should invite skepticism (as opposed to a healthy circumspection in confidence) about the project of pursuing true physical theories.

7   *WHICH* EXISTENCE QUESTION?

We are now in a position to see that certain ways of formulating the question regarding contingent existence that is to be answered make questionable assumptions about the form an explanation schema for existence must take. It is commonly put thus: *Why is there anything at all?* But this very general formulation admits importantly distinct ways of making it more precise: Why are there contingent things? What are there contingent things rather than there being nothing contingent at all? Why do *these* contingent things exist? And why do *these* contingent things exist rather than *those* apparently possible others?

I suggest that the *best* formulation of the question is this:

The Basic Question of Contingent Existence

Are there contingently existing objects, and if there are, why do those particular contingent objects there are exist and undergo the events they do?

The reason to prefer this formulation is that it presumes the least about what is there to be explained and what form a true explanation may turn out to have. Spinoza questioned the common assumption that there are any contingent truths at all. The second half of the *Basic Question* sets a *minimum bar* for precluding brutely (wholly inexplicable) contingent existences or occurrences in reality. Some explanations consistent with PCE I and the more general PCE II are not consistent with PSR and are no worse for that. Contingency rooted in indeterministic causes need not be brute.

Finally, let me try to clarify a subtle issue in the neighborhood.[18] We start by noting that all noncontrastive explanations for *P* appear to provide, in trivial fashion, the materials for corresponding contrastive explanations of *P rather than not-P*—the limit case, we might say, of contrastive facts. Since *P* is equivalent to *not-not-P*, explaining why *P* plausibly provides the resources for explaining why *not-not-P*. (There are niceties to be explored here that turn on the intensionality of explanations, but I don't think these suffice to call into question the claim I just made.) And to explain why *P* and (thereby) why it's not the case that *not-P* seems tantamount to explaining why *P rather than not-P*.

But now consider the question *Why is there something contingent rather than there being nothing contingent?*, a question that has the form of *Why P rather than not-P?* I have been arguing, it seems, that there could be an adequate noncontrastive explanation of the first disjunct (*there is something contingent*) in terms of its being indeterministically caused by God in accordance with certain (resistible) reasons. If so, and if *Why is there something contingent rather than there being nothing contingent?* is asking for a *trivially* contrastive explanation, the requisite answer should fall out of the noncontrastive explanation. But this contrastive question appears *not* to be answered by appeal to a nonnecessitating cause that need not have caused anything contingent at all. So what's going on here?

We have gone astray, I believe, in the very first step, where it was supposed that the contingent activity of a necessary being noncontrastively explains the fact that there is something contingent. For this question is implicitly contrastive, and thus so must be any adequate answer to it. Unpacked, it asks, *Why does one of these possibilities—the ones that involve contingently existing things—obtain, rather than none of them?* Whether it has an answer depends on the details of the proposed theistic scenario. One might suppose that while it was undetermined which contingent reality God produced, it was necessary that God produce some reality or other. (One reason to think this might be so comes from the Platonic-medieval thesis that Goodness naturally diffuses itself.)[19] In that case, there will be available an explanation for our implicitly contrastive question. But if we do not suppose this, then we also do not have reason to suppose an explanation of *there is something contingent*. In this scenario, the question that has an

---

18. Thanks to William Lane Craig for raising this matter in discussion.
19. For discussion, see Kretzmann (1988) and O'Connor (2008: ch. 5).

explanatory answer is *Why is there this contingent reality?*, a different question from *Why is there anything contingent?*

8   ON THE DISPARAGEMENT OF 'RATIONALISM'

I turn to a final objection. Endorsing a metaphysical explanation schema for contingent existence, empiricists complain, is indulging in an extreme and outmoded variety of 'rationalism'. John Mackie (1982), for example, scorned the assumption that our world is 'intelligible through and through', or completely intelligible, in the way that would be the case if existence itself admitted of explanation.

Such a charge, when made explicit, is either mistaken or liable to be turned back on the one who makes it. If Mackie is right that our universe is *not* intelligible, then a necessary being that either constitutes all of reality or serves as the source of an independent contingent reality doesn't just happen to be absent, as it happens to be the case that there are no unicorns; its existence is *impossible*. For it cannot be that while there *is* no necessary being, there *might* have been one. The concept's peculiar logic precludes that. (This is the lesson of the modal ontological argument.) The concept of a necessary being is of one that could not have failed to exist, absolutely speaking. For such a being to be possible, it must be such that it would exist in every possible circumstance, including the actual one.[20] (That's precisely why the question of *its* existence cannot arise, thereby ending the regress of explanation nonarbitrarily.) Thus, in opposing a 'rationalist' commitment to the complete intelligibility of our world, the critic is thereby advancing an equally strong thesis, implicitly held as a *necessary* truth: it is necessarily the case that there is no complete explanation. Given that our natural, intuitive assent is toward our world's *being* completely intelligible (as the pervasive tendency to raise the question of the explanation of existence indicates), it is hard to motivate the Mackian attitude. Furthermore, note the distinctness of two 'rationalist' theses:

(1) Existence has an explanation. (Reality is intelligible 'through and through'.)
(2) Human beings are capable of laying bare the full intelligibility of reality.

Attacks on rationalism are quite plausible when directed at (2), a thesis held by very few, if any, philosophers of tradition. As I've emphasized, it is

---

20. I here assume with many that S5 is the correct logic of absolute necessity: facts concerning what is possible or necessary are invariant, in the sense that whatever might have contingently been the case, what is actually possible or necessary would still have been so.

enough to seek, not a comprehensive complete explanation, but the outline of an explanation (or range of possible explanations, if there is more than one that is viable on sustained reflection). Schematic answers may suffice for very significant constraints on general metaphysics. Antirationalist attacks are far less plausible when directed at (1), once we see the equally strong necessity claim that its repudiation commits us to and we further recognize that it is entirely independent of the inflated optimism embodied in (2).[21]

REFERENCES

Armstrong, D.M. (1997). *A World of States of Affairs*. Cambridge: Cambridge University Press.

Bird, A. (2007). *Nature's Metaphysics*. Oxford: Oxford University Press.

Della Rocca, M. (2010). 'PSR', *Philosophical Imprints* 10 (7): 1–13.

Ellis, B. (2001). *Scientific Essentialism*. Cambridge: Cambridge University Press.

Forrest, P. (2009). 'Review of Timothy O'Connor, Theism and Ultimate Explanation: The Necessary Shape of Contingency', *Analysis* 69 (3): 589–91.

Goldman, A. (1999). 'A Priori Warrant and Naturalistic Epistemology' in Tomberlin, J. *Philosophical Perspectives* 13. Malden, MA: Blackwell, 1–28.

Hume, D. (1779). *Dialogues Concerning Natural Religion*. In J.A.C. Gaskin (ed.), *Dialogues and Natural History of Religion*. Oxford & New York: Oxford University Press, 1993.

Jacobs, J. D. 'Powerful Qualities, Not Pure Powers', *The Monist* 94 (1): 81-102.

James, W. (1911). *Some Problems of Philosophy*. New York: Longmans, Green, 1911; excerpted in van Inwagen, P. and Zimmerman, D. (eds.). *Metaphysics: The Big Questions*. Cambridge, MA: Blackwell, 1998, 415–8.

Koons, R. (1997). 'A New Look at the Cosmological Argument', *American Philosophical Quarterly* 34: 193–211.

———. (2000). *Realism Regained*. New York: Oxford University Press.

———. (2001). 'Defeasible Reasoning, Special Pleading and the Cosmological Argument: A Reply to Oppy', *Faith and Philosophy* 18: 192–203.

---

21. Versions of this material were presented to audiences at the Center for Philosophy of Religion at the University of Notre Dame; the Butler Society at Oriel College, the University of Oxford; the Philosophy of Cosmology conference at St. Anne's College, also at Oxford; Wheaton College, St. Louis University, The University of London's Institute of Philosophy, Baylor University, Davidson College, Biola University, the University of Nebraska, Omaha, and as a plenary address at the annual meetings of the Evangelical Philosophical Society in New Orleans. I hope the present paper is considerably clearer as a result of the helpful criticisms and suggestions I received. I wish to thank in particular Robert Audi, John Bishop, Todd Buras, John Churchill, William Lane Craig, Thomas Crisp, Thomas Flint, John Greco, John Hare, Jeff Koperski, Matthew Lee, Brian Leftow, Michael Murray, Samuel Newlands, Alex Pruss, Michael Rea, Chris Tweedt, and, finally, Sir Martin Rees, my commentator at the cosmology conference. I have also benefited from reading reviews of *Theism and Ultimate Explanation* by Peter Forrest, Robert Koons, T.J. Mawson, Samuel Newlands, Graham Oppy, and Tom Senor.

———. (2008). 'Epistemological Foundations for the Cosmological Argument', in J. Kvanvig (ed.), *Oxford Studies in Philosophy of Religion*, Vol.1. Oxford: Oxford University Press, 105–33.

———. (2009). 'Review of Timothy O'Connor, Theism and Ultimate Explanation: The Necessary Shape of Contingency', *Mind* 118 (July): 862–7.

Kretzmann, N. (1988). 'A General Problem of Creation: Why Would God Create Anything at All?' in Macdonald, S. (ed.). *Being and Goodness*. Ithaca, NY: Cornell University Press, 208–28.

Leslie, J. (1979). *Value and Existence*. Oxford: Blackwell.

———. (1997). 'A Neoplatonist's Pantheism', *The Monist* 80 (2): 218–31.

———. (2001). *Infinite Minds*. Oxford: Clarendon Press.

Lewis, D. (1986a). *On the Plurality of Worlds*. Oxford: Blackwell.

———. (1986b). *Philosophical Papers*, Vol. 2. Oxford: Oxford University Press.

Lipton, P. (1990). 'Contrastive Explanation' in Knowles, D. (ed.). *Explanation and Its Limits*. Cambridge: Cambridge University Press, 247–66.

Mackie, J. (1982). *The Miracle of Theism*. Oxford: Clarendon Press.

Mawson, T.J. (2009). 'Review of Timothy O'Connor, Theism and Ultimate Explanation: The Necessary Shape of Contingency', *Religious Studies* 45: 237–41.

Molnar, G. (2003). *Powers*. Oxford: Oxford University Press.

Newlands, S. (2010). 'Review of Timothy O'Connor, Theism and Ultimate Explanation: The Necessary Shape of Contingency', *Philosophical Quarterly* 60 (239): 438–42.

O'Connor, T. (2008). *Theism and Ultimate Explanation: The Necessary Shape of Contingency*. Oxford: Blackwell.

———. (2010).). 'Replies to Senor, Oppy, McCann, and Almeida', *Philosophia Christi* 12: 307-14.

Oppy, G. (1999). 'Koons' Cosmological Argument', *Faith and Philosophy* 16: 378–89.

———. (2000). 'On "A New Cosmological Argument"', *Religious Studies* 36 (3): 345–53.

———. (2004). 'Faulty Reasoning About Default Principles in Cosmological Arguments', *Faith and Philosophy* 21: 242–9.

———. (2008). 'Review of Timothy O'Connor, Theism and Ultimate Explanation: The Necessary Shape of Contingency', *Notre Dame Philosophical Reviews* 2008 (6) [online].

———. (2009). 'Cosmological Arguments', *Noûs* 43 (1): 31–48.

———. (2011). 'O'Connor's Cosmological Argument' in J. Kvanvig (ed.). *Oxford Studies in Philosophy of Religion*, Vol. 3. Oxford: Oxford University Press, 166–86.

Parfit, D. (1998). 'The Puzzle of Reality: Why Does the Universe Exist?', in van Inwagen, P. and Zimmerman, D. (eds.). *Metaphysics: The Big Questions*. Cambridge, MA: Blackwell, 418–27.

Plantinga, A. (1993). *Warrant and Proper Function*. New York: Oxford University Press.

Pruss, A. (1998). 'The Hume-Edwards Principle and the Cosmological Argument', *International Journal for the Philosophy of Religion* 43: 149–65.

———. (2006). *The Principle of Sufficient Reason*. Cambridge: Cambridge University Press.

Pruss, A. and Gale, R. (1999). 'A New Cosmological Argument', *Religious Studies* 35 (4): 461–76.

Quine, W.V.O. (1961). 'Two Dogmas of Empiricism', in *From a Logical Point of View*. Cambridge: Harvard University Press, 20-46.

Reid, T. (1788/1969). *Essays on the Active Powers* of Man, ed. Baruch Brody. Cambridge, MA: MIT Press.

Rowe, W. (1984). 'Rationalistic Theology and Some Principles of Explanation', *Faith and Philosophy* 1: 357–69.

Senor, T. D. (2010). 'On the Tenability of Brute Naturalism and the Implications of Brute Theism', *Philosophia Christi* 12: 271-77.

Sider, T. (2011). *Writing the Book of the World*. Oxford: Oxford University Press.

Tegmark, M. (2008). 'The Mathematical Universe', *Foundations of Physics* 38: 101–50.

Tooley, M. (1987). *Causation: A Realist Approach*. Oxford: Clarendon Press.

Van Fraassen, B. (1988). *Laws and Symmetry*. Oxford: Clarendon Press.

Van Inwagen, P. (1996). 'Why Is There Anything at All?', *Proceedings of the Aristotelian Society*, Supp. Vol. 70: 95–110.

Wright, C. (1980). *Wittgenstein on the Foundations of Mathematics*. London: Duckworth.

———. (1986). 'Inventing Logical Necessity', in Butterfield, J. (ed.). *Language, Mind, and Logic*. Cambridge: Cambridge University Press, 187–209.

3   Ultimate Naturalistic Causal Explanations

Graham Oppy

There are various kinds of questions that might be asked by those in search of 'ultimate explanations'. Why is there anything at all? Why is there something rather than nothing? Why is there causal stuff? Why is there causal stuff rather than a complete absence of causal stuff? Why is there causal stuff that behaves as it does? Why is there causal stuff that behaves as it does rather than causal stuff that behaves in other ways?

In this chapter, my focus will be on 'ultimate causal explanations' and 'ultimate explanations of the natural world'—or, more exactly, on the *relative merits* of theistic and naturalistic 'ultimate causal explanations' and 'ultimate explanations of the natural world'. If we suppose that there are noncausal things—abstracta and the like—then we will not suppose that this discussion exhausts what there is to say about the relative merits of theistic and naturalistic ultimate explanations. However, I leave discussion of the relative merits of theistic and naturalistic accounts of the existence of noncausal things—abstracta and the like—for another day.

It is not part of my project to argue for the *absolute* virtue of the naturalistic ultimate causal explanations that will be canvassed in this article. The explanations in question depend on controversial assumptions about causality, modality, the meaningfulness of talk about 'ultimate explanation', and perhaps other things as well. What I do want to argue is that, against the background of these controversial assumptions, there is good reason to prefer naturalistic ultimate explanations to theistic ultimate explanations. Moreover, I shall argue that, if I am right in thinking that naturalistic ultimate explanations are better than theistic ultimate explanations, then those considerations alone are sufficient to defeat all cosmological arguments for the existence of God.

1   MODALITY

My favourite theory of modality goes like this. Wherever there was objective chance, there were alternative possibilities. Wherever there is objective chance, there are alternative possibilities. Wherever there will be objective chance, there will be alternative possibilities. Possible worlds are alternative ways that the actual world could have gone, or could go, or could one day go; possible worlds all 'share' an initial history with the actual world and 'branch' from the actual world only as a result of the outworkings of objective chance. Since the laws that govern the evolution of possible worlds do not vary over the course of that evolution, all possible worlds 'share' the same laws. If there was an initial state of the actual world, then all possible worlds 'share' that initial state; if there was no initial state of the actual world, then all possible worlds 'share' some 'infinite' initial segment with the actual world, and hence any two possible worlds 'share' some 'infinite' initial segment with one another.

My favourite theory of modality does not assume that there are objective chances. However, if there are no objective chances, then, on my favourite theory, there is just one possible world: the actual world. I take it that quantum mechanics affords some reason to suppose that there are objective chances. However, I note that the interpretation of quantum mechanics remains fraught, and, in any case, I note further that the inconsistency of quantum mechanics with general relativity provides us with good reason to suppose that quantum mechanics does not yet tell us the ultimate truth about natural reality. If it turns out that there is just one possible world, then the actual world is fully deterministic: any state of the world is both necessary and sufficient for all other states of the world.

My favourite theory of modality has the evident advantage of theoretical frugality. On the one hand, if there are objective chances, then any theory of modality is surely committed to the possibility of the outcomes that lie in the relevant objective chance distributions. On the other hand, it is not clear that we have good reason to commit ourselves to any possibilities beyond those that are required by whatever objective chances there might be; at the very least, any expansion of the range of possibilities clearly requires some kind of justification.

Of course, my favourite theory of modality is controversial: there are many who suppose that it omits further possibilities. For example, some suppose that (a) there might not have been anything at all; (b) the initial state of the world—or the entire beginningless history of the world—might have been different; (c) the laws might have been different; (d) the laws might change as the state of the world evolves; and perhaps there are yet other suppositions that might be entertained. On my favourite theory, these alternative suppositions are purely doxastic or epistemic: while they are ways that *it might be supposed* that the world could have gone, could go, or could one day go, they are not ways that the world could have gone, could go, or could one day go.

I do not suppose that it needs pointing out that what I have called 'my favourite theory of modality' is really only a fragment of a full theory of modality. For example, I have here taken no stance on the metaphysics of possible worlds: for all that I have said, the correct theory of possible worlds could be realist, ersatzist, primitivist, or perhaps something else again. All that I have been discussing here is what might be called 'the range of possibilities'—what is and isn't possible—and the ways in which the range of possibilities is related to what is actually the case.

2   CAUSAL REALITY

Causal reality has parts that stand in a fundamental external relation. If we are naturalists, we can suppose that the fundamental external relation is spatiotemporal. However, if we are supernaturalists, we cannot suppose that the fundamental external relation is spatiotemporal (though we may perhaps suppose that it has a temporal 'dimension').

For the purposes of the following discussion, I shall just take it for granted that the fundamental external relation uniquely partitions causal reality into maximal parts that (a) themselves have no parts that stand in causal relations and (b) are totally ordered under the relations of causal priority and causal anteriority. In particular, I assume (i) *irreflexivity* (no maximal part is causally prior [anterior] to itself); (ii) *antisymmetry* (if maximal part A is causally prior [anterior] to maximal part B, then maximal part B is not causally prior [anterior] to maximal part A); (iii) *transitivity* (if maximal part A is causally prior [anterior] to maximal part B, and maximal part B is causally prior [anterior] to maximal part C, then maximal part A is causally prior [anterior] to maximal part C); and (iv) *completeness* (for any pair of distinct maximal parts A and B, either A is causally prior [anterior] to B, or B is causally prior [anterior] to A).

While I make these assumptions for the purposes of subsequent discussion, I do not suppose that it is actually *true* that the fundamental external relation uniquely partitions causal reality into maximal parts that (a) themselves have no parts that stand in causal relations and (b) are totally ordered. Speaking very impressionistically, we can say that, for naturalists, this assumption is analogous to supposing that there is a unique global foliation of a general relativistic space-time. I think that it is quite clear that the argument I am developing would not have a different outcome if we instead developed a suitable 'extension' of the idea that there may be no unique general foliation of relativistic space-time to the fundamental external relation as it is manifest in supernatural causal reality.

I take it that the standing of the other assumptions is similarly contentious. For instance, there are well-known disputes about the possibility or impossibility of causal loops. Nothing in the forthcoming argument turns on the outcome of those disputes. On my favourite theory of modality, I'm inclined to think that causal loops really are impossible; on more permissive theories of modality, matters seem to me to be rather less clear. However, even if there are acceptable theories of modality on which there might be causal loops, there are no acceptable theories on which there might be single-membered causal loops, i.e. cases in which something stands in an unmediated causal relation to itself.

3   HYPOTHESES ABOUT CAUSAL REALITY

There are various hypotheses that one might make about the global shape of causal reality. In framing these hypotheses, we make no assumptions about the contents of causal reality; i.e. we make no assumptions about the relative extents of the natural and the supernatural. Moreover, in framing these hypotheses, we consider only their simplest versions.

1. *Regress*: Causal reality does not have an initial maximal part. That is, it is not the case that there is a part of causal reality which (a) has no parts that stand in causal relations to one another and (b) is not preceded by some other part of causal reality which has no parts that stand in causal relations to one another.
2. *Necessary Initial Part*: Causal reality has an initial maximal part, and it is not possible that causal reality had any other initial maximal part. On the assumption that the initial maximal part involves objects, both the existence and the initial properties of those objects are necessary.
3. *Contingent Initial Part*: Causal reality has an initial maximal part, but it is possible that causal reality had some other initial maximal part. On the assumption that the initial maximal part involves objects, at least one of the existence and the initial properties of those objects is contingent.

If we adopt my favourite theory of modality, then we get the following consequences.

According to *Regress*, every possible world shares an 'infinite' initial segment with the actual world. More accurately: in every possible world, there is no part of causal reality which (a) has no parts that stand in causal relations to one another and (b) is not preceded by some other part of causal reality which has no parts that stand in causal relations to one another; and every possible world shares an initial segment with the actual world.

According to *Necessary Initial Part*, every possible world has the same initial maximal part. In particular, then, every possible world has the same initial maximal part as the actual world. If the initial maximal part involves objects, then both the existence and the initial properties of those objects are necessary. If there is more then one possible world, then other possible worlds differ from the actual world because the evolution of the total state of the world is chancy: the laws and the initial properties of the objects that exist in the initial maximal part do not fully determine the subsequent history of the world.

Of course, on my favourite theory of modality, *Contingent Initial Part* is ruled out: on my favourite theory of modality, it cannot be that at least one of the existence and the initial properties of the objects that belong to the initial maximal part of the actual world is contingent. In order to accommodate theories according to which at least one of the existence and the initial properties of the objects that belong to the initial maximal part of the actual world is contingent, we need to retreat to a view on which the initial maximal part of the world might have been different: either because different things might have existed in that initial maximal part, or because those necessary existents that belong to the initial maximal part might have had different properties in that initial maximal part from the properties that they actually had in that initial maximal part, or because there might have been nothing at all.

4   NATURALISM AND THEISM

Naturalism and theism are, at least inter alia, competing hypotheses about the contents of global causal reality. According to naturalism, global causal reality is exhausted by natural causal reality: there are none but natural items—objects, events, states—related by natural causes, and none but natural properties involved in the causal evolution of those items.

According to theism, there is more to global causal reality than natural causal reality: for, apart from anything else, God is the supernatural creator of natural causal reality. Of course, many theists make more than this minimal supposition. On the one hand, many suppose that God's causal relation to natural reality involves much more than an initial act of creation: for example, they may suppose that God's supernatural agency is required to sustain the existence of natural reality, or they may suppose that God makes supernatural interventions in the natural causal order, or, in other words, causes miracles of one kind or another; etc. And, on the other hand, many theists suppose that the supernatural realm contains much more than God: there are angels, demons, and a whole host of other supernatural entities who God brings into existence and who have causal commerce with God and with the natural order. However, for the purposes of this paper, we shall focus our attention solely on the suggestion that God is the (lone) cause of the existence of the natural causal order: God brings into existence both the initial maximal part of the natural causal order and the laws that govern its evolution.

These characterisations of naturalism and theism are lean. Many discussions of 'naturalism' and 'theism' build much more into the definitions of these terms. For example, many theists suppose that there is much more to the essence of God than merely being the supernatural creator of natural causal reality. However, it is not my intention to here provide *analyses* of naturalism and theism. For the purposes of the forthcoming argument, all I need to suppose is that these characterisations supply necessary conditions:

naturalism *entails* that global causal reality is exhausted by natural causal reality, and theism *entails* that there is a supernatural lone creator of natural causal reality.

Even though my characterisations of naturalism and theism are lean, they are plainly not unproblematic. In particular, they take for granted a robust understanding of the distinction between the natural and the supernatural. Perhaps there are serious difficulties involved in the detailed explanation of this distinction. However, even if that is so, it is not clear that this is a threat to the argument that I shall be developing. After all, there are serious difficulties involved in the detailed explanation of just about any philosophically interesting distinction, and yet philosophers manage to continue to ply their trade, making use of terms that are intended to draw philosophically interesting distinctions. It seems to me that the distinction between the natural and the supernatural is in sufficiently good standing to bear the weight of subsequent argument; in consequence, at the very least, I think that I would need to be provided with strong reasons to retreat from this considered view.

5   HYPOTHESES COMPARED

The central idea behind my argument is that we can compare the merits of naturalism and theism, considered as hypotheses about the contents of global causal reality, under the various different assumptions that we might make about the global shape of causal reality. That is, for each hypothesis that we can frame about the global shape of causal reality, we can ask whether naturalism or theism should be preferred on that hypothesis about its shape, *all else being presumed equal*. If it turns out that, on each hypothesis that we can frame, we should prefer naturalism to theism, *all else being presumed equal*, then we can conclude that the global shape of causal reality gives us reason to prefer naturalism to theism, *all else being presumed equal*. And even if it only turns out that there is no hypothesis that we can frame on which we should prefer theism to naturalism, *all else being presumed equal*, we shall still be able to conclude that the global shape of causal reality gives us no reason to prefer theism to naturalism, *all else being presumed equal*.

This brief presentation of the central idea behind my argument raises at least two significant questions that require further comment. *First*, there is the question of what considerations we should take into account when deciding between theism and naturalism (on the various different hypotheses about the contents of global causal reality). *Second*, there are some questions about the role and significance of the insistence that all else should be presumed equal when we make our decision between theism and naturalism (on the various different hypotheses about the content of global causal reality).

I assume that, in the general case, there are a range of considerations that bear on choices between hypotheses or theories: *simplicity* (which is a matter of minimisation of theoretical commitments, taking into account ontological commitments, ideological commitments, and whatever other theoretical commitments there might be), *goodness of fit with data, explanatory scope and power, fit with other accepted hypotheses and theories*, and so forth. However, in the case that all else is presumed equal, I take it there are just three considerations that bear on the choice between hypotheses: simplicity, goodness of fit with data, and explanatory scope and power. (Even if this isn't right, and there are further considerations that bear on the choice between hypotheses when all else is presumed equal, I do not think that the subsequent argument will be affected. If necessary, we can return to consider this point further.)

What, then, is it for all else to be presumed equal? It is, essentially, for all other considerations to be ignored. If we ask whether naturalism or theism should be preferred on a hypothesis about the global shape of causal reality, all else being presumed equal, then we ask whether naturalism or theism should be preferred given that *that* hypothesis about the global shape of causal reality is the *only* thing that is being taken into account.

Why would it be an interesting result to establish that, on each hypothesis that we can frame about the global shape of causal reality, we should prefer naturalism to theism (or, at least, *not* prefer theism to naturalism)? Because, I take it, this result would decisively defeat all cosmological arguments for theism. On the one hand, it is obvious that the result would defeat all logical ('deductive') cosmological arguments, since *all else* is certainly ignored in these arguments. On the other hand, it is no less obvious that the result would defeat all evidential ('probabilistic') cosmological arguments, since such arguments rely on the assumption that all else is properly ignored. (This observation extends to some cases in which evidential cosmological arguments are supposed to contribute to a cumulative case for theism, namely, those cumulative case arguments in which each of the cases makes an *independent* incremental contribution to the overall case.) Of course, the result would not defeat arguments in which the global shape of causal reality is taken to be just one of several factors that are being *jointly* considered in the comparative assessment of theism and naturalism. (We shall have reason to return to this point towards the end of the chapter.) It hardly needs to be added that arguments in which the global shape of causal reality is taken to be just one of several factors that jointly serve to support theism over competing hypotheses are *not* properly called 'cosmological' arguments.

6   THE ARGUMENT

With various preliminaries behind us, it is a straightforward matter to state the central argument. We consider, in turn, each of the hypotheses that we might make about the global shape of causal reality.

Regress: If there is a global causal regress, then (a) according to naturalism, there is a regress of global natural causal states; and (b) according to theism, there is a regress of global natural+supernatural causal states. (Here, I allow that 'global natural+supernatural causal states' might lack a natural component, whereas it cannot lack a supernatural component. In fact, I suspect that the only version of this view that cannot be ruled out on other grounds is one in which there is a 'finite' series of global natural+supernatural states preceded by a regress of global supernatural causal states. However, nothing in the subsequent argument turns on the correctness of this supposition.)

In the nature of the case, it is obvious that, on the assumption that there is a global causal regress, neither naturalism nor theism fits better with the data or provides an explanation with greater scope or power—both views appeal to regress to answer the question why there is something rather than nothing, etc. However, it is equally obvious that naturalism scores better than theism on the count of theoretical commitment: naturalism has fewer ontological commitments than theism (fewer kinds of things to which it is committed) and fewer ideological commitments than theism (fewer primitive predicates that are required for the development of the theory), and naturalism plainly does no worse than theism in point of whatever other theoretical commitments there might be. Spelling out what I take to be obvious: naturalism is committed to one kind of entity (the natural), one kind of external relation (the spatiotemporal), one kind of causation (the natural), one kind of non-topic-neutral property (the natural), and so forth, whereas theism is committed to two kinds of entities (the natural and the supernatural), two kinds of external relations (the natural and the supernatural), two kinds of causation (the natural and the supernatural), two kinds of non-topic-neutral properties (the natural and the supernatural), and so on.

Moreover, even if one is inclined to dispute this assessment of the matter, I do not see how one could reasonably deny that, under the hypothesis that there is a global causal regress, there is no explanatory advantage that accrues to theism over naturalism when it comes to the answering of ultimate questions: Why is there anything at all? Why is there something rather than nothing? Why is there causal stuff? Why is there causal stuff rather than a complete absence of causal stuff? Why is there causal stuff that behaves as it does? Why is there causal stuff that behaves as it does rather than causal stuff that behaves in other ways? Etc. For, as I noted above, *both views appeal to regress in exactly the same kind of way* in order to provide whatever answers they provide to these ultimate questions, and it is not in question that naturalism does *no worse than* theism in point of theoretical commitments.

On my favourite theory of modality, given that there is a global causal regress, that regress is necessary (though, on the assumption that objective chance is ubiquitous, no part of the regress is necessary). That is, there is no possible world that fails to share an initial part of the actual world's global causal regress, even though, for any noninitial part of the actual regress, there are possible worlds that 'branch off' from the actual world prior to that noninitial part. On other, more permissive theories of modality, it may be that, given that there is a global causal regress, that regress is contingent.

But assessing our hypotheses according to those more permissive theories of modality does not change the relative explanatory standings of naturalism and theism: it remains the case that we have no better (or worse) fit with data or explanatory scope and power in the one case than we do in the other (and we still have it that naturalism does better than theism in point of minimisation of theoretical commitments).

In short, if there is a global causal regress, we should prefer naturalism to theism (or, at the very worst, we should not prefer theism to naturalism).

Necessary Initial Part: If there is a necessary initial part of the global causal order, then (a) according to naturalism, there is a necessary initial natural part of the global causal order that precedes a 'finite' series of natural parts; and (b) according to theism, there is a necessary initial supernatural part of the global causal order that precedes a 'finite' series of supernatural parts that in turn precedes a 'finite' series of natural+supernatural parts. (Here, I allow that the finite series of supernatural parts of the global causal order might be null: it might be that the creation of the natural causal order is immediately consequent on the necessary initial supernatural part of the global causal order. However, in order for it to be the case that the natural order has a supernatural cause, there must at least be an initial purely supernatural part of the global causal order.)

Of course, the argument that there is good reason to prefer naturalism to theism—or, at the very least, not to prefer theism to naturalism—on the hypothesis that there is a necessary initial part of the global causal order is exactly the same as it was in the case of the hypothesis that there is a regress. On the one hand, insofar as it is the necessity of the necessary initial part that is carrying the entire explanatory load, there is no advantage in the fit with data or the explanatory scope or power that accrues to theism above naturalism. But, on the other hand, naturalism is the leaner theory. All else being presumed equal, we have reason to prefer theories with fewer theoretical commitments, but there is no question that, insofar as we are only taking into account considerations that bear on global causal order, naturalism carries a substantially lighter theoretical load.

Perhaps it might be objected that there are reasons to prefer the hypothesis that there is a necessary initial global supernatural causal state to the hypothesis that there is a necessary initial global natural causal state. However, it is very hard to see how such a view might be defended. In particular, it is worth noting that my favourite theory of modality is almost inescapable on the supposition that there is a necessary initial global causal state. Certainly, it is just built into the view that all possible worlds share the same initial global causal state (and hence the same initial 'laws' governing the evolution of global causal state). Perhaps it might be denied that the only way that worlds can 'diverge' from the actual world is via the outworkings of objective chance—but, at the very least, considerations of simplicity militate against that denial. But given that it just falls out of the associated theory of modality that there is a necessary initial global causal state, I cannot see how one could hope to motivate the suggestion that it is more theoretically virtuous to suppose that that initial global causal state is supernatural rather than natural.

Some may feel that there is more to say here. For example, given that all noninitial global natural causal states are contingent, isn't there a good inductive argument to the conclusion that an initial global natural causal state would also be contingent? I don't think so. After all, given that all noninitial creators are contingent, surely there would be an equally good (or bad) inductive argument to the conclusion that any initial creator would also be contingent. Of course, I don't deny that many theists have the intuition that the hypothesis that there is a necessary initial state involving a necessarily existent supernatural creator (with necessary initial properties) is more theoretically virtuous than the hypothesis that there is a necessary initial state that involves nothing supernatural. However, it seems to me that this is pretty plainly a case in which the intuition is consequent on the prior adoption of theory: there just is nothing *intrinsically* more virtuous in the supposition that there is a necessarily existent supernatural creator (with necessary initial properties) than there is in the supposition that there is a necessary initial global natural causal state.

Contingent Initial Part: If there is a contingent initial part of the global causal order, then (a) according to naturalism, there is a contingent initial natural part of the global causal order that precedes a 'finite' series of natural parts; and (b) according to theism, there is a contingent initial supernatural part of the global causal order that precedes a 'finite' series of supernatural parts that in turn precedes a 'finite' series of natural+supernatural parts (as before, I allow that the finite series of supernatural parts of the global causal order might be null: it might be that the creation of the natural causal order is immediately consequent on the necessary initial supernatural part of the global causal order).

If there is a contingent initial natural part of the global causal order, then we can suppose either (a) that there is at least one necessarily initially existent natural entity—'the initial singularity'—at least some of whose initial properties are contingent, or else (b) that there are only contingently initially existing natural entities which may or may not have only essential initial properties. (Of course, the label 'the initial singularity' is not meant to be taken seriously: I am not assuming that natural reality is something like a standard big bang universe. However, it will be convenient to have a tag to use in the subsequent discussion.) If there is a contingent initial supernatural part of the global causal order, then we could suppose either (a) that there is at least one necessarily initially existent supernatural entity—God—at least some of whose initial properties are contingent, or else (b) that there are only contingently initially existing supernatural entities which may or may not have only essential initial properties.

Given that our interest in is theism—i.e. in the hypothesis that there is exactly one initially existent supernatural entity—we need only compare theism with versions of naturalism on which there is just one initially existing entity. If we do this, then, on the one hand, we compare the hypothesis that there is a necessarily existent initial singularity at least some of whose initial properties are contingent with the hypothesis that there is a necessarily existent supernatural creator at least some of whose initial properties are contingent; and, on the other hand, we compare the hypothesis that there is a contingently existing initial singularity which may or may not have only essential initial properties with the hypothesis that there is a contingently existing supernatural creator which may or may not have only essential initial properties.

The argument that there is good reason to prefer naturalism to theism—or, at the very least, not to prefer theism to naturalism—on the hypothesis that there is a contingent initial part of the global causal order is exactly the same as it was in the case of the hypothesis that there is a necessary initial part. On the one hand, as before, there is no advantage in the fit with data or the explanatory scope or power that accrues to theism above naturalism. But, on the other hand, naturalism is the leaner theory: it does better in point of ontological commitment, ideological commitment, and whatever other kinds of theoretical commitments there might be. Of course, on my favourite theory of modality, it is not even possible that there is a contingent initial natural part of the global causal order; in that case, these alternative theories do not even furnish possible answers to our ultimate questions. However, even if we retreat from my favourite theory of modality to views on which it is possible that there is a contingent initial natural part of the global causal order, we do not arrive at any views on which theism provides better answers to those ultimate questions than naturalism provides. (I suppose that there have been few, if any, theists who have wished to say that there is a contingently existing supernatural creator which may or may not have only essential initial properties; however, we lose nothing by including this hypothesis among the class on which we are comparing theism with appropriate naturalistic alternatives.)

The upshot of the considerations rehearsed in the argument is clear: if we are only interested in the global shape of causal reality, and if we set all other considerations aside, then we have no reason at all to prefer theism to naturalism (and, very plausibly, we have good reason to prefer naturalism to theism).

7   OTHER EXPLANATIONS?

Regress, Necessary Initial State, and *Contingent Initial State* afford three different kinds of answers to ultimate questions: Why is there anything at all? Why is there something rather than nothing? Why is there causal stuff? Why is there causal stuff rather than a complete absence of causal stuff? Why is there causal stuff that behaves as it does? Why is there causal stuff that behaves as it does rather than causal stuff that behaves in other ways?

Regress says: There has always been something; there has always been something rather than nothing; there has always been causal stuff; there has always been causal stuff that behaves as it does; etc. (Of course, *Regress can also say*: It had to be that there has always been something, something rather than nothing, causal stuff, causal stuff that behaves as it does, etc.) *Necessary Initial State says*: There had to be something; there had to be something rather than nothing; there had to be causal stuff; there had to be causal stuff that behaves as it does. *Contingent Initial State (involving necessary existents) says*: There had to be something; there had to be something rather than nothing; there had to be causal stuff; there had to be causal stuff, but there is no explanation why it is the way it is rather than some other way that it could have been. *Contingent Initial State (involving only contingent existents) says*: There might have been nothing, and there is no reason why there is something rather than nothing; there might have been no causal stuff, and there is no reason why there is causal stuff rather than an absence of causal stuff; there might have been no causal stuff, but given that there is causal stuff, it had to be the way that it is (or, alternatively, there might have been no causal stuff, and given that there is causal stuff, there is no explanation why it is the way that it is rather than some other way).

Considered as answers to ultimate questions, it is controversial whether each of *Regress*, *Necessary Initial State*, and the two versions of *Contingent Initial State* is acceptable. Some suppose, for example, that *Contingent Initial State (involving only contingent existents)* and the weaker version of *Regress* could not possibly be supposed to afford acceptable answers to ultimate questions. However, I hope that it is obvious that this controversy has no implications for the argument that I have just developed. Showing that there is something unacceptable or even impossible about *Contingent Initial State (involving only contingent existents)* and the weaker version of *Regress* cannot contribute anything at all towards showing that theism gives a better answer to ultimate questions than naturalism does, so long as it is true that naturalism dominates theism, i.e. so long as it is true that, on each hypothesis that one might make about the global shape of causal reality, naturalism is more theoretically virtuous than is theism.

Of course, there is something that would contribute towards showing that theism gives a better answer to ultimate questions than naturalism does: namely, the identification of a different kind of answer to ultimate questions than those that are canvassed in the course of my argument. Perhaps there is some other hypothesis about the global shape of causal reality on which theism outscores naturalism? Or perhaps there is an answer to my ultimate questions that does not essentially amount to an assumption about the global shape of causal reality?

I think that both of these suggestions can be fairly quickly dismissed. On the one hand, it seems to me to be quite implausible to suppose that there is a hypothesis—however outré—concerning the global shape of causal reality on which theism turns out to be more theoretically virtuous than naturalism (in the sense required by the argument that I have developed). On the other hand, it seems to me to be no less implausible to suppose that there are promising candidate answers to our ultimate questions that do not amount to assumptions about the global shape of causal reality.

This is not to say that the literature has not thrown up other candidate answers for ultimate questions. In particular, some have been driven to suppose that the questions might be given the following kinds of answers: there is something because it is good that there is something; there is something rather than nothing because it is good that there is something rather than nothing; there is causal stuff, causal stuff rather than absence of causal stuff, causal stuff that behaves as it does, causal stuff that behaves as it does rather than in other ways, etc., because it is good that there be such.

While this axiarchial strategy seems hopeless to me—it's no explanation at all of why something exists to observe that it is good that it exists—I don't think that I need to insist on this in order to respond to the suggestion. For it seems to me that naturalists can be just as satisfied (or dissatisfied) with the suggestion that the initial singularity exists *because* it is good that it exists as theists can be with the suggestion that God exists *because* it is good that God exists. While the reasons may not be exactly the same in each case, it seems clear to me that the axiarchial hypotheses are a very poor explanatory fit for both naturalism and theism: in each case, the axiarchial hypotheses are ad hoc noncausal additions to a fundamentally causal explanatory framework. Few theists suppose that goodness is explanatorily prior to God; few naturalists suppose that goodness is explanatorily prior to global natural causal reality.

8   OTHER CONSIDERATIONS?

Even if it is granted that, *all else being presumed equal*, naturalism gives better (or, at any rate, no worse) answers to ultimate questions than theism does, it might be suggested that this is not a particularly significant or interesting result. After all, what really matters is whether naturalism gives better answers to ultimate questions *all things considered*. Perhaps, all things considered, theism gives better answers to ultimate questions than naturalism does, because the additional theoretical commitments that are incurred by theism provide explanatory advantages elsewhere: better fit with data, greater explanatory scope and power, better fit with established hypotheses and theories, and so forth.

I think that there is one sense in which this response is clearly not correct. Even if it turns out that, all things considered, theism gives better answers to ultimate questions than naturalism does, because the additional theoretical commitments that are incurred by theism provide explanatory advantages elsewhere, it would actually still be significant and important if it were established that, *all else being presumed equal*, naturalism gives better (or, at any rate, no worse) answers to ultimate questions than theism does. The reason for this is that contemporary discussion of cosmological arguments would be significantly transformed if the conclusion of my argument were broadly accepted. As I noted earlier, acceptance of the conclusion of my argument would sound the death knell for (i) logical cosmological arguments, (ii) probabilistic cosmological arguments, and (iii) discrete cumulative case cosmological arguments. For, in each of these categories, the arguments in question proceed by considering nothing apart from the shape of global causal reality.

If we set aside implications for the debate about cosmological arguments, it is clear that there is a sense in which the above point should be conceded. In the end, the most important question is whether naturalism or theism should be preferred, *all things considered*. When everything is taken into account, answers to ultimate questions may turn out to be a matter of spoils to the victor: if one hypothesis trumps the other in every other domain, on every other piece of relevant evidence, then we shall reasonably conclude that that hypothesis gives better answers to the ultimate questions as well. However, if this is right, then it is worth asking how far the kind of argument that I have developed in connection with the shape of global causal reality can be extended.

Suppose, for example, that we decide to compare theism and naturalism, taking into account both the global shape of causal reality and the fine-tuning for life of our part of causal reality: can we argue that naturalism still trumps theism on all of the hypotheses that we might frame about the shape of global causal reality and the point in that global causal reality at which the fine-tuning for life of our part of causal reality is first established? I think so! While I cannot develop the full argument here, I can at least outline how it goes. In essence, there are only two hypotheses about where in global causal reality the fine-tuning is first established (if, as we shall simply suppose for the sake of argument, it is really true that our part of causal reality is fine-tuned for life). On the one hand, the fine-tuning could be there in the initial state; on the other hand, the fine-tuning could first arise in some noninitial state. On the latter hypothesis—i.e. on the hypothesis that the fine-tuning arises in some noninitial state—it must be that the fine-tuning is simply the outcome of objective chance. On the former hypothesis—i.e. on the hypothesis that the fine-tuning is present in the initial state—we can go on to suppose either that the fine-tuning is a contingent feature of the initial state or that it is a necessary (or essential) feature of the initial state. But in every one of these cases, there is no difference in the ultimate ground of the explanation of the fine-tuning between theism and naturalism. That is, the situation turns out to be exactly the same as it was in the case of the global shape of causal reality: theism and naturalism are on a par with respect to everything other than theoretical commitments, and naturalism trumps theism (or, at any rate, plainly does no worse than theism does) on point of theoretical commitments. So, I say, it's not just the discussion of cosmological arguments that should be transformed by adoption of the kind of approach that I have sketched. If I'm right, there is a very similar argument that sounds the death knell for (i) logical fine-tuning arguments, (ii) probabilistic fine-tuning arguments, (iii) discrete cumulative case fine-tuning arguments, (iv) logical cosmological + fine-tuning arguments, (v) probabilistic cosmological + fine-tuning arguments, and (vi) discrete cumulative case cosmological + fine-tuning arguments.

Of course, I do not suppose that this argument admits of indefinite extension: I don't suppose that, waiting in the wings, there is an extension of this argument for the conclusion that naturalism should be preferred to theism *all things considered*. For all that can be argued along these kinds of lines, it might be that the theoretical economies of naturalism are trumped by the greater explanatory virtues of theism in connection with consciousness, reason, mathematics, miracles, religious experience, or what have you. However, that theism trumps naturalism in this way is clearly something that would remain to be argued and that has not hitherto been satisfactorily argued.

Perhaps there are a couple of further remarks that it will be useful to make here. First, the preceding discussion may have interesting implications for ontological arguments. In particular, acceptance of my favourite theory of modality has interesting implications for such descriptions as 'the greatest possible agent' and the like. On the version of metaphysical naturalism that is tied to my favourite theory of modality, a description like this, if proper, will pick out a possible natural agent (and perhaps even a possible human being)! Second, there are good reasons to suppose that Euthyphro-style considerations rule out the suggestion that theism gains an advantage over naturalism from considerations about mathematics, meaning, morality, modality, and a host of related domains. So, while I do not suppose that, waiting in the wings, there is an extension of the presented argument to the conclusion that naturalism should be preferred to theism, all things considered, I do think that the presented argument contributes to the task of narrowing the turf on which battles between theism and naturalism might be conducted in the future.

9   *PERSONAL* EXPLANATION?

I anticipate that some may say that the argument that I have been developing improperly ignores a distinction that can be made between scientific explanation and personal explanation. In discussing explanations of fine-tuning, I asserted that theism has no explanatory advantage over naturalism if either (a) the fine-tuning is an outcome of objective chance or (b) the fine-tuning is a feature of the initial state of global causal reality. However, if the fine-tuning is an outcome of objective chance, then, whereas naturalism claims that this is just a result of the outworkings of natural law, theism claims that this is result of God's free creative decision. And if the fine-tuning is a feature of the initial state of global causal reality, then, whereas naturalism claims that this is a brute (though perhaps necessary) feature of the initial state of global causal reality, theism claims that this is a brute (though perhaps necessary) feature of the (initial state of the) mind of God. Might someone reasonably object that objective chances are more theoretically virtuous if attributed to free creative decisions than if attributed to the outworkings of natural law? Might someone reasonably object that brute (though perhaps necessary) features are more theoretically virtuous if attributed to the mind of God than if attributed to the initial state of the natural world?

I don't think so. If the thought is that personal explanations—explanations in terms of beliefs, desires, intentions, and the like—come at no theoretical cost, then the thought is evidently forlorn. And if the thought is that personal explanations come at a lower theoretical cost than explanations in terms of the outworkings of natural law, then, again, that thought is surely forlorn. A contingent desire to bring about a fine-tuned natural reality incurs no less theoretical cost than does a contingent fine-tuned natural reality; a necessary desire to bring about a fine-tuned natural reality incurs no less theoretical cost than does a necessary fine-tuned natural reality; an objectively chancy causing of the fine-tuning of natural reality by a free creative decision incurs no less theoretical cost than an objectively chancy causing of the fine-tuning by the outworking of natural law. No matter which hypothesis we entertain about the fine-tuning of natural reality, there just is no theoretical advantage that accrues to the 'personal' version of that hypothesis.

Of course, in our ordinary practice of giving personal explanations—i.e. for the behaviour of human agents—we typically don't need to worry about the theoretical costs involved in the postulation of the relevant beliefs, desires, intentions, and so forth. I can have great confidence in my attribution of beliefs, desires, intentions, and the like to human agents, without having much at all by way of knowledge of the causal aetiology of those beliefs, desires, intentions, and so forth. Nonetheless, when I causally explain the behaviour of those agents in terms of those beliefs, desires, intentions, and the like, I do *not* suppose that the relevant beliefs, desires, intentions, and so forth have no causes. The theoretical costs involved in the giving of personal explanations may typically escape our notice when we give those explanations, but this is not good grounds for supposing that there are no such costs.

10   *METAPHYSICAL* NATURALISM?

I anticipate that some may say that the argument that I have been developing involves an inadequate or improper conception of naturalism. The *metaphysical* naturalism that I have been discussing will surely be anathema to many contemporary naturalists: methodological naturalists, scientific naturalists, and the like. Whatever the merits of the view that I have been defending, isn't it simply inconsistent with mainstream contemporary naturalistic philosophies?

Not at all! Of course, I grant that I have been discussing theories of modality, causality, ultimate explanation, and so forth, which are regarded as anathema by some contemporary naturalists. But there is nothing in the argument that I have developed that required *endorsement* of any of those theories. If those theories of modality, causality, ultimate explanation, and so forth are properly eliminated on other grounds, then, pretty clearly, the standard metaphysical arguments for theism—cosmological arguments, fine-tuning teleological arguments, and the like—are properly eliminated as well (since those arguments cannot even be framed without the support of those theories). But even naturalists who are quite certain that these theories of modality, causality, ultimate explanations, and the like are properly eliminated on other grounds can still ask, *What if we are wrong about that?*

So, of course, the point of the argument that I have been developing is not to argue for the absolute merits of the metaphysical naturalism under discussion. Rather, the point of the argument that I have been developing is to argue for the absolute lack of merit of standard metaphysical arguments for theism. If you want to buy into the controversial theories of modality, causality, ultimate explanation, and so forth that are the stock in trade of the standard metaphysical arguments for theism, then, it seems to me, there is a pretty compelling case to be made that the arguments that you can erect on those foundations provide more support for the metaphysical naturalism outlined in this paper than they do for theism (and, at the very least, it is surely plain that those arguments provide no less support for the metaphysical naturalism outlined in this paper than they do for theism).

11   CONCLUDING REMARKS

I don't claim to have original answers to offer to questions about ultimate explanation. I suppose that, at some level, there are only three competing views: (i) nothing is impossible, (ii) nothing is possible (but not actual), and (iii) nothing is actual. On my favourite theory of modality, (i) turns out to be correct: it is not possible for there to be nothing. If I am pushed to make a choice, this is the view I favour. However, I take it that (ii) remains a serious contender: there are alternative theories of modality on which it is possible for there to be nothing, even though it is not actually the case that there is nothing. View (iii) is, I think, definitely ruled out. (If you are an ontological nihilist, and if you insist that there is nothing but first-order quantification, then you can insist on the literal truth of the claim that there is nothing. However, it is clear that the informal statement of (i)–(iii) is premised on the assumption that we are not restricted to first-order quantification: in the relevant sense, even ontological nihilists do not accept that there is nothing.)

It seems to me that metaphysical naturalists do not need to suppose that they have answers to ultimate questions in order to justify the claim that consideration of those ultimate questions gives them grounds to favour metaphysical naturalism over theism. It seems to me that metaphysical naturalists can properly be utterly agnostic about the shape of global causal reality—perhaps regress, perhaps loop, perhaps necessary origin, perhaps contingent origin, perhaps something else . . . —while nonetheless being confident that considerations about the shape of global causal reality favour naturalism over theism. Of course, there is a sense in which this kind of 'agnostic' metaphysical naturalism is more complicated than competing views that settle on a definitive answer, but the complexity in question is not one that speaks to the greater theoretical virtues of those competitors (whether theistic or naturalistic). There is no good methodological precept that militates against reasonable withholding of judgement; yet, as things stand, it is very hard to see any good reasons to favour any particular class of answers to ultimate questions (regress, or loop, or necessary origin, or contingent origin, or something else again . . .).

4 Reasoning Without the Principle of Sufficient Reason

Shieva Kleinschmidt

According to Principles of Sufficient Reason, every truth (in some relevant group) has an explanation. One of the most popular defenses of Principles of Sufficient Reason has been the *presupposition of reason* defense, which takes endorsement of the defended Principle of Sufficient Reason to play a crucial role in our theory selection. According to recent presentations of this defense, our method of theory selection often depends on the assumption that, if a given proposition is true, then it has an explanation, and this will be justified only if we think this holds for *all* propositions in the relevant group. I will argue that this argument fails even when restricted to contingent propositions, and even if we grant that there is no nonarbitrary way to divide true propositions that have explanations from those that lack them. Further, we can give an alternate explanation[1] of what justifies our selecting theories on the basis of explanatory features: the crucial role is not played by an endorsement of a Principle of Sufficient Reason but rather by our belief that, prima facie, we should prefer theories that exemplify *explanatory power* to greater degrees than their rivals. This guides our theory selection in a manner similar to *ontological parsimony* and *theoretical simplicity*. Unlike a Principle of Sufficient Reason, our belief about explanatory power gives us a prima facie guiding principle, which provides justification in the cases where we think we have it, and not in the cases where we think we don't.[2]

---

1. Alexander Pruss (2006) discusses this option but rejects it, due to worries that we would not be able to provide justification for our belief that explanatory power is truth-tracking (at least, generally enough to support all of the instances of theory selection which we'd like to). More on this in §3.
2. The fact that it is merely a prima facie principle is crucial in blocking a direct argument from this view about explanatory power to Principles of Sufficient Reason. If we thought that the most explanatory theory is *always* the correct one, then the PSR would claim victory over its rivals. But the prima facie nature of this principle allows for overriding considerations (such as the belief that in some cases there are truths for which we cannot even imagine how an explanation might go; note, for instance, this volume's primary subject matter).

In §1 I will present the recent version of the *presupposition of reason* defense that has been put forward by Michael Della Rocca and Alexander Pruss.[3] In §2, I will discuss cases where we seem tempted to posit unexplained truths, and I will focus on the Problem of the Many. This case is particularly difficult for the proponent of the inductive presupposition of reason defense, because it seems relevantly like a paradigm case where our theory selection is based on an attempt to avoid unexplained truths, but in this case we do not reject the theory that requires an unexplained truth. I will argue that this gives us good reason to reject the inductive argument for Principles of Sufficient Reason. Finally, in §3, I will briefly explain how appealing to explanatory power as a truth-tracking theoretical virtue can explain our differing responses to these very similar cases, while allowing us to claim that both responses are justified and without requiring us to accept a Principle of Sufficient Reason.

1   THE PRESUPPOSITION OF REASON DEFENSE

Principles of Sufficient Reason (PSRs) are formulated in a variety of ways. The fully general PSR is the following:

> *The General Principle of Sufficient Reason (G-PSR)*: Every true proposition has an explanation.

There are also restricted versions.[4] The two that will be relevant in the following discussion are the following.

> *The Principle of Sufficient Reason for Contingent Truths (C-PSR)*: Every contingent, true proposition has an explanation.

> *The Principle of Sufficient Reason for Necessary Truths (N-PSR)*: Every nonanalytic, necessary, true proposition has an explanation.

What one's PSR amounts to will also depend on the features we require explanations to have. I will not take a stand on whether the explanation must be complete (explaining every component of a proposition), or ultimate (in that it does not itself stand in need of explanation), or sufficient (in that it

---

3. Pruss 2006: ch. 16, and Della Rocca 2010.
4. However, not every restriction of the domain of propositions will result in a PSR; for instance, I believe that there is an explanation for why it's true that there's a Christmas tree in my house. However, I do not take myself to thereby endorse a PSR. When I speak of defenders of the *presupposition of reason* defense claiming that we must endorse a PSR in order for some group of beliefs to be justified, I am not suggesting that they believe that a purported PSR restricted to any group of propositions you choose will be sufficient.

entails what it explains). Further, if one finds something particularly problematic about talk of propositions, PSRs can be taken to be about events, states of affairs, facts, or the existence of objects. My comments will apply regardless. Further, the worries I raise in this paper will be problematic for every PSR that is either fully general or nonarbitrarily restricted.

One of the most popular defenses of PSRs has been the *presupposition of reason* defense. Leibniz claimed that we cannot successfully engage in reasoning without endorsing a PSR. More moderate presentations of the defense simply claim that some of the beliefs we take to be justified will not be if we do not endorse the PSR being defended. One might claim that we presuppose the relevant PSR when we form these beliefs and that it plays a direct and crucial role in justifying those beliefs. But an alternative means of arguing for PSRs has been presented,[5] on which it's noted that, in forming such a belief, we often make an assumption that, for some particular proposition in some class C, if that proposition is true, then it has an explanation. Further, within C, it does not seem that there is a nonarbitrary way to divide propositions with respect to this feature. And if there is not a nonarbitrary division, then we will not be justified in simply assuming any particular member of C has this feature unless every member of C does. So, if we take ourselves to be justified in forming the beliefs in question, we should believe that there is an explanation of every truth in C. If we take C to be the class of contingent propositions, then we should endorse the PSR.[6] In other words:

The Inductive Argument for the PSR

1. For some proposition,[7] P, which is a member of class C, and some theory about P, T, our justifiably assuming that if P is true, then P has an explanation, plays a crucial role in our justified acceptance or rejection of T (if it is justified).
2. Our acceptance or rejection of T is justified.
3. *So*, we justifiably assume that there is an explanation of P.
4. For any proposition, Q, if Q is a member of C, then Q is relevantly similar to P.[8]

---

5. Pruss 2006: ch. 16, and Della Rocca 2010.
6. Michael Della Rocca (2010) presents this argument, but he does not restrict the class of truths. He argues for the G-PSR, requiring explanations for all necessary truths as well.
7. This argument could just as easily involve states of affairs, events, or the existence of entities. Substitute as you prefer.
8. By 'relevantly similar to' here, I do not mean to imply that they are alike with respect to whether, if true, they have explanations. Rather, I intend to claim that they are alike with respect to whether there is anything that *grounds* their having an explanation. If there is not, they may still differ with respect to whether they have explanations, but no nonarbitrary division between them can be drawn to explain why.

5. *So*, we should believe that for any truth, Q, that is a member of C, there is an explanation of Q.
6. *So*, we should believe the Principle of Sufficient Reason about truths that are members of C.

A version of this argument can be given for each brand of PSR. If the relevant class of propositions, C, contains all and only the contingent propositions, then the argument will be for the C-PSR. I'll call this the Contingent Inductive Argument (C-IA). If the relevant class of propositions contains all and only the nonanalytic, necessary propositions, then it will provide an argument for the N-PSR. I'll call this the Necessary Inductive Argument (N-IA).[9]

There are many ways to respond to these inductive arguments. For instance, we might reject premise (4), claiming that we *can* draw a nonarbitrary division between members of the relevant class, to explain why some true claims in C have explanations and others don't. For instance, if C is restricted to contingent propositions, and we think that explanations necessitate their explananda, we may claim that merely all of the contingent truths that do not describe instances of agent causation have explanations.[10] For the moment, I am going to set aside this sort of worry, grant that premise (4) is true (at least, for the C-IA and N-IA), and examine other alternatives for responding to the argument. I will return to worries about this premise in §2.4.

2 FISSION AND THE PROBLEM OF THE MANY

In presenting the inductive argument for the C-PSR, we might support premise (1) by pointing to ordinary cases where we expect explanations. For instance, suppose we find small blue handprints along the wall, and we notice that the blue frosting is gone from its bowl and some is on the hands, face, and torso of a nearby five-year-old. When wondering what happened, we will not be tempted even for a moment by the alternative the child wishes to bring to our attention, namely, that the handprints are on the wall for no reason, that they are *simply there*. But if truths about events like these all have explanations, on what grounds could we claim that there is not an explanation of a truth describing a larger event, say, one that happens to include all of the smaller events?

To support premise (1) of the inductive argument for the N-PSR (or, as Della Rocca does, the G-PSR), we must present cases where, for some necessary proposition, we assume that if it is true, it must have an explanation. Della Rocca provides a host of examples, among which are our rejection of

---

9. This version of the inductive argument can be found in Pruss 2006: 12–13.
10. Pruss (2006) defends the C-PSR while rejecting the claim that explanations must necessitate their explananda, appealing to God's free action in explaining the existence of the universe.

dispositional differences between qualitative duplicates, our endorsement of the Uniformity of Nature, and our response to Wiggins's and Parfit's *fission* cases.[11] I'll focus on the last of these.

Here is the structure of the rest of this section. I will present two metaphysical puzzles: fission cases and the Problem of the Many. I will note that in the fission case, we reject a view that requires an unexplained truth but that in the Problem of the Many, we're compelled to accept a view that requires an unexplained truth. I will not take a stand on whether the relevant (nonanalytic) propositions, if true, would be contingent or necessary. However, I will claim that the similarities between the cases suggest that, if true, the propositions would either both be contingent or both be necessary. I will then present this dilemma: if they are contingent, then the unexplained truth required in response to the Problem of the Many will be a straightforward counterexample to the C-PSR (and any PSR that entails it). If they are nonanalytic and necessary, we have a counterexample to the N-PSR and should reject the N-IA. And if we are justified in rejecting the unexplained truth in the fission case while accepting the unexplained truth in response to the Problem of the Many, then the similarities between the N-IA and C-IA, in conjunction with our belief that the necessary propositions are at least as hard to nonarbitrarily divide as the contingent ones, should lead us to also reject the C-IA. Thus, regardless of what we take the modal statuses of the relevant propositions to be, we should reject the C-IA. Rejecting this argument is compatible with endorsing the C-PSR, but we no longer have this piece of inductive support for it. Let us begin.

Fission Cases

Consider a case where a subject, S, is cut in two, and each half is immediately paired up with a newly created replacement of the half it just lost, so now it appears there are two people, Lefty and Righty. That is, prior to the fission, a person, S, is made of two halves, L and R (and we'll suppose L and R are relevantly similar). Then, L and R are separated, but each is immediately paired with a new half that is relevantly similar to the old one. Post fission, there seem to be two people: Lefty, made of L and R^*, and Righty, made of L^* and R.[12]

There are many things you can claim about this case: you might think that no subject can survive such fission, or you might think that in any such case, there were two coincident people to begin with and they simply part ways when fission occurs.[13] However, according to one response, there is a single person at the start, and either that person survives as Lefty, or the person survives as Righty, but not both. We tend to reject this alternative simply because we assume that, if the subject in these circumstances survives as one rather than the other, then there must

---

11. Della Rocca 2010: 2–6.
12. These cases have been presented by Wiggins (1967: 50) and Parfit (1984: 254–61). The presentation of fission cases that I've used is borrowed from Ross (unpublished).
13. For the four-dimensionalist version of this view, see Lewis 1976.

be an explanation for this. But if the person is split evenly, and we imagine that the halves of the person were relevantly similar to begin with, and that the new halves they're paired up with are also relevantly similar, then Lefty and Righty will each be equally good candidates for being identical to our subject. Without any relevant dissimilarities, it seems nothing can explain why the subject in these circumstances is, after the fission, made of one pair of halves rather than the other. That is, the following proposition must lack an explanation:

> T1: In circumstances *C*, where Lefty and Righty are relevantly similar, exactly one person undergoes fission, and post fission, that person is made of *L* and *R** (/*L** and *R*) rather than *L** and *R* (/*L* and *R**).

Della Rocca claims that, in reflecting on a variety of cases like these, we should think that if *this* proposition's truth would require an explanation, then any (at least nonanalytic) truth must.

However, many philosophers take there to be some nonanalytic, necessary truths that lack explanations. For instance, it is not uncommon to think that there is a true, general moral principle which is both necessary and lacks an explanation. Or that there are some necessary, unexplained rules governing part/whole relations (like Strong Supplementation or Unrestricted Composition). And it is not uncommon to take some (but not all) truths of mathematics to be nonanalytic, necessary, and without explanation.

The Problem of the Many

I'm now going to focus on one piece of motivation for thinking that there is a truth that lacks an explanation. We will return shortly to the question of its modal status.

Consider Unger and Geach's Problem of the Many.[14] Though the problem can be raised for a variety of objects, I'll follow Hud Hudson's presentation, focusing on the problem as it applies to people.[15] There is some group of atoms that makes up you. (For the nonmaterialist who may think souls play

---

14. Unger 1980, and Geach 1980.
15. Hudson 2001: ch. 1. Focusing on the problem as it applies to people allows us to rule out some responses which we might think were acceptable if, for instance, we were talking about clouds instead. For instance, one response to the Problem of the Many is to say that there are many different spatially overlapping objects of the relevant kind whenever there is one object of the relevant kind. This response might not seem bad when the relevant objects are clouds, but it seems very problematic if the relevant objects are people. Another example: Peter van Inwagen's nihilism with respect to all nonliving things (van Inwagen 1990b) may help him escape this puzzle with respect to things like clouds, because he will deny that there are any clouds and thus needn't claim that there are many overlapping clouds in order to avoid arbitrariness. But this response does not help him when the puzzle is raised for people. (Van Inwagen instead responds by saying that claims about parthood can be true to degrees other than 1 and 0.)

an important role in what makes up a person, consider this problem as it applies to, say, ants, or peonies.) But there is another group of atoms that has all the same members, minus an atom right at the tip of your left pinkie finger, and with the addition of an atom right off the tip of your right pinkie finger. These two groups of atoms seem to be equally good candidates for being all and only the atoms that make up a person. However, we want to say that there is exactly one person overlapping the space you occupy. Thus, exactly one of these groups of atoms succeeds in composing a person, and there is no explanation for why it is one group rather than the other that is successful, given these circumstances (which include the arrangement of the atoms and the like).

This problem is frequently taken to be paradoxical because we are resistant to this arbitrariness that is involved in what is otherwise the preferable solution. However, the other solutions, which involve things like the denial that there are any people, the positing of many spatially overlapping people,[16] or the positing of ontological vagueness, seem even more problematic.[17] Because we seem to have no other good alternatives, we may accept that there are some unexplained truths.

If we *do* think that this is an unexplained fact, then we have a counterexample to the G-PSR. Further, if we think this unexplained fact is contingent, it will also be a counterexample to the C-PSR. If we think it is necessary, we should reject the N-PSR, N-IA, and, I will argue, the C-IA. But what is this truth's modal status?

The Unexplained Truth as Contingent

First, we should specify exactly which proposition we're claiming is unexplained. It is not simply this (where we're taking G1 and G2 to be two overlapping groups of atoms which are equally good candidates for composing a person):

T2: The atoms in group G1 rather than those in G2 compose a person.

If T2 is true, it does seem to be contingent. For the atoms in G1 could have failed to exist, or they could have existed but been scattered across the

---

16. We focused on only two relevantly similar groups of atoms, but there are many, many overlapping groups that seem to be equally good candidates for making up a person anytime one group succeeds in doing so.
17. There are other responses as well. For instance, Hud Hudson presents the claim that each relevant group of atoms *does* make up a person but that the distinct groups each make up the same person, and that person is simply multiply located (and has different parts at each location he or she occupies). However, Wasserman (2003) has raised worries about this solution's inability to solve a higher-order version of the Problem of the Many. Also, I have argued that we should avoid positing even the mere possibility of multilocation, due to its incompatibility with central axioms of mereology (Kleinschmidt 2011).

cosmos. However, T2 seems to have an explanation (though perhaps not an ultimate one). For instance, we might explain it by saying: (i) in any world with these circumstances, arrangement of atoms, and histories of atoms (etc.), the group of atoms with feature F will compose a person, and the group of atoms with feature H will not compose a person; (ii) the actual world has the circumstances, arrangement of atoms, and histories of atoms (etc.) referred to in (i), and G1 has feature F and G2 has feature H. We might supplement this explanation by describing how the atoms came to be in those arrangements. The relevant truth that *lacks* an explanation seems to be this one:

> T3: Given the circumstances, and the arrangement and histories[18] of the atoms in the world, the atoms in group G1 compose a person and the atoms in group G2 do not.

It is plausible to take T3 to be necessary. However, theorists will think it is contingent if they think that composition facts involving persons do not supervene on facts about the arrangement and histories (and the like) of atoms in the world.

Further, if you think that intrinsic duplicates are possible, you might be persuaded by the following argument for the contingency of T3. (Though anyone who thinks intrinsic duplicates are impossible, especially due to independent tension with a PSR, will not be swayed.)

The Problem of the Many and Unexplained Contingent Propositions

1. Possibly, there are two groups of atoms, G1 and G2, which have the following features: (i) G1 and G2 overlap spatially and share almost all of their members, (ii) G1 and G2 are intrinsic duplicates of one another, (iii) G1 and G2 bear relevantly similar relations to all of the other entities in their world (with the exception of parthood relations),[19] and (iv) G1 composes a person, or G2 composes a person, but not both.
2. If two groups of atoms, G1 and G2, have the features described above and are in circumstances C (which include facts about the arrangement and histories of all of the atoms in the world), and G1 rather than G2 composes a person, then there exists a possible world where a duplicate of G2 composes a person in circumstances C.

---

18. I hereby cancel any implication that I think the arrangement and history of the atoms are all that's relevant. If there are other relevant features (and they don't involve haecceities), consider them included here.
19. So, for instance, for any distance relation, R, there exists an atom, x, that G1 bears R to iff there exists an atom, y, that G2 bears R to. However, it will not follow that the groups are indiscernible.

3. If there is a possible world where a duplicate of G2 composes a person in circumstances C, then, possibly, G2 composes a person in circumstances C.
4. *So*, for any groups of atoms with the features described in (1), if one group rather than the other composes a person in some set of circumstances, then this is a contingent truth.

So, for instance, we can imagine a person-involving instance of the Problem of the Many involving groups of atoms which mirror one another perfectly.[20] And we can imagine that those atoms are embedded in a world with similar features: for any atom that is, say, exactly 300 light-years to the left of a member of our first group of atoms, there is an atom that is 300 light-years to the right of the counterpart member of our second group of atoms. There may still be irrelevant differences between those faraway atoms, however; for instance, perhaps two subatomic particles to the far, far left of our first group have the same spin, and the corresponding subatomic particles to the far, far right of our second group differ in spin from one another. These differences in faraway atoms, however, will not be relevant for the composition of persons.

A similar argument can be given for the claim that T1, the explanation-lacking proposition that fission cases drew our attention to, would be contingent if it were true:

Fission and Unexplained Contingent Propositions

1. Possibly, a fission case, *F*, occurs where Lefty and Righty (as well as *L*, *R*, *L**, and *R**) are intrinsic duplicates,[21] and there are no important differences in the relations they stand in to objects disjoint from *L*, *R*, *L**, and *R**.[22]
2. If in *F* exactly one person undergoes fission, and that person survives as Lefty rather than as Righty, then there exists a possible world where

---

20. Though the two groups needn't be incongruent counterparts. For instance, we can stipulate that the groups are embedded in space extended in more dimensions than the groups are, so our groups of atoms can be duplicates in the same way that a 'p' and 'q' embedded in 3-dimensional space can be duplicates—though, again, if we're worried that positing intrinsic duplicates begs the question against a PSR, we can allow for irrelevant differences between them. See discussion on this below.
21. Or, at least, similar in every minimally important respect.
22. Ross (unpublished) provides an example of this sort: he has us consider a fission case involving a subject made up of cells such that each cell's halves are intrinsic duplicates of one another. He then has us imagine that fission occurs when the halves of each of these cells are all simultaneously separated from one another and provided with new duplicate halves to replace the now-displaced ones. (We can imagine that the arrangement of the cells is held fixed.)

exactly one person undergoes fission, and that person survives as an intrinsic duplicate of Righty.[23]

3. If there is a possible world where the subject who undergoes fission survives as an intrinsic duplicate of Righty, then, possibly, the subject who undergoes fission survives as Righty.

4. *So,* if in a fission case where Lefty and Righty are intrinsic duplicates, exactly one person undergoes fission, and that person survives as Lefty rather than as Righty, then it is a contingent truth that in a case like this the subject survives as Lefty rather than as Righty.

Of course, there are several ways one might reject these arguments. For instance, a transworld identity theorist may deny the third premise of each. And a counterpart theorist might deny the third premise if he or she believes worldmates cannot be counterparts. Alternatively, one might present this dilemma: either the intrinsic duplicates mentioned in the first premise of each argument are indiscernible (i.e. not only do they have all of the same qualitative intrinsic features, but they have all the same qualitative relational features as well), or they are not. If they are, we may deny the first premise, due to thinking that distinct indiscernibles are impossible. If they are not, then we can deny the third premise. That premise claims that, for any possible x and y, we can infer that x is possibly G if, possibly, y is G. But, our detractor may claim, there's a restriction: we can make this inference only when, in the world where y is G, nothing is more similar to how x actually is than y. I think there is good reason to reject this restriction,[24] but if you accept it, here's how it can be used to cause trouble. If the intrinsic duplicates appealed to in my arguments are distinct indiscernibles, then they will meet this requirement and we do not have a problem. But if, for instance, Lefty stands in a relation that Righty does not stand in, then Lefty will not be at least as similar to Righty as anything else in its world, because Righty will be more similar to itself than Lefty is to it. Thus, we will have grounds for denying the third premise.

---

23. For the four-dimensionalist, this premise will read: If in F exactly one person undergoes fission, and the person's postfission temporal parts are all and only Lefty's postfission temporal parts rather than Righty's, then there exists a possible world where there is exactly one person who undergoes fission and the person's postfission temporal parts are all and only the members of a group of temporal parts that is an intrinsic duplicate of the group of all and only Righty's postfission temporal parts.

24. For instance, imagine a world that contains a bunch of qualitatively indiscernible statues. It seems plausible that one of the statues could have been shorter while the rest stayed the same. But then, in that other world, the other statues will be more like the actual statue than the shorter statue will be. Thus, if we endorse the proposed restriction, we will have to deny that this sort of unique shortness is possible for our statue.

I have mentioned just some of the ways of responding to my arguments, and I do not want to give defenses of those arguments here. Instead, I merely wish to note that there is *some* motivation for thinking that, if we posit unexplained facts due to the Problem of the Many, we ought to take those facts to be contingent. And if we do, then we must reject the C-PSR and G-PSR.

The Unexplained Truths as Necessary

What if, instead, we take the T1 and T3 to be necessary truths rather than contingent ones? The two claims do not seem to be analytic. Very specific facts about which arrangements of atoms in which circumstances will result in the composition of a person may be true as a matter of necessity, but they do not follow from, say, the analysis of *person*. So, if T1 and T3 are necessary, then they are nonanalytic necessary truths. And if T3 is true, then we have a counterexample to the N-PSR and G-PSR.

If we also believe that we are justified in rejecting T1, then we have a problem. Because it seems that our rejection of T1 depends on the justified belief that T1 must, if true, have an explanation, and since there is no explanation available, it must not be true. But how can our rejection of T1 be justified when we fail to reject a relevantly similar proposition, T3? That is, it does not seem that we can draw a nonarbitrary division between T1 and T3. So something is wrong with the N-IA. Either we are not justified for the reasons we assumed, or there really is a nonarbitrary way we can divide the nonanalytic, necessary truths with explanations from the nonanalytic, necessary truths without them.

Here is how this causes trouble for the C-IA. The two arguments are very similar. The methodology we use in rejecting T1 seems *just like* the methodology we use in rejecting the five-year-old's suggestion that the blue handprints on the wall were *simply there*. So the first premise of the C-IA and the first premise of the N-IA will stand or fall together: whatever explains the justification for our theory selection in one case should also explain it in the other.

Further, it seems that if we're justified in endorsing (4) and the inference to (5) of the C-IA, then we'll be justified in endorsing them for the N-IA as well. T1 and T3 are the same kind of proposition, about the very specific conditions under which some entities can compose a person. It seems remarkably hard to find any grounds for T1's having an explanation that T3 would lack. Thus, it is unclear how we might be able to draw a nonarbitrary division between these propositions that would allow us to reject one on the basis of its not having an explanation but accept the other in spite of its lacking an explanation. If, in spite of this significant similarity, there *is* a nonarbitrary difference between T1 and T3, then premise (4) of the N-IA will false. And if a lack of a nonarbitrary difference between T1 and T3 does not mean we should treat them similarly, then the inference to (5) is false. But if we must opt for one of these options with such remarkably similar propositions as T1 and T3, then what hope can we have of endorsing (4) and (5) for the wide range of contingent truths? If the N-IA fails in this way, it seems the C-IA will as well.

So, if we believe that T1 and T3 are necessary, nonanalytic truths, and that we are justified in rejecting T1 and in accepting T3, then the N-IA fails. But any way in which it fails gives us reason to reject the C-IA as well. Thus, even if T1 and T3 are necessary, the C-IA does not give us sufficient motivation to endorse C-PSR.

Generalisation

There are two important objections I'd like to note. First, one might respond by claiming that I have given the wrong response to the fission case or to the Problem of the Many. For instance, someone who believes there are no people at all will think that the Problem of the Many does not give us reason to endorse an unexplained proposition like T3. If this is correct, then I have not yet shown that we can justifiably reject an unexplainable proposition in one case and endorse an unexplainable proposition in another. Similarly, one might claim that T1 is a plausible alternative for what happens in fission cases and that we shouldn't expect it to have an explanation. Again, if this is correct, I will not have succeeded in showing that these relevantly similar propositions differ with respect to whether they have explanations.

Alternatively, one might respond by claiming that T1 and T3 are not relevantly similar after all, because they differ in their modal status. Consider, for instance, someone who believes there can be distinct indiscernibles and accepts my argument that in the fission case, if T1 is true, then it is contingent. However, suppose this same theorist believes that in a world with the sort of symmetry required for there to be mostly overlapping groups of atoms that are qualitatively indiscernible, any people that exist and are made of such atoms will have a member of one group of atoms as a part only if they have the corresponding member of the other group of atoms as a part. This theorist will reject premise (1) of my argument for the contingency of T3. Hence, the theorist can claim that T1 is contingent and T3 is necessary, and so we have a nonarbitrary division between them. (But notice that any theorist rejecting the possibility of distinct, qualitatively indiscernible entities will not endorse this response.)

Both of these responses would be quite worrisome if the problems I'm raising depended on our responses to these two particular puzzles. However, the points I'm making are more general. The idea is this: it is very common for philosophers to think that some nonanalytic, necessary truths lack explanations, while others have them. But it is notoriously difficult to nonarbitrarily divide those two groups of propositions from one another. It is not at all clear what (if anything) it is in virtue of that some of these propositions have explanations and others do not.

For example, you might think that, necessarily, no composite objects are point-sized. And you may think this has an explanation that contains the following components: (i) to be point-sized is to lack extension, and to be composite is to have more than one part, so anything composite and point-sized will have colocated parts, and (ii) necessarily, colocation is impossible. But (ii) is an excellent candidate for being an unexplained truth; at the very least, we will not reject it on the basis of a lack of explanation. And a host of other truths fall into this category, like the view that any objects have a fusion, or the view that objects persist four-dimensionally, etc. It is not clear what we can say to divide these truths.

Similar worries arise involving truths about mathematics and some logics; various axiomatisations are possible, and we take the axioms to be unexplained. But if we think math is not analytic, then we will have some non-analytic, necessary truths, but they'll be so similar to the explained truths that we can debate about which truths go into which categories.[25] There may be examples in other domains as well.[26]

Some contingent truths do seem relevantly dissimilar from the rest. For instance, the truth that there's something rather than nothing seems dissimilar from ordinary contingent claims. If we think that propositions like that one lack explanations, we may hope to be able to nonarbitrarily separate them from the propositions that do have explanations. But in the case of nonanalytic necessary truths, the project looks harder. And yet, in spite of not being able to draw a nonarbitrary division among these truths, we reject some necessary claims on the basis of their not having explanations, just as we do with some contingent propositions. The C-IA tells us that use of this methodology gives us good reason to accept the C-PSR. But we know this can't be right in the necessary case. And if the necessary argument fails, we can expect the same of the contingent one.

3 THE EXPLANATORY POWER OF EXPLANATORY POWER

If the C-IA and N-IA fail, then we cannot use the C-PSR or N-PSR to explain our justified rejection of theories that require unexplained truths. How, then, might we explain it?

---

25. This point is made in Pruss 2006: 12.
26. For example, consider these propositions: (i) It is impermissible to cause pain for no reason; and (ii) it is impermissible to throw acid on someone for no reason in conditions where that will cause pain. The first principle is a candidate for a fundamental moral truth, but the second isn't. In fact, the second may be explained via appeal to the first. But it is not the case that, for any necessary truths, if one is stronger than (and entails) the other, and they are equally natural, then the stronger truth explains the weaker one. Consider: (iii) If one object is part but not all of another object, then the second object has a part that is not had by the first object; (iv) if one object is not part of another, then there is some part the first object has that the second object does not. Principle (iii) is Weak Supplementation, and is entailed by (iv), Strong Supplementation (Simons 1987: ch. 1). But it is commonly believed that (iii) is not explained by (iv). (Note: This will only be an example of the sort we want if we take Weak Supplementation to be nonanalytic.)

Pruss has discussed an alternative, namely, that in these cases we are making inferences to the best explanation.[27] Of course, sometimes the theory we're endorsing simply states that there *isn't* an explanation, so I'll describe it in this way: the general principle doing the work in justifying our responses in many of these cases is not a principle saying that, for some group of propositions, *every* member in the group has an explanation. Instead, the principle is this:

EP: Explanatory Power is a truth-tracking theoretical virtue.

That is, all else being equal, we should take the theory with more explanatory power to be more likely to be true. Further, we attach significant weight to this theoretical virtue: it takes a lot to make something's *completely lack* of an explanation seem worth accepting.

So, for instance, in the handprint case, we reject the theory that the handprints simply appeared for no reason, because we can see how some explanations might go, and some of the explanations are such that endorsing them won't have disastrous theoretical consequences. Similarly, in the fission case, we reject the alternative on which exactly one person enters the process and then survives as exactly one of Lefty or Righty, because we can see how some alternative theories might go, and at least some of these theories (such as, for instance, the four-dimensionalist's response) do not have disastrous consequences.[28]

However, in the Problem of the Many, there are no alternatives that do not seem highly problematic. For instance, it is significantly implausible that there are many people overlapping where you are right now. It is also significantly implausible that there are no people. Finding ourselves only with alternatives that are revisionary to an unacceptable extent, we choose the option that lets us say a host of completely reasonable things but that requires that at least one of those lacks an explanation.

Thus, since EP is a principle guiding theory acceptance rather than a principle drawing divisions between things in the world, it allows us to give different responses to cases which seem relevantly similar, at least with respect to whether we'd otherwise expect an explanation to exist. In this way, the principle works like Ontological Parsimony. We tend not to endorse a fixed, general principle that says that any simple state of affairs involves at most *n* kinds of entities. We might initially think that such a fixed principle can help us explain our justified rejection of theories that require us to posit more than *n* kinds of entities. But the principle is too inflexible: it will fail to account for our occasional justified acceptance of theories that violate the principle.

---

27. Pruss 2006: ch. 16 and 17.
28. Though this is contentious. For arguments that four-dimensionalism itself has disastrous consequences, see, for instance, Thomson 1983 and van Inwagen 1990a. For arguments that each response to fission cases has disastrous (or at least highly revisionary) consequences, see Ross unpublished.

However, we can instead simply think that, all else being equal, the theory which involves positing fewer sorts of entities is more likely to be true. If we think that Ontological Parsimony is truth-tracking in this sense, then it can justify our rejection of less parsimonious theories in some cases (where other considerations don't outweigh it) and fail to justify such rejections in other cases (where we think other considerations push us to accept the less parsimonious theory).

Pruss denies that something like EP is doing this justificatory work for us. Among his reasons is this: we might wonder why, if there are *some* unexplained truths, we are so reluctant to posit them in any given case. Why does it take a complete lack of nondisastrous alternatives to get us to accept an unexplained proposition?[29]

In response to Pruss, we might give an analogy.[30] We tend to be very reluctant to explain a student's being late for class via appeal to their being hit by lightning, unless the evidence for that explanation is quite strong. This is so even in spite of our knowing that people are sometimes struck by lightning. And we have this reluctance even when we have not yet seen the student, and thus cannot tell the student apart from those who are lightning-struck.

In the lightning case, we can explain our reluctance by noting that we justifiably believe, partly due to induction, that lightning strikes rarely. We might hope to give a similar explanation of our endorsement of EP. However, worries have been raised about appeals to induction for such an explanation.[31] Addressing these worries is beyond the scope of this paper. However, it is worth noting that similar questions arise involving ontological parsimony. We can see that, in some cases, several kinds of entities are required to explain some state of affairs. Why, then, in other cases where the data don't *require* us to posit many kinds of entities, are we very reluctant to do so? What justifies our use of the principle of ontological parsimony? It seems reasonable to hope that whatever justifies our use of this principle will also justify our use of EP.

Something seems to be playing the role of justifying our explanation-related beliefs. I have given reason to think that it is not a PSR. EP is perfectly suited for playing the role and justifies exactly the beliefs we would like it to. And though we have yet to explain why we are licensed to believe EP, it seems to work in a way relevantly similar to other principles that are frequently taken to govern our reasoning.

Of course, nothing in this paper tells us that there is no true PSR or that there is not an explanation for why there is something rather than nothing. However, at least we can take some degree of comfort while tackling that

---

29. Pruss 2006: ch. 17.
30. This response was suggested by Jake Ross.
31. Pruss 2006: ch. 16.

formidable topic: the justification of our beliefs in a wide variety of other areas does not directly depend on the outcome.[32]

REFERENCES

Della Rocca, M. (2010). 'PSR', *Philosopher's Imprint* 10, no. 7: 1–12.
Geach, P. (1980). *Reference and Generality* (3rd ed). Ithaca, NY: Cornell University Press.
Hudson, H. (2001). *A Materialist Metaphysics of the Human Person*. Ithaca, NY: Cornell University Press.
Kleinschmidt, S. (2011). 'Multilocation and Mereology', *Philosophical Perspectives* 25: 253–76.
Lewis, D. (1976). 'Survival and Identity', in Rorty, A.O. (ed.). *The Identities of Persons*. Berkeley: University of California Press, 17-40.
Parfit, D. (1984). *Reasons and Persons*. Oxford: Oxford University Press.
Pruss, A. (2006). *The Principle of Sufficient Reason: A Reassessment*. New York: Cambridge University Press.
Ross, J. (Unpublished). 'Any Way You Slice It: Fission, Fusion, and the Weighing of Welfare'.
Simons, P. (1987). Parts: A Study in Ontology. Oxford: Oxford University Press.
Thomson, J.J. (1983). 'Parthood and Identity Across Time', *Journal of Philosophy* 80: 201–20.
Unger, P. (1980). 'The Problem of the Many', *Midwest Studies in Philosophy* 5: 411–67.
Van Inwagen, P. (1990a). 'Four-Dimensional Objects', *Nôus* 24: 245–55.
———. (1990b). *Material Beings*. Ithaca, NY: Cornell University Press.
Wasserman, R. (2003). 'Review of Hud Hudson's *A Materialist Metaphysics of the Human Person*', *Philo* 6: 307–13.
Wiggins, D. (1967). *Identity and Spatio-Temporal Continuity*. Oxford: Basil Blackwell.

---

32. I am grateful to Rima Basu, Alexander Pruss, and especially Jake Ross for invaluable comments.

5   The Principle of Sufficient Reason and the Grand Inexplicable

Jacob Ross

It is widely held that the Principle of Sufficient Reason (PSR) proves too much. It is conceded that, if the PSR were true, then on its basis we could conclude a great deal, including that a necessary being exists. For everyone grants that contingent beings exist, and if the PSR were true, then the existence of the contingent would have to have an explanation, which only a necessary being could provide. It is also argued, however, that the PSR couldn't possibly be true. For it implies not just that the existence of contingent beings has an explanation but that every true proposition has an explanation. And it is argued that, necessarily, there are certain true propositions that couldn't possibly have explanations.

In what follows, I will argue that the position sketched in the above paragraph is wrong on all counts, and I will defend a very different view of the PSR and its implications. My chief aim will be to defend the PSR against arguments to the effect that, necessarily, there are true propositions that can't have explanations. Each of the arguments I will be considering puts forward some particular proposition (which I will call the Grand Inexplicable) and argues that it constitutes a counterexample to the PSR, since the supposition that this proposition has an explanation leads to a contradiction. These arguments fall into two types. First, there are arguments where the proposition that plays the role of the Grand Inexplicable is a conjunction of some vast collection of propositions, such as the conjunction of all contingently true propositions. Second, there are arguments where the Grand Inexplicable is an existential claim, such as the claim that the universe exists or that something exists. I will consider these two kinds of arguments in the first and second sections of my paper, respectively. I will argue that none of these arguments succeeds, and I will provide a diagnosis for why they fail. In the third section, having considered arguments against the PSR, I will turn to one of the most prominent arguments that employs the PSR, namely the argument from contingency for the existence of a necessary being. And I will argue that this argument requires the very same kind of false assumption that serves as the basis for Grand Inexplicable arguments *against* the PSR. Once we recognize that we must reject this kind of assumption, we can defend the PSR against the view that it leads to contradiction, but at the same time we deprive the PSR of much of the power it has been traditionally thought to have. In the concluding section, I will argue that while the PSR lacks some of the implications that have traditionally been ascribed to it, it has others that are no less surprising.

1   GRAND CONJUNCTION ARGUMENTS

Consider the following argument from Peter van Inwagen:[1]

Argument 1

(A1) Suppose the following thesis is true.
   PSR: For every true proposition A, there is a true proposition B that is sufficient to explain A.

(A2) Let C be the conjunction of all true contingent propositions.

(A3) Since any conjunction with contingent conjuncts is contingent, C is contingent.

(A4) Since C is a true proposition, it follows from our supposition that there is a true proposition (call it D) such that D is sufficient to explain C.

(A5) Since only contingent propositions can suffice to explain contingent propositions, D is contingent.

(A6) For any propositions A and B, if A is sufficient to explain B, then B is true in every possible world in which A is true.

(A7) Thus, C is true in every possible world where D is true.

(A8) The only possible world in which C is true is the actual world.

(A9) Thus, D is true in every possible world in which C is true.

(A10) For any propositions A and B, if A and B are true in exactly the same possible worlds, then $A = B$.

(A11) Thus, $C = D$.

(A12) Thus, from (A3) and (A11), D is sufficient to explain D.

(A13) But no contingent proposition is sufficient to explain itself.

(A14) Hence, the supposition that the PSR is true entails a contradiction, namely the conjunction of (A4), (A12), and (A13).

(A15) Therefore, the PSR is false.

This argument relies crucially on a coarse-grained conception of propositions, according to which, for every set of worlds, there is at most one

---

1. Van Inwagen 1983: 202–4.

proposition that is true in all and only these worlds. For such an account is implied by premise (A10).[2] But the defender of the PSR needn't accept such a coarse-grained account of propositions, as she may instead accept an account on which propositions are more fine-grained than sets of possible worlds. She might, for example, adopt a view on which every proposition consists in, or at least is representable by, an ordered series of constituents corresponding to the constituents of the sentences by which they would be expressed in a canonical language. And there are well-known advantages in adopting a more fine-grained conception of propositions. For the coarse-grained account that van Inwagen assumes implies that the two sentences in each of the following pairs express the same proposition:

(B1) All bachelors are unmarried.
(B2) Fermat's Last Theorem is true.

(C1) Jack runs.
(C2) Jack runs and Jack is a mammal.

Hence, assuming that propositions are the objects of belief and assertion, this view has the problematic implication that one couldn't believe or assert that all bachelors are unmarried without believing or asserting that Fermat's Last Theorem is true, and similarly that one couldn't believe or assert that Jack runs without believing or asserting that Jack runs and Jack is a mammal.

---

2. Van Inwagen states his argument not in terms of propositions but in terms of states of affairs. Hence he is arguing not against the PSR as we have defined it but rather against the following:

    PSR*: For every *state of affairs* that obtains, there is a sufficient reason for its obtaining.

    On van Inwagen's version of the argument, the analog of premise (A10) is as follows:

    (A10*) *States of affairs* are identical whenever they obtain in exactly the same set of possible worlds.

    However, on van Inwagen's conception of states of affairs, they stand in a one-to-one relation with propositions (1983: 171), and so, for him, (A10*) stands and falls with (A10). Of course, one might hold a coarse-grained account of states of affairs while holding a fine-grained account of propositions. Hence, one might accept (A10*) and endorse van Inwagen's argument against the PSR*, while re-jecting (A10) and hence rejecting the argument given above against the PSR. But if one adopts this kind of position, then one will be left without an argument against the defender of the PSR who understands the latter as a claim about propositions. Moreover, as I will go on to argue, there is strong reason to understand explana-tion as a relation that obtains between fine-grained entities. Hence, if one adopts the position in question and holds that states of affairs are coarse-grained while propositions are fine-grained, then one will have strong reason to state the PSR in terms of propositions, and hence to regard PSR, not PSR*, as the best formulation.

Moreover, when we consider the nature of explanation, we can see that the entities that stand in the explanation relation must be more fine-grained than sets of possible worlds, and hence that the propositions that figure in the PSR can't be coarse-grained entities. This can be seen if we consider the following sets of propositions:

(D1) If the other two sides of a right triangle are 3 and 4 units long, respectively, then the hypotenuse is 5 units long.

(D2) In any right triangle, the square of the hypotenuse is equal to the sum of the squares of the other two sides.

(D3) All bachelors are unmarried.

Here, (D2) explains (D1), but (D3) does not. Similarly, consider an example involving *a posteriori* propositions:

(E1) When water molecules are divided, oxygen and hydrogen are formed.

(E2) Water is H_2O.

(E3) Hesperus is Phosphorus.

Here, (E2) explains (E1), but (E3) does not. Similarly, consider an example involving contingent propositions:

(F1) Ten billion years after the Big Bang, the universe is in state S_2.

(F2) The universe is governed by deterministic laws L, and at the time of the Big Bang, the universe is in state S_1.

(F3) The universe is governed by deterministic laws L, and twenty billion years after the Big Bang, the universe is in state S_3.

Once again, given the right values of L, S_1, S_2, and S_3, (F2) will explain (F1), but (F3) will not. Note, however, that in each of these cases, the second and third propositions in each trio are true in exactly the same possible worlds. Thus, if we want to maintain that the second proposition explains the first, whereas the third proposition does not, then we need to maintain that the second and third propositions are distinct, and so we need to reject premise (A10).

However, not all Grand Conjunction arguments against the PSR require (A10). Consider an argument that begins with (A1) through (A5), and then continues as follows:

Argument 2[3]

(G1) Since C is the conjunction of all true contingent propositions, and D is a true contingent proposition, D is a conjunct of C.

(G2) For any propositions A and B, if A is sufficient to explain B, then A is sufficient to explain every conjunct of B.

---

3. A similar argument can be found in Pruss 2006: 97–8.

(G3) Thus, since D is sufficient to explain C, and D is a conjunct of C, D is sufficient to explain D.

(G4) But no contingent proposition is sufficient to explain itself.

(G5) Hence, the supposition that the PSR is true entails a contradiction, namely the conjunction of (A5), (G3), and (G4).

(G6) Therefore, the PSR is false.

Like Argument 1, Argument 2 aims to show that if every proposition had a sufficient explanation, then D (the proposition that explains the conjunction of all true propositions) would have to explain itself. But this time this claim is supported not on the basis of D's supposed identity with C but rather on the basis of D's being a conjunct of C.

Furthermore, like Argument 1, Argument 2 relies on the stipulation that C is the conjunction of all true contingent propositions. Is this a legitimate stipulation? That will depend on our conception of propositions. Suppose we identify a proposition with the set of all possible worlds in which it is true. Then we can define the conjunction of any propositions as the set of worlds that are contained in each of these propositions. Since, on this view, the true propositions will be the sets of possible worlds that contain that actual world, and since the only world that all these sets have in common is the actual world, it follows that, on this view, the conjunction of all true contingent propositions is the set containing only the actual world. Since, presumably, there is such a set, it follows that on this coarse-grained account of propositions, there will indeed be a conjunction of all true propositions.

But recall that our reason for moving from Argument 1 to Argument 2 was in order to be able to adopt a more fine-grained account of propositions. And so suppose we adopt such an account and regard propositions as consisting in, or at least representable by, an ordered series of constituents corresponding to the constituents of the sentences by which they would be expressed in a canonical language. On such an account, for every proposition, there will be a corresponding set of the constituents of this proposition. And a conjunction will have its conjuncts as constituents. And so it follows that, for every proposition, there will be a set that includes all of its conjuncts. On such a view, therefore, there will be a *conjunction* of all true contingent propositions only if there is a *set* of all true contingent propositions. But is there a set of all true contingent propositions? Alexander Pruss offers an argument that there can be no such set. His argument requires the controversial assumption that for every cardinality k, it is possible that k is the cardinality of objects in the universe. Later in this paper I will be arguing that the defender of the PSR should reject this kind of assumption. But we don't need this kind of controversial assumption. For, given the structured account of propositions we are considering, it's easy to argue that there can be no set of all true contingent propositions, without any assumptions about what the world might be like. For it is well known that there are too many *sets* for there to be a set of all sets.

And for every set S, there is a distinct *necessary* proposition of the form $S = S$. And for each of these necessary propositions, we can form a true contingent proposition by conjoining it with a given true contingent proposition (say, the proposition that Caesar crossed the Rubicon). These contingent propositions will all be distinct, since they will differ in one of their constituents. And there will be one such proposition for every set. Hence, since there are too many sets to fit in a set, it follows that there are too many true contingent propositions to fit into a set. Hence, on the account of propositions we are considering, we should deny that there is any conjunction of all true propositions.

Pruss has proposed a variant of Argument 2 that dispenses with the assumption that there is a conjunction of all true contingent propositions. In this alternative argument, the Grand Conjunction is instead the conjunction of all propositions of the following kinds:

(i) All true basic contingent propositions
(ii) All logically uncompounded true propositions reporting causal relations

His argument can be reconstructed as follows:

Argument 3

(H1) Suppose the following thesis is true.
PSR: For every true proposition A, there is a true proposition B that is sufficient to explain A.

(H2) Let E be the conjunction of all propositions of kinds (i) and (ii).

(H3) Since any conjunction with contingent conjuncts is contingent, E is contingent.

(H4) Since E is a true proposition, it follows from our supposition that there is a true proposition (call it F) such that F is sufficient to explain E.

(H5) Since only contingent propositions can suffice to explain contingent propositions, F is contingent.

(H6) Every proposition that explains any of the propositions of kinds (i) and (ii) is constructable out of propositions of kinds (i) and (ii).

(H7) Hence, since F is explanatory, and since E is the conjunction of all propositions of kinds (i) and (ii), F is constructable out of the conjuncts of E.

(H8) For any propositions A, B, and C, if A is sufficient to explain B, and B is a conjunction out of whose conjuncts C is constructable, then A is sufficient to explain C.

(H9) Therefore, since F is sufficient to explain E, and E is a conjunction out of whose conjuncts F is constructable, F is sufficient to explain F.

(H10) But no contingent proposition is sufficient to explain itself.

(H11) Hence, the supposition that the PSR is true entails a contradiction, namely the conjunction of (A5), (H9), and (H10).

(H12) Therefore, the PSR is false.

I believe Pruss's revised argument is not convincing, for it faces a dilemma. If we have a sufficiently narrow conception of "basic propositions," then while (H2) is acceptable, (H6) is dubious; but if we don't have such a narrow conception of basic propositions, then while (H6) may be acceptable, (H2) is dubious. Let's begin with the first horn of the dilemma. On a natural construal of "basic propositions," the true contingent basic propositions will state the Humean facts; that is, they will indicate what qualities are present at what spacetime points. Assuming there are only continuum many spacetime points, there will presumably be only continuum many such true basic contingent propositions. Or, in any case, there will be few enough such propositions to fit into a set. Similarly, we should expect the propositions of type (ii) reporting causal relations to be manageable in number as well, since presumably there won't be more of those than there are pairs of events, and there will be only continuum many events. And so if the basic propositions are understood in this Humean manner, then we should expect all the propositions of types (i) and (ii) together to form a set, and so we should expect there to be a conjunction of such propositions, as (H6) requires.

But in this case, premise (H6) will be suspect. For it seems there could be law-stating propositions that explain the Humean and causal propositions without supervening on, and hence without being constructible in terms of, the Humean and causal propositions they explain. Here's an illustration. Imagine two worlds, w_1 and w_2, that have identical initial conditions, and whose laws differ in only the following respect. In w_1, it is a law of nature (call it L_1) that the attractive force a struon exerts on a fluon is proportional to the charge of the struon. Thus, if a struon is positively charged, then it attracts fluons, and the greater the charge the greater the attraction; but if a struon is negatively charged, then it repels fluons, and the greater the charge the greater the repulsion. By contrast, in w_2, it is a law of nature (call it L_2) that the attractive force a struon exerts on a fluon is proportional to the *absolute value* of the struon's charge. Thus, the greater the charge of a struon, be it positive or negative, the more strongly it attracts fluons. In both worlds, struons pick up their charge by colliding with thruons (which give them positive charge) and shmuons (which give them negative charge). It just so happens that in both worlds, the struons never collide with the shmuons, and so, while they could easily have acquired negative charge, they never do. Now, since these two worlds have the same initial conditions, and with respect to their laws differ only in that L_1 prevails in w_1 and L_2 prevails in w_2, and since these laws diverge only when struons have negative charge, which never obtains in either world, these two worlds will be identical with respect to true Humean propositions and with respect to the true propositions concerning causal relations between particular events. But these worlds will differ with respect to what explains these true propositions. When a struon attracts a fluon in w_1, this is explained by L_1, whereas when a struon attracts a fluon in w_2, this is explained by L_2. And so these laws explain some of the Humean and causal propositions without being constructable out of the Humean and causal propositions. And so (H6) is false.

Now consider the second horn of the dilemma. Suppose we adopt a broader conception of the basic contingent propositions. Suppose we hold that these include not only the Humean and causal propositions but also the law-stating propositions. In this case, there's no guarantee that there will be few enough basic propositions for them all to fit into a set. And so there's no guarantee that there is any conjunction of the kind stipulated in H2. Moreover, the proponent of the PSR is likely to deny that there are so few propositions. For she may hold that for every set of laws, there is a further law that explains the conjunction of these laws. And from this it follows, on pain of paradox, that there must be too many laws to include in any set.[4] Thus, if the basic propositions include the laws, then it can't be assumed, without argument, that there are few enough laws to fit into a set, since such an assumption appears to beg the question against the PSR.

To sum up, in order to provide a Grand Conjunction argument against the PSR, one would need to assume that there is some *set* of contingent propositions such that any proposition that explains any proposition within this set would have to be somehow included within this set (either by being one of its elements or by being constructable out of these elements). But the defender of the PSR can simply deny this. She can maintain that while every contingent proposition is explained by another contingent proposition, these contingent propositions are too numerous to form a set, and for any set of propositions one must go beyond this set to find the proposition that explains their conjunction.

2 GRAND EXISTENTIAL ARGUMENTS

In the preceding section, we considered Grand Inexplicable arguments against the PSR in which the proposition that served as the Grand Inexplicable was a conjunction of vastly many contingent propositions. In the present section, we will consider a different kind of Grand Inexplicable argument where this role is played by some existential proposition that is of cosmic significance. One such proposition, which will no doubt be salient to the reader of this

---

4. Suppose there were few enough to include in a set. Then there would be a set *S* of all laws. But, *ex hypothesi*, for every set of laws, there's a further law that explains their conjunction. And so there must be some further law, not in *S*, that explains the conjunction of the laws in *S*. But *S* includes all the laws. So we have a contradiction.

volume, is the proposition that *there exists anything at all*. It might seem that this proposition does not admit of any explanation, and hence that it can serve as a counterexample to the PSR. One could argue as follows:

Argument 4

(I1) Suppose the following thesis is true.
PSR: For every true proposition A, there is a true proposition B that is sufficient to explain A.

(I2) Let G be the proposition that there exists some being.

(I3) Thus, by our supposition, there is a true proposition (call it H) that is sufficient to explain G.

(I4) For any kind K of beings, the proposition that there exists something of kind K can be explained only by a proposition that appeals to the existence of beings that are not of kind K.

(I5) Thus, since H is sufficient to explain G, and since G is the proposition that there exists something that is a being, H must appeal to the existence of beings that are not beings.

(I6) And so, since no true proposition appeals to the existence of beings that are not beings, H is not true.

(I7) Hence, the supposition that the PSR is true entails a contradiction, namely the conjunction of (I3) and (I6).

(I8) Therefore, the PSR is false.

The crucial premise of this argument is (I4). This premise has some prima facie plausibility. After all, one might hold that any explanation of an existential claim would need to involve another existential claim. But if one attempted to explain the existence of Bs by appealing to the existence of Bs, then this putative explanation would appear to be viciously circular. And so it may seem, *prima facie*, that any explanation of the existence of Bs must appeal to the existence of non-Bs. And so (I4) has some plausibility. Nonetheless, we should reject (I4). Here's a counterexample. Consider the following proposition:

(J1) There is something that undergoes gravitational attraction.

This proposition could be explained by the following proposition:

(J2) There are at least two massive bodies, and every massive body is gravitationally attracted to every other massive body.

But while (J2) explains (J1), (J2) doesn't appeal to the existence of anything that is not of the kind posited by (J1). For the only objects to whose existence (J2) appeals are massive bodies, and all these objects undergo gravitational attraction. And so this pair of propositions constitutes a counterexample to (I4).

But maybe there's a way of construing the claim that something exists in such a way that it can serve to refute the PSR without appealing to (I4). Perhaps it can be understood not as the claim that there exists something in the kind *beings* but rather as the claim that there exists something in set S, where S happens to be the set of all beings. For there is an important difference between explaining why there are things of kind K and explaining why there are members of set S: it seems you can explain why there are things of kind K without explaining why any of the things in kind K exist—this is what the case above illustrates, for here we explain why there are things that undergo gravitational attraction, without explaining why it's true that any of the things that happen to undergo gravitational attraction exist. By contrast, since sets contain their members essentially, you can't explain why there are members of a given set without explaining why it's true that any of the members of the set exist.

It seems, therefore, that we could solve the problem faced by Argument 4 by replacing premises (I2) and (I4) with the following two premises respectively, and by revising the other premises accordingly:

(K2) Let S be the set of all beings, and let G be the proposition that there exists at least one member of S.

(K4) For any set S of beings, the proposition that there exists at least one member of S can be explained only by a proposition that appeals to the existence of beings that are not in S.

Premise (K4) is much more plausible than (I4), and it is immune to the counterexample that (I4) faces. To see why, let S be the set of objects that undergo gravitational attraction. Suppose there were three objects that undergo such attraction, and call them Peter, Paul, and Mary. Thus, S = {Peter, Paul, Mary}. While (J2) may explain why there are objects that undergo gravitational attraction, it doesn't explain why Peter, Paul, or Mary exists, and so it doesn't explain why there exists at least one member of S. And so this example is not a counterexample to (K4).

But there's a problem. While (K4) is perfectly acceptable, (K2) is not. For (K2) assumes the existence of a set of all objects. But there is no such set. For there are too many objects to fit into a set. This follows from the fact that there are too many sets to fit into a set, and the fact that all sets are objects.

Thus, it's not so easy to refute the PSR using the claim that something exists. For, where this is understood as the proposition affirming the existence of something in the kind *beings*, an appeal to this proposition can refute the PSR only when combined with something like (I4), which, as we have seen, is false. If, on the other hand, the claim that something exists is understood as the proposition affirming the existence of something in the *set* of *beings*, then it is doubtful that this could be a true proposition, for it is doubtful that there is any such set.

What about the proposition, not that something exists, but that *everything* exists? Could this serve as a Grand Inexplicable in an argument against the PSR? Might we argue that, if there were an explanation of the existence of everything, it would have to appeal to the existence of something outside of everything, which is impossible, and hence that there can be no explanation of the existence of everything?

Now, on one construal of the claim that everything exists, it's a tautology, and it would be true even if nothing existed. Clearly, if the claim is construed in that manner, its explanation would not require positing the existence of anything, let alone the existence of anything outside of everything. But there are other construals of the claim that everything exists on which it is not a tautology. For it could be understood as the proposition that everything in S exists, where S is the set of all objects. One might argue that any explanation of this principle would need to appeal to the existence of something outside of S. But, as before, we should reject any such argument. For such an argument would have to assume that there is a set of all objects, and it is doubtful that there is any such set.

Lastly, we might understand the claim that everything exists as the proposition that F exists, where F is the fusion or mereological sum of everything that exists. And we might argue that the existence of this Grand Fusion could never be explained, since any explanation would have to appeal to the existence of something outside that fusion, and there is no such thing. Thus we could formulate a variant of Argument 4 in which (I2) and (I4) are replaced by the following premises, and the other premises are revised accordingly:

(L2) Let F be the fusion of all beings, and let G be the proposition that F exists.

(L4) For any fusion A, the proposition that A exists can be explained only by a proposition that appeals to the existence of something disjoint from A.

The problem here, however, is that while (L2) may be unproblematic, (L4) is not. For it seems that fusions can be explained by their parts. As an illustration, let J be the fusion of Cleopatra's nose and Mount Everest. Now it seems that the following proposition:

(M1) J exists.

can be explained by this proposition:

(M2) Cleopatra's nose exists, and Mount Everest exists, and for any two disjoint objects, the fusion of these objects exists.

But while (M2) explains (M1), (M2) doesn't appeal to the existence of anything disjoint from *J*. And so this case constitutes a counterexample to (L4).

It seems, therefore, that we can no more refute the PSR by appealing to the claim that everything exists than we can by appealing to the claim that something exists. Neither of these appears to correspond to a proposition that is essentially inexplicable.

3 ARGUMENTS FROM CONTINGENCY

Having seen why the Grand Existential arguments get into trouble, we are in a position to appreciate the weakness of arguments from contingency. Consider the following version of the latter argument:

Argument 5

(N1) Let *L* be the proposition that there is a contingent being.

(N2) PSR: For every true proposition *A*, there is a true proposition *B* that is sufficient to explain *A*.

(N3) Since *L* is a true proposition, it follows from the PSR that there is a true proposition (call it *M*) such that *M* is sufficient to explain *L*.

(N4) For any kind *K* of contingent beings, the proposition that there exists something of kind *K* can be explained only by a proposition that appeals to the existence of beings that are not of kind *K*.

(N5) Thus, since *M* is sufficient to explain *L*, and since *L* is the proposition that there exists some contingent being, *M* must appeal to the existence of something that is not a contingent being but is instead a necessary being.

(N6) But if a true proposition appeals to the existence of a necessary being, then there must be a necessary being.

(N7) Therefore, there is a necessary being.

Van Inwagen presents an argument of this form, and he claims that if only the PSR were true, this argument would be sound.[5] It is now clear, however, that van Inwagen is mistaken in this assertion. For (N4) is simply (I4) from Argument 4 restricted to contingent beings. And (N4) is vulnerable to the same counterexample as (I4). For recall the proposition *there is something that undergoes gravitational attraction*. The kind that figures in this proposition (things that undergo gravitational attraction) is a kind of contingent beings. And so (N4) has the false implication that whatever explains this proposition would have to appeal to the existence of things that don't undergo gravitational attraction.

---

5. Van Inwagen 2009: 148–50.

As before, we might try to solve this problem by replacing premises (N1) and (N4) with the following premises:

(O1) Let *S* be the set of all contingent beings, and let *L* be the proposition that there exists at least one member of *S*.

(O4) For any set *S* of contingent beings, the proposition that there exists at least one member of *S* can be explained only by a proposition that appeals to the existence of beings that are not in *S*.

But, once again, the first premise is problematic, since it assumes the existence of a set of all contingently existing objects. And it can easily be argued that there can be no such set. For we know that there are too many sets to fit into a set. Now, if all the contingently existing sets belonged to a set, and all the necessary existing sets belonged to a set, then all sets would belong to a set. Hence, either there are too many necessary sets to fit into a set, or there are too many contingent sets to fit into a set. But there are at least as many contingently existing sets are there are necessarily existing sets. For, for every necessarily existing set, we can construct a distinct contingently existing set by pairing it with some contingently existing object, such as Jack. Hence, if there are too many necessarily existing sets to fit into a set, then there are too many contingently existing sets to fit into a set. And so we may conclude that there are too many contingently existing sets, and hence too many contingently existing objects, to fit into a set.

Maybe we can solve this problem by focusing not on contingent objects in general but on contingent concrete objects. This way, we'd exclude sets from the class of relevant objects, thereby allowing for the possibility that these objects could be sufficiently few to fit into a set. We could thus revise our argument by replacing (N1) and (N4) with the following premises:

(O1) Let *S* be the set of all *contingent concrete* beings, and let *L* be the proposition that there exists at least one member of *S*.

(O4) For any set *S* of *contingent concrete* beings, the proposition that there exists at least one member of *S* can be explained only by a proposition that appeals to the existence of concrete beings that are not in *S*.

If these premises were true, then, together with the PSR, they would allow us to conclude that there is a necessary, concrete being. But, again, we should be skeptical of the first premise, for we should be skeptical of the assumption that there is any set of contingent concrete beings. Why couldn't these be too numerous to fit into a set? It is plausible that the objects that could fit into a single spacetime continuum would have to belong to a single set. But there might be lots of disconnected spacetime continua, including duplicate, qualitatively identical spacetime continua. And if we allow that, then it's hard to see what constraints there could be on how many spacetime continua there could be. And so it's hard to see why there would be any constraints on how many concrete contingent objects there could be.

Moreover, it seems that if one accepts the PSR, and if one accepts (O4), then one will have reason to maintain that the concrete contingent objects are too numerous to fit into a set. For if one accepts (O4), then one will have reason to accept the following strengthening of that principle:

> (P1) For any set *S* of *contingent concrete* beings, the proposition that there exists at least one member of *S* can be explained only by a proposition that appeals to the existence of *contingent concrete* beings that are not in *S*.

After all, one might think that whatever was sufficiently explained by the existence of a necessary being would have to be necessitated by the existence of the necessary being, and so it would have to be necessary. Thus, one might think that whatever it is whose existence explains the existence of contingent beings must itself be contingent. But from (P1), together with the PSR, it follows that there can be no set that includes all contingent concrete beings, since, for any set of contingent concrete beings, there must be contingent concrete beings outside that set.

Thus, the kind of arguments we have been considering in this section will enable us to infer the existence of a necessary being from the PSR only if we assume that there is a set of all concrete contingent objects. But anyone who accepts the PSR will have reason to be skeptical of the existence of any such set.

4   THE REAL IMPORT OF THE PSR

I have argued that the PSR doesn't have the implications it is widely thought to have. Contrary to what many of its *detractors* claim, the PSR doesn't entail any contradictions. But at the same time, contrary to what many of its *proponents* claim, the PSR doesn't entail the existence of a necessary being. Does this mean the PSR is not a very interesting principle? Far from it. For the PSR has very striking implications. In particular, if it is true, then it implies that the world is a very complicated place. It's a place that's so complicated that there is no set of first principles, however large, on the basis of which all other truths can be explained.

Suppose we lived in a simple world. In such a world, there would be some set of propositions that jointly explained all the less fundamental propositions. These might in turn be explained by some simpler set of propositions. But assuming that explanations need to be simpler or more unifying than what they explain, it follows that as we moved to deeper and deeper explanations, we'd eventually reach a set of explanatory propositions the conjunction of which is at least as simple and unifying as anything one might adduce to explain it. So, eventually, we'd reach a point where explanation must come to an end.

The defender of the PSR is committed to claiming that the world is more complicated than that. Indeed, she must claim that the actual world is delicately poised between order and chaos. It must be sufficiently orderly that every fact has an explanation. But at the same time it needs to be sufficiently complicated for there to be no fact or set of facts that explains all the less fundamental facts and that is sufficiently simple and unifying as to admit of no further explanation.

Traditionally, the PSR has often been thought of as a fundamental principle of reasoning, or Law of Thought. Furthermore, it has often been thought that the principles of reasoning guide us to favor simple theories over complicated ones, and hence that they involve a kind of presumption that the world is a simple and orderly place. It now seems, however, that these two thoughts can't both be true. If the PSR is indeed a principle of reasoning, then reason dictates that we presume that the world is overwhelmingly complicated.[6]

REFERENCES

Pruss, A. (2006). *The Principle of Sufficient Reason*. Cambridge: Cambridge University Press.
Van Inwagen, P. (1983). *An Essay on Free Will*. Oxford: Oxford University Press.
———. (2009). *Metaphysics* (3rd ed.). Boulder, CO: Westview Press.

---

6. I would like to thank Kenny Easwaran, Shieva Kleinschmidt, Alexander Pruss, and Gabriel Uzquiano for their tremendous generosity in discussing and providing comments on earlier drafts of this paper. Without them, this paper could not have been written.

6 Contingency, Dependence, and the Ontology of the Many

Christopher Hughes

1 THE CONTINGENCY-DEPENDENCE ARGUMENT

In his book *Metaphysics* (1993), Peter van Inwagen sets out an intriguing argument for the existence of a necessary being. The gist of the argument is as follows:

> First, some terminology. Call a being *contingent* if it might or might not have existed. Call a being *independent* if it doesn't depend on anything outside itself for its existence, and *dependent* if it does depend on something outside itself for its existence. Perhaps necessary beings can be partitioned into independent necessary beings and dependent necessary beings, but contingent beings cannot be partitioned into independent contingent beings and dependent contingent beings: there couldn't be independent contingent beings. (In other words, necessarily, whatever exists and might not have existed, depends on something not only distinct from but also outside it.) So all beings are contingent only if all beings are dependent. It might look as though it could be that all beings are both contingent and dependent. But consider: all the "smaller" beings there are jointly compose a "larger" being that we may call *the World*. Given that there is nothing outside the World, the World cannot be a dependent being. But, as we have seen, only a dependent being could be contingent. (*Only dependent beings could be contingent* is equivalent to *all contingent beings must be dependent*). So the World is a necessary being. So there is at least one necessary being (the World). (Indeed, it seems as if there are at least two necessary beings, since it seems that nothing could be a necessary being, if it is composed exclusively of contingent beings.)

Van Inwagen concedes that the claim that, necessarily, all contingent beings are dependent (henceforth, for brevity, *the contingency-dependence principle*) is "at least somewhat plausible" (1993: 111). But, he argues, even if the truth of the contingency-dependence principle is granted, the above argument does not go through. For as well as relying on the contingency-dependence principle, it relies on the principle that there is such a being as the World; and there are good reasons to suppose that there is no such being.

But isn't it a truism to say that there is such a being (such a thing) as the World? Van Inwagen's view appears to be the following: when we talk about the World, we are not talking about a single composite being; we are speaking "collectively" about many different beings. (As he puts it: ". . . [A]ny use of the phrase 'the World' is a mere manner of speaking: use of this phrase is no more than a device for speaking about all individuals" [1993: 112].)

Why does van Inwagen suppose that the phrase "the World" is a device for speaking about many different individuals, none of which is the World, rather than a singular term referring to an individual composed of many different individuals? His argument seems to be (roughly) the following: suppose that what there is is God, parts of God (should He have parts), and creatures. There is surely a possible world in which there are no creatures, and all that there is is God and parts of God (should He have parts). But if there were such a thing as the World, there couldn't be such a possible world—at least on the assumption that, necessarily, all contingent beings are dependent. Why not? Well, given that assumption, if the World exists, it is a necessary being (by the above argument). So the World exists in every possible world, including the possible world in which all there is is God and parts of God (should God have parts). This implies that in the possible world in which all there is is God and parts of God, either the World = God or the World is a part of God. It cannot be true in that possible world that the World = God. For it is true in that possible world that the World might have had parts that were not parts of God. But it is, of course, not true in that possible world that God might have had parts which were not parts of God. So it is true in that possible world that God and the World are discernible (with respect to their modal properties) and thus distinct. Could it be true in that possible world that the World is part of God? It seems "fairly evident" (1993: 113), van Inwagen says, that the World is not the right sort of thing to be part of God, whether or not God has parts. (The World is the right sort of thing to have God as a part but not the right sort of thing to be a part of God.) So (assuming the contingency-dependence principle) the supposition that there is such a thing as the World is incompatible with the supposition that there is a possible world containing only God and His parts, and should for that reason be rejected.

The argument just summarized is directed against "Worldly" theists (i.e. theists that believe there is such a thing as the World) rather than "Worldly" atheists, and van Inwagen is not entirely explicit about why atheists shouldn't be "Worldly". It seems to me, though, that the argument van Inwagen offers, despite the way he presents it, is not essentially an argument against Worldly theism. It depends on the idea that we can locate, in the actual world, an individual (distinct from the World) that could have existed, even if none of the actual individuals outside it had existed and no other (nonactual) individuals (outside it) had existed. But an atheist might well accept this principle, and a theist might well reject it. (A theist who agreed with Norman Kretzmann that [i] God necessarily exists, [ii] God is necessarily perfectly good, and [iii] necessarily, a perfectly good being will create something, because *bonum est diffusivum sui*, would deny that there is a possible world in which God exists but nothing outside God exists. Moreover, she would deny that there is a possible world in which some individual, and nothing outside that individual, exists. (Any possible world will contain God [by God's necessary existence], and any possible world that contains God will contain something outside God [by God's necessary creative generosity]. So a theist who shares Kretzmann's view of God will reject van Inwagen's argument against the existence of the World.))

Suppose, however, that a Worldly metaphysician (be she a theist or an atheist) accepts that the World is a necessary being and that some actual being (other than the World) could have existed, even if nothing outside it had existed. Is her position untenable?

Perhaps I have missed something, but it's not clear to me that it is. Suppose that the Worldly metaphysician is a theist, and her individual (other than the World) that could have existed even if nothing outside it had existed is God. She could say something like this:

> Consider a sweater made from a single (very long) thread. The sweater is not the very same thing as the thread, since the sweater came into existence after the thread did, and *a came into existence after b did* implies *a ≠ b*. Neither is the sweater a *part* of the thread. (Can we imagine anyone (uncorrupted by philosophy) saying, "the best part of this thread is the sweater"?) If, however, the sweater is not a part of the thread, how is it related to the thread? Well, in negative terms, we can say that the sweater is not *outside* the thread (in the way that a sweater made from a completely different thread would be). In positive terms, we can say that the sweater *shares a decomposition* with the thread, where a decomposition is a set of smaller parts that jointly compose a bigger thing. The sweater and the thread (or the statue and the portion of bronze) can be "decomposed" into the same set of molecules, atoms, and subatomic particles.
>
> Now suppose that, in the actual world, God and creatures exist, and in an alternative possible world, God exists, and nothing outside God exists. Is the alternative possible world inhabited only by God and His parts (should He have any)? *Pace* van Inwagen, no. For in our alternative possible world, the World exists, and is distinct from God (since it does not have all the same modal properties as God), and—as van Inwagen intuits—is not a part of God. So (in our alternative possible world) how is the World related to God? It depends. If (in that possible world) God has parts, we can say that (in that possible World) the World shares a decomposition with God. (For example, if in our alternative possible world God = the Trinity, and the Trinity is composed of three divine Persons, then in our alternative possible world the World and God are both composed of those three Persons.) What

if, in our alternative possible world, God has no parts at all? (As van Inwagen notes, it is often supposed that God is entirely without parts.) If God has no parts to share, we won't be able to say that the World shares a decomposition with God. We will have to say that the World is disjoint from (i.e. shares no parts with) God, since *a* can't share a part with *b* if *b* has no parts. Still, we will be able to say in negative terms that the World is not (wholly or even partly) outside God. So there are possible worlds in which there is nothing (even partly) *outside* God and His parts (should He have any), but there are no possible worlds in which all that there is is God and His parts (should He have any). (Here someone might object that it makes no sense to affirm that in a possible world with a partless God and no creatures, there is something *disjoint from* God, and to deny that in that possible world there is something *outside* God: *a is outside b* and *a is disjoint from b* come to the same thing. But if *a is disjoint from b* means *a and b share a part*, and if [as seems plausible] there can be things that have no parts, it would seem possible for *a* to be disjoint from *b* even though *a* is not outside *b*. Suppose that *a* is partless, *b* has parts, and one of *b*'s parts is *a*. If *a* has no parts, *a* and *b* must be disjoint [i.e. cannot share a part]. But if *a* is a part of *b*, *a* cannot be outside *b*. So *a* is disjoint from but not outside *b*.)

As best I can see, the position just sketched is coherent. It's true that it doesn't assort with what classical mereologists say about the part-whole relation. To start with, for mereologists, nothing can be completely without parts, since necessarily everything is a part of itself (an "improper" part of itself, as mereologists say, in acknowledgement of the oddity of the idea that the part-of relation is reflexive rather than irreflexive). Also, classical mereologists hold that whenever *a* shares a decomposition with *b*, *a* is an (improper) part of *b*. But it's not as though classical mereology is an uncontroversially correct account of the part-whole relation.

Nor is the account sketched above the only one available to the Worldly theist. Perhaps she thinks that, upon reflection, we can see that classical mereologists are right to maintain that everything is a part—albeit an improper part—of itself, and can see that things that share a decomposition are parts of each other (albeit improper parts). In that case she can take the line that in a possible world in which God exists, and nothing outside God exists, the only things that exist are God and His parts—that is, God, His proper parts (should He have any), and His improper parts (including, at least, God and the World). On this sort of account, the initial apparent oddity of the view that the World is a part of God (or that the sweater is part of the thread) could be attributed to our difficulty in keeping sight of the fact that things can have improper as well as proper parts.

Suppose that those who believe in the World can tell a coherent story about the relation of the World to (say) God in a possible world in which there is nothing outside God. It might still be that, as van Inwagen supposes,

"World-talk" is just a way of talking collectively about many things, rather than a way of talking about a single thing composed of many things.

Well, it might be, and it might not be. There seem to be terms that are, as it were, grammatically plural and logically singular: it seems plausible that *the Badlands* is, from a logical point of view, just as singular a term as *the Gobi Desert*. It likewise seems perfectly possible that there are terms that are grammatically singular and logically plural. That said, I find it hard to find clear cases of such. One might have thought that a term such as *that pair of objects on the table* was a clear case: isn't that-pair-of-objects-on-the-table talk collective talk about two objects, and not talk about a single being composed of two objects? After all, someone might say *a pair of objects* is just another way of saying *two objects*, and *that pair of objects* is just another way of saying *those two objects*; and *those two objects* is surely not a singular term!

Still, a mereologist might say that the term *that pair of objects on the table* is a (logically) singular term that refers to the "mereological fusion" of the "mereological atoms" of the objects on the table (though for the usual reasons, I don't think this will work). A believer in aggregates as construed by Tyler Burge (cf. Burge 1977) might (more plausibly, to my mind) maintain that the term *that pair of objects on the table* is a (logically) singular term that refers to the Burgean aggregate of the two objects on the table.

To avoid a possible misunderstanding: it's not that I think the World could plausibly be identified with either a mereological fusion of mereological atoms or a Burgean aggregate of "member-components" (roughly, ordinary individuals, as opposed to aggregates thereof). For it seems plausible to suppose that mereological fusions or Burgean aggregates are essentially composed of the mereological atoms or member-components they are actually composed of, and it doesn't seem at all obvious that the World is essentially composed of the things it is actually composed of. (The proponent of [what I shall call] the Worldly argument for the existence of a necessary being will presumably want to deny that the World is essentially composed of the things—the individuals, or the mereological atoms, or the member-components—it is actually composed of, given the apparent contingency of those components.) The point is just that if *that pair of objects on the table* isn't a clear case of a grammatically singular but logically plural term, it seems unlikely that *the World* is.

When a term *t* refers to a (unique) entity, let us call the thing that *t* refers to *Ref(t)*. If, say, *t* is the numeral seven, Ref(*t*) will be the number seven. If *t* is a (referring) logically singular term, presumably the statements *just one thing is Ref(t)* and *there is exactly one thing that is Ref(t)* will be true. And it seems plausible to suppose that if *t* is not a (referring) logically singular term, then the statements *just one thing is Ref(t)* and *there is exactly one thing that is Ref(t)* will not be true (or, at least, not true on their most straightforward construal).

If this is right, we have a kind of "test" for the (referring) logical singularity or otherwise of a term. Is "the Badlands" a (referring) logically singular term? If (as I believe) *just one thing is the Badlands* and *there is exactly one thing that is the Badlands* are true, then "the Badlands" is indeed a (referring) logically singular term. (Some readers may worry about the apparent lack of grammatical agreement in *just one thing is the Badlands*, but it seems no more problematic than the apparent lack of agreement in *the United States is a big country.*) Is the (grammatically plural) term "those two things on the table" a (referring) logically singular term? It seems not. For, it seems, neither *just one thing is those two things on the table* nor *there is exactly one thing that is those two things on the table* is true. What about the (grammatically singular) term "that pair of things on the table"? Is it a (referring) logically singular term? Someone might wonder about whether it could be true that just one thing is that pair of things on the table. But it seems to me that it could be. If (as could happen) just one pair of things is on the table, then just one thing is the pair of things on the table. If (as could happen) there is exactly one pair of things on the table, then there is exactly one thing that is the pair of things on the table. (Notice that if this is right, it seems that "those two things" is not simply synonymous with "that pair of things", inasmuch as *there is exactly one thing that is that pair of things* is true, and *there is exactly one thing that is those two things* is not.) What about the (grammatically singular) term "the average man"? I take it that it is not a (referring) logically singular term, since I take it that *just one thing is the average man* and *there is exactly one thing that is the average man* are not true. (If it were true that just one thing is the average man, it would likewise be true that there is such a thing as the average man, and there is no such thing as the average man.)

Finally, what about "the World"? I see no obvious reason to deny that *just one thing is the World* and *there is exactly one thing that is the World* are true. Capitalization aside, *there is just one World* sounds like a truism and seems to imply *just one thing is the World*. (Conversely, I see no obvious reason to suppose that *there's no one thing that's the World* is truistic, in the way that *there's no one thing that is the average man* is.)

Much more could be said about these issues, and indeed has been said by van Inwagen in *Material Beings* (1990). I hope to have explained, though, why I think it is nowhere near as clear that "the World" is not a (referring) logically singular term as it is that, say, "the things in the World" and "the average man" are not (referring) logically singular terms.

Suppose, though, that van Inwagen is right and that just as there is no such thing as the average man, there is no such thing as the World. Then, even if the contingency-dependence premiss is granted, the argument for a necessary being set out in *Metaphysics* clearly fails, since it only gets to *there is a necessary being* via *there is an independent being*, and it only gets to *there is an independent being* via *the World is an independent being*.

The argument for a necessary being that van Inwagen discusses is just one of a range of such arguments that rely both on (some version of) a contingency-dependence principle and on the existence of some sort of "sufficiently inclusive" being. (In the van Inwagen argument, the sufficiently inclusive being is the World; in other versions it might be a set. For example, if our contingency-dependence principle were that every set all of whose elements are contingent depends for its existence on a being outside that set, then the "sufficiently inclusive" being might be the set of [all] contingent ur-elements—that is, elements of sets that are not themselves sets.) It is worth pointing out that van Inwagen's critique of the Worldly argument for a necessary being does not in any obvious way generalize to cover arguments for a necessary being in which the sufficiently inclusive being is a being of a different sort from the World. At any rate, I see no reason to think that the kinds of worries van Inwagen raises about the existence of the World arise for, say, the existence of a set of (all) contingent ur-elements. (The worries van Inwagen raises about the existence of the World turn on the idea that the World is composed of different beings in different possible worlds; as we have seen, there is no obvious reason to think that the composition of a set varies from possible world to possible world.)

But there is another respect in which, it seems to me, van Inwagen's critique of the Worldly argument does not generalize. I used to think (along with Peter Geach, I believe) that the family of arguments for a necessary being to which the Worldly argument belongs essentially depended on a contingency-dependence premiss (which implied that if everything was contingent, then everything was dependent) and an existence-of-a-sufficiently-inclusive-being premiss (which implied that not everything was dependent). But I now think that perhaps someone arguing for a necessary being doesn't need to make any assumptions about the existence of sufficiently inclusive beings, as long as she has a strong enough version of the contingency-dependence principle (one that implies, but is not implied by, the version of the contingency-dependence principle in the Worldly argument).

Aquinas, Scotus, Leibniz *et alii* held that

> If a being is contingent, then there is some being outside that being on which that being depends.

But they also held that

> If two beings are (both) contingent, then there is some being outside both of those beings, on which at least one of those beings depends.

> If three beings are (all) contingent, then there is some being outside all three of those beings, on which at least one of those beings depends.

. . . and so on. That is, Aquinas *et alii* held that

> If any being is contingent, or any two or more beings are (all) contingent, then there is some being outside that being or outside (all) those beings, on which that being or at least one of those beings depends.

Equivalently:

> If any being is contingent, or any beings are (all) contingent, then there is some being outside that being or outside (all) those beings, on which that being or at least one of those beings depends.

This principle—which we may call *the singular-and-plural contingency-dependence principle*, inasmuch as it involves both a singular universal quantifier ("any being") and a plural universal quantifier ("any beings")—implies but is not implied by the ("merely singular") contingency-dependence principle of the Worldly argument. If the singular-and-plural contingency-dependence principle is true (and there are beings), then there is a necessary being.

If this is not immediately clear, it may be helpful to go at things contrapositively. Suppose there are beings, and all beings are contingent. Then there are some beings—to wit, all the beings there are—that satisfy both these conditions: (i) (all) those beings are contingent, and (ii) there is no being outside (all) those beings on which at least one of those beings depends (since there are no beings outside [all] those beings full stop). But if there are some beings that satisfy conditions (i) and (ii), then the singular-and-plural contingency-dependence principle is false. (Let us say that one of some beings is *exodependent* just in case one of those beings depends on something outside (all) those beings. The singular-and-plural contingency-dependence principle says that if any beings are (all) contingent, then at least one of them is exodependent. But if there are some beings that satisfy (i) and (ii), then there are some beings [namely, all the beings there are] that are (all) contingent, even though none of them is exodependent [inasmuch as they are all the beings there are].) So if there are beings, and all beings are contingent, then the singular-and-plural contingency-dependence principle is false. Contraposing, if there are beings, and the singular-and-plural contingency-dependence principle is true, there is at least one necessary being.

We have arrived at an unWorldly argument for the existence of a necessary being, in which the (strengthened) contingency-dependence principle does all the work, obviating recourse to an additional assumption concerning the existence of a sufficiently inclusive object. Does this mean that those who want to argue for the existence of a necessary being can do so simply on the basis of a (suitably formulated) contingency-dependence principle, within an ontological framework that does not go beyond ordinary individuals?

One might certainly think so. The singular-and-plural contingency-dependence principle does not explicitly say anything about the World, or mereological fusions, or Burgean aggregates, or sets; it only says things about beings (about any being or beings). And the same obviously goes for the additional premiss needed to get to the existence of a necessary being (*there are beings*). It might accordingly be thought that the premises of the unWorldly argument for the existence of a necessary being are not about and (to use the jargon) do not "ontologically commit us to" anything over and above beings.

If I have understood his views correctly, this is how George Boolos would see the matter. Naturally, Boolos does not discuss the unWorldly argument. But he does argue that the celebrated Geach-Kaplan sentence—*some critics only admire each other*—is not about and does not ontologically commit us to anything over and above critics and persons, and is equivalent to:

> There are some critics each of whom admires a person only if that person is one of them, and none of whom admires himself. (1985: 328)

By Boolos's lights, when we "quantify over" critics singularly, we incur an ontological commitment to critics. And when we quantify over critics plurally, we again incur an ontological commitment to—critics. As far as ontological commitment is concerned, the only difference between *some critic admires himself* and *some critics admire only each other* is that the latter, unlike the former, commits us to there being more than one critic: the latter statement certainly doesn't commit us to more kinds of things than the former—say, (nonempty) sets of critics, and not just critics.

If Boolos is right about what is often called the "ontological innocence" (i.e. ontological noncommittalness) of plural quantification, then we can get from a (suitably strong) contingency-dependence principle to the existence of a necessary being, without making any assumptions about what kinds of beings there are (hence, without making any assumptions about the existence of "sufficiently inclusive" beings).

Not all philosophical logicians or metaphysicians agree with Boolos about the ontological innocence of plural quantification, though. Some defend the "older-fashioned" Quinean view on which *some critics only admire each other* is about (implies the existence of, ontologically commits us to) sets (or something rather like sets) of critics. The champions of the Quinean view say that *there are some critics each of whom admires a person only if that person is one of them* is just another way of saying something like *there is a (nonempty) set of critics each element of which admires a person only if that person is an element of that set*. (As they see it, in a statement such as *there are some critics each of whom admires a person only if that person is one of them*, the term *them* is as it were grammatically plural and logically singular: for someone to be one of *them* is for someone to be a member of a particular set [or set-like entity]. And, as they see it, saying *for any being and any beings* is just another way of saying something like *for any being and any set of beings*.)

I don't think it's obvious who is right in this dispute. On the one hand, it's not unnatural to think that *for any being or any beings* amounts to *for any being or any group of beings*, and a group of beings is a set of beings, or something very like a set of beings. (Unless perhaps we run the argument in the reverse direction, and say that since *a group of beings* amounts to *some beings*, *a group of beings* is grammatically singular but logically plural and that talk about groups of beings does not commit us to anything over and above beings, in the same way that—it was suggested earlier—talk about that pair of shoes does not commit us to anything over and above those two shoes?) On the other hand, there is something at least initially plausible about the idea that *there is a (nonempty) set of critics each element of which admires a person only if that person is an element of that set* is unlike *some critics don't admire anyone who isn't one of those critics* in that the former but not the latter is about and ontologically commits us to sets. Also, as Boolos notes, *there are some sets that are all and only the sets that aren't members of themselves* seems to be true, but it is not clear how it could be true on a view according to which plural talk is talk about sets, given that (for Russellian reasons) there is no set of all sets that are not members of themselves.

For our purposes, though, we needn't take sides in the Quine-Boolos dispute about the ontological innocence (or otherwise) of plural quantification. The crucial point is that if the truth of sentences involving plural quantification implies the existence of sets or set-like entities—of what we may call *pluralities*—then ontological commitment to pluralities is unproblematic: after all, it's clear that some statements involving plural quantification are true.

The moral is that—despite what one might have suspected from van Inwagen's discussion of the Worldly argument—arguments from (some version of) the contingency-dependence principle to the existence of a necessary being may or may not involve ontological commitment to sufficiently inclusive entities but in any case need not involve any problematic ontological commitments. If Boolos is right, we don't need to believe in pluralities (of beings) to run the unWorldly argument (all we need to believe in is beings). If the Quinean view is right, we do need to believe in pluralities (of beings) to run the unWorldly argument, but this can't be a weak point of the unWorldly argument, because we need to believe in pluralities, whether or not we run the unWorldly argument.

At this point I shall try to draw a few threads together. Contingency-dependence arguments for the existence of a necessary being take various forms, at least some of which have premises that imply the existence of some kind of "sufficiently inclusive" being (the World, or the set of contingent ur-elements, or the like). But if we think of "the contingency-dependence argument" as something that can come in various versions (in the way people think of "the cosmological argument" or "the argument from evil"), then for the purposes of evaluating the contingency-dependence argument, issues about the existence or otherwise of various kinds of sufficiently inclusive objects drop out. The crucial questions are, (i) is it true that there are, or perfectly well could be, contingent but independent beings? and (ii) is it true that there are, or perfectly well could be, contingent beings none of which depends on any being that isn't one of them? If upon reflection we decide the answer to one of these questions is "yes", we should not accept the contingency-dependence argument; otherwise, we should accept it.

2 EVALUATING THE CONTINGENCY-DEPENDENCE PRINCIPLE

So, after all that, should we or should we not find the contingency-dependence argument—say, in the version I called the unWorldly contingency-dependence argument—cogent? I'm inclined to believe there is no answer to this question, until we know who "we" are.

Some people have an immediate, strong, and stable intuition that contingent beings, as such, are incapable—singly or jointly—of existing without an external "ground". If you are one of these people, and you can follow a bit of reasoning, then you will find the unWorldly contingency-dependence argument convincing (if you are exposed to it). In that case, to my mind, it's quite possible that you are reasonable ("doxastically responsible", "doxastically irreproachable") in finding that argument convincing. For I take it that if you have an immediate, strong, and stable intuition that contingent beings, as such, are incapable—singly or jointly—of existing without an external ground (and you are exposed to the unWorldly argument, and you can follow a bit of reasoning), then you will find that argument convincing, and you will be *prima facie* justified in doing so. So you'll be *ultima facie* justified in finding that argument convincing, unless perhaps there is what epistemologists call a "defeater" of your *prima facie* justification. And while there *might* be a defeater of your *prima facie* justification (e.g. a deep need to believe in a necessary being, which undermines your capacity to rationally evaluate arguments for a necessary being), there is no obvious reason to think there would have to be.

Of course, as I shall discuss, not everyone intuits that contingent beings, as such, are incapable—singly or jointly—of existing without an external ground. If you do so intuit (immediately, strongly, and stably), does the fact that not everyone else does (or the fact that you are aware that not everyone else does) mean that you are not *ultima facie* justified in believing what you intuit and thus in finding the unWorldly contingency-dependence argument convincing? It is not obvious that it does, even supposing you can't give a noncircular argument for why your intuitions are better than the intuitions of those who disagree with you about the principle at issue.

Take an analogous case. I think (and I have argued elsewhere; see Hughes 2002) that when we reflect on the "existence conditions" of certain kinds of composite (natural and artificial) objects, we can see that there are good (though not irresistible) reasons to suppose that such objects could go out of existence and subsequently come back into existence. So (unlike Aristotle and Locke) I think that things could come back from nonexistence. Suppose we say that a being is annihilated (reduced to nothing, as opposed to reduced to its parts) just in case that being and all its parts go out of existence. Then I am inclined to think that things could come back from annihilation as well as from nonexistence: as various mediaevals have said, if it is within God's power to bring a creature into existence from nothingness, it is also within His power to bring a creature back into existence from nothingness. So (unlike Aquinas) I am inclined to think that things can come back from annihilation as well as from nonexistence. That said, I don't know of any (good, noncircular) arguments that will take us from (relatively uncontroversial) premises about the existence conditions of certain kinds of beings to the conclusion that annihilation needn't be forever. At the end of the day, I am inclined to believe that things can come back from annihilation, because that just *looks* possible to me. But I know that not everyone shares my intuitions about this. Some people (e.g. Peter van Inwagen) strongly intuit that nothing existing after the annihilation of x could be the very same thing as x, even if it were a perfect duplicate thereof. I don't want to say that van Inwagen's belief that nothing can return from annihilation is unjustified, even though I think differently (and even though, as it happens, he knows I think differently). Given how things look to me, I tend to think, my belief that things can come back from annihilation isn't unjustified; given how they look to van Inwagen, I tend to think, his belief that things cannot come back from annihilation also isn't unjustified. For it seems perfectly possible that since our intuitions about the possibility or otherwise of returning from annihilation are different, our total evidence is different, so what we can justifiably believe about the possibility or otherwise of returning from annihilation is different.

In his discussion of the Worldly argument for the existence of a necessary being, van Inwagen notes that many of us intuit that any particular contingent being, as such, is incapable of existing without an external ground. Interestingly, he doesn't go so far as to say that many of us immediately, strongly, and stably intuit this; rather, he says that when we consider allegedly possible cases in which a particular contingent being exists without an external ground, "we may feel a certain metaphysical unease" (1993: 109): we (or at least a good many of us) doubt that such cases are genuinely possible. This seems right, and important, inasmuch as not a few of us have uncertain and wavering and conflicting intuitions about whether there could be a contingent and independent being. For some of us, on the one hand, the idea of a contingent and independent being does seem (as van Inwagen puts it) "weird", but on the other hand, the pair of properties <contingency, independence> does not look like a pair of clearly and blatantly incompatible properties, in the way that, say, the pairs <being red all over, being blue all over> and <being identical to 7, being greater than 8> do. For some of us, the idea of a contingent but independent being seems of doubtful possibility, rather than of clear impossibility (or possibility).

Van Inwagen does not explicitly discuss whether a good many of us intuit that contingent things, as such, are jointly incapable of existing without an external ground, since he considers only the "merely singular" version of the contingency-dependence principle. Certainly one could intuit the truth of the (weaker) merely singular contingency-dependence principle, without intuiting the truth of the (stronger) singular-and-plural contingency-dependence principle. In my experience, though, people accept both principles, or neither. I know philosophers who think every being is contingent (so that the singular-and-plural contingency-dependence principle is false). But I don't know any who think that since every being is contingent, and every contingent being is dependent, then—whatever current or future physical theories might suggest—the cosmic egg must depend on something else that depends on yet another thing that depends on. . . . The philosophers I know who are happy with the idea that everything is contingent (so that the singular-and-plural contingency-dependence principle is false) are also happy to say it's perfectly possible that physics will discover that there is a first contingent being (so that the merely singular contingency-dependence principle is likewise false). Conversely, the philosophers I know who think that a contingent being, as such, is incapable of existing without an external ground think that groups of contingent beings are just as incapable of existing without an external ground as are single contingent beings.

As I have suggested, many people do not strongly and consistently—or even weakly and fitfully—intuit the impossibility of contingent and independent beings. Atheists typically believe, as Bertrand Russell did, that something or other (the cosmic egg, or the universe, or mass/energy, or . . .) is both contingent and independent. Since these atheists hold that contingent and independent beings actually exist, they *a fortiori* hold they are possible. But as well as believing that contingent and independent beings are in fact possible, they (at least typically) believe contingent and independent beings don't—even initially—*look* impossible. Compare: Certain (noneliminative) materialists believe that phenomenal properties are a (nonempty) subclass of physical properties. So they believe that it is, and *a fortiori* could be the case, that one and the same property is both physical and phenomenal. They may nevertheless admit that—initially at least—physicality and phenomenality appear to be incompatible (higher-order) properties (say, because it looks as though [i] there couldn't be any more to a phenomenal property than how it feels but [ii] there has to be more to a physical property than how it feels). Indeed, some materialists who think that physicality and phenomenality are co-exemplified and *a fortiori* compatible may think that physicality and phenomenality are not going to stop looking incompatible to us until we acquire radically new concepts that will make the appearance of incompatibility go away. Some materialists go further and think that physicality and phenomenality will *never* look compatible to us: the facts that explain how a property can be at once physical and phenomenal are "cognitively closed" to us. By contrast, I don't know any atheists who think that although contingency and independence are co-exemplified and hence compatible, their compatibility is currently and may forever remain deeply mysterious. All the atheists I know think that something's being contingent and independent is conceivable and not (even initially) apparently impossible.

But it's not just atheists who see things this way. There are theists who see no apparent impossibility in the idea of a contingent and independent God (a contingently existing all-powerful, all-knowing, all-good, uncreated

Creator of everything outside Him). It is true that many philosophical theists have supposed that God is a necessary being, just as many philosophical
theists have supposed that God is an absolutely simple being. But just as it
is not clear that theists (as such) have any more reason to think God is absolutely simple than atheists have to think that (say) the cosmic egg is simple,
it is not clear that theists (as such) have any more reason to think that God
is necessary than atheists have to think that the cosmic egg is necessary.

Myself, I am with the theists (and atheists) to whom the existence of
a contingent and independent being looks—at least initially—like a genuine possibility, or, at least, doesn't look like an impossibility. I agree with
van Inwagen that the existence of a contingent and independent being isn't
blatantly and obviously a genuine possibility, in the way that, say, my never
having existed seems to be. But whatever propensity I have to doubt that it
is a genuine possibility is no stronger than my propensity to doubt that it is
an impossibility. That's why *I* don't find either the Worldly or the unWorldly
argument convincing—which, again, is not to say that *you* won't find either
of those arguments convincing or that you shouldn't find either of those
arguments convincing.

Two concluding remarks: In both the Worldly and unWorldly versions of the contingency-dependence argument, the relevant contingency-
dependence principle is unsupported by anything else in the argument. (The
same is true for various mediaeval versions of the contingency-dependence
argument. As I read Scotus and Aquinas, they do not try to motivate or
defend the assumption that anything that might not have existed depends
on something outside it: I think they regard it as axiomatic and at least
as plausible as anything that could be said in its defence.) But given how
many people regard the existence of an ungrounded contingent being, or
an ungrounded series of contingent beings, as clearly possible, or at least
not clearly impossible, a defender of the Worldly or unWorldly argument
might try to expand (and bolster) that argument by folding a defence of the
(relevant) contingency-dependence principle into it. For example, she might
argue *modo Leibniziano* that every fact has a (complete, or at least partial)
explanation but that the existence of a contingent and independent being
couldn't have even a partial explanation. (Van Inwagen is aware that someone might try to motivate the [merely singular] contingency-dependence
principle in this way but holds that the attempt will fail, inasmuch as the
supposition that every fact has a [complete, or at least partial] explanation
is more problematic than the merely singular contingency-dependence principle.) Whether (some version) of the contingency-dependence principle is a
not immediately compelling principle that can nevertheless be made compelling by the right argument is, sadly, an issue that goes beyond the scope of
this paper.

Finally, both the Worldly and the unWorldly argument make use of a contingency-dependence principle that is, in one way, surplus to requirements.
If there is a World (that nothing is outside of), and if in fact there are no

contingent and independent beings, then there is a necessary being: to get to a necessary being, we needn't suppose that there *couldn't be* contingent and independent beings. Similarly, as long as, in fact, any contingent being and any contingent beings have an external ground, we needn't suppose that there *couldn't be* some contingent being or some contingent beings without an external ground, in order to get to a necessary being. This suggests that defenders of the Worldly or unWorldly argument might want to bolster that argument, not by folding into it an argument for the relevant contingency-dependence principle, but rather by folding into it an argument for a weak-ened ("denecessitated") version thereof. After all, why make a job harder than it needs to be? Again, whether or not some denecessitated version of the contingency-dependence principle is a not immediately compelling principle that can nevertheless be made compelling by the right argument is, sadly, an issue I cannot pursue here.[1]

REFERENCES

Boolos, G. (1985). 'Nominalist Platonism', *Philosophical Review* 94, 3: 327–44.
Burge, T. (1977). 'A Theory of Aggregates', *Nous* 11, 2: 92–117.
Hughes, C. (2002). 'Starting Over', in Bottani, A., Carrara, M. and Giaretta, P. (eds.). *Individuals, Essence, and Identity*. Dordrecht, the Netherlands: Kluwer, 451–75.
Van Inwagen, P. (1990). *Material Beings*. Ithaca, NY: Cornell University Press.
———. (1993). *Metaphysics*. Boulder, CO: Westview Press.

---

1. Many thanks to Tyron Goldschmidt for his encouragement and his patience!

7 Conceiving Absolute Greatness

Earl Conee

1 INTRODUCTION

Anselm argued for the existence of a Greatest Conceivable Being (GCB).[1] Anselm's argument for a GCB relies on a contingent truth. It assumes that the Fool understands something. We shall see that if the argument at its best is a success, then all contingency is eliminable. A GCB would have to exist. If a GCB has to exist, then there couldn't have been nothing.

Anselm's argument at its best fails. Peter Millican (2004) has described a difficulty that turns out to be insuperable. The Anselmian argument that Millican's critique targets can be improved. The argument has three eliminable weaknesses. First, a premise is open to counterexamples that an Anselmian can avoid without cost. Second, the sort of entity to which the argument attributes greatness is not best thought to be great in the way that the argument requires. Another bearer of greatness is available that is more congenial to the argument's goal. And, third, the argument relies on the doubtful assumption that all great-making properties have maxima. A kindred argument needs no such assumption.

A revised Anselmian argument will be offered here. It is intended to be optimal for Anselm's purposes. This version will be seen to fail. A diagnosis of the failure will be proposed. If the diagnosis is correct, the difficulty is ineluctable.

2 IMPROVEMENTS

The premise that needlessly weakens the Anselmian argument that Millican criticizes concerns the greatness of a nature. The greatness of natures turns

---

1. Indefinite articles like "a" will be used throughout for the quantity of what Anselm's argument is supposed to prove to exist. Nothing in the argument gives reason to think that there is a unique being than which a greater cannot be conceived. It may be that other reasoning could establish that the sort of being who would qualify as greatest must be unique. For instance, being ultimately great may require creating everything else. Meanwhile, it is harmless to the argument for it to conclude with the existence of one GCB.

out not to be maximally advantageous for the argument. The premise can be improved.

In preparation for this, let's remind ourselves of Anselm's original work and then see how Millican formulates the reasoning and objects. Here is a standard translation of Anselm (Mann 1972: 260–1):

> Thus even the fool is convinced that something than which nothing greater can be conceived is in the understanding, since when he hears this, he understands it; and whatever is understood is in the understanding. And certainly that than which a greater cannot be conceived cannot be in the understanding alone. For if it is even in the understanding alone, it can be conceived to exist in reality also, which is greater.[2] Thus if that than which a greater cannot be conceived is in the understanding alone, then that than which a greater cannot be conceived is itself that than which a greater can be conceived. But surely this cannot be. Thus without doubt something than which a greater cannot be conceived exists, both in the understanding and in reality.

To a first approximation, the reasoning goes like this. Something is considered—a GCB, or a concept of one, or something else that pertains in the right way to a GCB. This something embodies an ultimate in greatness. Because existence would contribute to the greatness, the supposition that a GCB does not exist reduces to absurdity. The ultimate greatness of what is considered requires existence actually to make that contribution. This implies that a GCB actually exists.

An argument like this needs a mental topic, and a sort of greatness, and it needs them to match up in the right way. The mental topic, the thing in the Fool's mind that gets the argument going, is either a GCB or some appropriate proxy. In any case, the greatness that pertains to the mental topic is what must somehow require the existence of a GCB.

Millican's rendition of Anselm's argument is about the greatness of a nature. These natures are entities composed of combinations of properties. Millican quite reasonably supposes that Anselm's aim was to prove the existence of something that has traditionally divine properties such as

---

2. Millican relies on an importantly different translation of this sentence. His translation replaces this sentence with the following: "For if [a GCB] exists in the mind alone, something that is greater can be thought to exist in reality also" (2004: 439). Millican (ibid.: note 2) credits Alexander Broadie for this translation. The crucial difference is that in Millican's preferred translation, what is greater is just "something" that exists in reality, perhaps *any* existing thing. Millican gives evidence that this is the correct translation. This translation supports Millican's attribution to Anselm's argument of the premise that is argued below to be needlessly problematic. Whether Millican's version is Anselm's premise or not—a historical issue that will not be addressed here—it will be contended below that an improvement is available.

omniscience, omnipotence, omnicreation, and perfect goodness. To designate a nature that is composed of that conjunction of properties, Millican uses the term "<God>" (2004: 453).

Millican's version of the argument has as its explicit topic whatever nature meets the following specification: a nature than which no greater can be thought. If the argument succeeds, then this specification is met by the nature with the traditional divine properties, <God>. The argument is an attempt to prove that <God> is instantiated. Here is how Millican states it:

Millican's Anselmian Argument (MAA)

(1') The phrase "a-nature-than-which-no-greater-nature-can-be-thought" is clearly understood by the Fool, and apparently makes sense.

(2') Hence we can take the phrase "a-nature-than-which-no-greater-nature-can-be-thought" as successfully denoting some specific nature.

(3') A nature which is instantiated in reality is greater than one which is not.

(4') So if a-nature-than-which-no-greater-nature-can-be-thought were not instantiated in reality, then it would be possible to think of a nature that is greater (for example, any nature that is in fact instantiated in reality).

(5') But this would be a contradiction, since it is obviously impossible to think of a nature that is greater than a-nature-than-which-no-greater-nature-can-be-thought.

(6') Therefore a-nature-than-which-no-greater-nature-can-be-thought must indeed be instantiated in reality. (2004: 457–8)

Millican criticizes this argument as follows.[3] <God> is the nature to which the description in (6'), "a-nature-than-which-no-greater-nature-can-be-thought", is intended to apply. The consequent (4') is about something that is supposed to be possible, on the condition of the antecedent. This amounts to the condition that <God> is not actually instantiated. So, one term of the greatness relation in (4')'s consequent is how great <God> is, on the condition that <God> is uninstantiated. Premise (3') asserts that any nature that is instantiated is greater than any nature that is uninstantiated. It is therefore easy to see that (4') follows from (1')–(3') when the possibility in (4')'s consequent can hold in virtue of a comparison between the greatness of some instantiated nature and the greatness of <God> if <God> is uninstantiated. Yet precisely because the possibility asserted by the consequent of (4') is established by a greatness comparison between some instantiated nature and the uninstantiated <God>, (5') is quite doubtful. Premise (5') denies the possibility of thinking of any nature that is greater than <God>,

---

3. The following exposition of the objection leaves out some details. See note 4 below.

the referent of "a-nature-than-which-no-greater-nature-can-be-thought". Contrary to (5'), it is not at all contradictory to think of a nature that is instantiated here and thereby think of one that is greater than <God> is here. Premise (3'), with its assertion that instantiation trumps all else when it comes to the greatness of a nature, makes it easy to understand how that is consistent.

The consequent of (4') can be interpreted to be about a different comparison, one that (5') would quite plausibly assert to be a contradiction. The consequent of (4') can be interpreted to assert the possibility that the nature that is thought of, <God>, *as that nature is in reality*, is greater than that same nature, <God>, *as that nature is in reality*. That is evidently impossible, whether or not <God> is instantiated. But nothing in the premises (1')–(3') even suggests that (4'), so interpreted, follows from them. Those premises plainly allow that the nature <God> is exactly as great as it is, instantiated or not. Nothing about the greatness of instantiation according to (3') so much as hints at a reason to think otherwise.

Finally, the consequent of (4') can be interpreted to assert the possibility that <God>, as that nature is thought to be when instantiated, is greater than <God>, as that nature is thought to be when instantiated. This again gives us a consequent of (4') asserting that something is possible that is plainly impossible, as (5') requires. But again nothing in (1')–(3') even suggests that (4') follows on this interpretation. The greatness <God> is thought to have when instantiated is as great as it is. This greatness is entirely unaffected by whether <God> is instantiated, and the premises (1')–(3') do not suggest otherwise. Thus the argument fails, no matter which greatness comparison is made—one that is about how great <God> is, one that is about how great <God> is thought to be, or one that compares the former to the latter.[4]

This line of objection is very valuable. If we are to evaluate any one definite argument, then, just as the objection requires, we must attend to the settings in which greatness is supposed to be had when we consider the merits of the premises that make claims about relative greatness. The content of the argument is fully determinate only when the terms of the greatness relation are specified.

MAA is not optimal for Anselm's purposes, however. Premise (3') causes the argument avoidable trouble. For one thing, it is a liability that (3') is about the greatness of natures. And, for another thing, (3') makes a needlessly implausible claim about the role of instantiation in greatness.

Millican makes MAA about the greatness of a nature, rather than the greatness of a being who has the nature of a GCB, in order to avoid certain traditional objections. For one thing, there is the accusation that the Anselmian

---

4. Again, this is a simplified version summary of Millican's critique. He also discusses potential referents other than <God> of the phrase "a-nature-than-which-no-greater-nature-can-be-thought". The full discussion is in Millican (2004: 463–8).

argument relies on at least the mental reality of something that really is a GCB—some object of thought that has in some way the relevant greatness, whether or not it actually exists. The reality of any such entity can be reasonably doubted. In contrast, it is quite reasonable to take for granted the nature in question and make allegations about its greatness and what that requires. This procedure does not assume that the nature is actually had by some being. It is an ordinary Platonist view that properties can exist without being instantiated and that natures are entirely constituted by combinations of properties. So an argument about the greatness of <God> can be given, for the purpose of establishing the conclusion that <God> is in fact instantiated, with the nature's existence taken for granted. Clearly, if some nature like <God> is instantiated, then a being exists with great credentials for being a GCB.

The trouble with this strategy for formulating the argument is that the greatness that pertains specifically to natures is not suited to Anselm's purposes. There is a readily recognizable sort of greatness that can be had by entities other than natures. This greatness would be had by a substantial entity *exemplifying* properties such as omniscience and creation. Having those properties would be wonderful and awe-inspiring. Such properties are great-making in an easily understandable way. But MAA relies on a greatness that is possessed by natures. Specifically, MAA requires the nature <God> to have this greatness. Yet <God> does not have impressive properties like omniscience and creation. That nature is not an all-powerful creator. <God> must rather have the requisite maximal greatness by being *composed of* such properties.

It is quite unclear that natures are made great by the familiar great-making capacity of the properties that compose them. The greatness of a nature seems rather to be determined by whatever enhances the magnificence of an abstract object that is composed of properties. Perhaps this enhancement is affected by the great quantity of the properties that compose it, or by their great diversity, or by the intricacy of the logical relationships among them.

It may seem that we can simply set aside all such musings about the true nature of the greatness of natures. We can simply take it for granted that the relevant sort of "greatness" of a nature is the familiar greatness of *having* the nature.

This interpretation ruins the Anselmian argument. The argument relies on the crucial greatness comparison to deliver the existence of a GCB. That can happen only if the existence of a GCB at least makes some sort of positive difference to how much of the relevant greatness is possessed by the relevant bearer of greatness. Natures are the bearers of greatness in MAA. So the positive difference that the argument needs from existence would have to be made, not by *the existence of the nature*, that being assumed, but rather by the nature *having an existing instance*. That instantiation is what would get us the existence of a GCB. But we are now supposing that the greatness of a nature is determined by the familiar greatness that a being would get by instantiating that nature. The trouble is that it makes no positive difference to *this* greatness for the nature to have an existing instance. The greatness is measured by what instantiating the nature *would* do for a being by having it. This is a necessary property of the nature, whether or not any existing thing has the nature.

We could seek another understanding of the greatness of natures, hoping to find a sort of greatness for them where existence helps, while <God> remains at least a contender for greatest. Unfortunately, premise (3') of MAA makes such an extreme claim about the instantiation of natures that the prospects of finding a suitable notion of greatness are quite dismal. Premise (3') asserts that any instantiated nature is greater than any uninstantiated one. This assumption implies that if something does possess the composing properties of a nature, then no matter how unimpressive those properties are—indeed, no matter how insignificant or even evil they make their possessors—that instantiated nature is "greater" than the most impressively composed uninstantiated combination. So, for example, the nature that is constituted of all the evils of the worst villain in the history of the world is a "greater" one, according to this premise, than is the most saintly nature that no one ever quite attained. That ranking of any sort of quality among natures is just not credible.[5]

3   AMELIORATION

We seek an optimal version of Anselm's argument. A best version best combines these features: it makes minimal assumptions, each premise has maximal plausibility, each derivation is valid, and the conclusion asserts something that is sufficient for the existence of a GCB. A best version of Anselm's argument also implements "Anselm's way of arguing". That classification is clearly murky. Its application is contestable on both textual and charitable grounds. The intention here is to favor argumentative strength over textual fidelity.

Anselm's way of arguing in outline is this. The argument aims to derive the existence of a GCB from the Fool's own understanding. A priori reflection is supposed to reveal that the nature of the concept of a GCB implies that it applies to an existing being. In more detail, the argument has three main working components. First, it relies on a conception of a being as maximally great. Second, it relies on existence making a positive difference

---

5. In a critical discussion of Millican's version of Anselm's argument, Yujin Nagasawa (2007: 1034) observes that the argument does not need this particular premise. Nagasawa offers as a replacement premise the more limited assumption that existence is a great-making property—a nature is greater if it is instantiated than if it is uninstantiated (ibid.: 1035). In note 10 Nagasawa suggests that a further improved version of the premise might limit the great-making that is done by existence to natures that are not intrinsically malevolent. The further improved version is also problematic. There are uninstantiated natures that would be worthless, e.g., a nature that would slightly enlarge a dust mote that is floating where it could never affect anything sentient. It is reasonable to think that natures composed of worthless properties like that would not be made greater by being instantiated. In any event, it is argued below that the best Anselmian argument does not address natures at all.

toward that greatness. And, third, using a reductio assumption that denies that the conception applies to anything, the argument derives from the maximality of the greatness that this denial is an absurdity.

4   ABSOLUTE GREATNESS

Before attempting an optimal formulation, we should avoid one more potential obstacle to a successful Anselmian argument. Some great-making properties have no apparent maxima. For instance, benevolence and omnipotence are traditional great-makers. The more intentional good someone does, the greater the person seems to be. There is no limit on how much good an omnipotent being would be able to do.[6] Similarly, making momentous and valuable free choices seems to add to a being's greatness, and there is no limit on how many of these free choices an omnipotent being would be able to make. It could create new vast quantities or types of flourishing sentient creatures and sizably improve their lot in any number of ways. Finally, creating infinitely more seems to be greatness enhancing. Creating an infinitely more extensive universe seems greater than creating a less extensive one. The cardinality of the infinite magnitudes in possible universes seems to have no maximum.

If anything like these reflections on open-ended great-makers is right, then no possible being has the maximum of all the great-making properties, since some of them have no upper limit. It thus seems that for each possible possessor of great-making properties, there is another that would be greater. A greatest conceivable being is impossible.

Fortunately, even without a maximum for some sorts of greatness, fundamentally the same Anselmian argument can be made. Several traditional divine great-making properties have maxima. These include omniscience, omnipotence, and necessary existence. Let's use the phrase "absolutely greatest being" to express the concept of a being that is, for one thing, greatest in all such ways—it has all of the "absolutes" of greatness.[7] Furthermore,

---

6. For further discussion, see Conee (1994).
7. Arguments exist for an incompatibility among absolute great-making properties. For example, David Blumenfeld (1978) argues that being omniscient requires having experiences that an omnipotent being could not have. Blumenfeld holds that feeling fear is required to know some propositions. Yet according to Blumenfeld belief in personal danger is needed to feel fear, and an omnipotent being would be unable to have that belief, since it would know the belief to be false (1978: 95–6). But omnipotence must include being able to self-induce any belief. Knowing the belief to be false would not be an insuperable obstacle to any omnipotence worthy of the name. That much seems plain. Indeed, omnipotence seems to require being able to do anything whatsoever. (This is defended in Conee [1991].) Quite generally, arguments for incompatibilities among absolute great-makers seem ineffective. But it is harmless to substitute the following as the requirement for an "absolutely greatest being": having an overall greatest maximal combination of absolute great-makers.

the being is at least infinitely good in any great-making ways that are open-ended. In other words, an absolutely greatest being has all of the great-making properties that *do* have maxima and also has, to some infinite degree, any other great-making properties that do *not* have maxima. Proving the existence of an absolutely greatest being would leave open the possibility of an even greater conceivable being. But it would be proving the existence of something tremendously great.[8]

We should also adjust the Anselmian argument by employing a suitable greater-than relation. The adjustment should allow the argument to do its job of proving the existence of something absolutely greatest—if all else goes well—while leaving open the possibility of great-making properties that do not have maxima. The adjustment should ensure that any such great-makers do not prevent there being a relevantly "greatest" conceivable being.

Let's use "absolutely greater" to express the familiar greatness relation of beings, except as it applies to any great-making properties that do not have maxima. If there are any of those, then for one being to be "absolutely greater" than another is for the being either to be greater in the familiar way (e.g., the one being is greater in virtue of having an additional absolute great-making property or the one is greater in virtue of having a higher finite degree of some open-ended great-maker) or to have to an infinite degree one or more additional open-ended great-making properties that the other does not have to any infinite degree.[9] Thus, although larger infinities of great-making properties are larger quantities, on this account just having a larger infinity of a great-maker does not make a being absolutely greater. Crucially for an Anselmian argument, employing this absolutely-greater-than relation continues to allow the absolute property of existence (or necessary existence) to be at least eligible as an improvement in greatness. So a premise in the argument can assert that it is an improvement, without immediately running afoul of the definition.

---

8. Necessary existence is a maximum of existence. There are no further levels or extents of existence that could enhance it. So perhaps necessary existence is maximally great with respect to existence. Still, it might be that an Anselmian argument can successfully utilize contingent existence as a great-making property. That sort of argument is what will be discussed later in the body of the text. But necessary existence is also available to play that role in an argument about a conceivable absolutely greatest being. A version of the argument that is explicitly about necessary existence is not as faithful to the cited Anselm text. However, we seek a maximally strong Anselmian argument. A version of the proposed optimal argument that is about necessary existence will be discussed in the notes below. It will be argued to be no more successful.

9. When I say here that the one has "additional" great-makers it is intended that the two beings otherwise have the same great-makers.

5   AN OPTIMAL ANSELMIAN ARGUMENT

Here is a formulation that takes into account the need for improvement that we have seen in MAA. It is intended to provide a best Anselmian argument.[10]

Optimal Anselmian Argument (OAA)

P1   An absolutely greatest being is conceivable.

P2   An absolutely greatest being that exists is absolutely greater than is an absolutely greatest being that does not exist.

Therefore,

C1   If an absolutely greatest being does not exist, then it is possible for a conceivable being to be absolutely greater than an absolutely greatest being.

P3   It is not possible for a conceivable being to be absolutely greater than an absolutely greatest being.

Therefore,

C2   An absolutely greatest being does exist.

Here are some assets of this version of the argument. First, OAA makes no contingent assumptions. One thing that OAA is about is something's being conceivable. That is, OAA is partly about a concept that might have been possessed by someone. The possibility of a concept being possessed is a necessary fact. OAA is also about a greater-than relation. It asserts something about how existence bears on the extension of that relation. The truth-value of the OAA claim about the bearing of existence on this greatness derives entirely from the nature of the greatness. It does not depend on any contingency. Since the argument requires only some necessary facts about conceivability and greatness, if the premises are true, they necessarily true. If the derivations are valid, then the conclusion is a necessary fact. There would have to be an absolutely greatest being.

A second asset of OAA is that P1 requires nothing more ontologically extraordinary than a concept of an absolutely greatest being. The possibility of someone having this concept is all it takes for an absolutely greatest being to be conceivable.

It is another asset of OAA that it gives the great-making potential of existence its least ambitious role in an Anselmian argument. P2 requires only

---

10. Those who think that every great-making property has an intrinsic maximum can ignore the "absolutely" qualifiers throughout.

that the existence of an absolutely greatest being would be the existence of a being with more absolute greatness than the being would have without existence. P2 does not imply that existence is a great-maker for anything else. P2 does not even imply that existence is a great-maker for an absolutely greatest being. P2 implies only that an absolutely greatest being is absolutely greater with existence than without it. The modesty of this assumption can be seen by considering some highly plausible principles that defend P2. Like P2, the principles have the asset of not implying that existence would be good for things that would be bad or neutral, were they to exist. For example, P2 could be true without existence itself being any good for anything. P2 could be true because of the truth of the principle that nothing is any way at all without existing. P2 could be true because of the truth of the principle that any potentially good being has that goodness only by existing with it, and so such a being is better with existence than without it.[11] And P2 could be true because of the truth of the principle that existence is needed for necessary existence and that property is positively great-making, at least for an absolutely greatest being.

The validity of the implication of C1 is not quite straightforward. This is a desirable feature of OAA. The argument at its best turns out to have a problem. This derivation is as good a place as any for part of the problem to lurk without being too obvious. The consequent of C1 needs careful interpreting. It is easy to read C1 so that it clearly follows. C1 follows when it is read to say: without the actual existence of an absolutely greatest being, there is a conception of a being that *requires of* the being more greatness than a nonexistent absolutely greatest being *actually has*. The conception that requires more absolute greatness calls for that greater greatness in virtue of requiring the ultimate of a sort of greatness that P2 tells us existence enhances. It is the conception of a being that has all that it takes to be absolutely greatest, which by P2 includes actual existence. P1 tells us that this sort of being is conceivable. Clearly, without the existence of an absolutely greatest being, "it's" actual status falls short of this ultimate in conceivable greatness. When C1 is read to say this, C1 clearly follows from P1 and P2. We shall have to return to the content of C1.[12]

---

11. These first two principles offered on behalf of P2 do not defend a premise that replaces P2 with the assertion that *necessarily* existing is absolutely greater than not existing necessarily. Contingent existence is clearly sufficient for having properties, whether they are good, bad, or indifferent. The replacement premise thus would make a version of OAA that was about necessary existence less defensible. But if necessary existence is the most plausible sort of existence to serve as an absolute greatness-maker, then that version may still be optimal overall.

12. In a version of OAA where C1 is about necessary existence, the counterpart point holds about a plainly valid interpretation: a conception that requires necessary existence requires more absolute greatness than is had by a being that lacks necessary existence, given the presence in this version of OAA of a premise claiming that necessary existence is relevantly better.

P3 also turns out to call for careful interpreting. Again this is an asset of OAA. The problem for the best version of Anselm's way of arguing should not be entirely in any one place in the argument, where it might be readily isolated and identified. Like C1, P3 has a clearly true reading. It can be read to say: the concept of an absolutely great*est* being cannot be outdone, in how much absolute greatness it requires to apply, by any concept.

OAA is not formally a reductio ad absurdum. But the antecedent of C1 amounts to a reductio assumption. The consequent of C1 is supposed to state an absurdity. P3 is supposed to make the absurdity explicit by asserting the consequent to be impossible. The validity of the derivation of the second conclusion, C2, depends on P3 denying what the consequent of C1 asserts. It can easily appear that P3 does deny that. The C1 consequent says that something is possible. The syntax makes it at least appear that P3 denies that very possibility. With C1 and P3 understood in this way, C2 follows.

C2 asserts the existence of a being that has all absolute great-making properties and infinite degrees of any other sort of great-maker. Proving that conclusion would be sufficient for a successful Anselmian argument.

6   EVALUATION OF OAA

Let us now investigate how well OAA works. P1 is quite acceptable. It asserts only that a concept can be had—the concept of an absolutely greatest being. We have that concept, so it can be had. Note that P1 does not say that there is, or that there could have been, some entity to which this concept applies. P1 does not say that we are in a conceiving-of relation to any being to which the concept applies. P1 is a claim only about the content of a certain plainly available way of conceiving.

P2 is substantial, but it is nearly rationally irresistible. If some existing thing does answer to the concept of an absolutely greatest being, then it really has all of the great-making properties that go into being absolutely greatest. For instance, the being actually knows all. Its knowledge is just as genuine as ours, and entirely comprehensive to boot. That is impressive. If no absolutely greatest being exists, then at most there is some nonexistent Meinongian object that somehow qualifies as an absolutely greatest being. The nonexistent being is omniscient in just the way that the Meinongian nonexistent gold mountain is a mountain made out of gold. Whatever that way of being made out of gold is, it does not excite prospectors. Gold that exists is way better. Similarly, a defender of P2 can quite reasonably contend that genuinely existing with great properties like omniscience is a greater way to be. So if some absolutely greatest being is real but nonexistent, then P2 is right that an existing absolutely greatest being would be absolutely greater.

Suppose that we set Meinongianism aside. Suppose that there is no absolutely greatest being with any kind of reality, if one does not exist. Instead, when we reflect on the idea of a GCB, we are just conceiving of how such a thing would be. This conception has no object at all, and so none that is any actual good. In contrast, the real thing would be terrifically great. Clearly, the real thing would be absolutely greater than its absence. So P2 is acceptable, with or without nonexistent objects.[13]

C1 requires careful handling. Loosely speaking, C1 says that without an existing absolutely greatest being, there is a concept of something greater than that nonexisting being. But we must be fastidious in answering this question: *where is the absolute greatness of these things supposed to be manifested as the basis for comparison?* Evidently, given the antecedent of C1, the inferior being is supposed to be getting its inferiority from its lack of actual existence. So we are to rate it as it is when not existing here, in the actual world. In other words, given C1's antecedent, what is at stake is the actual absolute greatness of an absolutely greatest being on the assumption that it does not exist here. Next we should ask: where is the greatness manifested of the being that the consequent asserts to be absolutely greater than that? Well, to make use of P2, the larger absolute greatness must derive partly from its existence. So evidently the consequent is supposed to be assessing that greatness *on the condition that the assessed thing does exist.* The absolutely greater thing is supposed to be absolutely greater in virtue of a requirement of existence being built into the concept. So we must *not* assess the absolute greatness of the absolutely greater being *here.* It exactly matches *here* the absolute greatness of an absolutely greatest being as it is here. It is identical to such a thing. The greatness of its *conception*, as that greatness is elaborated by P2, is clearly supposed to be crucial to its being greater. So it is reasonable to employ instead a comparison to the absolute greatness that the concept requires for its application: the absolute greatness that something *would* have *if* it answered to the conception of an absolutely greatest being.[14] By P2, this greatness includes having actual existence, and so it plainly requires more greatness than a nonexisting absolutely greatest being actually has. In other words, we have arrived at this reading of C1:

C1* If an absolutely greatest being does not exist, then it is possible for a being to be conceived of so as to be absolutely greater than an absolutely greatest being actually is.

---

13. These thoughts do not defend a premise about necessary existence. Contingently having all of that absolute greatness would still be better than having it in a Meinongian way or being nothing at all. The necessary-existence version of P2 would have to be defended instead by something like the sheer impressiveness of necessary existence versus any less extensive mode of existence. Perhaps that is defense enough.
14. The being need not be metaphysically possible. This term of the evaluative comparison is determined by how great a being that answered to the concept of an absolutely greatest being would thereby have to be.

C1* is a necessary implication of P1 and P2.[15] Now we must be strategic in our interpretation of P3, aiming to make sure that C2 follows validly. P3 currently reads:

> P3 It is impossible for any conceivable being to be absolutely greater than an absolutely greatest being.

To reiterate, what the consequent of C1* is about is *not* some being whose absolute greatness is superior to that of another being in one and the same situation. Rather, the consequent is about a possibility of the absolute greatness of one being *as that being is conceived to be* versus that of one being *as that being actually is*. So *that* greatness comparison is the possibility that P3 should deny. Then C1* and P3 logically imply C2. For P3 to deny that possibility, it must read like this:

> P3* It is impossible for a being to be conceived of so as to be absolutely greater than an absolutely greatest being actually is.

C1* and P3* plainly entail:

> C2 An absolutely greatest being does exist.

Now we have an adequately interpreted argument. And now OAA is in big trouble. The trouble is that P3* is not reasonably thought to be true. It is quite clear that if no absolutely greatest being exists, then *we just did* conceive of something as being absolutely greater than a nonexistent absolutely greatest being is. We did it simply by entertaining the concept of an absolutely greatest being. P2 tells us that this conception requires existence. So having existence would make an absolutely greatest being that answered to this conception absolutely greater than a nonexistent absolutely greatest being actually is.[16]

On the other hand, if we had good reason to think that an absolutely greatest being does exist, then we would thereby have reason to think that

---

15. The step is not formally valid. We have just worked out why C1* would have to be true under any conditions in which P1 and P2 were true. So C1* is necessarily implied. The version of C1 in an argument about necessary existence has a counterpart consequent. That version of C1 is about a possibility that compares a being that lacks necessary existence with a being that meets the requirement of necessary existence that the necessary-existence version of P2 implies is built into the concept of maximal absolute greatness. The consequent would claim the possibility that the latter is absolutely greater than the former. That possibility is equally plausible and also follows validly from its premises.

16. The counterpart objection applies equally well against the version of P3* about necessary existence. The complaint would be that we just did conceive of something as being absolutely greater than a being that does not necessarily exist, in virtue of our conception of an absolutely greatest being with the requirement of necessary existence that is assured by the necessary existence counterpart of P2.

it would be as absolutely great as an absolutely greatest being would be where it existed. It would itself be precisely such a being. P3* would be true. The credibility for us of P3* thus depends on our having some reason to accept the existence of an absolutely greatest being. Absent that, P3* is unjustified. Having justification for P3* in a way that allows the premise to help OAA to justify its conclusion requires having some reason to believe that an absolutely greatest being exists that is independent of OAA. That is, we would have to have some independent reason to believe the conclusion of OAA. So, at best, OAA could give its conclusion supplemental support. We would have to have some other good reason to believe in the existence of a GCB.

Posing the problem as a lack of justification for P3* understates its severity. Anselm's reasoning is a reductio ad absurdum. It needs an absurdity, not merely an assertion of impossibility for which we might seek some sort of justification. The nonexistence of a GCB must entail something that is "surely" impossible. It is clear that this absurdity is supposed to be an entailment to the effect that something is greater than a greatest thing. If any such entailment did exist, then the argument would work. Any claim of the following form is indeed absurd: a thing X has more greatness than a greatest thing Y has. In contrast, all that the consequent of C1* delivers is a plainly coherent claim: it is conceivable for something to have been absolutely greater than the actual greatness, if any, of an absolutely greatest being, if any. That is no absurdity. Without absurdity there, the Anselmian reasoning fails.

There is a ready interpretation of P3 on which it does assert a manifest impossibility. In the interest of finding the optimal Anselmian argument, we should turn to that interpretation. The relevant circumstance for an absolutely greatest being, in its comparison with a genuinely absolutely greatest being, is how great an absolutely greatest being is required to be by that very conception. It would be manifestly incoherent to suppose that any conceivable being was absolutely greater than that. So, in order to express the relevant incoherence, P3 should read:

> P3' It is impossible for any conceivable being to have been absolutely greater than the absolutely greatest being is conceived of as being.

The absolute greatness of the absolutely greatest being is specified by P3' to be at the maximum. It is manifestly impossible for any being to have been greater in this way than the greatest in this way would be. So P3' gives us an Anselmian absurdity.

To give us a valid argument for C2, P3' must deny the consequent of the other premise. This is currently C1*:

> C1* If an absolutely greatest being does not exist, then it is possible for a being to be conceived of so as to be absolutely greater than an absolutely greatest being actually is.

The possibility asserted in the consequent of C1* has something *conceived of* as greater than something *actually is*. P3' comes nowhere near to denying the possibility of that. The impossibility of P3' has something *possibly* greater than something is *conceived of as being*. There is no appearance of a clash between the C1* consequent-asserted possibility and the P3'-asserted impossibility. All it would take for both to obtain is for there to be a certain fact of the form: something could have been greater than something actually is, but the former could not have been greater than the latter is conceived of as being. There seem to be countless mundane facts of that form. For instance, I could have been greater with respect to virtue than I actually am, by having been more virtuous than I actually am. Nonetheless, I could not have been greater with respect to virtue than I am conceived of as being, when I am conceived of as being maximally virtuous. The same goes for the absolute-greatness comparison at issue. It is quite coherent to suppose that an absolutely greatest being could have been absolutely greater than it actually is, perhaps having a considerable greatness deficiency owing to its nonexistence. But it could not have been absolutely greater than it is conceived to be, with that greatest greatness duly abetted by its conceived existence. We have no reason to think that the P3' impossibility is incompatible with the C1* consequent possibility. So we cannot validly infer negation of the antecedent of C1*. C2 is not implied.

For the sake of having C2 implied, we can revise the argument upward from P3'. We can adjust the consequent of C1 so that it is negated by P3':

> C1' If an absolutely greatest being does not exist, then it is possible for some conceivable being to have been absolutely greater than the absolutely greatest being is conceived of as being.

The consequent of C1' asserts to be possible just what P3' declares to be impossible. So the negation of the antecedent of C1' is implied, and this secures the implication of C2. But C1' does not follow from P1 and P2. The concept of an absolutely greatest being requires existence. So the superiority of existence, asserted by P2, is built into how great an absolutely greatest being is conceived of as being. There is no clue in P1 or P2 of how the nonexistence of an absolutely greatest being might support the possibility of a conceivable absolutely *greater* being. Instead, it is clear that the maximal absolute greatness that an absolutely greatest being is conceived to have is entirely unaffected by what does or does not exist. Thus, the first subargument in the current interpretation of OAA—P1 and P2, therefore C1'—is not valid.

In order to have a chance of validly deriving C1', we would have to change something further upstream, P1 or P2. No such alteration holds any prospect of success. The rational distance between the antecedent of C1' and its consequent is too great. The argument needs the consequent of its version of C1 to be an absurdity. If the absolute greatness that it must be absurd to exceed is that of how absolutely great an absolutely greatest being is conceived of as being, then no premise like P2 about actual existence stands a chance of securing the valid implication of the relevant C1. Matters pertaining to what actually exists just do not bear on the absolute greatness that things can be conceived to have.[17]

This problem is not eliminable. The argument has no chance of giving a proof based on the Fool's own understanding, or anything like that, unless its premises are defended a priori. The a priori defense of the maximal absolute greatness of a being must be a defense of how absolutely great it is conceived to be, just in virtue of its conception. So the greatness a being is conceived to have must be one term of the comparison. The argument also relies on a reductio assumption of the nonexistence of an instance of the concept. Yet the nonexistence of an instance cannot affect how much greatness is built into the conception. So the nonexistence of an absolutely greatest being has not been reduced to absurdity.

7   CLARIFICATION AND FURTHER DEFENSE OF THE OBJECTION

The problem that has been described for the Anselmian argument might seem to have a shaky basis. It might seem that the complaint can be conveyed by this slogan: you can't improve a concept by having something fall under it. More straightforwardly stated: a concept is not made greater by having an existing instance. That proposition might well seem doubtful. Maybe concepts that apply to existing things are more significant, more impressive, or something like that, while uninstantiated concepts are less great. Or maybe not. That issue can be reasonably disputed.[18]

The problem for the Anselmian argument, though, is not that it relies on the assumption that the crucial *concept* is maximally great only where it has an application. The argument is not about how great some concept can be. The argument is about the greatness that is required to fall under a concept. The GCB concept is supposed to be ultimate in what sort of being a concept can call for. The aspiration of the argument is that the greatness that is required to be a GCB would be absurdly exceeded by the greatness required by some other concept, in the absence of the actual existence of a GCB. The problem is that the GCB concept sets the requirements for falling under it essentially. It is the essential nature of a concept to have a certain content. In

---

17. In exactly the same way, the absence of a necessarily existing being does not affect how much absolute greatness the absolutely greatest being can be conceived of as having, on the supposition that this greatness requires necessary existence.

18. The greatness of concepts is a fairly obscure matter. The GCB concept seems to have some serious competition for greatness as a concept. For instance, ingenious and fruitful ideas of pure mathematics seem more impressive as concepts.

this case, the GCB concept is that of a being that is greatest among conceivable beings. Whether or not this specification applies to any existing thing just does not affect what the specification requires. Yet the argument needs a reductio premise to this effect: if a GCB does not exist, then this entails the absurdity that there is a concept of something even greater than a greatest conceivable being. This entailment holds only if the GCB concept having an existing application *does* affect how great the concept requires an instance to be. Since it is quite clear that application makes no such difference, the argument cannot be made to work.

There is one more potential source of doubt. It might be thought that describing the problem as was just done unjustifiably preempts a promising alternative. Perhaps we must have some *being* in mind in order to conceive of any sort of GCB, absolutely greatest or otherwise. Perhaps a being that "exists in the understanding" is required. It can seem that granting the mental existence of such a being is all that the argument needs. After all, the being is indeed a GCB, its greatness does indeed entail actual extra-mental existence, and so the extra-mental reality of a GCB is entailed and the argument succeeds.

An Anselmian argument begins with what the Fool must grant by his comprehending denial of God's existence. The argument ends with the existence of God. The Fool must grant only that he has a certain conception of an entity, namely, that of a GCB (or the proposed optimal replacement, the concept of an absolutely greatest being). Adding more to the presupposed ontology of the argument than a minimal ontology of having concepts weakens the argument. It builds more than a minimum into what the Fool's understanding brings with it. What the Fool must "have in mind" is the concept the Fool is considering in denying the existence of a GCB. The assumption that the Fool "has such a being in mind" is guaranteed by the conceptual activity of the Fool only if this phrase is a rewording of the fact that the Fool is thinking of how something would have to be for the concept to apply to it. This is conceiving of having a certain combination of properties. Nothing in that thinking relies in any apparent way on the actual possession of those properties by a being that has a mental existence. Any such further requirement of the Fool's understanding would need some additional defense.

Granting the mental existence of a GCB would not vindicate the reasoning anyway. The reductio assumption of the reasoning would have to be that a GCB has mere mental existence, whatever that might be. The reductio assumption would have to include that the being does not have the sort of existence that the argument aims to prove, what we might call "genuine" or "full-blooded" existence. By P2, as it would then be understood, genuine existence is greater for a GCB than its absence, including its absence owing to the being having merely mental existence. The trouble for the argument on these assumptions is that no absurdity gives any appearance of following from this reductio assumption. We assume that an entity is a merely mentally existing GCB. On this assumption it lacks full-blooded existence. So a premise tells us that it is not as great as a GCB is conceived to be, when existence is included. That is not at all manifestly impossible. The level of greatness of a mentally existing GCB might be contingent, precisely because that level depends on whether or not it genuinely exists. If so, then clearly a merely mentally existing GCB would not have as much greatness as we conceive of a GCB as having when existing.

8   CONCLUSION

The content of a concept cannot show us that an absolutely greatest being exists. Nothing can be shown to exist by what is required for some concept to apply.

REFERENCES

Blumenfeld, D. (1978). 'On the Compossibility of the Divine Attributes', *Philosophical Studies* 34, 1: 91–103.

Conee, E. (1991). 'The Possibility of Power Beyond Possibility', in Tomberlin, J. (ed.). *Philosophical Perspectives* 5. Malden, MA: Blackwell, 447–73.

———. (1994). 'The Nature and the Impossibility of Moral Perfection', *Philosophy and Phenomenological Research* 54, December: 815–25.

Mann, W. (1972). 'The Ontological Presuppositions of the Ontological Argument', *Review of Metaphysics* 26: 260–77.

Millican, P. (2004). 'The One Fatal Flaw in Anselm's Argument', *Mind* 113, 451: 437–76.

Nagasawa, Y. (2007). 'Millican on the Ontological Argument', *Mind* 116, 464: 1027–39.

8　A Proof of God's Reality

John Leslie

Does the existence of our universe prove that God is real? Yes; for it is extravagant to suppose that the universe exists reasonlessly, and the sole satisfactory explanation for it involves something worth calling "God".

1　SOME ATHEISTIC SOLUTIONS

First, let us look at explanations that do without God.

> I. It is sometimes said that an absence of one thing is always the presence of something else instead. An absence of all things is unthinkable.

I answer that it is easy to think of things vanishing one by one until there are just two things, then a single thing, then nothing.

"Universe" is a term with no fixed meaning. It may mean Everything in Existence, even including any divine person. Often, however, it means a gigantic region, perhaps with its own Space and even its own Time. Talk of "many actually existing universes" then becomes possible. Now, physicists have suggested that universes exist as quantum fluctuations ex nihilo, fluctuations against the background of absolutely nothing. They then sometimes declare that sooner or later each universe will suddenly vanish. Imagine their amazement if you told them that *at least one universe* would have to remain in existence!

> II. Some protest that asking "Why?" about the universe is illegitimate. One variant of this objection is that all possible scientific explanations appeal to physical laws, and these cannot operate until there is a universe. Another is that any explanation for the existence of something must point to some earlier thing that created it or that contained all the "stuff" that has now been rearranged so as to form it.

The best reply is that Plato has an explanation making no mention of physical laws or previous things or "stuff". I shall discuss it in due course.

III. Some say an explanation for the universe at any one moment is that it existed at the previous moment. Seeking any further explanation imitates the man who, noticing that humans have mothers, seeks a mother of the entire human race. That is Bertrand Russell's little jest.

Russell could have found it hard to explain a Big Bang that was a beginning of all things, but nowadays most cosmologists do not picture the Big Bang like that. In particular, Eternal Inflation is popular. According to this scenario, the cosmos stretches far beyond what our telescopes can see. Most of it is a scene of ceaselessly expanding violence, made possible by the fact that gravitational binding-energy is *negative energy* and so can balance the mass-energy of more and more light rays, material particles, and so forth. The expansion has been in progress eternally; each stage is the product of an infinite chain of earlier stages. Inside its violence there are countless Big Bangs, each the birth of a region very hot in its early moments but gradually cooling.

Note that it is standard physics to treat binding-energies as *negative*. When a star's protons fuse to form deuterons the result is a mass *increase*; but, being negative, the binding-energy of the protons compensates for this, even liberating some energy to heat up the star.

Is there not the difficulty, though, that talk of an infinite chain of causes cannot answer why the chain exists? Leibniz imagined an infinite series of geometry books. Could they be explained by saying that each book had been copied from an earlier one? Surely not, he pointed out, for this would leave unanswered why the books were about geometry.

Much the same difficulty arises if Time is viewed as finite but circular. Could each event be explained by another preceding it in the circle? Well, would not the following story be utterly absurd? A time machine existed in the year 2010; it had traveled forwards in time from the year 2000. And why did it exist in the year 2000? Answer: It had traveled backwards from the year 2010. A self-explaining loop!

IV. Peter van Inwagen, and earlier Robert Nozick, suggested that the existence of Something, not Nothing, might be infinitely probable on the following grounds. There is only one way of there being Nothing but infinitely many conceivable ways of there being Something.

Nozick commented that this assumes the Egalitarian principle that all conceivable situations are equally probable. To me such Egalitarianism looks wrong for two reasons. The first is that, with Leibniz, I think Nothing "simpler and easier"; if there were nothing in existence, then there would be nothing to be explained. For me that is a fundamental conviction. It cannot be proved right, but this does not make it unjustified. As Hume and Kant appreciated, we must start from various fundamental convictions if we are ever to reach conclusions about the world. While fundamental convictions never can be proved right, there is nothing wrong in having them. Consider the philosophical baby that keeps crawling into the fire. The baby lacks the fundamental conviction that the past will be a guide to the future. Yes, *in the past* it would have done better by assuming that the past would be a guide to the future; it then wouldn't have got burned repeatedly. But, says the baby, this supplies no logical basis for deducing that *in the future* the past will be a guide to the future. Well, Hume saw that logic like the baby's is correct, yet he would have called it a foolish baby.

My second reason for rejecting the Egalitarian approach is this. Suppose that the world had been selected randomly from among all logically possible worlds, each of which (including a totally empty world) had been blessed with an equal chance of being picked. It would then almost certainly be a scene of utter chaos, for utterly chaotic worlds form an overwhelmingly large majority of all logically possible worlds. This is the same point as destroys the Modal Realism of David Lewis.

> V. Do all logically possible worlds exist? David Lewis thought so. His Modal Realism maintains (as he himself cheerfully admitted) that all the Greek gods are real just so long as there is nothing self-contradictory in it. Provided they are not like round squares or married bachelors, Zeus and Aphrodite exist somewhere but of course not locally. They cannot be found in our world.

Lewis thought this doctrine gave a useful background to *counterfactuals*; asking what would have happened had a rock hit a window is asking how things are in other worlds very like ours, worlds in which such a rock did hit such a window. Influenced instead by the reasons that encourage physicists to speak of multiple universes, Max Tegmark has suggested that the doctrine would make physics super-elegant. In this he is like the philosopher Peter Unger, who views it as a superbly simple doctrine. To "What exists?" it gives a superbly brief answer: "Everything that is logically possible!"

Unfortunately, the doctrine ruins inductive predictions. Can the past be a guide to the future? Not if all logically possible worlds exist! There are countless logically possible ways in which you could die in the next five seconds through the future ceasing to resemble the past. You might vanish, burst, or turn into blackberry jam, pickled cabbage, a mountain, a pencil, a lump of uranium ... but mercifully five seconds have passed and no such disaster has destroyed you. If all logically possible worlds exist then you have just now benefited from fantastically much luck. It is better to believe that they do not.

Lewis thought he had an adequate reply. The worlds in which Induction fails cannot form a majority, he said. Those in which it fails and those in which it does not fail are equal in number since there are infinitely many in each category. However, this reply would not impress any sensible physicist. Some physicists think our universe infinitely large. It then presumably contains infinitely many puddles that boil all of a sudden through drawing heat from their cold surroundings. Thermodynamics says this would happen occasionally, and therefore on infinitely many occasions. But do not tell the physicists to expect to see it happening! In the case of each particular puddle it would be hugely improbable, no matter how large the universe.

> VI. Some argue that, for instance, two added to two must always make four *no matter what*—completely unconditionally. They then conclude that there must always exist at least two sets of two objects, perhaps apples or atoms, to supply "an ontological foundation" for this, or that there must always be at least one mind that asks itself about two and two.

I reply that, yes, two and two must make four, no matter what. What follows from this, however, is that two and two would make four even if the realm of existing things were empty. The reality that two and two make four is the reality that *if there ever were to exist* two sets of two whatnots, there would then exist four such whatnots. Supplying "an ontological foundation" in the form of actually existing things that could be counted, or of an actually existing mind thinking about two and two, is the sort of error Gilbert Ryle called "a category mistake": like saying that mathematical equations, as well as sometimes applying to racehorses, do actually watch them racing.

> VII. Edward Tryon noticed that our universe could have a total energy that was zero or almost zero: its gravitational binding-energy could cancel or almost cancel the mass-energy of everything in it. [Remember, binding-energies are *negative*.] This led him to picture the universe as a quantum fluctuation "of some larger Space", a gigantic, very long-lasting variant on the quantum fluctuations in which hugely many particles spring into existence every microsecond in your immediate vicinity, then vanishing quickly. "Borrowing" of the mass-energy needed for something to exist is allowed by Heisenberg's Uncertainty Principle just so long as "repayment" (vanishing) takes place fast enough. If a universe-sized fluctuation involved little or no borrowing, billions of years could pass without the need for repayment.

Could this truly be why our universe exists? There is the problem of where Tryon's "larger Space" came from, but other theorists have managed to do without one. In a model developed by James Hartle and Stephen Hawking our universe sprang into existence without springing from any Space external to it, and there was even, in the quantum fuzziness of its earliest moments, no definite time and place where it was born. And Alex Vilenkin, noting that his own very different model showed quantum-fluctuational universes as able to be born from smaller and smaller Spaces, proposed that universes can quantum-fluctuate from Spaces *of size zero* or in his words "literally nothing". Yet even if the Hartle-Hawking and Vilenkin models made sense quantum-physically there would still be the question, recognized by Hawking's talk of the need for something "to breathe fire into the equations", of why quantum physics worked.

We could write down an equation saying that the number of unicorns grows continually. Even if it starts at zero, the number increases by twenty-three unicorns per second. If it applied to reality, the equation would guarantee the existence of a world: one containing plenty of unicorns at least. But why would it apply to reality?

2   SOME THEISTIC SOLUTIONS

Next let us look at some theistic explanations that strike me as insufficient. They try to throw light on the existence of a deity able to create a universe.

A. Some suggest that such a deity must exist through mere logic. God is defined as perfect in power and in everything else. Now, a thing cannot possess all perfections unless it *exists*; or, alternatively, it cannot possess all perfections unless it has *necessary existence*. These are two Ontological Proofs of God.

Kant thinks the first proof fails because existence is not an attribute, something that could characterize ("be a predicate of") something. His reasoning is odd, for surely existence is an attribute of a sort. It characterizes some possibilities (the ones that are "actualized", the ones inhabiting not only the realm of the possible but also the realm of existing things like you and me), and it fails to characterize others. Agreed, existence is not an attribute entering into the constitution of anything, like the size of a coin in Kant's pocket, but any defects of that first proof must be sought elsewhere.

Still, it is easy enough find one. Even if existence were one of God's attributes, this would mean only that God would not be like, for example, the fact that two and two make four, which is a reality without being an existing thing. The "proof" would establish only that *if* God were real, then God would exist.

As for *necessary existence*, well, many philosophers think it not even a possible attribute. And at any rate we could not compel a Being to have it *just by definition*. Consider an Incomparably Dreadful Devil. Could we *define him into* possessing necessary existence? Could we support the project by saying that his dreadfulness would be perfected by possessing it, which would guarantee nobody could kill him? Surely not. For one thing, a devil could be exactly equally dreadful if nonkillable just as a matter of brute fact. And similarly with a Perfect Divine Person. He could be an exactly equally excellent reality even if he failed to exist necessarily. If he existed just as a matter of fortunate chance, but nothing could ever destroy him, then that would be quite enough.

The underlying difficulty, I suggest, is that deducing God's necessity from God's definition as a Perfect Being treats the necessity as a commonplace logical necessity. Yet commonplace logical necessities, affairs "logically necessary" in a sense widely accepted today, are matters simply of avoiding contradictions. Now, a round square would be self-contradictory, but the mere absence of something, God for instance, would provide nothing that could self-contradict.

B. Must God exist because God is Pure Being? Even if Pure Being were not nonsense—even if a deity possessing existence and no other characteristic were a logical possibility—how much would this prove? Only that *if* God were real, then certainly God would exist instead of being like the reality that two and two make four.

C. Richard Swinburne has suggested that God exists reasonlessly but with an existence intrinsically much more likely than the existence of a rock, for example. That is because God is supremely simple. No physicist could fully describe even a grain of sand. To describe God is far easier because of God's infinitude. What, for example, does God know? Answer: God knows all that is knowable. What can God do? The answer is equally simple.

This strikes me as quite an improvement on the universe-explanations I have so far discussed. Given the existence of an infinitely powerful God, the existence of everything else could be explained; Prefer Simplicity is a principle no scientist can afford to reject; and Swinburne's grounds for calling God simple are interestingly strong. Yet Swinburne's God, looked at from another angle, is an immensely complex being. Knowing all that is knowable would involve knowing infinitely many mathematical truths, for a start. In a good enough sense, would not this be far more complicated than knowing as much as you and I know? But, more crucially, I am very unhappy with the idea that anything could exist for no reason whatever. An absence of all existents would be so much simpler.

Still, if forced to choose between a reasonlessly existing universe and Swinburne's reasonlessly existing divine being, then I would probably choose the divine being.

3   A PLATONIC APPROACH

Now for an explanation I think adequate, a Platonic explanation. If, as I have tried to illustrate, other explanations for the world are unsatisfactory, and if Nothingness would be "simpler and easier" in a way that makes an explanation necessary, and if, finally, the Platonic explanation involves a reality deserving the name "God", then this little essay of mine may merit the name I have given to it.

Suppose existing things suddenly disappeared, every one of them. In the resulting emptiness, what would there be that might act creatively?

Infinitely many affairs would still be *real*. It would be real that a universe had once been there. It would be real that if two sets of two butterflies were ever to come into being, there would then exist four butterflies. It could be really and immensely fortunate that the emptiness had not quickly been replaced by a world crammed with people in torment. And it would genuinely be a pity, unfortunate as a matter of reality, that there existed no good universe. Replacement of the emptiness by a good universe would be what I call *ethically required*; for something can be required ethically, say I, even when it is not *a morally required action*.

To me, you see, the word "ethical" is like the word "Ethics". It covers goodness of all types instead of good actions only. Instead of "ethically required", say "axiologically required" if you prefer; it is what Nicholas Rescher says in this context, and what is the use of warring over language? The things I want to fight for are instead these: (1) that the existence of some situations can be fortunate *as a matter of reality* rather than, for instance, of people prescribing various actions without actually describing any reality (a curious "prescriptivism" once ruled the world of Oxford philosophy); (2) that the absence of good things would be unfortunate *even when nobody existed* to weep over it, let alone to have a duty to do something about it; and (3) that fortunateness, goodness, is not an ordinary property like redness or being spherical; it is instead a matter of being required, marked out for existence in a way I call "ethical". Call it "axiological" if you like, but do please recognize that talk of *required existence* throws light on what Ethics deals with.

To understand what Ethics deals with, you have to grasp that the evolution of intelligent life on Earth could have been something good even if there had existed no deity, demigod, or extraterrestrial with a duty to bring about its evolution—just as the suffering of a dinosaur could be bad even in the absence of folk morally obliged to prevent it. You must accept, too, that a thing's goodness is, and not just through human whim or a quirk of language, the fact that its existence is called for, needful, required. *A reason for that whatnot to exist* is what the goodness of any whatnot *is*. Yet we have to use common sense in interpreting talk of reasons or requirements here. It is not being said that ethical/axiological reasons or requirements must automatically be endowed with causal or creative success just because they truly are reasons or requirements for the existence of various whatnots: various situations, actions, minds, mental states, or whatever. So far as we can tell, they might have ethical authority yet never any actual power.

Still, it might instead be that some ethical requirement or set of compatible requirements does have creative success, bearing direct responsibility for why there is a world. When Plato thinks it, he has not wandered into idiocy.

In Book Six of his *Republic*, Plato suggests that The Good, a reality "beyond existence", is "what gives existence to things". In other words, the realm of existing things is something whose presence *is required ethically and with creative effect*. The ethical requirement for its presence is "beyond existence" because it does not depend for its reality on anything already existing, let alone on any person with a duty to recognize the requirement and then strive to give effect to it. This makes it a reality of at least the right sort—"in the right ballpark", as we North Americans say—for bearing responsibility for why there is Something and not Nothing: Something, that is to say, which exists as the world does, instead of having the kind of abstract reality possessed by inhabitants of Plato's realm of Forms.

Plato's suggestion is tentative, and certainly he attempts no logical proof of its correctness. However, the ethical requirement that there exist a good situation might create that situation—might manage to bring about its existence if it did not yet exist, or might be responsible for its eternal existence—without this being a logically provable affair. Plato's approach could therefore deserve the influence it has had over the years. Numerous thinkers have accepted Hermann Lotze's principle that "the true beginning of Metaphysics lies in Ethics" since we should "seek in *what should be* the ground of that which is". "The Good is that on which all else depends" (Plotinus); "Goodness is that whereby all things are" (Dionysius); "Goodness as a cause is prior to being", and "Even non-existent things seek a good, namely, to exist" (Aquinas); "The predisposing cause of God is his perfection itself, through which he is the cause of himself" (Spinoza); "The world is so determined that its opposite implies imperfection or moral absurdity" (Leibniz); Absolute Reality, a cosmic "Idea that thinks itself", is "not so impotent as to have merely a right to exist without actually existing" (Hegel); "Existence is the upholding of value-intensity" (A.N. Whitehead); God "is not a being" but is instead both an ethical factor, "something that has a claim upon us", and "the power of being", "the creative ground of existence" (Paul Tillich); "Tillich stands in the classical Platonist tradition of Christian ontology" (J.A.T. Robinson, Bishop of Woolwich).

Some of those following in Plato's footsteps have pictured God as a divine mind whose eternal ethical requiredness is responsible for its existence, a mind that then creates all other things. This notion has recently attracted the Idealist philosopher A.C. Ewing, the physicist-turned-philosopher John Polkinghorne, and the philosopher-turned-theologian Keith Ward. Others, however, have stuck closer to Plato, for they see Value as directly creating all things. "God", if that word is to be used, may then mean the creative effectiveness of ethical requirements whenever they are not overruled by other ethical requirements. Plotinus, Dionysius, many in the Greek Orthodox church, the Catholic theologian Hans Küng joining hands with Tillich among the Protestants—all fall into this school. But beware here of seeing some deep distinction between the theories (a) that God is the creative effectiveness of world-creating ethical requirements, (b) that God is the ethical requirements that are world-creating, (c) that God is the world's creative ethical requiredness, and (d) that God is the world, considered as meriting the name "God" because it possesses creative ethical requiredness. Spinoza, for instance, will be found to have chosen (d)—when, that is to say, you read him carefully, unlike those who forget his *Short Treatise* and are deaf to how its Platonic creation story reappears in his *Ethics*. Yet he could instead have chosen (a), (b), or (c) because any differences here would be simply in how he would have chosen to use *the word* "God". In each case the situation described with the help of that word would obviously have been exactly the same.

How successfully, though, can any of this account for the evidence of our senses, the world that we see?

4   INFINITE MINDS

For a start: We see a world that has causal orderliness. This could well be considered a contribution to its goodness——though it often has nasty consequences, so that it might be better to have a dreamlike world without the causal laws that scientists find beautiful, a world without harsh struggles, needs for courage, frustrations, headaches, plagues, or earthquakes.

Next, the world seems "fine-tuned" for the evolution of intelligent life—another possibly great good. No doubt Schopenhauer was not clearly unreasonable when he wrote that Earth would better have remained like the moon, a lifeless mass, because of all those frustrations, plagues, and suchlike. Perhaps it would be good if hydrogen bombs annihilated all living things. But it is plausible that the fine-tuning makes a worthwhile world possible, and hence is something Plato's theory could explain. And a popular alternative way of explaining it seems none too satisfactory. Often cosmologists theorize that there exist multiple universes with very varied characters. In our universe the strengths of physical forces, the masses of elementary particles, the expansion rate at early times, the degree of turbulence, and various other affairs all appear to have needed tuning, often with extreme accuracy, for intelligent life to be possible; but, say the cosmologists, such things as force strengths and particle masses *vary from universe to universe*. A plausible reason for this would be that physical symmetries were broken differently in the different universes by scalar fields (the Higgs field has been a popular choice) whose strengths differed randomly from universe to universe. Given sufficiently many universes it would then be no surprise that a few chanced to have life-permitting characteristics, and no surprise, either, that we living beings found ourselves in one of those few. Yet, although eager to believe in multiple universes with very varied characters, I argue (see chapter 3 of my *Universes*, for instance, or chapter 6 of my *Infinite Minds*) that they could not by themselves suffice to explain the observed fine-tuning. For a force strength or a particle mass often needs tuning to within the same narrow limits *for several different reasons simultaneously.*

Consider electromagnetism. Its strength needs accurate tuning for quarks not to be converted into leptons, making atoms impossible; for protons not to decay quickly, meaning there would soon be no more atoms; for proton-proton repulsion to be weak enough to allow for chemistry; for there to be stars like the sun, burning peacefully for billions of years; and so on down quite a long list. Well, why didn't electromagnetism need to be tuned to one strength to achieve a first fortunate result, to a second very different strength to achieve a second, to a third strength to achieve a third, and so forth? Yes, fundamental laws might lead to different force strengths and particle masses in different universes, perhaps thanks to differing scalar fields, but why is there *even a single mixture* of force strengths, particle masses, etcetera that is life-encouraging? Why aren't all possible mixtures equally unsatisfactory? The problem could not be solved just by saying, "Fundamental laws themselves differ from one universe to the next, and ours is a universe whose laws do not lead to the problem". For science, based as it is on respect for Induction, could never by itself justify accepting that laws that are genuinely fundamental (rather than matters such as force strengths, settled by factors such as scalar fields) *vary* from one universe to another. Our fine-tuned universe can therefore point toward something worth calling "God": something that made fundamental laws vary or else forced them to be laws of just the right sort for producing life. And therefore, I would say, it can help show the correctness of a Platonic creation story.

There is, though, a gigantic difficulty with how stories of this general kind are typically developed. The situation typically pictured is vastly inferior to what could be expected if such stories were right.

Axiarchism is my name for the doctrine that Value is creatively influential, either directly or else thanks to the benevolence of a Creator perhaps himself existing reasonlessly. Axiarchists often rather oddly suggest that there exists only a single universe, but this could easily be remedied. Leibniz, for instance, although insisting that by "world" he means "the whole succession and whole agglomeration of existing things", appears never to have considered that there might be infinitely many huge realms of the type cosmologists now call "separate universes", yet a reincarnated Leibniz could quickly incorporate this idea into his axiarchistic world picture, arriving at a "best possible world" far better than the one described in his *Theodicy*. The gigantic difficulty lies elsewhere. It is this. If Value were creatively influential, then what would be created? Only the very best, presumably. However, no possible existent would seem better than a mind worth calling "divine", a mind contemplating everything worth contemplating—this including, we might well think, every detail of possible universes in infinite number and endless variety. Well, then, *why would there exist anything except* a mind or minds of that supremely desirable sort? Why do axiarchists so very typically believe in hugely many other minds, each with an existence fully separate from that of its companions, whose experiences are so immensely inferior that Schopenhauer could judge them worse than worthless?

For anybody like me, not just an axiarchist of some kind but a defender of creative ethical requirements, the only plausible answer is that there in fact exists nothing outside divine thinking. Pantheism much as defended by Spinoza will have to be accepted; the order and succession of the world's things must be nothing but the order and succession of ideas in a mind worth calling "divine". Your thought patterns and mine, together with the patterns of all the things and events surrounding us, are carried by the mind in question.

This involves no conflict with science or with the evidence of our every conscious moment. Think of John Barrow. Professor of mathematical physics at Cambridge, Barrow has speculated that conceivably our world is a pattern inside an enormous artificial mind, a computer of cosmic complexity. How could this ever be refuted by any physical experiment, let alone by what every child knows about its own consciousness? Physics studies only the world's structure. It has no use for talk of "good, solid stuff that could not possibly be nothing but a computer's information-processing, or nothing but divine thinking". Physicists working at physics describe the complex patterns of our universe and the laws that control their development over time. They never discuss whether those patterns, including of course the patterns of our thinking brains, exist inside a mind that, contemplating them in all their details, thereby gives them all the existence that they ever have—a mind whose infinite complexity could make it worth calling "divine".

But when able to contemplate absolutely anything worth contemplating, why would a divine mind contemplate our world with its frustrations and plagues? Might it not be much better to contemplate beautiful mathematics, music finer than Mozart's, scenes of the sort we would call "hallucinatory splendors"? The answer is that such things, whether or not much better, *could also* form part of what that mind contemplated. All that pantheists need claim is that our universe would be among the things deserving a place inside such a mind. It might not even be particularly fine among possible universes. There might be infinitely many others that were better. But then the patterns of those other universes would be contemplated *also*, in all their details, with such universes therefore existing side by side with ours inside the mind in question.

How, though, could any pantheist explain a world of perpetual change? Spinoza's *Short Treatise* tells us that the all-inclusive divine mind must be changeless "because never able to change into anything better"; now, how could this be compatible with a world of falling apples and speeding bullets? Einstein supplies an answer. He writes that our world is without "sections which represent 'now' objectively", making it "natural to think of physical reality as a four-dimensional existence instead of, as hitherto, the evolution of a three-dimensional existence". In Einstein's eyes, change is always only a relative matter. The world certainly changes in a sense, yet so does the pattern of a carpet's interwoven threads. It changes at successive points along the carpet.

Einstein found this comforting. As he explained to the mourning kinsfolk of his dead friend Michele Besso, life never was lost in any absolute way. I think we could describe this view as follows. Although no longer among things existing in the present, Besso's life remained in existence "back there along the fourth dimension". In an important sense, everything ever in existence is something that exists forever. "Forever in what sort of Time?" you ask. Well, why not reply, "In a Time in which absolute changes might be taking place, although in point of fact such absolute changes never occur"? In Einstein's world, as in Spinoza's, no situation is ever replaced by another in an absolute fashion, yet presumably such replacement would be logically possible nonetheless. Even if a four-dimensional continuum formed a whole that never in fact altered, it could be altering so far as Logic was concerned; it could even vanish entirely.

Might Einstein's world then give us something worth calling *immortality*? Einstein himself resisted using that word, but I see no strong reason to avoid it. The kind of immortality Einstein could be said to offer us is the immortality of lives that never become wiped out in an absolute manner. When we had died we would not exist *then*, yet we would exist "back there". Still, we might also have immortality in a more generally accepted sense. Suppose that the divine mind, thinking about a man, considered his earthly death, the point at which the working of natural laws destroyed his body. Why would not that mind think of this man's consciousness as continuing onward, perhaps coming to share progressively more of the wonders of divine knowledge? It would necessitate no miraculous breakdown of how those natural laws operated inside our universe. And if it would be a good for it to happen, then Creative Value would make it happen.

Would there be only a single infinite mind? The suggestion strikes me as weird if a Platonic creation story is accepted. We must not argue that a situation containing a single infinite mind would have infinite goodness and therefore could never be improved on. For suppose there existed two infinite minds, each filled with infinitely many worthwhile thoughts. Would it be quite all right to annihilate one of the minds "because Reality would continue to have the same infinite worth as before"? Surely not. That would be like saying, "It would be quite all right to kill your wife, for Reality would afterwards still contain God's wondrous infinitude and so would be in no way worse". Yet if the annihilation of one of those two infinite minds would be a misfortune, then its never having existed would have been a misfortune also, and, similarly, it would be a misfortune if there had not been three such minds, and if there had not been four, and if there had not been five, etcetera. In short, if the realm of existing things owes its reality to its creative ethical requiredness, then it must contain not *just one* infinite mind but infinitely many. Each contemplates absolutely everything worth contemplating. *Or*, if what philosophers call "Identity of Indiscernibles" is correct, then there exists just one mind that contemplates absolutely every-thing worth contemplating, plus infinitely many other minds each failing to contemplate some little something that is contemplated by that first mind: a different little something in each case so that Identity of Indiscernibles is not violated.

Identity of Indiscernibles is the principle that says that if angels have no extension (like the "point particles" imagined by some physicists) and are identical in all but their spatial positions, then no two angels can be brought to the very point of an infinitely sharp pin. The principle would allow the existence of two separate universes, each in a Space of its own, just so long as those universes differed with respect to a single atom. Logic, the principle says, would prevent any such last trivial difference from disap-pearing. Rather than the logical catastrophe of having it disappear, one or both universes would have to vanish, or perhaps they would have to fuse. Believe in such logic if you can!

5 NECESSITY

As I hope to have shown, talk of *creative ethical requiredness* can lead to a very attractive world picture. It is tempting to treat this as reason enough for rejecting all such talk. ("Wishful thinking carried to fantastic extremes!") However, anything markedly less attractive would be flatly incompatible with a Platonic creation story—and if such a story is wrong, then how else could we explain why there is Something and not Nothing?

We do, though, need to look carefully at the concept of creative ethical requiredness. May it not contain some absurdity?

1. A first objection is that nothing as abstract as an ethical need could possibly do anything. But cannot we reply that this simply assumes Plato's wrongness? Could we not protest, even, that abstract factors, whether or not they are doing things all by themselves, do constantly influence the world? Toss fifty coins. You might get Heads fifty times, but you would be fifty times more likely to get it only once. Just try explaining it without mentioning anything abstract!
2. A next objection is that ethical requirements are at least never seen to do anything all by themselves. All we ever see is people putting such requirements into effect by their actions or, alas, acting very differently.

Obviously, this objection has some force. Plato's creation story might be far more evidently correct if the hungry, instead of needing to be fed by the charitable, always found meals materializing out of thin air. Superb cathedrals that were self-constructing, or superb music without any com-poser, might be dramatic evidence to support the story. Still, exactly how would the absence of such evidence destroy it? Though we may lack firm knowledge that ethical requirements create things, do we not see things that could well have been created by them? (i) Is there not a universe instead of a blank? (ii) Do we not witness elegant causal orderliness? (iii) Are not causal laws "fine-tuned" with startling accuracy in ways making life's evolution possible? (iv) Is not our world in many respects a wonderful place, making many of us feel fortunate to be parts of it? No doubt it cannot be *known* that these four matters are results of ethical requirements acting by themselves. Yet which philosophers cry out most vigorously that ethical requirements "never are seen acting"? In my experience, by far the loudest cries come from folk who treat these very same matters as *visible evidence* of a deity's benevolent actions. Well, why cannot we instead view them as what ethical requirements have produced without help from anybody's actions? And when those same folk protest that they never see meals appearing out of thin air or self-constructing cathedrals, do they not deserve a *tu quoque*, a cry of "You're in the same boat"? The absence of self-constructing cathedrals is no better at dismissing Plato's approach than it is at refuting Swinburne's God, a deity whose benevolence has not produced self-constructing cathedrals or an absence of evil men and destructive earthquakes.

Evil men and earthquakes? The sad fact is that the need for some goods could often overrule the need for others, it being impossible to have all goods simultaneously. It could, for example, be good that not everything was done for us, as in a dream world, a world without the causal laws that lead to earthquakes, and that we could sometimes decide for ourselves what to do instead of being mere puppets. It could then sometimes be the case that various ethical requirements would be satisfied only if we decided to give our support to them, and that sometimes we would decide not to give it——the need for the requirements to be satisfied then being overruled by the need for us not to be puppets. Reasoning of this sort is commonplace in philosophy of religion. Why must followers of Plato be banned from using it? Why cannot Genghis Khan and the Lisbon Earthquake exist in a world created by ethical requirements, just as much as in one produced by Omnipotent Benevolence?

It need not be held that absolutely every causally ordered universe would contain destructive earthquakes. *Some* universes among the infinitely many that existed inside an infinite mind might have causal orderliness without any disasters whatever. But could it not be good for that mind to contain, *as well*, universes like the one we inhabit? (Suppose that our universe did exist inside such a mind. Ought we then to do our best to annihilate it "so as to improve the goodness of the whole"?)

3. "Yet how could an ethical requirement *as such* ever create anything? It's no part of the concept of such requirements that they ever do that kind of work!" —We can reply that there is certainly a sense in which no ethical requirement "as such" could create anything, but equally there is a sense in which, while cows "as such" are female,

no cow as such is ever brown. This does not mean brown cows cannot be real.

4. "But", you want to know, "what could make any ethical requirement creatively powerful?" —The answer is: *Nothing whatever*. The whole point of Plato's theory is that nothing would do any *making* here. No magic wands would be at work, no divine commands, and no cogwheels either. Instead, one or more ethical requirements would have created our world in which cogwheels do things. The Platonic theory is that some ethical requirement or set of compatible ethical requirements *has itself* acted creatively. You might almost as well want to know what "made" a state of mind filled with boredom and misery any worse intrinsically than one filled with interest and happiness. To that the answer would have to be that not even Omnipotence could "give" intrinsic worth to anything. Things just do sometimes have intrinsic worth; or maybe they just do not, for I cannot see how we could prove firmly that anything is ever better than anything else—that good and bad are more than fictions. But, even if unprovably, it could still be real that some things are indeed better than others, and also that this is so necessarily.

That last point is crucial. It could not be, for example, that one state of mind happened to be good intrinsically—good when considered in itself and without looking at its "instrumental" goodness or badness, the goodness or badness of its consequences—while another exactly similar state of mind was intrinsically bad. The language of good and bad can guarantee that much, whether or not good and bad are fictions. (Whether or not dragons are fictions, the language of talk about dragons guarantees that any dragon breathes flames.) Intrinsic worth could never be a mere matter of chance. It would be a necessary matter. And similarly with Plato's suggestion that some ethical requirement or requirements acted creatively. Either that is right, or it is wrong. Logic cannot prove that it is right or that it is wrong. But if it is wrong, then this is no matter of chance; it is a necessary matter. And if it is right, then this is no matter of chance either; it, too, is something necessary. The creative power of some ethical requirement or requirements could not be an affair of pure happenstance. *Not being logically necessary* is fully compatible with *being firmly necessary*: necessary absolutely but in an other-than-logical way.

Such an idea should not be found too difficult. Think of how phenomenal red—the color red as experienced, for example, in the afterimage of a bright light—is nearer to phenomenal orange than to phenomenal yellow. That is not a matter of chance, but neither is it like the fact that every bachelor's son has an unmarried father. It is no mere result of defining the word "orange" with the words "reddish-yellow", for even cavemen without language would have seen that strawberries looked more color-similar to oranges than to lemons. It is a matter of firm necessity nonetheless, necessity that forces us to accept "reddish-yellow" as another way of saying "orange".

6   GOD'S REALITY PROVED?

Could these arguments have proved God's reality, in some suitably weak sense of "proved"? My position is heavily Spinozistic, and Spinoza has often been called an atheist. His God differs greatly, at any rate, from what is preached from many a pulpit, so call him an atheist if you wish, and then call me an atheist as well. Still, his ideas about why the universe exists strike me as rather closely allied to fairly standard theological Platonism. And his ideas about our place in the universe call to mind prayers to a deity "in Whom we live and move and have our being". Though not myself religious, I see sense in those words.

Am I going too far, though, when I claim that an ocean of infinitely many infinite minds, something than which nothing better could be conceived, could justifiably be called "God"?[1]

---

1. For more ideas like these, please see my *Value and Existence* (Blackwell: Oxford 1979); *Universes* (Routledge: London 1989); chapter four of *The End of the World: The Science and Ethics of Human Extinction* (Routledge: London 1996); *Infinite Minds* (Oxford University Press: Oxford 2001); *Immortality Defended* (Blackwell: Oxford 2007); and 'How Many Divine Minds?', in *Consciousness, Reality and Value*, editors P. Basile and L.B. McHenry (Ontos Verlag: Frankfurt 2007), 123–34; also my edited *Modern Cosmology and Philosophy* (Prometheus: Amherst, Mass. 1998). Important recent works developing Platonic creation stories are A.C. Ewing, *Value and Reality* (Allen and Unwin: London 1973) (in chapter 7, Ewing uses such a story to explain why a divine person exists); Mark Wynn, *God and Goodness* (Routledge: London 1999); a book by Hugh Rice with exactly the same title, *God and Goodness* (Oxford University Press: Oxford 2000); and books by Nicholas Rescher including *Nature and Understanding* (Oxford University Press: Oxford 2000) and *Axiogenesis: An Essay in Metaphysical Optimism* (Lexington Books: Lanham, Md. 2010).

9 Methodological Separatism, Modal Pluralism, and Metaphysical Nihilism

David Efird and Tom Stoneham

In this chapter we aim to clarify the debate over the particular question of whether there might have been nothing, and the more general question of the nature of modality, by introducing the concept of a Modal Theory and investigating its form. We begin by arguing that the question of whether there might have been nothing can be pursued independently of the question of the nature of possible worlds; that is, we can investigate what possibilities there are without having to investigate what possibilities are. A theory that governs what possibilities there are we call a 'Modal Theory'. We then draw attention to the fact that modal theorists, to date, have typically assumed that modal theories are single-criterion, that is, that they have the form: p iff $\Diamond q$ for nondisjunctive p.[1] In response, we challenge the reasons we take for this assumption and then present an argument for Modal Theory having multiple criteria, a view we dub 'modal pluralism'. We then investigate the forms of the axioms of such a multiple-criterion Modal Theory, and we conclude by drawing lessons for the debate over whether there might have been nothing.

1 METHODOLOGICAL SEPARATISM

In earlier work (2005a, 2005b, 2006, and 2008), we have insisted on the distinctness of two philosophical questions one might ask about modality and, more importantly, on the methodological separability of the projects of answering each question.[2] In this section we further articulate this methodological thesis and defend it against a recent criticism by John Divers (forthcoming).

---

1. Here and throughout we use p and q as schematic letters for well-formed formulae or grammatical sentences without any presumption that they are logically simple, excepting, of course, in the definition of a single-criterion theory as one for which p is not a disjunction.
2. We are not alone in this view, for methodological separatism is exploited in Cameron 2012 and encouraged in Gregory 2011.

The two questions relate, respectively, to the *extent* of possibility, what possibilities *there are*—that is, what is possible—and the *nature* of (unactualized) possibility, what (unactualized) possibilities *are*—that is, what possibility is. Clearly the questions are logically distinct, so the substantive issue is whether the philosophical project of answering each is distinct or whether they can only be addressed together. Of course, one does not have a fully adequate philosophy of modality unless one has answered both questions, so, in a sense, they are parts of a single project. Even so, however, it leaves open the issue of whether we should answer one question, at least in part, by answering the other; specifically, whether our account of the nature of possibility should partially determine the answer to the question of what is possible, or whether we should address them separately, though under the overarching constraint that our answers be mutually consistent.

It seems that there are four possible views about the relation between these two questions. A 'nature-first' theorist would hold that we must answer the question of what unactualized possibilities are first and that the answer to that question should constrain our answer to the question of extent. Perhaps Quine exemplifies this attitude, for he seems to think ontological scruples about possible fat men in the doorway should lead us to restrict what possibilities we allow (1953: 4). In contrast, an 'extent-first' theorist would hold that we begin by working out what is possible and then populate the world with possibilia to match. Quine's 'Wyman', who is a close relative of Meinong, has this view. Third, we might seek a 'reflective equilibrium' between our answers to the two questions, sometimes rejecting a claim about what is possible on the grounds of nature and sometimes doing the reverse. We suspect that this approach is in fact the one taken by most metaphysicians. We want to defend the fourth option, dubbed 'separatism'. While this may have very similar results to the third option, there are great benefits in dialectical clarity. According to the separatist, there is one project of determining the best answer to the question of extent and another project of determining the best answer to the question of nature—and a third project of coming up with a consistent set of overall philosophical views. The first two projects are part of the public academic activity of philosophy. The third is a more personal matter: what is an appealing trade-off between ontology and ideology for one philosopher may be unacceptable to another. Some have a taste for desert landscapes, others for biodiversity. By confusing matters of the objective evaluation of theories with more subjective questions of what overall package of views someone can be brought to accept, metaphysics does itself a disservice conducted in the sphere of public reason. The separatist merely points out that by maintaining consistency with some other views, a philosopher may be accepting a much worse answer to the question of extent or nature or . . . There is no such thing as a free lunch, but someone needs to calculate the bill.

In our earlier work, we have described answers to the two questions about modality as 'theories' and the data which they draw on as 'intuitions'. For these purposes, we can regard any assertion or belief which organizes some data, usually by categorizing it or deriving it from some variables, as theoretical with respect to that data (which may, in turn, be theoretical with respect to some other data). In this sense, any philosophical account of X is a theory of X. Thus, traditional philosophical analyses, such as the tripartite account of knowledge, are theories (in this case, asserting that knowledge is a function of three variables—and the majority of responses to the Gettier counterexamples can be seen as attempting to find a fourth, 'hidden' variable), as are ontological reductions, such as the bundle theory of objects.

While any theory is theoretical only relative to some data, and thus some data are data only relative to some theory, we may reasonably think that there must be some data which are not theoretical relative to anything, on pain of regress.[3] These data are the ultimate subject matter for all theorizing and must include empirical data, such as observation and experience. But philosophical theorizing also draws on other data, and that is what we have indicated with the term 'intuitions'. The nature of these data is highly controversial (see Williamson 2007 for a lengthy discussion), with some taking them to be concepts or conceptual schemes, others linguistic knowledge, others a priori knowledge. We intend to remain neutral on these issues, using 'intuitions' to refer to that body of beliefs about a subject matter on which we can reach general, though rarely universal, agreement prior to philosophical theorizing. Determining exactly what falls into the class of intuitions is not easy, and we do not rule out the relevance of experimental philosophy (Alexander 2012), nor do we think that pre-philosophical beliefs about X need to be unreflective beliefs about X. Thus we allow that on reflection there may be agreement on a belief which is different from that held by the majority prior to reflection (which is just to say that by 'agreement' we mean the product of a process of discussion rather than the summing of a set of independent opinions).[4] And because the process of agreement is reflective, it can also involve ensuring consistency with our knowledge in general, and especially our scientific knowledge.

With these definitions in hand, we can state the thesis of methodological separatism a little more clearly. The data for the theory of the extent of possibility, of what is possible, are intuitions about what is possible, intuitions about propositions of the form '$\lozenge p$' (where an intuition about a proposition

---

3. This is not to say that the data may not be theory-laden, merely that they are themselves not theoretical in the sense defined above.
4. A better term than 'intuition', and one which links the thought to its history, might be 'common notions'.

can be that it is true or that it is false).[5] Since the theory aims to establish the extent of what is possible, it will consist of a series of propositions of the form 'if p then $\Diamond q$' (and perhaps also 'if p then $\sim\Diamond q$', though see below for discussion of this point). There is no reason to restrict p to nonmodal propositions, and, in fact, if we want some of the axioms of modal logics such as S4 to be part of this theory, then we will have to allow modal antecedents.

Strictly speaking, the data for the theory of the nature of (unactualized) possibility are just intuitions about what kind of thing (unactualized) possibilities are.[6] These are sparse, though the famous 'incredulous stare' which Lewis's Genuine Modal realism so often met (Lewis 1986: 133) suggests there are some implicit beliefs about these matters, and Peter van Inwagen has articulated a specific intuition thus: 'How *could* one suppose that the (unactualized) possibility that the universe is thus-and-so is a thing that has a mass of 3.4×10^{57} grams and is rapidly expanding?' (1986/2001: 226). However, we can also include in the data for this theory intuitions about what sorts of things there are or are not which have consequences about what unactualized possibilities are, even if those consequences need careful drawing out (see e.g. the discussion of the null individual in our 2005a). While that exhausts the data proper to the theory, it is a general feature of a theory of the nature of Xs that it may have consequences for which Xs exist, if any. Furthermore, that may be one of the primary interests in constructing such a theory. This might lead one to think that intuitions about which Xs exist, in this case the intuitions which are the data for the theory of the extent of possibility, are data for the theory of the nature of Xs. However, the methodological separatist denies this, insisting instead that the only data for the theory of the nature of possibility are intuitions about the nature of unactualized possibilities and that intuitions about what is possible do not directly constrain that theory. They do, however, indirectly constrain the theory via the requirement that all our theories be mutually consistent and, consequently, that the theory of the nature of possibility be consistent with the theory of the extent of possibility. If the former has a consequence which is inconsistent with the latter, one or the other will have to be modified.

We have pursued the separatist methodology through a series of papers on metaphysical nihilism, which is the claim that there might have been nothing concrete. To begin, we (2005b) argued for this claim on the basis of a theoretical claim in the theory of the extent of possibility, namely, that all contingent concreta possess the modal property of subtractability,[7] which

---

5. Strictly speaking, this rests on a prior philosophical theory, the duality of the modal operators, which takes as its data all modalized intuitions.
6. Intuitions about what properties possibilities have, including such properties as being knowable, can be included here because they have consequences for what kinds of things those possibilities are.
7. This way of putting the point was intended to head off E.J. Lowe's objection to the argument (Lowe, this volume).

was itself grounded in intuitions about what is possible. Then, we (2005a, 2006) argued that despite claims to the contrary, metaphysical nihilism is, in fact, consistent with, respectively, Lewis's (1986) and Armstrong's (1989) theories of the nature of unactualized possibility. Finally, we (2008) argued that the plenitude objection to Lewis's (1986) theory of the nature of unactualized possibility misconstrues the role of the Principle of Recombination, which is, in fact, part of the theory of the extent of possibility and not a proper part of Lewis's theory of the nature of unactualized possibility.

However, Divers (forthcoming) has recently launched an important challenge to methodological separatism. He notes that separatism has consequences for what is and is not relevant to evaluating the success of a theory[8] of modality, such as Lewis's, but that evaluation of a theory is possible only once we have fully defined our conception of analysis, which involves specification of 'its intended components, structure, aims, methods and criteria of success' (1). Divers then presents a clear specification of Lewis's conception of analysis and argues that, on this conception, methodological separatism is mistaken. As he is well aware, this does not show that methodological separatism is, in fact, mistaken, for the result is only conditional, but it does pose a significant challenge to the separatist to offer an equally well-defined conception of her philosophical project which does not have the same consequence.

According to Divers, on the Lewisian conception, an analysis consists of three components: <Opinion, Analytic Hypotheses, Metaphysical Base>. Opinion is pre-philosophical belief, which includes and may be identical with the sum of all intuitions, as defined above. The Analytic Hypotheses give a 'sense' or 'truth-condition' (9) for the subset of Opinion, which is the target of the analysis, typically in the form of a bi-conditional, and the Metaphysical Base is an existential statement, which, given the Analytic Hypotheses, determines the truth-values of the target sentences and, quite possibly, other sentences in the Opinion. Thus, in the case of the analysis of modality, we get the following (4):

(Opinion)   It is possible that there be [Fs, e.g.] talking donkeys.
(Analytic Hypothesis) It is an F-possibility iff there unrestrictedly exists an F^*.
(Metaphysical Base)   There (unrestrictedly) exist $x, y \ldots$ such that $\ldots H^*x, y \ldots$

where H^* is a primitive expression of the kind that figures at the end of a chain of Definitions of the arbitrary nonmodal predicate F^*.

---

8. Divers talks only of 'analysis', but that is a type of theory on our definition.

Such an analysis is evaluated against the dual virtues of Conservative-ness (of Opinion) and Economy (of Metaphysical Base) in the following manner (10): we hold the Analytic Hypotheses constant and consider the various pairings of Opinion and Metaphysical Base which result from their co-variation established in the Analytic Hypotheses. If some such pairing is adequate with respect to both Conservativeness and Economy, then the analysis is accepted, but if none is, the analysis is rejected.

Since Opinion includes beliefs about what is and is not possible, beliefs which have a direct bearing on the extent of possibility, considerations of Economy in the Metaphysical Base have direct consequences for the extent of possibility. Thus, to take a well-known example, Opinion includes, or at least is committed to, the possibility of 'island universes', that is, pos-sible universes with spatio-temporally unconnected parts. But the Analytic Hypothesis requires that all possibilities are parts of worlds, and the Meta-physical Base tells us that worlds are maximally spatio-temporally intercon-nected mereological sums. Thus, Lewis (1986: 71) is faced with the choice of modifying the Metaphysical Base or rejecting an aspect of Opinion, and he takes the latter course. This seems a clear violation of methodological separatism, justified by the conception of analysis.

Divers's challenge to the separatist is to give an equally well-defined and clear conception of analysis which does not have this consequence. Given what was said above, the separatist could perfectly well adopt the Lewis-ian conception of analysis as an account of the theory of the nature of X, with one change, namely, that 'Opinion' be restricted to intuitions about the nature of X or about what kind of thing there is or is not, that is, to proper data for the theory.[9] This move immediately blocks the consequence that the evaluation of an analysis such as Lewis's involves making a judge-ment about the extent of possibility. In fact, we can grant that intuitions about what unactualized possibilities are are entirely neutral on the ques-tion of island universes and thus that the savings in Economy provided by a Metaphysical Base in which all worlds are maximally spatio-temporally interconnected mereological sums has no cost to Conservativeness at all. However, given the Analytic Hypotheses, it does entail that island universes are not possible. But even if we grant that intuitions about what is possible include island universes, we do not yet have a loss of Conservativeness, for we do not know whether the best theory of the extent of possibility captures or rejects that intuition. Suppose Modal Theory does capture that intuition. Then our best theory of the extent of possibility is inconsistent with Lewis's

9. Is the intuition that island universes are possible an intuition about the nature of unactualized possibility? Well, it is an oddity of the Lewisian metaphysics that unactualized possibilities have the properties that are said to be possible, so every claim about what is possible entails a claim about the nature of an un-actualized possibility. But since that entailment is mediated by the very theory we are evaluating, the consequence cannot be regarded as data for the theory.

theory of the nature of unactualized possibility, and we have a hard theory choice to make, comparing not merely the virtues of each theory but also those of the next best theory. Suppose, instead, that Modal Theory does not capture the intuition. Then, in our overall account of modality, there is a loss of Conservativeness. But, crucially, this is held against Modal Theory, the theory of what is possible, not the Lewisian theory of what possibilities are. So, should there be some inconsistency discovered with some third theory, we can properly evaluate which part of our overall account of modality has that particular weakness.[10]

However, this is not an adequate separatist response to Divers's challenge, for there is as yet no well-defined conception of the components, structure, aims, methods, and criteria of success for a separate theory of the extent of possibility. Without such a conception, it remains open that the only adequate way to address the question of extent is by an analysis of the nature of possibility and its consequences for the extent of possibility.

From what was said above, an account of the extent of possibility, of what is possible, appears to have two parts corresponding, respectively, to data and to theory, namely, <Intuition, Principles>. The intuitions will be those about propositions of the form '$\Diamond p$'. The principles will be conditionals of the form 'if p then $\Diamond q$' and perhaps also 'if p then $\sim\Diamond q$'. In order to count as a theory of the intuitive data, the principles must nontrivially entail those data (i.e. not because they have the form 'if $\Diamond p$ then $\Diamond p$'). Furthermore, the theory is interesting or useful or explanatory in virtue of having principles which each generate significant numbers of data points.

However, in order for the principles to generate any possibilities at all, we need a third element in the theory, corresponding structurally to the Metaphysical Base. Now, if there are a small number of principles with a limited variety of antecedents, then this third element can be quite small, but we cannot know that in advance. So, it is best if the third element contains all the antecedents of all the possible Principles. Since we are interested only in true antecedents, let's call this 'Fact'. Fact includes all of Intuition and all consequences of the conjunction of Fact and Principle, for the antecedents of Principles can be modal. So we have the following structure: <Intuition, Principles, Fact>. We can spell this out schematically:

Intuitions: $\Diamond p_1, \Diamond p_2, \ldots, \Diamond p_n$
Principles: If p^*i then $\Diamond p_j$
Facts: $p^*_1, p^*_2, \ldots, p^*m$

The Principles are not analytic, for their consequents contain information not in their antecedents. Rather, they are meant to explain the Intuitions (in

10. This paragraph is a more abstract version of the argument at Efird and Stoneham 2008: 484.

conjunction with the Facts). So how do we evaluate such a theory? There seem to be four criteria of evaluation:

1. *Consistency*: If Intuition contains $\sim\Diamond q$, Facts contains p, and Principles contains *if p then* $\Diamond q$, revision of something is required. It might be thought that Facts will never be subject to revision on the basis of conflict with modal Intuitions and Principles, but (i) Facts include modal propositions, and (ii) Facts may include analyses of what unactualized possibilities are, so they do not have any clear priority over the other two elements.

2. *Fit to data*: If we have two theories which are both consistent, we can evaluate their relative merits by considering which has a better fit to the data, that is, which captures more of the Intuitions. However, if the Principles only generate possibilities, that is, propositions of the form '$\Diamond p$' (see below for discussion of this issue), we need to take care to distinguish between a theory which fails to fit the Intuition that $\sim\Diamond p$ by generating $\Diamond p$, and one which fails to fit the Intuition that $\Diamond p$ by failing to generate $\Diamond p$. In the former case, this is clearly a theoretical vice, but the latter case may not be such unless we know independently that the theory is complete. If we allow the possibility of multiple Principles, we may be able to rectify the latter failure to fit the data by adding more Principles. As we see in the next section, many philosophers seem to assume that there can be only one Principle generating possibilities.

3. *Simplicity*: If we have two theories which are both consistent, we can evaluate their merits by how well they organize the data. Simplicity is very hard to make precise, but it is a widely accepted theoretical virtue in many fields, so the issue of assessing it is a general problem in the account of theory choice and not one specific to this area.

4. *Power*: If we have two theories which are both consistent and roughly equal in their balance of fit to data and simplicity, then we can evaluate their merits by their ability to extrapolate or interpolate new data points. For example, suppose Intuition is silent on whether talking fleas are possible or not. If theory A has the consequence that talking fleas are possible (or not) but theory B has no such consequence, then—ceteris paribus—we have a reason to prefer theory A over B in virtue of its being more powerful.

Clearly more detail can be given, but from this sketch it should be clear that there can be a well-defined conception of the separate account of the extent of possibility, so Divers's challenge is met.

2 SINGLE-CRITERION MODAL THEORIES AGAINST METAPHYSICAL NIHILISM

Michael Dummett (1959/1978: 169) poses the 'philosophical problem' of necessity thus: '[W]hat is its source, and how do we recognize it?' Posing the problem in this way presupposes that modal claims, if true, are not 'barely true', in terminology Dummett (1991: 328) develops later; that is, they are true in virtue of some other class or classes of statements. Whether modal claims are true in virtue of a single class of statements or multiple classes of statements has, to date, not been investigated. It has simply been assumed that, following a certain reading of Dummett's posing of the philosophical problem of necessity, necessity has a single source rather than multiple sources. Through investigating the nature of Modal Theory, we aim to go some way towards opening up space for necessity having multiple sources as opposed to a single source.

A Modal Theory is a theory which tells us which propositions are and which are not possible. Such a theory has the form

(P) $\Diamond p$ iff . . .

where a single-criterion Modal Theory fills in the ellipsis in (P) with just one clause, while a multiple-criterion Modal Theory fills in the ellipsis with a disjunction of clauses. That is, the single-criterion theory has one Principle of the form ' if p then $\Diamond q$', whereas the multiple-criterion theory has several such Principles. According to a single-criterion Modal Theory, there is only one way for a proposition to be determined possible; according to a multiple-criterion Modal Theory, there are multiple ways for a proposition to be determined possible. That Modal Theory is, or should be, single-criterion is typically assumed in arguments of the form: state of affairs S does not meet criterion C, so p, the proposition describing S, is not possible. For this argument to be valid, it must be that criterion C gives the only criterion for a proposition describing a state of affairs to be possible. Thus, the argument relies on Modal Theory being single-criterion. But this assumption has not been articulated, let alone defended. In what follows, we draw attention to this unarticulated and undefended assumption and the role it plays in two recent arguments against the possibility of nothing.[11]

---

11. This assumption, that Modal Theory has, or should have, a single criterion, is made throughout much of the literature on Modal Theory and not merely in the dialectic concerning the possibility of nothing. As a further example, George Darby and Duncan Watson (2010: 439) criticize our (2008) formulation of Lewis's principle of recombination on the grounds that it 'doesn't entail that there's a world at which there's no gunk'. However, nowhere do we assume that the principle of recombination is the only principle by which possibilities, that is, possible worlds, on Lewis's (1986) view, are generated. On the contrary, we were well aware that, following John Divers and Joseph Melia (2002), the principle of recombination does not deliver possibilities regarding alien individuals and properties, but if, as Divers and Melia (2002: 34) argue, the principle that '[e]very way that a part of [a] world could be is a way that a part of some world is', these possibilities are indeed generated but at the cost of undercutting Lewis's (1986) reductionist ambitions. Darby and Watson's criticism thus assumes a single-criterion Modal Theory, an assumption they never articulate and so never defend.

One of the most prominent single-criterion modal theories is

(Con)   <*p*> is possible iff it is conceivable that *p*.

Such a theory is described by Tamar Szabó Gendler and John Hawthorne thus:

> We have, it seems, a capacity that enables us to represent scenarios to ourselves using words or concepts or sensory images, scenarios that purport to involve actual or non-actual things in actual or non-actual configurations. There is a natural way of using the term 'conceive' that refers to this activity in its broadest sense. When we engage in such conceivings, the things we depict to ourselves frequently present themselves *as possible*, and we have an associated tendency to judge that they *are possible*. Indeed, when invited to consider whether something is possible, we often engage in a deliberate effort to conceive of it; upon finding ourselves able to do so, we conclude that it is. We may even decide that something is impossible on the basis of our inability to conceive of it. (2002b: 1–2; emphasis in the original)

As an illustration of this Modal Theory at work, John Campbell (2002) seems to assume something like it in his interpretation of Berkeley's thought when he considers Berkeley's so-called 'master argument' (Gallois 1974: 55):

> But say you, surely there is nothing easier than to imagine trees, for instance, in a park, or books existing in a closet, and no body by to perceive them. I answer, you may so, there is no difficulty in it: but what is all this, I beseech you, more than framing in your mind certain ideas which you call *books* and *trees*, and at the same time omitting to frame the idea of any one that may perceive them? But do not you your self perceive or think of them all the while? This therefore is nothing to the purpose: it only shows you have the power of imagining or forming ideas in your mind; but it doth not shew that you can conceive it possible, the objects of your thought may exist without the mind: to make out this, it is necessary that you conceive them existing unconceived or unthought of, which is a manifest repugnancy. (Berkeley 1710/1975: §23)

Campbell (2002: 127) writes, 'Berkeley famously claimed to be unable to conceive of existence unperceived, from which he famously concluded that existence unperceived is impossible'. Similarly, in commenting on the version of Berkeley's (1713/1998) 'master argument' in the *Dialogues*, André Gallois seems to read this same single-criterion Modal Theory in Berkeley's thought when he interprets Berkeley's argument thus:[12]

---

12. However, Gallois's reading of Berkeley's argument appears to be a misreading, as Berkeley endorses explicitly only the claim that if it is conceivable that there are unperceived things, then it is possible that there are unperceived things. See Stoneham 2002: 134–9 for details.

(1) Hylas thinks that possibly $(\exists x)(x$ is perceivable and x is unperceived).
(2) If what Hylas thinks is true, then the concepts being the possible object of some perception and being the object of some perception do not necessarily apply to the very same things.
(3) In order to sustain the claim that something could be both perceivable and unperceived, it must be possible to have an image of a perceivable which is not an image of something perceived.

([3] follows from [2] in conjunction with an imagistic criterion of necessity, the demand that Hylas be in a position to mention the kind of thing that could be both perceivable and unperceived, and, finally, that he can image appropriately something of this kind if he is to qualify as having the concept of an unperceived perceivable.)

(4) Hylas cannot meet the condition embodied in (3), and his failure in this respect is not the result of a contingent limitation of Hylas's powers of imaging.

The desired conclusion that nothing could be both perceivable and unperceived follows. (Gallois 1974: 63–4)

What underwrites both Campbell's Berkeley's inference and Gallois's Berkeley's argument is the left-to-right direction of (Con), and the assumption that possibility is uniquely constituted by conceivability, a single-criterion Modal Theory. Now, Bede Rundle seems to be making just this sort of argument when he argues against the possibility of nothing thus:

> We might insist that it is not possible that there should be, or have been, nothing at all; whether animate or inanimate, material or immaterial, there had to be something. On the other hand, it may well be that of no particular thing can one say that it is inconceivable that it should not have existed; our galaxy did not have to exist, nor did galaxies quite generally. (2004: 110)

In this passage, Rundle seems to take impossibility to be interchangeable with inconceivability and, as a consequence, to thereby endorse, at least implicitly, the single-criterion Modal Theory (Con). This comes out more clearly in the following argument against the possibility of nothing, where, on the assumption that we are unable to imagine nothing, it follows that there had to have been something, at least a setting:

> ... I suspect that our attempts at conceiving of total non-existence are irredeemably partial. We are always left with something, if only a setting from which we envisage everything having departed, a void which we confront and find empty, but something which it makes sense to speak of as having once been home to bodies, radiation, or whatever. ... [T]alk of imagining there was nothing—which is what is

called for—does run the risk of being treated as if a matter of imagining nothing, and that is refraining from imagining anything. Either that, or, I suggest, it is to imagine things lacking where there might have been something: we suppose we can imagine the stars ceasing to exist one by one—like so many lights going out—but we still look to where they were. . . . We have not discarded the setting; something we might search in vain, but something—a previously occupied region—none the less. (2004: 110–1)

Rundle's argument is valid only if, again, inconceivability entails impossibility, in which case, it would seem, possibility is constituted by conceivability, a single-criterion Modal Theory. This assumption goes unarticulated and so undefended. So, one way of attacking Rundle's argument, rather than simply denying that there is any connection whatsoever between conceivability and possibility, is to maintain that while conceivability gives one way for a proposition to be possible, there are others as well. Sothe inconceivability of *p* does not rule out the possibility of <*p*>. Now, it's likely that Rundle will resist this line of argument, given that he takes the source of necessity to be relations between concepts (2004: 98, see also p. 109), which then gives rise to a single-criterion Modal Theory. However, for the objection to metaphysical nihilism to be cogent, Rundle needs to argue that this is the *only* source of modality.[13]

A second example of this unarticulated and so undefended assumption can be found in Graham Oppy's recent argument against the possibility of nothing. He describes his 'favourite theory of modality' thus:

Wherever there was objective chance, there were alternative possibilities. Wherever there is objective chance, there are alternative possibilities. Wherever there will be objective chance, there will be alternative possibilities. Possible worlds are alternative ways that the actual world could have gone, or could go, or could one day go; possible worlds all 'share' an initial history with the actual world and 'branch' from the actual world only as a result of the outworkings of objective chance. Since the laws that govern the evolution of possible worlds do not vary over the course of that evolution, all possible worlds 'share' the same laws. If there was an initial state of the actual world, then all possible worlds 'share' that initial state; if there was no initial state of the actual world, then all possible worlds 'share' some 'infinite' initial segment with the

---

13. In fairness, we should note that Rundle does indirectly address this issue by arguing that the possibilities not licensed by his single criterion are meaningless (e.g. 2004: 112–3). This requires him to regard many modal intuitions as mere illusions of meaningfulness. Whether this move has the same sort of cost of Conservativeness to a theory as denying the intuitions is a difficult point to adjudicate, but we expect most readers of this volume to be reluctant to accept that they are speaking as much nonsense as Rundle claims.

actual world, and hence any two possible worlds 'share' some 'infinite' initial segment with one another.

My favourite theory of modality does not assume that there are objective chances. However, if there are no objective chances then, on my favourite theory, there is just one possible world: the actual world. (this volume: 46–7)

Notice that Oppy begins with a sufficient criterion for a proposition's being possible, namely, if there was, is, or will be an objective chance that *p*, then <*p*> is possible. However, after taking possible worlds to be 'alternative ways that the actual world could have gone, or could go, or could one day go', he then concludes that all possible worlds ' "share" an initial history with the actual world and "branch" from the actual world only as a result of the outworkings of objective chance'. This inference is valid only if there being an objective chance that *p* is not only a sufficient but also a necessary condition for <*p*>'s being possible—that is, that there being an objective chance that *p* is a single-criterion theory of modality. This assumption can be seen to be at work most dramatically in the last sentence of the passage, where he draws the consequence that if there are no objective chances, then there is only one possible world, the actual world. Following this outline of his 'favourite modal theory', he outlines what he takes to be its controversial consequences, which, again, follow only if the Modal Theory he is offering is a single-criterion Modal Theory:

Of course, my favourite theory of modality is controversial: there are many who suppose that it omits further possibilities. For example, some suppose that (a) there might not have been anything at all; (b) the initial state of the world—or the entire beginningless history of the world—might have been different; (c) the laws might have been different; (d) the laws might change as the state of the world evolves; and perhaps there are yet other suppositions that might be entertained. On my favourite theory, these alternative suppositions are purely doxastic or epistemic: while they are ways that *it might be supposed* that the world could have gone, could go, or could one day go, they are not ways that the world could have gone, could go, or could one day go. (this volume: 47; emphasis in the original)

In what follows, we will challenge this assumption that Modal Theory should be single-criterion and thereby challenge these arguments from Rundle and Oppy, not by denying that it being conceivable that *p* or that there being an objective chance that *p* is a sufficient criterion for <*p*>'s being possible but rather by asserting that they are not necessary for <*p*>'s being possible, opening up space in the dialectic for multiple-criterion modal theories.

3   MODAL PLURALISM

There is always going to be a trade-off between simplicity and fit to the data in constructing any theory, and there is plenty of evidence that single-criterion theories of what is possible, while simpler than multiple-criterion theories, always lose too much of the data. For example, while we might accept that if p is conceivable, then $\Diamond p$, to make this the only criterion of possibility amounts to adding the much more controversial claim that if p is inconceivable, then $\sim\Diamond p$. This claim faces a dilemma. On the first horn, if conceivability is relative to an actual historical circumstance—that is, is what actual people in an actual context have the ability to conceive when they try—then possibility also becomes so relativized. Consequently, we would find ourselves saying that what used to be impossible is now possible and what is now impossible is possibly . . . possible (because we can conceive of beings who can conceive of beings who . . . who can conceive of it). There is a debate to be had here, but for many this is too big a conflict with intuition. On the second horn, we consider conceivability under some idealization, so that what is conceivable for us is thereby ideal-conceivable for previous generations and what is conceivably . . . conceivable for us is ideal-conceivable. But then the theory has been modified to:

$\Diamond p$ iff $\Diamond$(conceivable that p).

Now, while a pluralist theory can readily allow claims of the form '$\Diamond p$ then $\Diamond q$', a single-criterion theory cannot have this form. For if it did, it would fail to be a theory of the data, the modal intuitions, since all it would allow us to do would be to deduce new modal claims from old ones, without providing any *explanation* of the original intuitions.

We find similar sorts of difficulties with other candidates for single-criterion theories. Take, for example, the Principle of Recombination (Lewis 1986: 87), which is often treated as if it was a single-criterion theory. In our formulation, this is (2008: 489, original numbering preserved):

(7)   For any sequence of intrinsically distinct objects $x_1, x_2, x_3, \ldots, x_m$ and any sequence of cardinals $(n_i \geq 0)$ $n_1, n_2, n_3, \ldots, n_m$ and any spatiotemporal relation between those objects, there exists a possible world which contains: exactly n_1 duplicates of x_1, exactly n_2 duplicates of x_2, exactly n_3 duplicates of x_3, . . ., exactly n_m duplicates of x_m in that spatiotemporal relation.

To make this fit the form of a single-criterion Modal Theory, let's define a PR-world as a possible world the existence of which is a consequence of (7). Then the single-criterion Modal Theory becomes:

(PR) $\Diamond p$ iff there is a PR-world at which p is true.

Now, this theory does really well in establishing possibilities, such as there being more or fewer of certain kinds of objects, or objects that have existed in different places and times. But it is far less clear how it can establish that talking donkeys are possible. Presumably, if talking donkeys are possible, there is some reconfiguration of matter, specifically donkey cells, probably with additional neurons and also muscles around the throat and tongue, which is sufficient for there to be a talking donkey (setting aside, for present purposes, the question of whether there is some PR-world in which a donkey talks in virtue of the transmigration of a human soul into a donkey body). And the Principle of Recombination tells us that there is a PR-world with that reconfiguration of matter. But it does not tell us that talking donkeys are possible because it does not tell us that that reconfiguration of matter is sufficient for there to be a talking donkey. So (PR) does not determine whether it is possible that there are talking donkeys.

Assuming for a moment that, even on reflection, we do have the intuition that there might be talking donkeys, then (PR) fails to fit the data in this respect. It also fails to fit the data in respect of any other intuition we might have that $\Diamond p$, where p is not a fact about the distribution of objects but one which supervenes on it. This has the consequence that if (PR) were the correct single-criterion Modal Theory, certain vexed debates in philosophy would be quickly resolved. For example, it would become a mere triviality that zombies are possible. To avoid this consequence and fit the data rather better, (PR) needs to be supplemented by 'connecting axioms' (Lewis 1986: 155) telling us which supervenient facts hold at which PR-worlds. These connecting axioms will be strict conditionals, but for Modal Theory what is important is not the strict conditional but the consequences of the form 'if $\Diamond p$ then $\Diamond q$', where p is entailed by the existence of a PR-world and q is some supervenient fact. That is to say, either (PR) fails to fit the data, or it needs to be supplemented with some further Principles of Modal Theory.

We have no general proof that a single-criterion theory which fits the data well can be constructed, but it should be clear that the burden of proof is on the one who proposes just a single criterion. Those of us who allow multiple criteria will always have a better fit to the data because we can take any proposed single criterion and add a further criterion to improve the fit. But that might be thought to be a cost in terms of simplicity which needs to be weighed in the balance.

It is worth pausing for a moment to consider the dialectical position with respect to those partisans of desert landscapes who think that a poor fit with the data of modal intuition is not a cost to Modal Theory but rather a benefit, for possibility is intrinsically suspect and should be allowed only in the most limited of cases.[14] From the point of view of Methodological

---

14. Oppy (this volume) seems to be an example of this attitude since he is happy to discard all intuitions that there are possibilities with different histories in return for reducing all possibility to objective chance.

Separatism, what is going on here is that a weak Modal Theory—'weak' in the sense of not doing a good job of theorizing the data—is being preferred over much stronger alternatives on the basis of consistency with *independent* metaphysical views. While that is a perfectly legitimate move to make, when we are scorekeeping in the metaphysical game we must not lose sight of the fact that a significant cost has been incurred.

So far, we have drawn attention to the fact that many modal theorists seem to assume that Modal Theory is single-criterion, and we then argued inconclusively in favour of a multiple-criterion Modal Theory. We now consider one alleged advantage of a single-criterion theory, namely, that it does a better job of capturing our intuitions about necessity since we can infer impossibility from the failure of that single criterion. The obvious way for multiple-criterion theories to capture intuitions about necessity is to write them in as separate Principles, but that really does look ad hoc compared to the single-criterion approach. Another response would be to deny that Modal Theory must in fact capture a set of intuitions about necessity as well as about possibility. We explore this response by considering cases. The best candidates for intuitions about necessity are intuitions about essence. For example, how should Modal Theory capture the various principles of the necessity of origin, such as that I must have had the parents I did or that this table must have been made from the wood it was made from? These appear to have the form:

(NO) $(x) (Ox \rightarrow \Box\, Ox)$

Are these Principles of Modal Theory reached by systematizing our modal intuitions? Many philosophers assert that they are (e.g. Ballarin 2011: n. 2). However, on the face of it, we have a contrary intuition. Consider this table, made from the oak which blew down in the Great Storm of '87. The intuition is widely shared that it could turn out that this table here was not in fact made from that oak, that the carpenter had made a mistake and used the wrong wood. Surely, then, this is the intuition that it is possible that this very table had a different origin?

The defender of the necessity of origin will claim that the possibility just described, in which we discovered the table had a different origin from the one we believed it had, is distinct from the possibility that it has a different origin from the one it actually has. Is it a modal intuition, a pre-philosophical datum that Modal Theory must try to fit, that this is not possible, that *given that the table was made from that tree* it could not have been made from another? Kripke tells us that it 'seems so' to him but also that 'in many cases you won't become convinced of this, at least not at the moment' (1980: 113), suggesting that it takes some reflection to share the intuition. Can reflection which does not appeal to philosophical theories persuade us? Here is how that reflection might go (drawing on Kripke 1980: 114, n. 56): it is possible that as well as this table, made from the oak which fell in the storm of '87, there is another very similar table made at roughly the same time from a different oak, perhaps one felled deliberately in the week before the storm. Since there are two tables in this possibility, the latter is obviously not identical to the former. But then there is a third possibility in which the former is not made but the latter is. It would still not be identical with our original table, and since the choice of alternative origin was arbitrary, this shows that any possible table with a different origin is not identical with the table made from the oak which fell in the Great Storm of '87.

Kripke himself tells us that this argument rests on the necessity of distinctness, but as decades of attempts to reconstruct the argument have shown, it must rest on more than just that. A different line of reflection is offered by Dummett (1981: 130–1), who suggests that the necessity of origin follows from the thought that an essential property of an object is one which, at every time during its existence, it cannot 'cease to have'. Clearly, the circumstances of something's coming into existence fulfil this condition. But apart from the fact that this makes way too much essential (McGinn 1976: 130), this establishes the necessity of origin only if it is not possible for one thing to have different essential properties—on this definition of essence—in different possible worlds. And clearly the world in which the table was made from a different tree is an apparent counterexample to that claim. So no progress is made.

Perhaps we do not need an argument here at all; perhaps there is a modal intuition about naming which will rule out the possibility that this table could have had a different origin? In the last paragraph we took care not to name the table, but Kripke's discussion, and all that follow it, always introduce a name for the original table. So let us call the table actually made from the wood of the oak that fell during the Great Storm of '87 'Tabby' and make clear that this is a genuine singular term and not an abbreviated description. Now, consider the possible world in which no table is made from that tree but a very similar table is made from another tree. Is that table Tabby? One way of addressing that question is to ask about the name; that is, does the name 'Tabby', as we use it, refer to that table in that possible world? (Of course, the people in that world may have their own name for the table, and that may also be Tabby, but it is our name we are asking about.)

This question about naming could surely receive an intuitive answer only if semantic competence with the name involved grasping some principles of the form: $\Box(x)\,(Fx \to \text{'T' refers to } x)$. Now, Kripke of all people is not going to appeal to semantic intuitions about naming of that form. It seems instead that what is driving Kripke's intuition is that there are constraints on which possible objects a given actual name can refer to, that these constraints are not part of the intension, connotation, or sense of the name but rather must derive from some contingent causal connection between the name and the object. Thus, since our name 'Tabby' refers to a particular table only in virtue of that table's causal relations, for it to refer to a possible table, that possible table must have the right position in the causal order to be the referent of our name. It could then be argued (not easily, but one can see how the argument might proceed by ruling out alternatives) that only having the same origin as Tabby is sufficient to make it the case that the name 'Tabby' refers to that object.[15] If this is what underlies Kripke's conviction that a table with a different origin would not be '*this table*' (1980: 113; emphasis in the original), that is, would not be Tabby, then we can see that, far from the necessity of origin being a modal datum, the modal intuition that Tabby could have been made from a different tree is over-ruled by the *theoretical* requirement that there be a determinate fact as to whether our name 'Tabby' refers to a given merely possible table or not.[16]

The necessity of identity may have greater claim to be a modal intuition. However, when we examine this debate more closely, this is again not so obvious. For it seems that both sides agree that we have the intuition that the lump of bronze 'is' the statue and that it might not have been the statue (had it not been poured into the mould). Proponents of contingent identity claim that these intuitions are about the identity and thus their view conserves the data, whereas proponents of the necessity of identity claim that these intuitions are not about the identity of the bronze and the statue but some other relation such as constitution. So again we have a situation in which the intuitive data apparently conflict with the essentialist claim and have to be reinterpreted. When reinterpreted, the data do not support essentialism, but merely fail to conflict with it. The support for essentialism comes from a process of reflection which, typically, appeals to the necessity of self-identity and Leibniz's Law applied to modalized open sentences. However, this process of reflection is not one which produces general, let alone universal, agreement, so it does not look to be a good candidate for a modal intuition. Perhaps the necessity of self-identity will have to be an axiomatic Principle of Modal Theory, but that is hardly a great cost to simplicity. However, we might think that if, among the multiple modal Principles, there is to be one introducing necessities, it is most likely to be a version of the Rule of Necessitation: if p is known a priori,[17] then $\Box p$. This would explain the necessity of self-identity (we know the self-identity of each thing a priori) and analytic or conceptual

---

15. This is a metalinguistic version of Salmon's (1981: 206) premise (V).
16. Some may think that there is an intuition that it is determinate whether our name refers to any *actual* object or not. This might become a requirement that it be equally determinate whether it refers to any possible object or not, via the necessity of identity. But it is not clear that the necessity of identity is a modal intuition either.
17. Being a priori is analogous to being a theorem because a theorem rests on no assumptions and what is known a priori depends on no evidence. Note that it is important that p be *known a priori*: a priori warrants are defeasible, so we may have a priori warrant for some beliefs without knowing them (e.g. Flockemann 2011) and even without their being true.

truths such as 'All vixens are foxes' and 'Nothing is red and green all over at the same time'. And, of course, within a multiple-criterion Modal Theory, accepting this Principle does not rule out a posteriori necessities.

The objection was that we always have a reason to prefer a single-criterion Modal Theory because it directly entails intuitions of necessity, whereas a multiple-criterion theory will have to capture those intuitions by adding ad hoc Principles. But we have seen that the alleged intuitions of necessity are either no such thing or can be captured by the single Principle 'if p is known a priori, then $\Box p$'.

So we have seen that single-criterion theories will always have trouble providing an adequate fit to the data and that there is no such problem with multiple-criterion theories. Of course, there is always a trade-off between simplicity and fit, but we are left with no reason to think that only a single-criterion theory can find the appropriate balance. Thus the widespread, un-argued assumption that an adequate Modal Theory will be single-criterion is unjustified.

4   BURDENS OF PROOF AND METAPHYSICAL NIHILISM AGAIN

If a multiple-criterion Modal Theory consists of a collection of Principles of the form 'if p then $\Diamond q$' (and the Principle 'if p is known a priori then $\Box p$'), then our knowledge of the range of possibilities becomes, in a sense, open-ended. For in order to establish $\sim\!\Diamond p$, one would either have to know $\sim\!p$ a priori (and we are right to think that the scope of genuine a priori knowl-edge is probably quite narrow) or to know that some specific set of Princi-ples are *all* the Principles of Modal Theory and deduce $\sim\!\Diamond p$ from the failure of this complete Modal Theory to entail $\Diamond p$. However, once we accept the need for a multiplicity of criteria of possibility, it seems epistemically risky to make the assumption that one's Modal Theory is complete, since there is always the chance that some first-order axiom has been missed. Thus, for a given possibility not entailed by the (first-order) axioms, it is usually an epistemically open question as to whether that possibility is a genuine pos-sibility or not.

Now, if the extent of possibility is open-ended in this way, Hume's Razor, as formulated by Peter Forrest (2001; cf. Efird and Stoneham 2005a),

(HR)   Do not multiply necessities beyond necessity.

then follows. For in positing a necessary truth, the philosopher is taking a risk, since for all she knows, she has missed out an axiom of their corre-sponding Modal Theory which entails the possibility ruled out by the neces-sity they posited. Similarly, what might be termed 'Leibniz's Principle of the Presumption of Possibility':[18]

---

18. Leibniz (1703–5/1982: 438) writes,

(LP) One has the right to assume $\Diamond p$ until someone proves the contrary.

is also a good regulative principle in philosophy, since proving impossibility requires proving one has not overlooked some Principle which generates possibilities, and that is harder than proving the acceptability of some proposed Principle. In general, where theoretical certainty is lacking, pragmatic considerations can come into judgement-making.

John Heil (this volume: 171), following C.B. Martin (2008: 65), disagrees. He formulates the following principle:

(C) It is no good *assuming* that p is contingent in cases in which p's being contingent functions as a substantive premise in an argument.

And he comments, 'Where p is a substantive thesis that serves as a premise, the claim that p is contingent and the claim that p is not contingent are on all fours' (this volume: 171). In a note to this remark (n. 5), he writes,

> Roy Sorensen has reminded me that Martin's principle itself includes a commitment to 'modal fallibilism'. The principle assumes that modal truths have mind-independent truthmakers concerning which we could be wrong. I do not know how to discuss the issue at hand—the why-is-there-anything question—without making this assumption.

Now, it is ironic that Martin's and Heil's position is dependent on a form of modal fallibilism since it is also a form of modal fallibilism that is motivating our position, a position which supports the regulative (LP). For on our modal fallibilism, since we could have missed out one of the axioms of Modal Theory (of the form 'if p then $\Diamond q$'), it is safest to assume that those we do have are not all that there are, and so possibilities are, in general, never ruled out but rather ruled in. Consequently, it is then safest to presume that a putative possibility is genuinely possible unless we have positive reason to rule it out, which is just (LP).

Finally, not only does a multiple-criterion Modal Theory consisting of axioms of the form 'if p then $\Diamond q$' seem to support Hume's Razor and Leibniz's Principle of the Presumption of Possibility, two popular and deeply held methodological principles, but it also seems to leave open the epistemic possibility of impossible worlds. For the modalized Principle of Noncontradiction

(NC) $\sim\!\Diamond(p \;\&\; \sim\!p)$

And it is already something that by this remark it is proved that given that God is possible, he exists, which is the privilege of Divinity alone. One has the right to presume the possibility of every Being, and above all that of God, until someone proves the contrary. So that this metaphysical argument already yields a moral demonstrative conclusion, which implies in the present state of our knowledge we ought to judge that God exists, and act accordingly.

is not one of the axioms of Modal Theory, since it is not of the form 'if p then $\Diamond q$'.[19] It is then an open question whether it could be rational to assert the possibility of a contradiction.[20]

This way of understanding the theory of possibility fits very well with a framework introduced by Nathan Salmon (1989). Salmon distinguishes *ways for the things to be* from *ways things might have been* (1989: 11), calling the former 'generic worlds' and the latter 'possible worlds'. Now, the possible worlds are clearly a subset of the generic worlds, though they may not be a proper subset. Salmon is primarily concerned to argue against the S4 axiom $\Box p \rightarrow \Box\Box p$ on the basis of examples where it is impossible that a given table T might have been made out of a certain block of wood w, even though it is possibly possible that it might have been. Thus, the world in which T is made from w is impossible relative to the actual world but possible relative to some other world. For this to make sense, we need a notion of worlds, the generic worlds, which is independent of the question of whether any given world is possible or not. And once we have this in place, we can allow that '[s]ome ways for things to be are not even possibly possibly . . . possible, for any degree of nesting. . . . As far as I can tell, worlds need not even be logically consistent' (Salmon 1989: 7–8).

There is no need for us to take a view here on which generic worlds, if any, may not be possible worlds. However, we should accept the metaphysically neutral translation schemata:

If $(p \lor \sim p)$ then there is a generic world at which p.
If $\Diamond p$ then there is a possible world at which p.

Rather, the distinction between generic and possible worlds allows us to understand the role of Modal Theory in the debate about whether there might have been nothing. For what a Modal Theory does is say of a generic world, whatever that might be, that it is a possible world; of a way for things to be, that it is a way things might have been. Now, there being nothing concrete is a way for things to be (pace Rundle): the empty world is a generic world.

---

19. It might be a theorem if $\sim(p \,\&\, \sim p)$ is known a priori. But the dialetheist takes the Liar and related paradoxes to cast doubt on precisely that.
20. One way of resolving this question is by considering the philosophical theory of propositional attitudes. Hintikka (1975: 475) puts the following claim forward:

> A sentence of the form 'a knows that p' is true in a world W iff p is true in all epistemic a-alternatives to W, i.e., in all the epistemically possible worlds which are compatible with everything a knows in W.

Now, this claim is not, strictly speaking, a part of Modal Theory, in the sense of the theorization of the pre-philosophical modal data. However, it does generate possibilities: if a does not know that p, then there is an epistemically possible world in which p is false. Furthermore, with some plausible assumptions, as Hintikka notes, it generates logically impossible worlds.

What an argument for metaphysical nihilism has to do is to give a principle of Modal Theory on which that way for things to be is a way they might have been. The Subtraction Argument as we reconstruct it (2005b) does precisely this by formulating and justifying the principle of subtractability. Similarly, we noted (2008) that one plausible formulation of the Principle of Recombination also entails that the empty world is possible. Thus, there are two candidate reasons to accept metaphysical nihilism, and we can endorse both.

All this goes to show that the burden of proof in the debate lies with one who denies that the empty world is a possible world. They must either offer an argument that regarding it as possible conflicts with some other piece of metaphysics (e.g. Lowe, this volume) and opt to reject the best Modal Theory in favour of one which does not have the plausible principles which entail metaphysical nihilism, or they must offer an alternative Modal Theory and argue that it is a better theory of our modal intuitions.

REFERENCES

Alexander, J. (2012). *Experimental Philosophy: An Introduction*. Cambridge: Polity.
Armstrong, D.M. (1989). *A Combinatorial Theory of Possibility*. Cambridge: Cambridge University Press.
Ballarin, R. (2011). 'The Necessity of Origin: A Long and Winding Route', *Erkenntnis*, online first, doi: 10.1007/s10670-011-9354-3.
Berkeley, G. (1710/1975). *The Principles of Human Knowledge*. London: Everyman.
———. (1713/1998). *Three Dialogues Between Hylas and Philonous*, ed. Jonathan Dancy. Oxford: Oxford University Press.
Cameron, R. (2012). 'Why Lewis's Analysis of Modality Succeeds in Its Reductive Ambitions', *Philosophers' Imprint* 12, no. 8.
Campbell, J. (2002). 'Berkeley's Puzzle', in Gendler, T.S. and Hawthorne, J. (eds.). *Conceivability and Possibility*. Oxford: Clarendon Press, pp. 127–43.
Darby, G. and Watson, D. (2010). 'Lewis's Principle of Recombination: Reply to Efird and Stoneham', *Dialectica* 64: 435–45.
Divers, J. (forthcoming). 'The Analysis of Possibility and the Extent of Possibility'.
Divers, J. and Melia, J. (2002). 'The Analytic Limit of Genuine Modal Realism', *Mind* 111: 15–36.
Dummett, M. (1959/1978). 'Wittgenstein's Philosophy of Mathematics', originally published in the *Philosophical Review* 68: 324–48; reprinted in Dummett, M. (1978). *Truth and Other Enigmas*. London: Duckworth, 166–85; page references are to the reprinted version.
———. (1981). Frege: Philosophy of Language, second edition. Cambridge, MA: Harvard University Press.
———. (1991). *The Logical Basis of Metaphysics*. Cambridge, MA: Harvard University Press.
Efird, D. and Stoneham, T. (2005a). 'Genuine Modal Realism and the Empty World', *European Journal of Analytic Philosophy* 1: 21–38.
———. (2005b). 'The Subtraction Argument for Metaphysical Nihilism', *Journal of Philosophy* 102: 303–25.
———. (2006). 'Combinatorialism and the Possibility of Nothing', *Australasian Journal of Philosophy* 84: 269–80.
———. (2008). 'What Is the Principle of Recombination?', *Dialectica* 62: 483–94.

Flockemann, R. (2011). *Epistemic Norms, the A Priori, and Self-Knowledge*. PhD thesis, University of York.

Forrest, P. (2001). 'Counting the Cost of Modal Realism', in Preyer, G. and Siebelt, F. (eds.). *Reality and Humean Supervenience*. Oxford: Rowman and Littlefield, pp. 93-103.

Gallois, A. (1974). 'Berkeley's Master Argument', *Philosophical Review* 83: 55–69.

Gendler, T.S and Hawthorne, J. (eds.). (2002a). *Conceivability and Possibility*. Oxford: Clarendon Press.

Campbell, J. (2002b). 'Introduction: Conceivability and Possibility', in Gendler, T.S. and Hawthorne, J. (eds.). *Conceivability and Possibility*. Oxford: Clarendon Press, pp. 1–70.

Gregory, D. (2011). 'Iterated Modalities, Meaning and A Priori Knowledge', *Philosophers' Imprint* 11: 1–11.

Hintikka, J. (1975). 'Impossible Worlds Vindicated', *Journal of Philosophical Logic* 4: 475–84.

Kripke, S.A. (1980). *Naming and Necessity*. Cambridge, MA: Harvard University Press.

Leibniz, G.F. (1703–5/1982). *New Essays on Human Understanding*, trans. Peter Remnant and Jonathan Bennett. Cambridge: Cambridge University Press.

Lewis, D. (1986). *On the Plurality of Worlds*. Oxford: Blackwell.

Martin, C.B. (2008). *The Mind in Nature*. Oxford: Clarendon Press.

McGinn, C. (1976). 'On the Necessity of Origin', *Journal of Philosophy* 73: 127–35.

Quine, W.V.O. (1953). 'On What There Is', in his *From a Logical Point of View*. Cambridge, MA: Harvard University Press, 1–19.

Rundle, B. (2004). *Why There Is Something Rather Than Nothing*. Oxford: Clarendon Press.

Salmon, N. (1981). *Reference and Essence*. Princeton: Princeton University Press.

———. (1989). 'The Logic of What Might Have Been', *Philosophical Review* 98: 3–34.

Stoneham, T. (2002). *Berkeley's World*. Oxford: Oxford University Press.

Van Inwagen, P. (1986/2001). 'Two Concepts of Possible Worlds', *Midwest Studies in Philosophy* 9: 185–213; reprinted in his *Ontology, Identity, and Modality*. Cambridge: Cambridge University Press. Page references are to the reprinted version.

Williamson, T. (2007). *The Philosophy of Philosophy*. Oxford: Blackwell.

10 Contingency

John Heil

147. That the absolutely impossible cannot be done by God or another agent.—An error, if impossible is understood according to
nature.

—From the Condemnations of 1277; Grant 1974: 49

What, then, is the importance of modern science for the argument
for the existence of God based on the mutability of the cosmos? By
means of exact and detailed research into the macrocosm and the
microcosm, it has considerably broadened and deepened the empirical foundation on which this argument rests, and from which
it concludes to the existence of an *Ens a se*, immutable by His very
nature. It has, besides, followed the course and the direction of
cosmic developments, and, just as it was able to get a glimpse of
the term toward which these developments were inexorably leading, so also has it pointed to their beginning in time some five billion years ago. Thus, with that concreteness which is characteristic
of physical proofs, it has confirmed the contingency of the universe
and also the well-founded deduction as to the epoch when the cosmos came forth from the hands of the Creator. Hence, creation
took place in time. Therefore, there is a Creator. Therefore, God
exists!

—Pope Pius XII, Address to the Pontifical Academy of Sciences,
22 November 1951

Nothing contains all things. It is more precious than gold, without
beginning and end, more joyous than the perception of bountiful
light, more noble than the blood of kings, comparable to the heav-
ens, higher than the stars, more powerful than a stroke of lightening,
perfect and blessed in every way. Nothing always inspires. Where
Nothing is, there ceases the jurisdiction of all kings. Nothing is without any mischief. According to Job the earth is suspended over Nothing. Nothing is outside the world. Nothing is everywhere.

—Otto von Guericke, *Experimenta nova (ut vocantur) Magedeburgica
de vacuo spatio*, 1672; quoted in Grant 1981: 216

Necessities will have to be earned, but so will contingencies.

—Martin 2008: 65

1 PHILOSOPHICAL LEGACIES

Why is there something rather than nothing? Why is there anything at all? Discussion of such questions as we now have it is rooted in a medieval theological vision according to which the universe and its characteristics, including its laws, are the result of a divine choice. Philosophers who would reject the theology out of hand are happy to retain the overall picture, a not uncommon occurrence in philosophy. By establishing a settled space of possibilities, an antique, discredited—or at any rate repudiated—thesis can continue to exert a powerful gravitational pull on our thinking.

You can begin to get a feel for what I have in mind by reflecting on mainstream philosophical approaches to laws of nature. The idea that the universe is subject to governing laws originated in the late medieval rejection of Aristotelian conceptions of the universe according to which nature was self-governing: what a thing does or would do is determined by the thing's nature. Such a picture threatens God's omnipotence. The solution is to strip objects of their powers and relocate the powers in God.

Start with the idea that the laws are God's decrees. Laws are external to, or separate from, whatever 'obeys' them. God *imposes* laws on the particles. God tells the particles what to do and when, and they do it. They have no choice. Or maybe God actively manipulates things; maybe God impels individual particles, nudging them hither and thither. In either case, laws could be understood to express divine policies, principles on which God acts.

Although few philosophers today would look favorably on the idea that laws of nature emanate from God, many apparently arrive at their conception of laws by accepting the picture minus God: laws *govern* the behavior of the particles; the particles *obey* the laws. But what is left when you subtract God? What is left to issue and enforce the laws? Moving God out of the picture is not a matter of changing a detail. Erasing God results in a dramatically different picture.[1]

Philosophers have stepped in with various God replacements. Hume substitutes *regularities* for God's decrees. Humean laws in no sense govern. Laws are true generalizations of the form 'Every *F* is a *G*'. David Armstrong reinstates the governing laws but identifies them with constituents of the universe, 'higher-order universals' (see, e.g., Armstrong 1997). Suppose *F* and *G* are universals, scientific kinds. There might be a law to the effect

---

1. Des Chene (forthcoming) discusses the seventeenth-century transition from an Aristotelian conception of natural occurrences, according to which objects governed themselves in ways determined by their various powers, to a conception of objects governed by laws. See also Milton 1998.

that the *F*s necessitate the *G*s: $N(F,G)$. This law implies—hence accounts for the fact—that every *F* is a *G*.[2] Others, Marc Lange, for instance, seem happy to allow laws to remain 'ungrounded' in the form of counterfactual truths with evil-smelling counterfactual truthmakers: contrary-to-the-facts facts (see Lange 2009).

In all these cases, two themes survive the removal of God from the original theological picture. First, laws of nature are *external* to whatever they govern. The appeal to laws distinguishes sharply between what something *is* (an alpha particle, a billiard ball, a neutron star) and what it *does* or *would do*. On the objectionable Aristotelian picture, in contrast, what something is determines what it does or would do. Second, laws of nature are *contingent*: the laws could have been otherwise; indeed, the laws could have been *any* (logically permitted) *way at all*. If that is so, the laws' being as they are is something that cries out for explanation. But what could such an explanation *be*? *What* could explain the obtaining of *this* collection of contingent laws?

Here the theological option reasserts itself. The laws are as they are because God so willed it. Given the dependence of life on the laws' being as they are, and given all the endless possibilities, it looks as though either we are stupendously, ridiculously lucky that things turned out as they did, or things turned out as they did for a reason. And what could that reason be if not the Creator's benevolence?

I am not suggesting that philosophers with interests in cosmology must be theists, even closet theists. What I *am* suggesting is that your starting place, the picture with which you begin, sets the problem—by making certain kinds of question salient—and configures a space of possible answers. The starting place, the initial guiding idea, can be abandoned by one generation of philosophers, while the picture emanating from that idea continues to exert a residual pull on successive generations.[3]

We expect scientists to operate with all sorts of assumptions concerning their respective fields of inquiry. Philosophers, in contrast, are supposed to put everything up for grabs, assume nothing substantive, nothing controversial. This was Descartes's dream, although Descartes himself contrived

---

2. The *alleged* fact; see Cartwright 1983, 1999.
3. Edward Grant (1981: 262) notes that this is how it was with the modern concept of space:

Scholastic ideas about space and God form an integral part of the history of spatial conceptions between the late sixteenth and eighteenth centuries, the period of the Scientific Revolution. From the assumption that infinite space is God's immensity, scholastics derived most of the same properties as did nonscholastics, and did so before the latter. As God's immensity, space had to be homogeneous, immutable, infinite, and capable of coexistence with bodies, which it received without offering resistance. Except for extension, the divinization of space in scholastic thought produced virtually all the properties that would be conferred on space during the course of the Scientific Revolution.

to regard as uncontroversial a host of substantive theses that others would find anything but.

No one—not you, not me, not anyone—is immune to this kind of insensibility. Questions that today strike us as the deepest—the question at hand, 'Why is there anything at all?'; the question how minds and bodies interact; the question how conscious phenomena stand to the physical world—did not, *could* not, have occurred to Aristotle, for instance. This is not because Aristotle was distracted, not because he had bigger fish to fry. It is because these questions presuppose broad philosophical attitudes that would have been utterly alien to Aristotle. (See Matson 1966; and see King 2007, for a medieval sequel.)

I mention all this, not in hopes of rallying support for one or another favored philosophical precept, but merely to call your attention to the fact that theses regarded as obvious—what everyone accepts, what needs no defense, theses taken as uncontroversial starting points—can, often enough, be wholly optional. And sometimes, when you appreciate their origins, when you come to see why they were originally propounded, their obviousness recedes, their attractiveness wanes.

2   APPARENT CONTINGENCY

One approach to the question 'Why is there anything at all?' sets out to establish that the existence of the universe is not after all contingent: the universe exists 'of necessity'; the universe could not have failed to exist. Such a thesis is widely regarded as in need of a serious metaphysically weighty defense. I have suggested that the question flows from particular ways of thinking about the universe, ways that are at bottom optional. I shall presently suggest an alternative way of thinking about the status of the universe, the status of being, the status of reality itself, that, while yielding other questions, does not obviously yield this one.

One reason the thesis that the universe exists of necessity is thought to require serious defense is its invocation of *necessity*. The guiding idea is that it is reasonable to suppose that the existence of the universe is contingent *unless* there are compelling reasons to think otherwise.[4] Indeed, *any* truth about the world is to be presumed contingent in the absence of such reasons.

Here I follow Charlie Martin's principle quoted at the outset: contingencies, no less than necessities, must earn their keep. Thus

---

4. One prominent source of the thought that the universe is contingent stems from a conception of God's omnipotence. God is not bound by natural necessities. God created the universe voluntarily, could have refrained from creating the universe, and could have created endless other universes. In this regard, the Bishop of Paris's Condemnations of 1277 is a modal watershed. See Grant 1981: 108–10.

(C) It is no good *assuming* that p is contingent in cases in which p's being contingent functions as a substantive premise in an argument.

Where p is a substantive thesis that serves as a premise, the claim that p is contingent and the claim that p is not contingent are on all fours.[5]
Many would disagree. Consider Timothy O'Connor's comment on Einstein's 'Spinozistic' contention that the universe exists necessarily.

> We could . . . try to follow Einstein and his hero Spinoza in thinking that, appearances to the contrary, the universe itself is a self-contained wholly necessary being, down to the last, most contingent-seeming fact. (As Spinoza would say, the appearance of contingency here is a result of our ignorance of the totality of causes.) (O'Connor, this volume: 32)

O'Connor speaks of 'the appearance of contingency'. But what is it to 'appear contingent'? What does contingency look like?
The pre-Copernican belief that the Sun revolves around the Earth is sometimes explained by pointing out that this is how it *appears* to terrestrial observers. The Sun appears to be moving across the sky, rising and setting, so the belief is perfectly natural. But ask yourself, how would the Earth's rotating toward and orbiting the Sun appear?[6] Just as it does. In the same way, were Spinoza right, were all the worldly truths absolutely necessary, everything would appear just as it does now. How could appearances provide any sort of indication of contingency?

3   ALTERNATIVE WORLDS

Loose talk of 'possible worlds' has done much to facilitate the easy thought that contingencies come for free. If you start with the idea that ours is merely one among myriad alternative worlds, then every feature of the world we happen to occupy that differs from a feature of at least one other world is contingent. At the same time, it seems incredible to regard the existence of genuine alternative worlds as a presumption that needs no defense. Suppose, however, that you thought, as many philosophers do think, that alternative worlds were *merely* possible, that alternative worlds are *abstracta*, sets of propositions, for instance. In that case the assertion that such worlds *are*

---

5. Roy Sorensen has reminded me that Martin's principle itself includes a commitment to 'modal fallibilism'. The principle assumes that modal truths have mind-independent truthmakers concerning which we could be wrong. I do not know how to discuss the issue at hand—the why-is-there-anything question—without making this assumption.
6. G.E.M. Anscombe (1959: 151) attributes the question to Wittgenstein.

possible amounts to little more than the assertion that the actual world, the actual universe, is contingent.

The trouble is, nowadays talk of possible worlds trips off the tongue and elicits no controversy. What trips off the tongue can easily escape scrutiny. Frank Jackson speaks for many in proclaiming that 'possible-worlds methodology has more than paid its dues' (1998: 11). This makes it sound as though appeals to possible worlds are not only philosophically upstanding, but that, in putting the worlds to work, we philosophers are actually *indebted* to them.

I see it differently. The introduction of possible worlds into the philosophical landscape undoubtedly facilitated solutions to problems that had long resisted solution. My sense, however, is that, overall, the impact of the deployment of possible worlds has been a disaster for the philosophical ecosystem comparable to the aftermath of the introduction of cane toads in Queensland.[7] The idea that the invocation of possible worlds is philosophically innocent lacks credibility. At the very least, appeals to possible worlds that serve as bases for metaphysical theses about the actual universe stand in need of defense.

Let me note in passing that Lewis himself, who was admirably candid ontologically, took alternative worlds to be fully 'concrete', no less real, and in that regard no less *actual*, than the universe we inhabit. Even so, Lewis accepted the idea that truthmakers for modal claims, claims invoking those other worlds, were to be found in our world, the universe as it is.[8] When a philosopher resorts to talk of possible worlds to support a claim about what is or might be the case, it is worth asking what feature of the universe as we have it might make the claim true. The danger is that easy talk of possible worlds screens us off from serious ontology.

In the interest of tribal harmony, however, I propose to step down from my high horse, relax, take a deep breath, and, at least for the moment, go with the flow of possible worlds.

So pretend that our world is just one among many alternative worlds. Now, the question 'Why is there anything at all?' might be thought to be representable as the question 'Why does some one of these worlds exist?'

What are the options? We have all of the alternative worlds, W_1, W_2, W_3, . . ., W_n. What could it be for *none* of the alternatives to exist? The

---

7. An exaggeration. Given the depressed standing of academic philosophy in the world at large, cane toads have proved vastly more environmentally and economically devastating than alternative worlds, which have, at worst, corrupted the youth in ways unlikely to lead to widespread social or psychological damage.

8. See Heil 2012: ch. 5. Lewis (1986: 22) puts it this way in discussing counterfactual truths: 'it is the character of our world that makes the counterfactual true . . . the other worlds provide a frame of reference whereby we can characterize our world'.

alternatives are, by design, exclusive and exhaustive. This suggests that nothing is not an option.

I think this is right, but I am in the minority here.[9] Many philosophers follow Peter van Inwagen (1996) in depicting the 'nothing at all' option as an 'empty' world. Consider the array of worlds in Figure 10.1. Let the actual world be W_1, and let W_3 be the 'empty' world.[10]

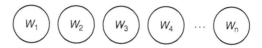

Figure 10.1

But what is W_3? W_3 is said to be empty. But an empty world is not a world with nothing in it. It is nothing at all. The 'empty' world is not a world that would cease to be empty were something *added* to it. The empty world is not a shell, a container with nothing inside it.[11] The empty world is not an *it*. Figure 10.2 provides a better representation of the situation. Nothingness, conceived of as the 'empty' world, is not one option, one world among others; it is not an option at all. The only possibilities are somethings.

Figure 10.2

I do not want to dwell on this line of argument because I regard the apparatus of possible worlds as metaphysically pernicious. I realize that few readers will share this assessment. And some of those will point to the empty set as providing a respectable model of the empty world. The empty set is the set with no members, the set with nothing in it. We 'quantify over' the empty set. The empty set has paid its dues. Perhaps the empty world is like this.

Sets are not objects alongside electrons, trees, and minds, however; sets are not somethings, and sets are not models of somethings, although, the empty set aside, their members can be: the empty set is not a something but not a nothing either. I side with E.J. Lowe in his discussion of the empty set in this volume (see also Lowe 1996). Elsewhere (Heil 2012: ch. 8) I have discussed in some detail Quine's criterion of 'ontological commitment', the idea that we are committed to the existence of whatever we ineliminably 'quantify over' in our best theories. My suggestion there is that Quine's

---

9. As was Lewis. See Lewis 1986: 73.
10. Discussion of the 'empty' world resembles medieval discussions of the vacuum, the infinite void presumed to surround the finite created world: is it a nothing or a something with nothing in it?
11. For extensive discussion of this topic, see Coggins 2003, 2010.

criterion is best understood as providing us with an inventory of *truths* to which we are 'committed'. This leaves open the nature of truthmakers for those truths. It leaves open, as well, whether a given truth requires a truthmaker.

We 'quantify over' numbers and sets. There is no prospect of 'paraphrasing away' talk of such things. It does not follow, however, that truthmakers for statements about numbers and sets are numbers and sets.

Some readers will object. Sets, numbers, and the like *are* objects, *abstract* objects. Abstract objects are special somethings.

I doubt that anyone has a very clear idea what an abstract object of the sort envisioned might be. As far as I can tell, contemporary thoughts of *abstracta* are the result of embracing Quine's criterion as an ontological arbiter: if you quantify over the empty set or the real numbers, there must be entities answering to predicates used to express truths concerning such things. And if these entities seem not to be 'concrete', seem not to be mutable occupants of space–time, they must be *non*concrete, shadowy items residing perhaps in an incorruptible Platonic realm.

All this takes us into turbulent philosophical waters, waters made turbulent by philosophers sparring with philosophers. As you can probably sense, my reservations about the empty world and the empty set do not stem from nuanced linguistic or metaphysical considerations, however. They stem from the conviction that sets are not self-standing entities alongside electrons, trees, and minds, not truthmakers for claims about sets, and that the empty set and the empty world are not empty somethings, containers of nonbeing. No argument, just a conviction. Acceptance of numbers and sets as fully fledged citizens of the universe does not come for free, however, and it certainly does not follow from the fact that we cannot but quantify over such things.[12]

4 THE NOTHING OPTION

Return to the question posed at the outset. When you ask, 'Why is there something rather than nothing?' what are the envisioned options: something and nothing? Well, there is the specific something we inhabit, the universe as a whole. So, why, you might ask, does the universe exist, rather than nothing at all?

Now the hard part. What exactly is *nothing at all*? What would nothing *be*? In what sense is nothing an alternative to something?

---

12. Thus I reject Peter van Inwagen's (1996) conception of the empty world as a world harboring only *abstracta*: propositions, numbers, sets, universals. In my view, *abstracta* are not eternal incorruptible entities unsullied by contact with lesser beings, but *concreta* considered without respect to their spatio-temporal natures. See Lowe 1996 and this volume, and Heil 2012: ch. 5.

In this context it would be a cheat to imagine God deciding whether to create something, a universe. God is a something. It is not as though, prior to creation, you have God plus nothing. You just have God. Now, take God out of the picture and try to imagine the nothing option. This is none too easy.

Some will see no particular difficulty: nothing is just nonbeing, the absence of being; *what's the big deal?* If you think that is the end of the story, I doubt that you will be much moved by what I have to say here. I remain convinced that our grasp of the idea of nothing is tenuous at best. You might try to get at nothing by imagining a universe with only a handful of objects, electrons, say, then subtracting these one at a time until no electron remains (Baldwin 1996). But the electrons are located somewhere in space. Their subtraction yields, not nothing, but empty space, a space empty of objects.

My guess is that most of us, in imagining nothingness, are imagining empty space. But a space, empty or not, is a something. It has, let us suppose, three dimensions; its regions are distinct. Physics tells us that empty space is substance-like; empty space has energy; empty space is 'unstable', forever finding ways to be nonempty (see Krauss 2012). Medievals endowed 'void space' with powers. How a body would behave in the void was a matter of controversy, but some medievals assumed that the void was not homogeneous (Grant 1981: 49–57). God could create a void by miraculously annihilating matter occupying the region between the earth and the lunar sphere. But the void would retain local characteristics of fire, air, water, and earth. Bodies moving about in the void would behave differently depending on where in the void they happened to be.

It is hard not to think of the void as extended spatially, hard not to think of it as a three-dimensional container unpopulated by bodies, hard not to think of the void as empty space. The void, so conceived, is a something, not a nothing. It is much harder to think of the absence of everything *including* the void. Start with a conception of a universe consisting solely of empty space, the empty universe. Now subtract the empty space. Is this something God could do? If space is a substance or is substance-like, why not? But now God, a manifest something, is back in the picture.[13]

I do not mean to suggest that space itself could not have arisen from something else during the Big Bang. I take this to be a serious option. But a precursor of the Big Bang is a something.

It is much harder to understand the nothing option than you might have thought. Everyday nothings, holes, for instance, require somethings to exist. A pothole in the highway requires the highway; an empty ballroom requires a ballroom. I find it hard not to think that the question 'Why is there anything?' or 'Why is there something rather than nothing?' makes sense only when the nothing in question is really a something: empty space, the void, the precursor

---

13. Might space annihilate itself spontaneously? I do not know. That depends on the nature of space, an empirical matter. Even if spontaneous annihilation were possible, it is a further empirical question whether it would leave a residue.

to the Big Bang. Thus understood, the question admits of an answer, although perhaps one we are barred from discovering owing to a lack of access to the pre–Big-Bang state of play. If, in contrast, nothing is understood as the absolute absence of being, the question cannot so much as be addressed.

5   WHY THE UNIVERSE?

Discussion of the possibility of an 'empty' world, a universe with nothing 'in' it, arose in response to the question 'Why is there anything?' But there are two other closely related questions, 'Why the universe?' and 'Why the universe as we find it?'

If you start with the apparatus of possible worlds, you will see this as a significant question, one that calls for explanation. There are all those worlds, W_1, W_2, W_3, . . ., W_n. Why do we have W_1, the actual world, the universe as we find it, rather than any of the others? This question persists even if the empty world is taken off the table.

Physics sometimes seems to tell us that the laws could have been other than they are, that the laws could vary across possible universes. Let that be so. Now ask yourself, what *grounds* the laws, what is responsible for natural laws in any universe? Could the laws be anything at all? Talk of alternative worlds makes this a trivial question. What could be easier than letting laws vary ad lib across worlds.[14]

But why credit ourselves with this God-like power? Why imagine that the idea that the laws could vary requires no defense? The fact, if it is a fact, that the laws would have been different, had things been different at the Big Bang, does not imply that the laws could have been anything at all. But if there are constraints, even very weak ones, on the possible laws, this suggests that reality itself, *being*, has a 'texture', a 'grain' (see O'Connor, this volume: 33).

Consider two possibilities.

(a) Our universe could not fail to have existed.
(b) A universe *resembling* ours (in its fundamental laws and general characteristics) could not fail to have existed.

If you accept (a), if ours is the only possible universe, then the existence of the universe as it is would call for no further explanation.

What of (b)? One way to understand (b) is to imagine that the Big Bang resulted from a spontaneous, perfectly random fluctuation in the vacuum,

---

14. 'Grounding' has recently replaced 'supervenience' as the weasel word of choice in metaphysics. By 'grounding' here I mean truthmaking. The question 'What grounds the laws?' is just the question 'What makes formulations of laws true?'

or the quantum field, or something. Were that so, there could be no explanation as to why *this* fluctuation occurred rather than some other, just as there is no explanation as to why a particular radium atom decayed *now* rather than at some earlier or later time. A universe quite like ours (in its fundamental laws and general characteristics) could, it seems, have existed as the result of a distinct fluctuation: a zygotic principle for universes.

I should say that by 'fundamental laws' here I mean the *really* fundamental laws, those constraining the range of possibilities for all the rest. You might doubt that there are such laws, but this amounts to denying that anything, literally *anything*, could have sprung from the Big Bang, *our* Big Bang. And that strikes me as something few cosmologists would be willing to countenance.

If the Big Bang resulted from a fluctuation, spontaneous or not, there must have been something to fluctuate. Nothing could not fluctuate; nothing could not be pregnant with being. This is not to say that the fluctuating something must have been something resembling the universe or any occupant of the universe as we find it. I prefer to think of a fluctuation as the onset of a mode of some substance, a dynamic way some substance is, but the nature of the substance is entirely open. It might not be thing-like at all; it might be a field; it might be space itself, or space–time, or some precursor of space–time.

6   A CONTINGENT UNIVERSE

I have suggested that it is important to distinguish three questions.

(1) Why does *a* universe exist?
(2) Why does *this* universe exist?
(3) Why is the universe as it is?

Question (1) is the question to which this volume is addressed. Taking the question seriously requires accepting that there might have been nothing at all, the empty possibility. It is one thing to ask why reality is as it is but another matter entirely to ask why there is being, why there is reality.

If, as seems distinctly possible, the universe resulted from a spontaneous event, a random fluctuation, then reality's being as it is would be no guarantee that any particular Big Bang occurs, no guarantee that any particular post–Big Bang universe exists. Nevertheless, reality, being itself, would subsist, embodying whatever it takes to give birth to a universe.

If the Big Bang was spontaneous, then, as noted already, there is no reason why *this* universe exists—question (2)—at least not if a distinct Big Bang would have resulted in a distinct universe. If the Big Bang was not spontaneous, this might be because it issued from the internal demands of being itself or because it was induced from the outside, by a Creator. If you regard an internally occasioned Big Bang as in need of further explanation, however, it is hard to see why an appeal to a Creator would not itself call for an explanation.[15] If the question is settled because it is of the nature of the Creator to induce the Big Bang, then why wouldn't it be settled by supposing that the Big Bang stemmed from the nature of being itself?

Is it crazy to think that the Big Bang was either a spontaneous product of being analogous to the decay of a radium atom or an unfolding of the nature of being comparable to the growth of a crystal? I do not see why. I do not see why the idea that reality itself has a texture is even especially controversial. What is, or ought to be, controversial is the idea that there are *no* constraints on the kinds of universe a Big Bang could yield.

Whether there is an answer to question (2) depends in part on whether the Big Bang, the apparent source of the universe as we find it, was or was not spontaneous. If it was spontaneous, there is no answer (for familiar reasons). If it was not spontaneous, then there is an answer, although we might never be in a position to work it out (again, for familiar reasons).

What of question (3)? If the question concerns only the most general features of the universe, then the answer lies in the fundamental laws. (As before, I mean by this the *really* fundamental laws, laws expressing the nature of being.) These laws stem from the character of reality itself, what I have called reality's texture. It is an open question whether the universe could have had different nonfundamental laws, but reality itself is what it is.

Where does this leave contingency? If, as physics now seems to tell us, there are genuinely spontaneous events in the universe, uncaused causes. The existence, indeed the ubiquity, of spontaneous occurrences guarantees an element of contingency even in an otherwise deterministic universe.

Suppose you thought of the universe as a dispositional matrix—a three-dimensional network, not a one-dimensional chain—in which everything is connected in some way to everything else. The overall shape of the network would be determined by the Big Bang. Were the Big Bang spontaneous, the network would be contingent. But given the network, everything within it is as it is of necessity.

Now keep the picture of a dispositional matrix or causal network, but infuse it with genuinely spontaneous occurrences. I have in mind the kinds of spontaneous occurrence that we seem to find in contemporary physical theory. If you mix such occurrences into an otherwise deterministic system, the result is a proliferation of contingency. The resulting contingency, however, is not something calling for explanation: contingency is rooted in spontaneity—and genuine spontaneity, spontaneity of the no-hidden-variable variety, forecloses explanation.

---

15. Medieval discussions of creation vacillated between two poles: creation as an expression of God's nature, and creation as an expression of God's unconstrained free choice. See Kretzmann 1991 for discussion.

7 LAWMAKERS

Earlier I evinced skepticism about laws conceived of as external constraints on occupants of the universe. What are the options? One possibility is that laws are 'built into' the universe's occupants. The particles, the fields, incorporate powers that determine how they behave or would behave. Are the powers laws?

Maybe laws are what the physicists seem to say they are: formulae, equations, principles. Maybe these, or some of these, the causal laws, in effect provide an accounting of the contribution of the various powers. Newton's laws of motion might, for instance, be thought to single out the contribution that mass makes to the behavior of whatever has mass.

So regarded, laws would not, as is sometimes contended, aim at telling us how an ideal body would behave under ideal circumstances. Why should anyone care? Laws would tell us how a body would behave qua massy. Bodies have other properties, other powers that, in concert with powers present in neighboring bodies and fields, and perhaps even in space or space–time itself, would affect their behavior as well. Sometimes, for some purposes, these other powers can be safely 'factored out', reasonably ignored. Still, how any particular body behaves depends on its total compliment of powers in concert with its circumstances. These circumstances comprise reciprocal powers inherent in items with which the body interacts.

Are the laws true of necessity? Particular powers might be thought to contribute of necessity as they do to the behavior of their possessors. A power *is* a power to manifest itself in particular ways with particular kinds of reciprocal manifestation partners. But what are powers? In what do powers reside? The short answer is that properties are powers but not *purely* powers; properties are *powerful qualities*.[16] Properties are particular ways substances are. *What* the substances and properties are is a matter of empirical discovery.

One question is whether the universe could have lacked bodies (or fields, or whatever, a qualification I shall assume without further explicit mention) possessing these powers or could have included bodies possessing different, 'alien' powers. The answer to that question is to be found in the nature of the fundamental laws, the texture of reality, the nature of being. Although it seems crazy to think that reality places no constraints whatever on the universe, if reality is such that the Big Bang could have been different in a way that yielded different kinds of fields and different kinds of particles, then there is an important sense in which laws governing the behavior of denizens of the universe could have been other than they are. The laws could have been other than they are because the denizens might have been

---

16. The idea that properties are powerful qualities is not new. In recent years, it has been most ardently defended by C.B. Martin. See Martin 2008; and see Heil 2003, 2012 for an extended discussion.

other than *they* are. And the question whether the denizens might have been other than they are is an empirical question, not something that could be worked out a priori by philosophers reflecting on goings-on in alternative worlds.

Why does the universe have the character it has rather than some other character? If the Big Bang is spontaneous and if Big Bangs yielding different kinds of particles and fields could have occurred, then the most you could hope for by way of an answer to this question would be provided by an accounting of the texture of reality. If the Big Bang issued nonspontaneously from the nature of being, if the Big Bang *channeled* the texture of reality, then there is a more definite answer to the question, although perhaps one forever beyond our reach. In that case it would be appropriate to regard the universe as originating from a truly transcendent being.

8   NOTHING FROM SOMETHING

Any discussion of the question 'Why is there something rather than nothing?' must begin with the fact that there is something: the universe exists. The question whether the universe might have failed to exist assumes that the universe's existence is contingent. What prompts that thought?

If the universe's existence is contingent, what are the alternatives? One alternative, a preexisting something that gives birth to the universe (but might have failed to do so), is beside the point. A preexisting something is a something. The pertinent alternative is nothing, nothing at all. But given that there is something, could there have been nothing instead? I do not see how. Thoughts of nothing require subtracting something. But starting with something and then subtracting introduces an irksome dependence of nothing on something, not the result you might have hoped to find.

If there is something there could not have been nothing.

This has the ring of a dramatic pronouncement. Why believe it? Begin with the thought that 'nothing comes from nothing': nothing lacks the resources to issue in something.[17] Had there been nothing, it would not have been possible for there to be something. Given that there is something, there could not have been nothing. No drama.

Might something have spontaneously popped into existence? Spontaneity requires something to be spontaneous. Even the idea that God could create material bodies ex nihilo starts with God.

Why is there something rather than nothing? Because there is no other option.[18]

17. Incidentally, neither can something become nothing. Crudely, there is no place to which something might retire.
18. This paper benefited from discussion with E.J. Lowe, Tyron Goldschmidt, Roy Sorensen, Harrison Hagan Heil, David Robb, Justin Clarke-Doane, Aubrey Townsend, and John Bigelow.

REFERENCES

Anscombe, G.E.M. (1959). *An Introduction to Wittgenstein's Tractatus*. London: Hutchinson.

Armstrong, D.M. (1997). *A World of States of Affairs*. Cambridge: Cambridge University Press.

Baldwin, T. (1996). 'There Might Be Nothing', *Analysis* 56: 231–8.

Cartwright, N. (1983). *How the Laws of Physics Lie*. Oxford: Clarendon Press.

——. (1999). *The Dappled World: A Study of the Boundaries of Science*. Cambridge: Cambridge University Press.

Coggins, G. (2003). 'World and Object: Metaphysical Nihilism and Three Accounts of Worlds', *Proceedings of the Aristotelian Society* 103: 353–60.

——. (2010). *Could There Have Been Nothing? Against Metaphysical Nihilism*. Basingstoke, UK: Palgrave Macmillan.

Des Chene, D. (forthcoming). 'Natural Laws and Divine Agency in the Later Seventeenth Century'.

Grant, E. (ed.). (1974). *A Sourcebook in Medieval Science*. Cambridge, MA: Harvard University Press.

——. (1981). *Much Ado About Nothing: Theories of Space and Vacuum From the Middle Ages to the Scientific Revolution*. Cambridge: Cambridge University Press.

Heil, J. (2003). *From an Ontological Point of View*. Oxford: Clarendon Press.

——. (2012). *The World as We Find It*. Oxford: Clarendon Press.

Jackson, F.C. (1998). *From Metaphysics to Ethics*. Oxford: Clarendon Press.

King, P. (2007). 'Why Isn't the Mind-Body Problem Medieval?', in Lagerlund, H. (ed.). *Forming the Mind: Essays on the Internal Senses and the Mind–Body Problem From Avicenna to the Medical Enlightenment*. Dordrecht, the Netherlands: Springer, 187–205.

Krauss, L.M. (2012). *A Universe From Nothing: Why There Is Something Rather Than Nothing*. New York: Free Press.

Kretzmann, N. (1991). 'A General Problem of Creation: Why Would God Create Anything at All?', in Macdonald, S. (ed.). *Being and Goodness: The Concept of the Good in Metaphysics and Philosophical Theology*. Ithaca, NY: Cornell University Press, 208–28.

Lange, M. (2009). *Laws and Lawmakers: Science, Metaphysics, and the Laws of Nature*. Oxford: Oxford University Press.

Lewis, D.K. (1986). *On the Plurality of Worlds*. Oxford: Basil Blackwell.

Lowe, E.J. (1996). 'Why Is There Anything At All?', *Proceedings of the Aristotelian Society*, Supplementary Volume 70: 111–20.

Martin, C.B. (2008). *The Mind in Nature*. Oxford: Clarendon Press.

Matson, W.I. (1966). 'Why Isn't the Mind–Body Problem Ancient', in Feyerabend, P.K. and Maxwell, G. (eds.). *Mind, Matter, and Method: Essays in Philosophy of Science in Honor of Herbert Feigl*. Minneapolis: University of Minnesota Press, 92–102.

Milton, J.R. (1998). 'Laws of Nature', in Garber, D. and Ayres, M. (eds.). *The Cambridge History of Seventeenth-Century Philosophy*. Cambridge: Cambridge University Press, 680–701.

Van Inwagen, P. (1996). 'Why Is There Anything at All?', *Proceedings of the Aristotelian Society*, Supplementary Volume 70: 95–110.

11 Metaphysical Nihilism Revisited

E.J. Lowe

Let us remind ourselves how the recent debate about metaphysical nihilism began. It began in 1996 with a paper by Peter van Inwagen concerning the question 'Why is there anything at all?'[1] He made it clear that his concern was with whether there might have been *no concrete objects*—that is, in the language of possible worlds, with whether there is an 'empty' world, in which no concrete objects exist. He was not concerned with whether there is a world in which no objects *at all*, either concrete or abstract, exist. In his opinion, there is an 'empty' world in this sense, but only *one* such world, from which—in conjunction with some other assumptions—he concludes that the probability of there being 'nothing at all' (in his sense) is zero. The other assumptions are that there are infinitely many possible worlds and that all of them are equiprobable.[2] In the course of his discussion of this issue, van Inwagen remarked that he could not see any way of arguing for the *impossibility* of there being 'nothing at all' other than by arguing for the existence of a necessary concrete being, such as God—and he does not consider that such an argument can be sustained, for reasons that he explains in the paper.

In my reply to van Inwagen's paper, I tried to advance an argument of a different sort for the conclusion that there is no 'empty' possible world.[3] Roughly, the idea was this. Some *abstract* objects exist necessarily, and so exist in every possible world. But all abstract objects *depend on* there being concrete objects—although not necessarily *the same* concrete objects in every possible world. Hence, concrete objects exist in every possible

I am grateful for comments received when an earlier version of this paper was presented at a Modality Workshop at the University of St Andrews in December 2005.

1. See van Inwagen 1996.
2. More accurately, van Inwagen's argument has the following four premises: (1) There are some beings; (2) if there is more than one possible world, there are infinitely many; (3) there is at most one possible world in which there are no beings; and (4) for any two possible worlds, the probability of their being actual is equal. See van Inwagen 1996: 99. By a 'being' he says that he means a concrete object, though he makes no attempt to define 'concrete': see p. 95.
3. See Lowe 1996. I refined the argument somewhat in Lowe 1998: 252–5.

world, even if there is no necessary concrete being. As putative examples of necessarily existent abstract objects, I cited the natural numbers. And in defence of the dependence thesis I appealed to a broadly Aristotelian conception of ontology.

Filling this out a little, my argument went roughly as follows. Arithmetical truths are truths about numbers, and they are also, very plausibly, *necessary* truths. Hence, the numbers that they are about must exist in every possible world. Consider, then, a world in which the numbers exist. What objects must exist in such a world? Well, obviously, the numbers themselves must. But what are they? Some would say that they are sui generis abstract objects. But that is not the most plausible, and certainly not the most popular, view to take of them. Some say that numbers are *sets*; others that they are *universals*. At the time at which I was writing, I myself took numbers to be universals whose particular instances are sets of appropriate cardinality.[4] Anyway, on any of these latter views, a world in which numbers exist must be a world in which either sets or universals or both exist. Perhaps, indeed, it could be a world in which the *only* abstract objects are sets and universals. That is perhaps the most economical hypothesis, so let us assume it. The question then is this: could this world be one in which *no other objects at all* exist, and hence one in which no *concrete* objects exist—in other words, could it be the 'empty' world, in van Inwagen's sense? I argued *not*, for the following reason. In a world in which there were, supposedly, only sets and universals, the sets would depend for their existence on the universals, and the universals would depend for their existence on the sets, generating a vicious circle which would deprive both sets and universals of the possibility of existing in that world. Here I was appealing to two 'Aristotelian' intuitions: that sets depend for their existence, and indeed for their *identity*, on their members, while universals depend for their existence, though *not* for their identity, on their instances. (I call the latter species of dependence *generic* existential dependence.) My conclusion was that there must, indeed, exist some concrete objects in any world in which the numbers exist, and hence in every possible world. I should add that by a 'concrete object', in this context, I mean one that exists *in space and time*—or at the very least *in time*.[5] However, it was crucial to my argument that I deny the existence of *the empty set* and hence the existence of so-called pure sets (sets which have *only other sets* in their transitive closure). In effect, this means that I had to deny the existence of the number zero.

What I offered at that time was, really, only a sketch of an argument, or rather of a *kind* of argument—an argument of a kind that van Inwagen said he was unable to envisage. My aim then was not so much to provide a watertight argument of this kind as to open up the prospect for developing

---

4. I had defended this view earlier, in Lowe 1993.
5. For discussion and a defence of this conception of concreteness, see further Lowe 1995 or Lowe 1998: ch. 10.

such an argument. Unsurprisingly, the particular argument that I did offer has come under attack from various quarters, first of all from Tom Baldwin, who objected to my rejection of the empty set.[6] His complaint was that I couldn't appeal to the standard conception of arithmetic as a body of necessary truths concerning the natural numbers while also rejecting a central element of that conception, namely, the existence of the number zero. Baldwin himself, of course, at the same time advanced a very interesting argument in favour of the existence of the 'empty' world—his 'subtraction' argument. Very roughly, it proceeds as follows. Surely, there is a possible world in which only finitely many—say, n—concrete objects exist, each one of which exists independently of the others. So, surely, it is true in that world that *one* of those objects could have failed to exist, leaving only the others. Iterating this inference $(n - 1)$ times, we arrive at a world in which just one of the original objects remains, which can then be 'removed' by one more step, to leave us with the 'empty' world. Baldwin's argument has been closely scrutinized by several critics and subjected to various objections and supposed improvements.[7] But my own view is that it is really question-begging and persuades, if at all, only by sleight of hand. For, surely, if one of the key premises is that there is a possible world in which only finitely many concrete objects exist, why start with a world in which *more than one* such object exists—why not start with a world in which *only one* such object exists, since 1 is as good an example of a finite number as any other? But if we do start with such a world and then assert that we can 'remove' that one concrete object without needing to suppose that any other concrete object exists in place of it, we are in effect assuming precisely what we sought to prove, namely, that there could be *no* concrete objects. We were softened up by the earlier stepwise 'removals' of objects into supposing that this final 'removal' was just like the rest—but it isn't, in the very respect that is crucial to the argument. For the previous steps are just steps between worlds in which concrete objects exist, whereas the last is a step from such a world to one in which no concrete objects exist.

I shall say no more here concerning the subtraction argument. As for my own argument against metaphysical nihilism—the doctrine that there is an 'empty' possible world—I have tried to refine it in the light of objections raised by Gonzalo Rodriguez-Pereyra.[8] I have also tried to explain more fully why I deny the existence of the empty set.[9] Very understandably, Rodriguez-Pereyra and other critics have, in order to focus their objections, attempted to lay out my argument in the form of an explicit set of premises and an explicit conclusion. The way that Rodriguez-Pereyra does it is as follows:

---

6. See Baldwin 1996.
7. See, especially, Rodriguez-Pereyra 1997, 2002; Paseau 2002; Efird and Stoneham 2005; and Cameron 2006.
8. See Rodriguez-Pereyra 2000 and Lowe 2002.
9. See, for example, Lowe 2003.

(RP1) Some abstract objects, like natural numbers, exist necessarily.

(RP2) Abstract objects depend for their existence on there being concrete entities.

Therefore,

(RP3) It is necessary that there are concrete entities. (2000: 335)

More recently, Ross Cameron has done it in this way:

(RC1) There are necessary truths the truth of which requires the existence of certain abstract objects.

(RC2) Necessarily there are abstract objects. (From [RC1])

(RC3) Necessarily, there are abstract objects only if there are concrete objects.

(RC4) Necessarily there are concrete objects. (From [RC2] and [RC3]) (2006: 209)

Yet another attempted formulation, by David Efird and Tom Stoneham, is the following (this time, no conclusion is explicitly stated, but it seems that we are supposed to take it to be 'Metaphysical nihilism is false'):

(ES1) The only abstract objects are sets and universals.

(ES2) Abstract objects exist necessarily.

(ES3) The empty set is impossible.

(ES4) It is possible that Fs are generically existentially dependent on Gs while Gs are identity dependent on Fs just in case the Fs have ontological priority over the Gs. (2005: 318)

I have no complaint about Rodriguez-Pereyra's and Cameron's formulations, as far as they go. Against Efird and Stoneham's I would certainly object that I nowhere affirm (ES2) but only that *some* abstract objects exist necessarily: indeed, I expressly affirm that *some* abstract objects are only contingent entities, such as sets all of whose members are contingent entities.[10] However, a more general difficulty is that some of these formulations include as 'premises' of my anti-nihilistic argument claims which I make in the course of *defending* those premises. I myself have nowhere attempted to set out in a list all of the claims to which I appeal in coming to my anti-nihilist conclusion, much less to formalize or even to *semi*-formalize my argument. It was, after all, only intended to be a sketch of an argumentative *strategy*.

But all of this is water under the bridge. Although I still think that my strategy is basically sound, I have changed my mind about some important issues relating to my previous defences of it. First of all, I am no longer inclined to think that numbers are abstract objects. This is not because I now think that they are concrete objects or that the abstract–concrete distinction

---

10. See Lowe 1996: 115.

is not exhaustive. Rather, it is because I am no longer inclined to think that numbers *exist*. I now consider that the concept of number is a purely *formal* concept, alongside those of *existence* and *identity*.[11] Just as I do not consider that existence is a *property*—whether one takes properties to be universals or 'tropes'—and do not consider that identity is a *relation*, so I do not consider that numbers are *objects*. They are not what I call 'elements of being'—that is, entities that belong to one or another of the fundamental ontological categories, as all entities must do. My own (broadly 'Aristotelian') view concerning these fundamental categories is that there are *four* of them—two categories of particulars and two categories of universals, to wit: (1) particular objects ('individual substances'), (2) particular properties and relations ('modes'), (3) the universals of which particular objects are instances ('substantial kinds'), and (4) the universals of which particular properties and relations are instances ('attributes'). The details need not concern us here.[12] The key thought for present purposes is that there are certain *formal ontological predicates*, such as 'is an object', 'exists', and 'is identical with', which do not denote items belonging to one or another of the fundamental ontological categories and hence do not denote *entities* that either do or could exist. Of course, *objects* exist and are entities, belonging to my first category. When I say that 'is an object' does not denote any entity, I am contrasting it with, for example, 'is square', which denotes a certain *universal*. In other words, I am saying that 'is an object' does not apply to an entity in virtue of some special *property* that the object has, the putative property of *being an object*—for there is no such property.

But how does all of this relate to talk about numbers? Well, consider a simple arithmetical truth such as 2 + 3 = 5. Previously, I considered that this was made true by a relation between numbers—the numbers 2, 3, and 5, which I took to be universals in my third category, having sets of appropriate cardinality as their particular instances. But I no longer think that there are such numerical universals. I took a two-membered set, such as the set of Mars's moons, {Phobos, Deimos}, to be an *instance* of two, very much as Mars itself is an instance of the substantial kind *planet*. I no longer believe this. I don't think that, in order to understand how such an arithmetical truth can be true, we need to suppose that 'two' denotes a *universal* of which all two-membered sets are instances. Rather, the arithmetical truth is grounded in the essence of any object, in virtue of the essential *unity* of objects. Any object is essentially *one*—a unit of its kind—and consequently any *plurality* of objects essentially has a cardinality: it is essentially two, or three, or four, or whatever.[13] And disjoint pluralities of two and three are, collectively, essentially five. The arithmetical truth that 2 + 3 = 5 is, thus, simply grounded in the essential unity of any actual or possible object. No further ontological

---

11. See further Lowe 2006: 83.
12. A full account appears in Lowe 2006.
13. See further Lowe 2003.

ground of its truth, in the shape of additional entities of any kind, is needed. Here it is crucial to recognize that essences, including the essences of objects, are not themselves further entities of any kind. An entity's essence is, in Locke's very apt phrase, 'the very being of any thing, whereby it is, what it is' (1975: III, III, 15). But the 'very being' of anything—its *identity*—is not some *further* entity.[14] As a consequence, arithmetical truths can be necessary truths—can be true in every possible world—even if there is a world in which *no objects at all* exist. For even in such a world these truths remain grounded in the essential unity of any *possible* object. Arithmetical truths, hence, are truths without truthmakers, if by 'truthmakers' we always mean existing *entities* of some sort.

However, none of this is really at all damaging to my original line of argument in response to van Inwagen. For recall that what van Inwagen was debating was whether or not there is an 'empty' world in which there exist no *concrete* objects but abstract objects *do* exist. To rebut this suggestion, one need show only that there cannot be a world containing *only* abstract objects. One does *not* have to show, however, that certain abstract objects, such as (supposedly) the numbers, exist in every possible world. So the fact that I no longer believe that numbers are such objects does not undermine my overall strategy for arguing against metaphysical nihilism. In other words, in the various formulations of my argument by its critics, the premises appealing to the necessity of arithmetical truths and the existence of some necessary abstract objects are really superfluous to requirements. These are premises (RP1), (RC1) and (RC2), and (ES2).

My strategy does still depend, however, on providing some sort of inventory of what abstract entities there are or could be. Originally, I proposed that all such entities are either universals or sets, the latter conceived as belonging to the category of particular objects. And this does fit in with the views of many of those metaphysicians who acknowledge the existence of abstract entities at all. As mentioned earlier, those of them who believe in numbers generally regard numbers as being either universals or sets. As for *propositions*—perhaps the other most important candidate for inclusion in the domain of abstract entities—these are again often regarded as being sets (for example, sets of possible worlds) or as being universals (for example, properties of possible worlds).[15] Alternatively, they may be regarded as being wholly composed or constituted in some ('non-mereological') fashion by

---

14. See further Lowe 2008: 23–48. My views about essence owe much to the work of Kit Fine on this topic: see, especially, Fine 1994.
15. What about possible worlds themselves? Of course, what *they* are is the subject of heated debate, but one popular view is that they are maximal consistent sets of propositions, and thus abstract particulars. If this view is taken, it will hardly do to regard propositions in turn as being sets of possible worlds, on pain of circularity, but the alternative account about to be described could be appealed to instead.

universals and particulars,[16] in which case, one would suppose, a proposition existing in a world devoid of concrete entities would have to be wholly constituted by universals and *abstract* particulars, such as sets. (Of course, on this view—according to which, I take it, propositions are themselves abstract particulars—some propositions could have *other propositions* amongst their particular constituents, but *elementary* propositions, by definition, could not.) Yet another alternative would be to regard propositions as sui generis entities, but this view is no more attractive than the corresponding view of numbers—indeed, if anything, it is less attractive. Perhaps we can at least say that the best candidates for the most *fundamental* species of abstract entities are universals and sets. Of course, some realists concerning universals *don't* regard them as being abstract entities, because they think that they are always 'wholly present' (in space and time) where their particular instances are.[17] But I am trying to be as generous as I reasonably can to the view that there is a world containing only abstract entities, so I shall set aside this 'concretist' conception of universals.

Anyway, let us see how well the hypothesis fares that the putative 'empty' world contains only universals and sets. Certainly, my critics have claimed that I have not succeeded in undermining the claim that there is such a world. As before, it is crucial to my argument from this point on that I deny the existence of the empty set, but I shall come back to that issue later. Let us assume, then, for the sake of argument, that the putative 'empty' world contains no empty set and hence no 'pure' sets. Here I need, however, a further assumption—that the *axiom of foundation* of set theory is true. This rules out infinitely descending or circular chains of set membership and consequently requires—in the absence of the empty set—the existence of *non*-sets of some sort. Of course, systems of non-well-founded set theory have been developed, which are no doubt of considerable interest to mathematicians.[18] But it is hard to take them seriously from an ontological point of view. The axiom of foundation represents a very reasonable demand that the existence of sets be suitably *grounded*, since a set depends ontologically on its members in an asymmetrical fashion: its members ground *its* existence, rather than vice versa. In earlier versions of my anti-nihilistic argument, I appealed at this point to the notion of *identity dependence*: a set depends for its *identity* on the identities of its members, but the reverse is not the case.[19] As I sometimes otherwise put it: it is *part of the essence* of a set that it has the members it does, but it is not part of their essence that they belong

---

16. For a comparable view of *states of affairs*, see Armstrong 1997. Some metaphysicians take 'propositions' to be entities that are rather like Armstrongian states of affairs.
17. This is David Armstrong's view: see Armstrong 1989: 98–9.
18. See Aczel 1988.
19. For more on the notion of identity dependence, see Lowe 1998: 147–51 and Lowe 2006: 198–200. See also Lowe 2010.

to it. However, what this notion of identity dependence does not, perhaps, immediately or obviously capture is the *ontological priority* of a set's members over the set of which they are the members. *They* ground *its* existence, rather than vice versa. This, rather than the notion of identity dependence as such, is really the crucial point.

Now let us turn to universals. I am assuming a version of *immanent* realism concerning universals. But it is a relatively weak version. Many metaphysicians understand by 'immanent realism' the view that universals are 'wholly present' (in space and time) where their instances are. I assume only that universals must *have* instances—that there cannot exist *uninstantiated* universals. For present purposes, I am not even assuming that all universals must have particulars—hence, non-universals—as their instances, since I am prepared to allow, at least for the sake of argument, that there can be 'higher-order' universals whose instances are other universals, the only constraint being that a universal of order n must have instances of order $(n - 1)$. Accordingly, particulars are of order *zero*. But what we have here, in effect, is another sort of axiom of *foundation*, applying to universals rather than sets. For even while we can acknowledge that lower-order entities must *instantiate* higher-order ones (that, for example, particulars must instantiate first-order universals), we still want to say—if we are immanentists in the Aristotelian tradition—that the existence of the higher-order entities is *grounded* in the existence of the lower-order ones that instantiate them, rather than vice versa. Again, it is a matter of *ontological priority*. The upshot is that there cannot exist universals in a world in which there are no particulars, for in that world the first-order universals would have no instances.

We now have *two* foundation or grounding principles at work, one of which demands that, in any world in which sets exist, there must exist non-sets that are ontologically more basic than any of the sets, and the other of which demands that, in any world in which universals exist, there must exist non-universals that are ontologically more basic than any of the universals. However, in a putative world in which there exist *only* universals and sets, the only *non*-universals are *sets* and the only *non*-sets are *universals*. And this presents a seemingly fatal difficulty for the view that there is such a world. For if the only *non*-sets in that putative world are universals, then the non-sets in that world that must be ontologically more basic than any of the sets must be *universals*, and this means that in that world *some universals are ontologically more basic than any of the sets*. On the other hand, if the only *non*-universals in that putative world are sets, then the non-universals in that world that must be ontologically more basic than any of the universals must be *sets*, and this means that in that world *some sets are ontologically more basic than any of the universals*. But it cannot be the case in any world that, in that world, some universals are ontologically more basic than any of the sets *and* some sets are ontologically more basic than any of the universals, because 'is ontologically more basic than' is evidently an asymmetrical relation. The problem with this putative world is that it is a world in which *nothing's existence is properly grounded.* I should emphasize here that it really doesn't help matters at all to point out, for instance, that in *other* worlds there are universals—perhaps even some of the *same* universals as those that supposedly exist in the 'empty' world—whose existence in *those* worlds is not grounded solely in the existence of particular sets. The problem is their lack of a ground for their existence *in the putatively 'empty' world.*

This is an appropriate point to examine an objection to my anti-nihilistic argument that is raised by Cameron. Cameron identifies the following as a principle that my argument assumes:

(P6) Aristotelianism about universals: Universals do not have ontological priority over particulars.

He remarks, however:

[T]here is an ambiguity in P6. Is the claim that no universal has ontological priority over *any* particular? Or is the claim that no universal has ontological priority over *all* the particulars in a world? If P6 is to be read in the latter way then Lowe's argument does not go through. Consider the world in which there is a universal U_1 which is instantiated by a set S_1 which has as its sole member the universal U_2 which is instantiated by the set S_2 which has as its sole member U_3 which is instantiated by the set S_3 ... and so on, ad infinitum. No universal has ontological priority over all the particulars; in fact for each universal, there is an infinity of particulars which are ontologically prior to it. ... We would only be forced into admitting that there was a universal which had ontological priority over all the particulars if we were forced into admitting that the chain had to stop somewhere. ... But we are not forced into admitting that the chain has to stop somewhere ... *unless* we have reason to believe that the stronger reading of P6 is true. The stronger reading of P6 says that universals are not ontologically prior to *any* particular. ... But surely that is too strong a premise ... far stronger than what one should accept simply from being an Aristotelian about universals. P6, on the stronger reading, entails that universals can never be in the transitive closure of a set. ... But Aristotelianism about universals should be compatible with the claim that for any possible being, the singleton of that being is also possible; the stronger reading of P6 denies this, since it rules out the possibility of singletons of universals. I conclude that Lowe's argument doesn't succeed. (2006: 217–8)

Now, certainly, I do not want to endorse Cameron's *stronger* reading of P6, according to which no universal has ontological priority over *any* particular. Of course we must allow that in any possible world that contains both universals and sets, some of the sets have universals as their members, in which case these universals have ontological priority over the particulars that are the sets to which they belong. So we must allow that this is the case in the putative 'empty' world, containing *only* universals and sets—but only, of course, if that really *is* a possible world. On the other hand, I *do* want to endorse Cameron's *weaker* reading of P6, according to which no universal has ontological priority over *all* the particulars in a world. Cameron contends, as we have just seen, that P6 on this weaker reading is consistent with there being an 'empty' world containing only universals and sets, if the universals and sets of that world are organized in an infinite chain of the sort that he describes. But from my point of view, the question that needs to be answered concerning Cameron's putative 'empty' world is whether it satisfies the two *principles of foundation* that I advanced earlier. Only one of those principles invoked an Aristotelian conception of universals, and, sure enough, it implies P6 on the weaker reading of the latter. The other principle was the *axiom of foundation of set theory*, which is very widely accepted as true—indeed, it receives even more widespread endorsement than does immanent realism concerning universals. Are these two principles of foundation *not* both satisfied in Cameron's putative 'empty' world? If so, why not? Each of the sets in Cameron's infinite chain $S_1, S_2, S_3, \ldots$ is a singleton, whose sole member is a universal. So it would seem that these sets present no challenge to the axiom of foundation of set theory. And each of the universals in Cameron's infinite chain $U_1, U_2, U_3, \ldots$ is a first-order universal, which is instantiated by a particular. So it would seem that these universals present no challenge to the foundation principle concerning universals. But if neither principle is challenged, how can the two principles together rule out the existence of Cameron's world?

At this point, we need to recall exactly what the implications of the two foundation principles are. What I said earlier was this (remembering that we are here assuming that there are no 'pure' sets):[20]

> We now have *two* foundation or grounding principles at work, one of which demands that, in any world in which sets exist, there must exist non-sets that are ontologically more basic than any of the sets, and the other of which demands that, in any world in which universals exist,

---

20. Of course, the 'axiom of foundation' of set theory, as *mathematicians* understand that principle, need not be construed as implying that non-sets have *ontological priority* over sets. Indeed, for mathematical purposes there is no need to suppose that the members of a set have ontological priority over the set of which they are the members. These claims concerning ontological priority are ones that are advanced only in the context of a metaphysical inquiry into the nature and ontological status of sets. But that does not, in my view, in any way diminish their cogency or cast doubt on their correctness. We should not suppose that mathematicians alone have the last word to say about sets.

there must exist non-universals that are ontologically more basic than any of the universals.

So what, in Cameron's putative world, are the non-sets that are ontologically more basic than any of the sets, and what are the non-universals that are ontologically more basic than any of the universals? Could they be, respectively, the universals $U_1, U_2, U_3, \ldots$ and the sets $S_1, S_2, S_3, \ldots$? Clearly not, because each of the universals $U_1, U_2, U_3, \ldots$ is ontologically less basic than the set that instantiates it, and each of the sets $S_1, S_2, S_3, \ldots$ is ontologically less basic than the universal that is its sole member. Consequently, the two foundation principles are not jointly satisfied in Cameron's world simply in virtue of its containing the infinite chain that he describes. In other words, he has not succeeded in describing an 'empty' world in which both of those principles remain unviolated. I conclude that his putative counterexample to my argument against metaphysical nihilism fails and that the argument goes through. We could not see any difficulty with Cameron's world when we considered each foundation principle *separately* with regard to the world. But when we consider the principles *jointly* with regard to that world, a problem does indeed arise.

Now I need to return to some unfinished business concerning *the empty set*. My argument against metaphysical nihilism does rely on a denial of the existence of the empty set, since if its existence is allowed, the axiom of foundation of set theory can be satisfied even in a world containing only sets—and hence, clearly, a world containing only pure sets and universals instantiated by them will satisfy both of my foundation principles. First, I have a preliminary point. This is that *Baldwin's* objection to my denial of the existence of the empty set now falls by the wayside, since that depended on my endorsement of the 'standard' view of arithmetic and the natural numbers, according to which the number zero exists. As I have already explained, I no longer think that numbers exist *at all*. This is not to say that I no longer believe in there being arithmetical truths or that I no longer believe such truths to be necessary. Quite the contrary. I still believe that $2 + 3 = 5$ is a necessary truth. But I don't believe that this requires the existence of the numbers 2, 3, and 5. By the same token, I don't believe that the truth of $1 - 1 = 0$ requires the existence of the numbers 1 and 0. If I am right about the nonexistence of numbers quite generally, however, one of the main reasons for advocating the existence of the empty set evaporates altogether, namely, the seeming requirement to find something to identify with the number zero. However, I don't just see no reason to believe in the existence of the empty set: I see reasons *not* to believe in its existence. The chief of these is that the identity of the empty set appears to be completely ungrounded, so that there remains an indissoluble mystery as to *what it is*. The identity of any *impure* set is perfectly well grounded, ultimately by the identities of the non-sets in its transitive closure. Thus, the identity of the set {Phobos, Deimos} is perfectly clear and determinate, being fixed by the identities of its two members. In my view, it is no use saying that the identity of the empty set is determinately fixed by the fact that it is the unique set that has *no* members and that this uniqueness is guaranteed by the axiom of extensionality of set theory—the axiom that states that sets are identical if and only if they have the same members. For putatively 'empty' sets have 'the same members' only in the Pickwickian sense that they have, supposedly, *no* members. If someone purported to identify the 'empty' *club* in such a fashion, he would be thought to be making a poor joke.

In earlier writings in which I have called into question the existence of the empty set, I have urged that just being told that the empty set is 'the set with no members' does not tell us *what it is*, because there are *many* things with no members in the set-theoretical sense—to wit, all the *non*-sets, such as you, me, and Mount Everest. The reason why none of the latter things can be the empty set is that none of them *is a set*. And the reason why none of them is a set is that, while all of them may have *parts*, none of them has *members* in the set-theoretical sense. But *the empty set*, likewise, is supposedly something that does not have members in the set-theoretical sense. So how does *it* manage to qualify as a set, whereas you, I, and Mount Everest do not?

Cameron thinks that this line of argument 'can be parodied to its discredit'. He writes:

> Lowe thinks that there is such a thing as the singleton of Socrates. Well if so, by the above reasoning, we need criteria of identity for the singleton of Socrates; in particular, why is it that *I* am not singleton Socrates? Because I do not have Socrates as a member? But that just begs the question. Because I am not a set? Because I am not the type of thing that could have Socrates as a member? Same response. . . . So if we have no worries with sets in general then we shouldn't have any worries about the empty set. (2006: 215)

I don't think that this 'parody' is fair—in fact, it *is* just a parody. The lesson of the parody is supposed to be that the alleged problem that I have raised concerning the identity of the empty set would, if it were genuine, be paralleled by a similar problem concerning the identity of the singleton of Socrates, {Socrates}. Now, in the first place, singletons are *not* in fact in as clearly good standing, ontologically speaking, as sets with more than one member, since it is not perfectly obvious what really distinguishes such a set from its sole member.[21] Sets with two, or three, or four, or however many more members *cannot*, of course, be identified with their members: for a two-membered set is *one* thing, whereas its members are *two*. But let us set aside this point for present purposes. Given that we have 'no worries with sets in general', then indeed we should have no specific worries with sets that have *three* or *two*

---

21. As David Lewis has remarked, 'Alas, the notion of a singleton was never properly explained; talk of collecting many into one does not apply to one-membered sets, and . . . I wonder how it is possible for us to understand the primitive notion of a singleton, if indeed we really do' (1991: vii).

members, or perhaps even just *one* member, for we can identify the sets in question by reference to their members. Indeed, it is *part of the essence* of singleton Socrates that it has Socrates as its sole member. How do I know that *I* am not singleton Socrates? Because I know, as clearly as I know anything, that it is *not* part of my essence to be related in any fashion to Socrates. Consequently, it does *not* 'beg the question' to say that I am not singleton Socrates because I do not have Socrates as a member, for what entitles me to say the latter is that I know that it is not part of my essence to be related to Socrates in *any* fashion and so a fortiori not in the fashion that singleton Socrates is related to Socrates, which is to have Socrates as a member. Very well, but can something similar be said on behalf of the empty set? In the case of singleton Socrates, I said the following: knowing which thing Socrates is, I know which set singleton Socrates is—it is the set that has Socrates as its sole member. But, plainly, I *cannot* say anything along these lines about the empty set. I cannot say anything of the form: knowing which thing X is, I know which set the empty set is—it is the set which is R-related to X. This makes the empty set utterly different from any other set, in respect of how it is to be identified. I simply cannot agree, then, with Cameron's blithe assertion that 'criteria of identity for singleton Socrates are no harder and no easier to give than criteria of identity for the empty set' (2006: 215).

The fact is, surely, that no one would for a moment countenance the existence of the empty set, any more than they would the existence of the empty *sum* in mereology or the empty *atom* in physics, if it were not that positing its existence is very useful for some set-theoretical purposes. Why not, then, simply regard it as a *useful fiction*, along with (or, indeed, in its guise as) the number zero—and, if I am right, all the other numbers? Why be *ontologically serious* about it? I am not complaining about the practice of mathematicians who talk about the empty set, just about metaphysicians who invest such talk with heavyweight ontological implications. Let me put the matter this way: if it is accepted that the only obstacle blocking my argument against metaphysical nihilism is the putative existence of the empty set in every possible world, is that *really* a good reason to resist the conclusion of my argument? Should a serious metaphysician resist that conclusion for the sake of something as little different from *nothing at all* as the empty set would appear to be? Indeed, in its guise as 'the number zero', isn't it fair to say that the empty set just *is* an illicitly reified *nothing*? In explaining the arithmetical equation $1 - 1 = 0$ to a child, we say that this means 'One take away one leaves *nothing*'. And nothing is not a peculiar kind of something, as is pointed out to all first-year logic students.

A final consideration that I want to address is this. The version of my anti-nihilistic argument that I have advanced in this paper no longer appeals to the necessary existence of certain abstract entities. Accordingly, it may be complained, it leaves entirely open the possibility that there is an *absolutely* empty world, in which nothing *at all* exists, either abstract or concrete. Doesn't that significantly reduce the metaphysical significance of the argument? Perhaps it does—though I hasten to emphasize once more that the existence or non-existence of such an absolutely empty world was never the primary question under discussion since the current debate about 'metaphysical nihilism' started. But notice, in any case, that I have not *denied* that there are any abstract entities whose existence is necessary. If it can be argued, for example, that there *are* some universals which exist in every possible world, then every world will contain at least universals and sets—and then my argument can be used to show that every world must contain other entities as well, which will have to be *concrete* if all abstract entities are either universals or sets. But it should not lightly be supposed that this will be an easy task. It would be facile, for example, to contend that *the property of self-identity* must exist in every possible world, perhaps on the grounds that every world must, at least, be identical with itself. For, as I indicated earlier, I think that it would be a serious mistake to suppose that the predicate 'is self-identical' denotes a property—that is, a *universal*—and thus some existing *entity*. To be perfectly honest, though, I suspect that the best hope for an argument against the existence of an *absolutely* empty world lies in the sort of argument that van Inwagen explicitly rejected—an argument for the existence of a necessary (concrete) being, in the shape of a version of the Ontological Argument.[22]

REFERENCES

Aczel, P. (1988). *Non-Well-Founded Sets*. Stanford, CA: CSLI.
Armstrong, D.M. (1989). *Universals: An Opinionated Introduction*. Boulder, CO: Westview Press.
———. (1997). *A World of States of Affairs*. Cambridge: Cambridge University Press.
Baldwin, T. (1996). 'There Might Be Nothing', *Analysis* 56: 231–8.
Cameron, R.C. (2006). 'Much Ado About Nothing: A Study of Metaphysical Nihilism', *Erkenntnis* 64: 193–222.
Efird, D. and Stoneham, T. (2005). 'The Subtraction Argument for Metaphysical Nihilism', *Journal of Philosophy* 102: 303–25.
Fine, K. (1994). 'Essence and Modality', in Tomberlin, J.E. (ed.). *Philosophical Perspectives, 8: Logic and Language*. Atascadero, CA: Ridgeview, 1-16.
Lewis, D.K. (1991). *Parts of Classes*. Oxford: Blackwell.
Locke, J. (1975). *An Essay Concerning Human Understanding*, Nidditch, P.H. (ed.). Oxford: Clarendon Press.
Lowe, E.J. (1993). 'Are the Natural Numbers Individuals or Sorts?', *Analysis* 53: 142–6.
———. (1995). 'The Metaphysics of Abstract Objects', *Journal of Philosophy* 92: 509–24.
———. (1996). 'Why Is There Anything at All?', *Proceedings of the Aristotelian Society*, Supplementary Volume 70: 111–20.

22. I have considerable sympathy for some versions of the Ontological Argument: see Lowe 2007.

———. (1998). *The Possibility of Metaphysics: Substance, Identity, and Time*. Oxford: Clarendon Press.

———. (2002). 'Metaphysical Nihilism and the Subtraction Argument', *Analysis* 62: 62–73.

———. (2003). 'Identity, Individuality, and Unity', *Philosophy* 78: 321–36.

———. (2006). *The Four-Category Ontology: A Metaphysical Foundation for Natural Science*. Oxford: Clarendon Press.

———. (2007). 'The Ontological Argument', in Meister, C. and Copan, P. (eds.). *The Routledge Companion to the Philosophy of Religion*. London and New York: Routledge, 331–40.

———. (2008). 'Two Notions of Being: Entity and Essence', in R. Le Poidevin (ed.). *Being: Developments in Contemporary Metaphysics*. Cambridge: Cambridge University Press, 23-48.

———. (2010). 'Ontological Dependence', in E. N. Zalta (ed.). *The Stanford Encyclopedia of Philosophy* (Spring Edition). http://plato.stanford.edu/archives/spr2010/entries/dependence-ontological/.

Paseau, A. (2002). 'Why the Subtraction Argument Does Not Add Up', *Analysis* 62: 73–5.

Rodriguez-Pereyra, G. (1997). 'There Might Be Nothing: The Subtraction Argument Improved', *Analysis* 57: 159–66.

———. (2000). 'Lowe's Argument Against Nihilism', *Analysis* 60: 335–40.

———. (2002). 'Metaphysical Nihilism: Reply to Lowe and Paseau', *Analysis* 62: 172–80.

Van Inwagen, P. (1996). 'Why Is There Anything at All?', *Proceedings of the Aristotelian Society*, Supplementary Volume 70: 95–110.

12 The Subtraction Arguments for Metaphysical Nihilism
Compared and Defended

Gonzalo Rodriguez-Pereyra

1 INTRODUCTION

The subtraction argument, originally put forward by Thomas Baldwin (1996), is intended to establish Metaphysical Nihilism, the thesis that there could have been no concrete objects. Some modified versions of the argument have been proposed in order to avoid some difficulties faced by the original argument.

In this paper I shall concentrate on two of those versions, the so-called subtraction argument* (presented and defended in Rodriguez-Pereyra 1997, 2000, 2002) and David Efird and Tom Stoneham's recent version of the argument (Efird and Stoneham 2005). I shall defend the subtraction argument* from Alexander Paseau's (2006) objection that because a crucial premise of the subtraction argument* may have no plausibility independent from Metaphysical Nihilism, the subtraction argument* is not suasive. Although Paseau focuses on the subtraction argument*, I shall point out that Efird and Stoneham could reply to Paseau's objection in the same way. Thus there are (at least) two suasive versions of the subtraction argument that establish Metaphysical Nihilism. But are those two arguments equally good? I shall argue that the subtraction argument* is preferable to Efird and Stoneham's argument.

2 THE SUBTRACTION ARGUMENTS

The informal version of the subtraction argument, as formulated by Baldwin, has the following premises:

(A1) There is a possible world with a finite domain of concrete objects.
(A2) These objects are, each of them, things which might not exist.
(A3) The nonexistence of any one of these things does not necessitate the existence of any other such things.

How do these premises support Metaphysical Nihilism? (A1) guarantees that there is a world with a finite number of concrete objects. Focus on one such world and call it w. Select any concrete thing x in w. By (A2) there is a world where x does not exist. By (A3) one of the worlds where x does not exist contains only the things that exist in w except everything whose nonexistence is implied by the nonexistence of x. In metaphorical terms, (A2) and (A3) allow us to subtract any concrete object that exists in w, without adding any other such objects. So if we start with a world like w, with a finite number of concrete objects, we eventually reach, by repeated application of the subtraction procedure guaranteed by the second and third premises, a world in which there are no concrete objects. Therefore, there could have been no concrete objects (Baldwin 1996: 232).

But is premise (A1) true? There are reasons to doubt that it is. First, one may think that necessarily all concrete objects have some spatiotemporal parts, that necessarily if something has a spatiotemporal part then it has infinitely many, and that necessarily the spatiotemporal parts of a concrete object are concrete objects. If so, it is necessary that concrete objects have infinitely many concrete parts.[1] Second, one may think that it is necessary that if something exists then sets having it as an ur-element exist, and that necessarily sets whose ur-elements are concrete are themselves concrete. If either of these thoughts is true then there is no possible world having some concrete objects and only finitely many such objects. If so, (A1) is not true.[2]

Of these thoughts I accept the first and reject the second, since I reject that sets with concrete ur-elements are concrete. But since both thoughts might be acceptable to some philosophers, and I would like Metaphysical Nihilism to be acceptable to as many philosophers as possible, I shall try to reformulate the subtraction argument so that the problems posed by these thoughts can be avoided. To this end I propose to modify the subtraction argument so as to apply to concrete* objects, where a concrete* object is an object that is (a) concrete, (b) non-set-constituted, and (c) a maximal occupant of a connected spatiotemporal region.[3]

By a *spatiotemporal region* I mean a sum of one or more spatiotemporal points; a region is connected if and only if any points in it can be joined by a path of points in it and disconnected if and only if it is not connected. An object x is a maximal occupant of a connected region if and only if x exactly occupies a connected region, and for all y all of whose parts occupy

---

1. Note that this is not the claim that all parts of a concrete object must be concrete (which is what Rodriguez-Pereyra [1997: 163] is committed to). This claim, together with certain assumptions about what mereological sums there are and what the mark of concreteness is, is false, as pointed out by Efird and Stoneham (2005: 313, n. 27).
2. I am assuming, without argument, and shall continue to assume, that spatiotemporal regions and points are not concrete.
3. This definition of concrete* object is a modification of the definition in my 1997 article. In that definition I required that a concrete* object be memberless, whereas I now require that it be non-set-theoretical. For the reasons for this modification see note 5 below.

spatiotemporal regions, if x is a proper part of y, then y occupies a disconnected region (cf. Rodriguez-Pereyra 1997: 163).[4]

By a *set-constituted object* I understand any object which is either a set, a proper class, or an ordered n-tuple, or which has a set, a proper class, or an ordered n-tuple as a part. A *non-set-constituted object* is one that is not a set-constituted object.[5]

I shall not propose any definition of concrete objects, but I shall uncontroversially assume that it is a necessary condition of any object being concrete that it is spatiotemporal. Clearly conditions (b) and (c) are compatible with condition (a), and, provided it is necessary that abstract objects are set-constituted objects, necessarily any object satisfying (b) is also a concrete object, in which case condition (a) is redundant. But since there is virtually

---

4. The clause 'all of whose parts occupy spatiotemporal regions' was not in the original definition. I have added it because I think it plausible that the following theses are true: (a) it is necessary that some non-spatiotemporal abstract objects exist, (b) sums of abstract and concrete objects are abstract objects, (c) such sums occupy the regions occupied by their concrete parts, and (d) unrestricted composition is necessarily true. If (a)–(d) are indeed true, then omitting the clause in question would mean that there could be no maximal occupants of connected regions and therefore that there could be no concrete* objects.

5. I am aware that ordered n-tuples are usually taken to be unordered sets, but I have wanted to be as neutral as possible in my definition of a non-set-constituted object. So the definition should be read as possibly redundant rather than as implying that ordered n-tuples are not sets. Similarly, the definition should not be taken to suggest any particular relation of constitution between sets and proper classes: even if in my technical sense of the term a proper class is a *set-constituted* object, this is simply because a proper class is a proper class, and being a proper class is sufficient for being a set-constituted object. I need a term to include the empty set plus all those objects which have members plus all those objects which have the empty set or membered entities as parts, and I have found no better term than *set-constituted object*. In my previous definition of concrete* object I required that concrete* objects be memberless, not non-set-constituted objects (Rodriguez-Pereyra 1997: 163). The idea was to rule out sets being concrete* objects, thereby ensuring the possibility of a world with only finitely many concrete* objects. But the requirement that concrete* objects be memberless cannot do what it was intended to do. To see this, assume that sets with concrete ur-elements are themselves concrete. Assume also, what is eminently plausible, that sums of concrete objects are concrete objects. Finally assume, what is not wildly implausible, that sets with concrete ur-elements are spatiotemporally located where and when the ur-elements are. Consider two concrete objects a and b such that $a + b$ is a maximal occupant of a connected region. The region occupied by $\{a\} + \{b\}$ is the region occupied by $a + b$. But then $\{a\} + \{b\}$ is a concrete memberless maximal occupant of a connected region. And so are $\{\{a\}\} + \{\{b\}\}$, $\{\{\{a\}\}\} + \{\{\{b\}\}\}$, and so on. But then, in general, there is no possible world with only a finite number of memberless maximal occupants of connected regions. But the new definition of concrete* object according to which a concrete* object is a non-set-constituted object, avoids this difficulty because such things as $\{a\} + \{b\}$ are set-constituted objects and therefore are not concrete* objects.

no consensus regarding the definition of abstract and concrete objects, I have added (a) to make sure that concrete* objects are concrete objects.

Is there a world with only finitely many concrete* objects? It seems so. At least its existence is not ruled out by the considerations above. For although whenever there are any concrete* objects, there are concrete objects, even if set-theoretical objects with concrete ur-elements are themselves concrete, no set-theoretical object is a concrete* object.

And even if concrete objects have necessarily infinitely many concrete parts, concrete* objects have no concrete* proper parts, for no spatiotemporal object that is a proper part of a concrete* object is itself a maximal occupant of a connected region, and therefore no proper part of a concrete* object is a concrete* object.

With the notion of a concrete* object on board, one may then run the subtraction argument*, which has the following premises:

(A1*) There is a possible world with a finite domain of concrete* objects and in which every concrete object is a (proper or improper) part of a concrete* object.[6]

(A2*) These concrete* objects are, each of them, things which might not exist.

(A3*) The nonexistence of any one of these things does not necessitate the existence of any other such things.

We then start from a possible world w_1, accessible from the actual world, with a finite domain of concrete* objects and where every concrete object is a part of a concrete* object, and then, after picking any of its concrete* objects x_1, we remove it completely—i.e. we remove x_1 and *all its parts*—and pass to a possible world w_2 that is exactly like w_1 except that x_1 has been removed completely. We repeat this procedure until we arrive at a world where there are no concrete* objects. That world will not contain any concrete objects. For the subtraction process does not add any objects to the worlds that are the result of subtracting concrete* objects from other worlds. And since that world will not contain any of the concrete* objects,

6. Originally, premise (A1*) of the original subtraction argument* was just the first conjunct of the present premise (A1*). I have added 'and in which every concrete object is a (proper or improper) part of a concrete* object' because if there are worlds in which some concrete objects are not part of a concrete* object, subtracting all the concrete* objects will not give a world in which there are no concrete objects. What would a world where some concrete objects are not parts of concrete* objects be like? One example would be worlds with concrete* objects coexisting with infinitely many occupied connected regions such that each one of them is a proper part of some of the others. Another example would be worlds with concrete* objects coexisting with scattered objects all of whose parts are scattered (that is, worlds which consist of concrete* objects plus what Aviv Hoffmann [2011: 50] calls 'scattered worlds'). Yet another example would be worlds which consist of concrete* objects plus what Hoffmann (2011: 49) calls 'Horsten worlds'.

or their parts, of the original world w_1, it will not contain any concrete objects.[7]

Efird and Stoneham avoid the problem arising from concrete objects having infinitely many concrete parts by defining a concrete object as an object that (a) exists at a location in space-time, (b) has some intrinsic qualities, and (c) has a natural boundary (2005: 314). The key condition here is (c), and it is intended to allow for the possibility of worlds with finitely many concrete objects, since not all parts of concrete objects have natural boundaries. They leave the notion of a natural boundary as an undefined primitive (2005: 315). In any case, as we shall see in section 6, (c) presents some problems whose possible solution is unclear.

But not everything is clear with premises (A3) and (A3*). Paseau (2002) has distinguished the two following readings of (A3*) and has claimed that on neither reading is the subtraction argument* valid (where o ranges over any concrete* objects and x over the concrete* objects mentioned in the first premise of the subtraction argument*):

> (α) $\forall x \forall o \exists w [\neg(x$ exists in $w) \wedge \neg(o$ exists in $w)]$
> (β) $\exists w \forall x [\neg(x$ exists in $w)]$

According to (α) the nonexistence of any of the xs does not necessitate the existence of any other such things in the sense that there is no concrete* object that exists in every possible world in which any of the xs does not exist. According to (β) the nonexistence of any of the xs does not necessitate the existence of any other such things in the sense that it does not necessitate that there is even one of the xs. Clearly, when (A3*) is interpreted in either of these two ways the subtraction argument* is not valid. But neither (α) nor (β) constitutes the intended reading of (A3*), as should be clear from the reasoning behind the subtraction argument. (α) and (β) are permissible interpretations of (A3*) as stated, but they are not plausible interpretations of that premise given the argumentative context in which it appears. The intended reading of (A3*) can be semiformally parsed as follows (where x ranges over the objects mentioned in premise [A1*]):

> (γ) $\forall w \forall x [x$ exists in $w \rightarrow \{\exists w^*(\neg(x$ exists in $w^*)) \rightarrow \exists w^{**}(w^{**}$ and w differ only in that in w^{**} neither x nor its parts exist)$\}]$.[8]

---

7. Note that I do not claim, as I did in my 1997 paper, that a world where there are no concrete* objects is a world where there are no concrete objects. This assumption was refuted by Hoffmann (2011). But all one needs to prove Metaphysical Nihilism is that at the end of the subtraction process there is a world where there are no concrete objects.

8. This is not exactly the way Paseau (2006: 148) parses (γ), nor is it exactly the way I parsed (A3*) in my 2002 work (p. 172). But I think it is the most accurate way to capture the intended reading of (A3*). Furthermore, Paseau seems to have understood (γ) in the way I am parsing it now, and his objections to the way he parsed (γ) are applicable to the way I am parsing it now. I shall therefore proceed as if Paseau had in mind (γ) as I have parsed it here.

Although in a more recent paper Paseau admits that when its third premise is understood as (γ) the subtraction argument* is valid, he argues that (γ)
cannot be a permissible interpretation of (A3*). Thus Paseau concludes that
there are two subtraction arguments*: the original and invalid one (where
the third premise is interpreted as either [α] or [β]) and the new and valid one
(where the third premise is interpreted as [γ]) (Paseau 2006: 149, 150–1).

I shall argue against these claims in section 3. Although Paseau made
his objection against the subtraction argument*, Efird and Stoneham, to
avoid Paseau's charge of invalidity, also interpret the third premise in a
way similar—but by no means equivalent—to (γ):

(B) $\forall w \forall x [x$ exists in $w \rightarrow \exists w^* \{\neg(x$ exists in $w^*) \wedge \forall y(y$ exists in w^*
$\rightarrow y$ exists in $w)\}]$.[9]

One notable feature of (B) is that, as Efird and Stoneham point out (2005:
309, n. 17), it makes premise (A2) redundant. For (A1) and (B) are sufficient
to entail Metaphysical Nihilism. I shall touch on the significance of this in
section 3. For now the important point is that the subtraction argument* is
valid when its third premise is interpreted as (γ), as is Efird and Stoneham's
version of the subtraction argument, with (A1) and (B) as premises.

3   THE INTERPRETATION OF (A3*)

Paseau argues that (γ) is not a permissible interpretation of (A3*). In effect,
he argues that any permissible interpretation of (A3*) must have a negated
universal, or equivalently an existential quantifier, as its leading world quantifier. Paseau says that (A3*) has the form:

Not-[A necessitates B]

If we interpret necessitation in the standard way in terms of possible worlds,
we obtain that (A3*) has the form:

Not-[$\forall w$(A holds at $w \rightarrow$ B holds at w)]

Thus Paseau concludes that any permissible interpretation of (A3*) must have
a negated universal or, equivalently, an existential quantifier as its leading
world quantifier. But the leading world quantifier of (γ) is universal. He concludes that (γ) cannot be a permissible interpretation of (A3*) (2006: 150).

But (γ) is a permissible interpretation of (A3*). To explain why, let me
start by noting and explaining an apparent discrepancy between (A3*) and

9. To maintain the unity of vocabulary between (γ) and (B) I have made some
slight alterations in the original formulation of (B) as it appears in Efird and
Stoneham 2005: 309. These changes do not alter its content but facilitate the
comparison of (γ) and (B).

(γ). This is that while in (γ) the subtractability of any of the xs is made to depend on there being a world in which x does not exist, nothing like this is mentioned in (A3*). The reason for this apparent discrepancy is that if one reads (A3*) as entailing the contingency of the xs, then (A2*) becomes redundant. Indeed, reading (A3*) as (α) or (β), Paseau's proposed permissible readings, makes (A2*) redundant, since both (α) and (β) entail that the xs are contingent. This means, by the way, that although (α) and (β) are permissible readings of (A3*), they are not plausible ones, since (A3*) was put forward as part of an argument in which (A2*) was supposed to play its role nonredundantly. Thus an interpretation of the argument that reads (A3*) as (α) or (β) neglects to take into consideration the context of the premise.

But (γ) is, on the contrary, a charitable interpretation of (A3*), given its context. But that it is a charitable interpretation does not mean that it is a permissible interpretation. And some might doubt that it is a permissible interpretation simply because the contingency of the xs is not guaranteed by (γ). But this is not a good reason to think that (γ) is not a permissible interpretation of (A3*). Sometimes we say things of the form 'P's being the case does not necessitate that Q is the case', without thereby incurring a commitment to P's being possible but, on the contrary, meaning that if P's being the case is possible, then P's being the case does not make Q be the case as well. For instance some believe that truths having truthmakers does not entail that there are facts. Such people might express this thought by saying, 'That truths have truthmakers does not necessitate the existence of facts'. But clearly not everyone who says this commits himself to the possibility that truths have truthmakers. Some might profess not to know whether truthmakers are metaphysically possible. Clearly, what they mean when they say that truths having truthmakers does not necessitate the existence of facts is not that there is a possible world with truthmakers but without facts but rather that if there is a world with truthmakers then there is a world with truthmakers but without facts.

Thus the apparent discrepancy between (γ) and (A3*) with respect to the contingency of the xs does not stop (γ) from being a permissible interpretation of (A3*). But it has not yet been shown that (γ) is a permissible interpretation of (A3*), since for all that has been said, the sense of (A3*) might be captured by (δ) or (ε), neither of which is capable, together with (A1*) and (A2*), of delivering the conclusion that there is a world where nothing concrete exists:

(δ) $\forall x \forall o [\exists w(\neg(x \text{ exists in } w)) \rightarrow \exists w^*(\neg(x \text{ exists in } w^*) \wedge \neg(o \text{ exists in } w^*))]$

(ε) $\forall x [\exists w(\neg(x \text{ exists in } w)) \rightarrow \exists w^* \forall x(\neg(x \text{ exists in } w^*))]$

What does (γ) say? It says that if the xs are contingent, then one can subtract any one x, without having to add anything, from every world in which any of them exist. What we need to see is that sometimes people say things of the form 'it is not the case that A necessitates B' meaning something like what (γ) means. To see this, imagine that there is a room with some number of people in it and some people outside it, and circumstances are such that no more than one person can leave the room at any one time and no more than one person can enter the room at any one time, and although it is possible for one person to leave the room simultaneously with another person entering the room, in no circumstance does the fact that someone leaves the room require that some other person enters the room. This situation can be naturally (partially) described by means of the phrase 'anyone's leaving the room does not necessitate anyone's entering the room'. And clearly in this case this means neither that it is possible that all the people who were in the room at the beginning have left the room at some time (this reading would be analogous to Paseau's [β]), nor that the leaving of the room by any person forces no particular person outside the room to enter into it (this reading would be analogous to Paseau's [α]). What it means is simply that, at any time, any of the persons in the room at the beginning can leave the room without anyone else entering the room. But if this is what 'anyone's leaving the room does not necessitate anyone's entering the room' can mean, then (A3*) can be interpreted as meaning what it was intended to mean.

Thus I think (γ) is a permissible interpretation of (A3*). But what I want to emphasise is that even if Paseau were right that (γ) is not a permissible interpretation of (A3*), it would not follow from this that there is a new subtraction argument* which is valid and whose third premise must be interpreted as (γ), and an old and original subtraction argument* which is invalid and whose third premise must be interpreted as either (α) or (β). On the contrary, since (γ) was the intended interpretation of the original subtraction argument*, all that would follow if Paseau were right that (γ) is not a permissible interpretation of (A3*) is that in the original informal formulation of the argument its third premise was not properly expressed. So either there is only one subtraction argument*, which is the valid old and original subtraction argument*, or there are two subtraction arguments*, the old and valid one in which (A3*) is interpreted as (γ) and the new and invalid one in which (A3*) is interpreted as either (α) or (β).

Can one argue that (B) is a permissible interpretation of (A3)? Yes, and on similar considerations to those that base my claim that (γ) is a permissible interpretation of (A3*), although in the case of (B) the case is simpler because there is no apparent discrepancy between (B) and (A3) with respect to the contingency of the xs. However, although (B) is a permissible interpretation of (A3), it is not a plausible one. For given the argumentative context in which (A3) appears, it is implausible to interpret it in any way that makes any of the other two premises redundant. So when we formalise the subtraction argument with only (A1) and (B) as premises, what we are doing is proposing a new subtraction argument.

This is not, of course, an objection against Efird and Stoneham's argument, nor is it an objection against their proposing such an argument, for what matters is to find (at least) one version of an argument that establishes Metaphysical Nihilism. And, indeed, they seem unconcerned with the fact that (B) makes (A2) redundant. But I find their lack of concern odd, for they seem to think that part of the advantage of (B) over (γ) is that it captures Baldwin's original intentions (Efird and Stoneham 2005: 309), but the fact that (B) makes (A2) redundant is (fallible but strong) evidence that (B) is not what Baldwin originally meant.[10]

4   THE SUBTRACTION PROPERTY

The idea or intuition behind (γ) and (B) is that necessarily if there are some concrete or concrete* objects, then there could have been fewer concrete or concrete* objects. One objection to this is that that idea or intuition presupposes that there is a world with no concrete or concrete* objects. For only if one believes that there is an empty world will one have reason to believe that necessarily if there are some concrete or concrete* objects then there could have been fewer of them. Thus no one who is not previously committed to the existence of a world with no concrete or concrete* objects would be moved by (γ) or (B) to accept Metaphysical Nihilism. This is, in a nutshell and extended to apply to (B), Paseau's objection against (γ) in his 2006 article. To meet this objection one needs to show that there are reasons to accept (γ), (B), or the intuition behind them.

Paseau argues that (γ) may have no plausibility independent of the existence of an empty world (2006: 154), in which case the subtraction argument* will fail to move those who are open-minded or agnostic about whether there is an empty world. Paseau does not establish, nor does he attempt to establish, that (γ) can be given no plausibility independent of the existence of an empty world. All he does is to show that certain ways of arguing for (γ) are unsuccessful, and then he issues metaphysical nihilists the challenge of trying to give independent reasons to accept (γ). In this section I shall argue that there are such reasons to accept (γ).

Paseau speaks indistinctly of a suasive argument having to convince someone who is agnostic about its conclusion and someone who is open-minded about its conclusion. I think the right thing is to demand of a suasive argument that it be capable of convincing someone who is open-minded about its conclusion. This is because agnosticism is compatible with dogmatism: there can be dogmatic agnostics. And suasive arguments need not convince dogmatic agnostics.

---

10. Although for reasons not having to do with the fact that it makes (A2) redundant, Efird and Stoneham think that (B) might be a replacement of (A3) (2005: 309, n. 18). This does not worry them, but for the reasons given above I think it should.

So a suasive argument must be capable of convincing someone who is open-minded about its conclusion, where a person is open-minded about a certain claim X if and only if as far as he knows he is not committed to any opinion as to whether X and is willing to examine reasons for and against X and also willing to let his judgement about X be rationally influenced by such reasons. What I am going to argue in this section is that independent reasons can be given in favour of (γ), reasons that should move anyone who is open-minded about whether there is an empty world. But Paseau's challenge to metaphysical nihilists is to provide reasons for (γ), not for the other premises of the subtraction argument*. So what I am going to do here is to provide reasons for (γ) that should move anyone who is open-minded about the possibility of an empty world and who accepts the other premises of the subtraction argument*.

Let us say that a contingent concretum* x is subtractable from a world w if and only if x exists in w and there is a possible world w^* such that x does not exist in w^*, and w^* and w differ only in that in w^* neither x nor its parts exist. Since the world mentioned in (A1*) has been arbitrarily chosen, its concreta* can be assumed not to be relevantly different from any other contingent concreta*, and, with this assumption, (γ) entails that every contingent concretum* is subtractable from any world in which it exists.[11] Let us say that a world has the *subtraction property* when all of its contingent concreta* are subtractable from it. Thus (γ) entails that every world with contingent concreta* has the subtraction property.

Paseau agrees that it is plausible that many-concreta* worlds have the subtraction property (2006: 152). If this is indeed possible, and I think it is, one might use it as a reason for (γ). How could this be done? One could argue that maintaining that many-concreta* worlds have the subtraction property without accepting (γ) puts one in a position to have to explain something that cannot be explained. One principle to implement this strategy might be (P1):

(P1)   If one thinks that a principle is true in most cases but might have some exceptions, one incurs the burden of explaining why these cases might be exceptional.

Paseau rejects this principle because, he says, it rules out some cases in which one is exercising due intellectual caution. He exemplifies this point with a case of someone who has reliably observed the voting behaviour of British women except the Scots. Such a person might have good reason to believe that British women vote Labour, the possible exception being Scots.

---

11. So (γ) entails that every contingent concretum* is subtractable in Efird and Stoneham's sense (2005: 322). Note that (γ) entails that every contingent concretum* is subtractable from any world in which it exists by requiring that every contingent concretum* is *individually* subtractable from any world in which it exists.

I agree that (P1) rules out cases of due intellectual caution, but not for the reasons Paseau gives. It is simply an exercise of intellectual caution to think that some principle that is not evidently universally true might have some exceptions. But it is one thing to think that what is not evidently universally true might have some exceptions, and another to believe of some cases that they might be exceptions to the observed rule. In this latter case one does incur the burden of explaining why these cases might be exceptional. Thus the following principle does not rule out cases of due intellectual caution:

> (P2) If one thinks that a principle is true in most types of cases but believes of some types of cases that they might be exceptions to the principle, one incurs the burden of explaining why these types of cases might be exceptional.[12]

Clearly (P2) is relevant to Paseau's case of the political preferences of British women. But (P2) does not rule out cases of due intellectual caution, because *due* intellectual caution is caution where there is a reason to be cautious. So if one is rational in thinking that a certain case might be an exception to the general case, one should have a reason why this *might* be the case, in which case one is in a position to explain why it might be exceptional. And there are lots of reasons why Scottish women might be an exception to the observed rule. After all, there are differences of culture, education, political history, and general political situation which are known to influence the voting behaviour of people—not to mention the fact that in Scotland there is a party, the Scottish National Party, that is not politically active in the rest of Britain.

Thus I take it that the demand imposed on explanations by (P2) is minimal: to explain why certain cases might be exceptional, all one is required to do is to provide some reason why they might be. Such a reason will typically be a reason that the potentially exceptional types of cases are not relevantly similar to the other ones. This suggests the following, more specific, principle:

> (P2*) If one thinks that a principle is true in most types of cases but believes of some types of cases that they might be exceptions to the principle, one incurs in the burden of showing why these types of cases might not be relevantly similar to the other ones.[13]

What (P2*) requires is that one be in a position to show why the potentially exceptional cases are not relevantly similar to the ones for which the principle is true. Since voting behaviour is influenced by education, culture, and political landscape, the burden is easily met in the case of Scottish women since one can

---

12. Note that this principle (P2) has nothing to do with Paseau's principle (P2) (Paseau 2006: 153).
13. (P2*) is similar to, but not the same as, Paseau's (P3) (2006: 153).

explain why they might be relevantly dissimilar to the other British women by pointing out that they differ or might differ from other British women in respect of culture, education, and the political landscape in which they act.

Now, according to premise (A1*) of the subtraction argument*, there is a possible world with a finite number of concreta*. If so, there must be some worlds which have the smallest domains of concreta*; that is, there must be some worlds which have at least one concretum* and no worlds that have fewer concreta* than they have. So anyone who accepts (A1*) should accept the following:

(1*) There is a world with the minimum possible number of concreta*.

The following principle is also plausible, and there is no reason why those who are open-minded about whether there is an empty world should not accept it:

(2*) If there is a possible world consisting of just n concreta*, then there is a world consisting of those n concreta* plus an additional concretum*.

Now, if one accepts (1*) and (2*) but suspends judgement with respect to there being an empty world, one has to meet the kind of explanatory demand imposed by (P2*). For if there is a nonempty world with the minimum possible number of concreta*, and for each world with a number of concreta* there is a world containing those concreta* plus an additional one, then most types of worlds have the subtraction property.

Thus, given the plausibility of (2*), it seems that those who are open-minded about the empty world ought to explain why some worlds with a certain number of concreta*, which might lack the subtraction property, are relevantly different from worlds with a higher number of concreta*, which have the subtraction property. How can this be done?

One way to do it would be to argue that there might be n necessarily existent concreta*, and so worlds with just n concreta* are relevantly different from worlds with more concreta* in that the number of things existing in the former is the number of necessarily existent concreta*, while this is not true of worlds with more concreta*. But this route is not available to our open-minded person, since this is someone who accepts premise (A2*) of the subtraction argument* and therefore believes that there are no necessarily existent concreta*.

Without resorting to necessarily existent concreta* the only other way seems to be to find a number n such that there might be some relevant difference between worlds with n concreta* and worlds with more concreta*, and such that that difference accounts for the fact that while worlds with more than n concreta* have the subtraction property worlds with just n concreta* might lack it. But if there is any chance of this to succeed then it is plausible to think that the number n in question is 1. This seems to accord with Paseau, since he says it is plausible to believe that there are one-concretum* worlds but seems open-minded about whether there is an empty world. Indeed, Paseau says that 'having just one entity as opposed to having more than one seems to be a highly relevant distinction for whether we can subtract something from a world and still be left with a world' (p. 154). Why is this a relevant difference? Paseau does not say, but there seems to be no relevant difference between one-concretum* worlds and two-concreta* worlds which is independent from the fact that there might be no empty world. For the difference in question must explain why one-concretum* worlds might lack the subtraction property while two-concreta* worlds have it. And no credible explanation can be given which makes no reference to the fact that subtracting its concretum* from a one-concretum* world results in an empty world, while this is not true of two-concreta* worlds (saying that the number 1, or one-concretum* worlds themselves, has magical or special properties that prevent subtraction from one-concretum* worlds would not be a credible explanation).

Paseau seems aware of this, but he draws from it the conclusion that the subtraction argument* cannot be suasive. This is what he says:

> For what it is worth, my own intuitions on the question of whether one can subtract its only concretum* from a one-concretum* world are none other than my intuitions about whether there is an empty world. If that is true more generally, the new subtraction argument cannot be suasive. It will lack the capacity to sway anyone who is agnostic about whether one-concretum* worlds have the subtraction property. The reason is that a subtraction premise [i.e. a premise like (γ)] will have no source of plausibility independent of the existence of an empty world, or at least no source that does not itself directly motivate the existence of an empty world. (2006: 154)

Paseau thinks that the subtraction argument* cannot be suasive because no one would accept that one-concretum* worlds are relevantly similar to two-concreta* worlds for reasons independent from there being an empty world. But one-concretum* and two-concreta* worlds are similar, and for reasons independent from there being an empty world: they contain at least one concretum*; they contain finitely many concreta*; they contain contingent concreta*; they contain less than three concreta*; they form part of series of worlds containing concreta* in which every member of the series has one more concretum* than the preceding one; if well chosen, the set of concreta* in the one-concretum* world is a subset of the set of concreta* in the two-concreta* world; and so on.

Clearly, the onus of proof is on those who say that one-concretum* and two-concreta* worlds are not relevantly similar. But the only relevant difference that would account for the fact that only one-concretum* worlds might lack the subtraction property would be that there might be no empty world. But if, as we are assuming with Paseau, there are one-concretum* worlds, then the fact that there might be no empty world *is* the fact that one-concretum* worlds might lack the subtraction property. But that one-concretum* worlds might lack the subtraction property is no relevant difference when it comes to explaining why one-concretum* worlds, unlike two-concreta* worlds, might lack the subtraction property.[14]

So if (P2*) is a constraint of rationality, one ought to abandon either (1*) or (2*), or else accept (γ). But the open-minded person we had in mind was someone who accepted premise (A1*) of the subtraction argument*, and therefore he is committed to (1*). And (2*) is a very plausible principle. Thus the rational thing to do would be to embrace (γ).

5   WHY THERE ARE WORLDS WITH ONLY ONE CONCRETUM*

I have been assuming that the relevant open-minded person knows that one-concretum* worlds are possible. But this assumption might be questioned. For someone might be open-minded about whether there is an empty world because he is open-minded about whether there must be something without knowing whether this might be the case because there must be at least one concretum*, or because there must be at least seven concreta*, or because there must be at least seven million concreta*, and so on. This would be a person who is not only open-minded about whether there is an empty possible world but who for every n, where $n > 0$, is open-minded about whether there is a world with just n concreta* because it might be that there must be more than n concreta*. He might say that most worlds have the subtraction property but that some might lack it because they are such that they might contain the minimum possible number of concreta*.

This person escapes the explanatory pressures imposed by (P2*). For although he believes that there might be some exceptions to a rule that obtains in most types of cases, he believes of no particular types of cases that they might be the exceptions. But it can be argued that there must be a world with just one concretum*. For the following principle is plausible:

(3*) If x and y are two concreta* existing in a certain world w, then there is a world w^* which differs from w only in that it includes a concrete thing z which does not exist in w and which connects x and y in w^*.

---

14. Geraldine Coggins raises a similar point to Paseau's, and it seems she would suggest that the relevant difference between one-concretum* worlds and two-concreta* worlds is that 'the nature of possibility or of what a possible world is seems to depend or be closely related to the question of whether or not [one-concretum* worlds have the subtraction property]' (Coggins 2010: 131). But this would be because for Coggins the possibility of an empty world has implications for the nature of possible worlds (Coggins 2010: 26–56). But, if so, one-concretum* and two-concreta* worlds would not differ for reasons independent from there being an empty world.

This principle is plausible since it is plausible that necessarily every two concreta* could have been joined together by means of some extra concrete object. That z connects x and y means that although the region occupied by $x + y$ is not connected, the region occupied by $x + y + z$ is. Thus in w^* x and y and z are not concreta* but merely parts of a concretum*.

What is important about (3*) is that it shows that one can always make one concretum* out of two, in the sense that every two concreta*, in any possible world, are not concreta* but parts of a third concretum* in another possible world. Thus (3*) entails that for every world with more than one concretum*, there is a world with exactly $n - 1$ concreta*. Thus if there is a possible world with a finite number of concreta*, as (A1*) states, then there is a world with just one concretum*.

Thus, given the initial credibility of (3*), unless the relevantly open-minded person has a positive reason to reject it, he ought to believe that there are worlds with just one concretum*. But then he ought to have a reason why one-concretum* worlds might be different from worlds with many concreta*, a reason that is independent from the fact that there might be an empty world. And this, I have argued, cannot be done. If so, given (P2*), (1*), and (2*), he ought to accept (γ).

6   THE SUPERIORITY OF THE SUBTRACTION ARGUMENT*

Since the relevantly open-minded person ought to accept (γ), given the validity of the subtraction argument* the relevantly open-minded person ought to accept the conclusion of the subtraction argument*. Clearly, the same kind of defence can be adopted by Efird and Stoneham to defend their argument from Paseau's objection (except that it is not clear how they could modify the argument in the previous section that there must be a world with just one concretum* to make it an argument that there must be a world with just one concrete object). So both arguments are valid, and there seem to be reasons to believe in their premises. Metaphysical Nihilism is in good shape.

Given this parity between the arguments, the issue is, then, which argument is better. I think the subtraction argument* is better than Efird and Stoneham's argument. I shall first consider their objections to the subtraction argument* and then explain my misgivings about their argument.

What do they find problematic with the subtraction argument*? Their main point seems to be that (γ) entails the existence of a world with a single concrete object and so does not allow for the existence of symbiotic objects, i.e. pairs of objects such that if one goes out of existence so does the other.[15]

---

15. Strictly speaking, what they have in mind is not (γ) but (R-P), which is their formalisation of the intended reading of (A3*). But I suppose they would probably have made the same objection to (γ).

But they think such objects should not be ruled out. Why? They think there are clear examples of such objects, namely mereological fusions of concrete objects (Efird and Stoneham 2005: 309).

But this objection leaves the subtraction argument* unscathed. First, what (γ) entails is not a world with a single concrete object but a world with a single concrete* object, since it is concrete* objects that (γ) talks about. And we have seen in section 5 that it can be argued, without presupposing (γ), that there is such a world. Some people might find repugnant the idea that there could have been just one concrete object (for instance those who believe that every concrete object must have concrete proper parts). But all the subtraction argument* commits one to is the idea that there could have been just one concrete* object. And this is not repugnant.

Second, (γ) and the subtraction argument* are consistent with symbiotic objects such as mereological fusions of concrete objects. For a mereological fusion of concrete objects is either a concrete, non-set-constituted, maximal occupant of a connected spatiotemporal region, or it is not. If it is, then it is a concrete* object, and so it is consistent with (γ) that its nonexistence entails the nonexistence of its parts, which although concrete are not concrete*. If it is not, then it is not a concrete* object, and so (γ) does not require that its nonexistence does not entail that of any other object.

Efird and Stoneham make other points against (γ), for instance that it is overly complicated. They think the argument can be simplified if one replaces (γ) with (B) (2005: 308–9). I do not think this objection has much weight, but in any case I shall argue below that (B) has serious problems, and these problems more than compensate for whatever advantage (B) gets from being simpler than (γ).

A more substantive point they make is that by restricting the application of the argument to concrete* objects, it is no longer possible to appeal to unphilosophical intuition to support the premises of the argument. Yet they do not argue for this substantive unobvious claim. But the only philosophical concept in the definition of concrete* object is that of a concrete object, a concept about which they think one can have unphilosophical intuitions.[16]

So the subtraction argument* has not been undermined by Efird and Stoneham's objections. I think, however, that their argument presents some serious problems, which arise from their conception of a concrete object.

---

16. Furthermore, why should we appeal to unphilosophical intuition when we are dealing with a philosophical argument? Should it also be uneducated, uninformed intuition? Presumably it must be educated, informed intuition. But then why should it not be informed by philosophical ideas? I cannot enter into this large methodological debate here, but I want to register my doubts about Efird and Stoneham's apparent assumption that philosophical ideas are better grounded on unphilosophical intuition.

Efird and Stoneham's original definition of a concrete object makes it necessary that concrete objects have natural boundaries (2005: 314). This makes it impossible that there be only one concrete object that takes up the whole of space. To avoid this unwanted conclusion, Efird and Stoneham have reformulated their definition of a concrete object by requiring of such objects only that if they have boundaries, they have natural boundaries (2009: 134). But this definition is still lacking, for then any extended concrete object will have infinitely many concrete objects as parts. Consider Efird and Stoneham's own example of a white card with a red circle in the middle (2005: 313). For any segment of the circumference of the circle there will be infinitely many parts of the circle which have that segment as a boundary and no other segment of the circumference as boundary. Those parts are located in space and time, they have intrinsic qualities, and they have a natural boundary. So they must count as concrete objects according to their revised definition.

I guess the solution is to require of concrete objects that if they have any boundaries, they have only natural ones.[17] But I doubt that this solution is entirely satisfactory. Think of a mountain, say Mount Olympus. Since Efird and Stoneham put a lot of emphasis on unphilosophical intuitions about the kind of object Metaphysical Nihilism is supposed to be about, surely they would want to count Mount Olympus as a concrete object.[18] Mount Olympus has some natural boundaries, but are all of its boundaries natural? Surely there is some boundary which delimits the base of Olympus from the rest of the part of the Earth on which it rests, but there seems to be no natural one. And this is not a problem about mountains not having precise boundaries. Indeed, they do not have precise boundaries. But the problem here is not that they are not precise but that not all of them are natural: no way of making the boundary between Olympus and its base precise would make it a natural boundary (cf. Efird and Stoneham 2005: 315).

It is not clear to me that this problem is not solvable, although at present I do not see what the solution is. One possible solution would be to say that mountains are not concrete. But it seems to me that whatever the intension of the concept of a concrete object, its extension must include mountains. Of course, one could, by modifying the definition again, accommodate the case of Mount Olympus so that mountains count as concrete. But, and this is admittedly an ad homines point, I suspect that by modifying it further Efird and Stoneham might make the definition of concrete objects such that 'it is no longer possible to appeal to unphilosophical intuition to support the premises of the argument' (2005: 313, footnote 27).

---

17. Or one can think of boundaries as complete, so that nothing is a boundary unless it delimits the totality of the object of which it is a boundary.
18. They count clouds as concrete objects (2005: 315), but counting clouds but not mountains as concrete would be rather peculiar.

Furthermore, the notion of a natural boundary, which is left undefined, does not seem to be totally clear. Is a boundary natural when the things occupying the two sides of the boundary have different natural properties or belong to different kinds? Efird and Stoneham think not, for they think there is a natural boundary between the legs and the top of a table when they are made from different pieces of wood. But they think that there must be some significant difference in kind between the things on the two sides of a boundary for this to be natural (Efird and Stoneham 2005: 315). But what a 'significant' difference is must be clarified.

The notion of a concrete* object is, on the other hand, much clearer than the notion of a concrete object defined in terms of natural boundaries. Thus I think that it is better to work with the notion of a concrete* object, about which it is possible to have clear (though perhaps not unphilosophical) ideas that support the premises of the argument: it is clear that Mount Olympus is not a concrete* object.

The subtraction argument* has not been undermined by Efird and Stoneham's objections. Their argument presents some serious problems; these are perhaps not unsolvable, but it is as yet unclear how they could be solved. This makes the subtraction argument*, for the time being at least, preferable to their argument. But whatever argument is best (if indeed one is better than the other), these are valid and persuasive arguments that establish Metaphysical Nihilism.[19]

REFERENCES

Baldwin, T. (1996). 'There Might Be Nothing', *Analysis* 56: 231–8.
Coggins, G. (2010). *Could There Have Been Nothing? Against Metaphysical Nihilism*. Basingstoke, UK: Palgrave Macmillan.
Efird, D. and Stoneham, T. (2005). 'The Subtraction Argument for Metaphysical Nihilism', *Journal of Philosophy* 102: 303–25.
——. (2009). 'Justifying Metaphysical Nihilism: A Response to Cameron', *Philosophical Quarterly* 59: 132–7.
Hoffmann, A. (2011). 'It's Not the End of the World: When a Subtraction Argument for Metaphysical Nihilism Fails', *Analysis* 71: 44–53.
Paseau, A. (2002). 'Why the Subtraction Argument Does Not Add Up', *Analysis* 62: 73–5.
——. (2006). 'The Subtraction Argument(s)', *Dialectica* 60: 145–56.
Rodriguez-Pereyra, G. (1997). 'There Might Be Nothing: The Subtraction Argument Improved', *Analysis* 57: 159–66.
——. (2000). 'Lowe's Argument Against Nihilism', *Analysis* 60: 335–40.
——. (2002). 'Metaphysical Nihilism Defended: Reply to Lowe and Paseau', *Analysis* 62: 73–5.

---

19. Thanks to Bill Brewer, Michael Clark, Ghislain Guigon, David Liggins, Alex Paseau, Matthew Soteriou, Ezequiel Zerbudis, and audiences in Belfast, Buenos Aires, Cambridge, Geneva, Manchester, Mexico City, Nancy, Nottingham, Oxford, and Warwick, where versions of this paper were presented.

13 The Probabilistic Explanation of Why There Is Something Rather Than Nothing

Matthew Kotzen

1 THE QUESTION

Our question is "Why is there something rather than nothing?" There are at least two different interpretations of this question. First, we might be asking why there are *material things* rather than no material things. Second, we might be asking why there is *anything at all*—material or immaterial—rather than nothing at all. In this essay, I will be addressing one particular explanatory strategy for addressing both questions. To make sure there is no confusion, I'll use "something" in this context to refer to anything at all, and I'll use "some material thing" in this context to refer to any material thing. Our two questions are why there is something rather than nothing, and why there are some material things rather than no material things.

The force of the "rather than" clauses in our questions also needs to be addressed. The explanation of why Laurie ordered chocolate cake for dessert rather than nothing might be different from the explanation of why Laurie ordered chocolate cake for dessert rather than strawberry ice cream; she ordered chocolate cake rather than nothing because she was still hungry, but she ordered chocolate cake rather than strawberry ice cream because she is allergic to strawberries.[1] Similarly, the explanation of why there is something rather than nothing, or of why there are some material things rather than no material things, might be different from the explanation of why there are *these particular* things, or *these particular* material things, rather than different ones. We are interested only in why there are some things *rather than nothing* and in why there are some material things *rather than no material things*; a full explanation of these contrastive facts might give us no insight at all into why the things that do exist are these particular ones rather than different ones. When we explain why *A* rather than *B* is true, I'll refer to *A* as the "explanatory fact" and *B* as the "explanatory foil."

---

1. For discussions of contrastive explanation, see Dretske 1972; Garfinkel 1981; Lipton 1990, 1991a, 1991b, 1993; Ruben 1987; and van Fraassen 1980.

This essay is about the Probabilistic Explanation of why there is something rather than nothing and of why there are some material things rather than none. The basic idea of the Probabilistic Explanation is that there is some legitimate sense in which there are "more ways" for there to be something than for there to be nothing, and hence that it was more likely that the Universe would contain something rather than nothing. Of course, we'll develop and critically discuss the Probabilistic Explanation below. But first we should get some preliminaries out of the way.

First, a lot of writers on explanation focus on causal explanation, and some writers can be reasonably interpreted to have argued that all or most explanation is causal in nature. Some philosophers think that even if there are some non-causal explanations, all explanation of *events* is causal.[2] I don't know whether the coming-to-exist of something, or the coming-to-exist of material things, is an event in the sense that these philosophers have in mind. But I think that the Probabilistic Explanation is best regarded as an example of a non-causal explanation of some fact or state of affairs; thus, if the coming-to-exist of something and the coming-to-exist of material things are events, then the Probabilistic Explanation is inconsistent with views according to which all event explanation is causal.

Second, some people might balk at the overtly probabilistic nature of the Probabilistic Explanation; they might argue that a genuine explanation of a fact or event must show why the fact or event *had* to occur, not just why it was *likely* to occur. But, quite independent of any considerations specifically to do with the Probabilistic Explanation, it is widely agreed that at least some legitimate explanations are probabilistic in nature.[3] When a coin that is heavily but not perfectly biased in favor of heads lands heads, we can't point to any considerations in virtue of which the coin was *guaranteed* to land heads—there are none, since the coin *wasn't* guaranteed to land heads—but it still seems as though the heavy heads bias of the coin explains the fact that it landed heads.[4] If you prefer an indeterministic case, change the coin into a quantum particle, and suppose that the particle is in a state (call it S) in virtue of which it's very likely—but not guaranteed—to emerge from the left aperture of the box that it has just entered. Again, when the particle does emerge from the left aperture, that fact seems to be explained by the fact that the particle was in state S when it entered the box, even though that fact merely probabilifies the explanandum. So, if there is a problem with the explanatory strategy of the Probabilistic Explanation,

---

2. Lewis (1986), for instance, defends this view.
3. The classic treatment of probabilistic explanation appears in Hempel 1965. Other important treatments include Humphreys 1989; Mellor 1976; Railton 1978; Salmon 1970; and Strevens 2000.
4. I think it's even clearer that the heavy heads bias of the coin explains why it landed heads in a very high percentage of a large finite number of flips, though here too the heads bias fails to guarantee the explanandum.

I don't think that it is plausibly diagnosed by pointing to the fact that it appeals only to factors in virtue of which its explanandum was likely rather than guaranteed.

2 THE INTUITION BEHIND THE PROBABILISTIC EXPLANATION

Consider the following three cases:

> **Case 1:** DICE. Marc rolls a pair of dice and observes that the sum of the numbers on the two dice is 7 rather than 12. Here is a candidate explanation of that fact: there is only one way to roll a 12—the left die has to land on 6, and the right die also has to land on 6. But there are more ways (namely, six) to roll a 7—the left die could land on n for any $n \in \{1,2,3,4,5,6\}$, and the right die could land on 7 − n. So, any particular dice roll is more likely to yield a total of 7 than a total of 12, which explains why Marc's roll yielded a total of 7 rather than 12.
>
> **Case 2:** GAS. A gas is initially contained by a partition in a small corner of a box. The partition is removed, and the gas quickly spreads out to occupy the entire box rather than staying contained in the small corner. Here is a candidate explanation of that fact: once the partition is removed, there are relatively few physically possible microstates of the gas that correspond to the gas remaining bunched up in the corner of the box, but there are (comparatively) far more physically possible microstates of the gas that correspond to the gas being approximately evenly dispersed throughout the box. So, once the partition is removed, any particular volume of gas is more likely to spread out than to stay bunched up, which explains why the gas in the box spread out rather than remaining bunched up.
>
> **Case 3:** BEACH. John decides to count all of the grains of sand on Daytona Beach.[5] After completing the count, he notices that the total is divisible by 8 but not by 7,296. Here is a candidate explanation of that fact: there are a lot more natural numbers that are evenly divisible by 8 than there are natural numbers that are evenly divisible by 7,296. So, it is more likely that any beach will have a number of grains of sand that is evenly divisible by 8 than a number that is evenly divisible by 7,296, which explains why Daytona Beach has a number of grains of sand that is evenly divisible by 8 rather than 7,296.

Each of the explanations above, I submit, has significant intuitive plausibility. By claiming this, I don't mean to be committing myself to the view that

---

5. Imagine that Daytona Beach has precise borders, so that there is no indeterminacy in whether a particular grain of sand is within its borders or not. This is, of course, quite implausible, but this idealization seems harmless in this context.

these explanations are exactly correct, or that they don't need to be made precise or developed in various ways; in fact, we'll be returning to these explanations below. But I hope that you agree that something in the general spirit of each of the above explanations is a very plausible candidate for explaining the relevant explanandum.

Now, consider the following cases:

> **Case 4:** SOMETHING. We look around and notice that there are some things, whereas there could have been none. Here is a candidate explanation of that fact: there are lots of possible ways for there to be some things—there could be exactly one proton, or there could be God and exactly one proton, or there could be two Gods and exactly one proton, or there could be two protons and one God, or there could be exactly 17 neutrons, etc. By contrast, there is only one way for there to be nothing—there are exactly zero protons, zero neutrons, zero electrons, zero people, zero tables, zero elephants, zero Gods, etc. So, the Universe was more likely to contain something than nothing, which explains why the Universe indeed contains something rather than nothing.
>
> **Case 5:** MATERIAL THINGS. We look around and notice that there are some material things, whereas there could have been none. Here is a candidate explanation of that fact: there are lots of possible ways for there to be some material things—there could be some protons, or some electrons, or some neutrons, or some of all three, etc. By contrast, there are comparatively fewer ways for there to be no material things—there would have to be no protons, or electrons, or neutrons, or any other kind of material object. So, the Universe was more likely to contain material things than none, which explains why the Universe indeed contains material things.

The idea behind the Probabilistic Explanation is that an explanation in the general spirit of the ones in SOMETHING and MATERIAL THINGS succeeds, just as in DICE, GAS, and BEACH. Notice that the explanations provided in SOMETHING and MATERIAL THINGS don't purport to explain why there are just *this* many material objects, or why there are *these* material objects rather than different ones; the explanations provided there are meant to explain only why there are some things rather than none. Similarly, the explanations in DICE, GAS, and BEACH endeavor only to explain why the relevant facts, *rather than their foils*, are true.

We should pause to note one difference between SOMETHING and MATERIAL THINGS. In SOMETHING, it is plausible that there is only one way for there to be nothing, since it seems as though we have fully specified what the Universe is like when we say that there is *absolutely nothing* in it.[6] By contrast,

---

6. Complications here might arise having to do with which laws, dispositions, or counterfactuals are true. On some views, specifying that there is *absolutely*

in MATERIAL THINGS, we haven't yet fully specified what the Universe is like simply by saying that there are no *material* things in it, since we've left unspecified whether there are immaterial things like Gods, numbers, properties, etc. (as well as how many of them there are and which ones there are), and thus there are lots of ways for there to be no material objects (there can be no material objects and one God, no material objects and two Gods, etc.). Arguably, DICE is more like SOMETHING, since in both cases there is only one way for the explanatory foil to be true,[7] whereas GAS and BEACH are more like MATERIAL THINGS, since in those cases there are multiple ways for the explanatory foil to be true (even though it is intuitive that there are *even more* ways for the explanatory facts to be true). In the end, I don't think that this difference will matter, since the core of the Probabilistic Explanation applies to any case in which there are intuitively more ways for the explanatory fact to be true than for the explanatory foil to be true. But this will play a role in my discussion of Peter van Inwagen's version of the Probabilistic Explanation in Section 4, so it is worth noting here.

Let's go back to BEACH. The explanation in BEACH appealed to the alleged fact that "there are a lot more natural numbers that are evenly divisible by 8 than there are natural numbers that are evenly divisible by 7,296." But the standard definition of the cardinality of a set entails that two sets have the same cardinality if their members can be placed in one-to-one correspondence with each other,[8] and it is possible to place the set of all natural numbers that are evenly divisible by 8 in one-to-one correspondence with the set of all natural numbers that are evenly divisible by 7,296. You simply place the members of each set in ascending order and associate the nth member of the former set with the nth member of the latter set; thus, 8 gets associated with 7,296; 16 gets associated with 14,592; 24 gets associated with 21,888; etc. Thus, on the standard definition of the size of a set, the size of the set of natural numbers evenly divisible by 8 is the same as the size of the set of natural numbers evenly divisible by 7,296. So, in this sense, it's false that "there are a lot more natural numbers that are evenly divisible by 8 than there are natural numbers that are evenly divisible by 7,296."

Does this mean that the explanation in BEACH fails? The intuition behind this explanation is extraordinarily gripping, and I think we should be very hesitant to give up the claim that there is something explanatorily legitimate

---

nothing in the Universe still leaves open which laws, dispositions, or counterfactuals are true. By contrast, on "Humean" views such as David Lewis's, this isn't so. For reasons of space, I have to ignore these complications here.

7. I say "arguably," because it's not completely clear that there is only *one* way for the sum of the dice to be 12; after all, both dice could land on 6 *and they land one inch from each other*, or both dice could land on 6 *and they land two inches from each other*, etc. Perhaps this complication could be avoided if we constrained the system more tightly, so that there really was only one way for both of the dice to land on 6. But, as will become clear below, I don't think that anything turns on this complication.

8. See, e.g., Potter 2004: chs. 4 and 9.

in the ballpark. One natural thought here is that even though the size of the set of natural numbers evenly divisible by 8 is the same as the size of the set of natural numbers evenly divisible by 7,296, we (and John) really know something more about beaches than just that they have *some* natural number or other of grains of sand; in particular, we know that every beach on Earth has fewer than some large finite number—10^{20}, say—of grains of sand. And the cardinality of the set of all natural numbers *that are less than 10^{20}* and are divisible by 8 is certainly not the same as the cardinality of the set of all natural numbers *that are less than 10^{20}* and are divisible by 7,296; the former set is many times larger than the latter. So, given that Daytona Beach has some number of grains of sand *that is less than 10^{20}*, it really is more likely that the number of grains of sand it has is evenly divisible by 8 rather than 7,296, since there really are more natural numbers less than 10^{20} that are evenly divisible by 8 than by 7,296.

The above all seems correct, but I don't think that the fact that we (and John) know that the number of grains of sand on Daytona Beach is less than 10^{20} (or any other finite number) plays an essential role in vindicating the explanation in BEACH. The reason for this is that an analogous explanation succeeds even in cases where we do *not* know that the relevant set of possibilities is finite.

Consider the following case:

> **Case 6:** DART. Keith is about to throw an infinitely sharp dart at a dartboard. Though he is guaranteed not to miss the dartboard entirely, Keith has no control over where the dart hits on the dartboard. Once the dart lands, he is going to draw a line segment from the point where it lands to the exact center of the bull's-eye. This line will form an angle with a vertical line segment that has already been drawn, beginning at the center of the bull's-eye and extending vertically upward. (The angle will be less than 180° if the dart lands on the right side of the dartboard and will be greater than 180° if it lands on the left side of the dartboard.) Keith will then measure the angle (in degrees) that the two lines form.[9] Keith throws the dart and measures the angle, and notices that the fifth decimal place of the angle is not 7. Here is a candidate explanation of that fact: there are more real numbers between 0 and 360 that have a digit other than 7 in their fifth decimal place than there are real numbers between 0 and 360 that have a 7 in their fifth decimal place. So, it is more likely that any particular dart (thrown by Keith) will form an angle that doesn't have a 7 in its fifth decimal place than that it will form an angle that does have a

---

9. For the purposes of this case, it won't matter whether we say that a dart that lands exactly on the vertical line forms a 0° angle or a 360° angle. If the dart lands precisely on the center of the bull's-eye, we'll stipulate that the angle formed is 0°.

7 in its fifth decimal place, which explains why the dart that Keith threw has a number other than 7 in its fifth decimal place, rather than a 7.

The explanation offered in DART seems to be very much like the explanation offered in BEACH. And the same criticism of the explanation in BEACH we considered above could be legitimately raised against the explanation in DART: the set of real numbers between 0 and 360 that have a 7 in their fifth decimal place can be placed in one-to-one correspondence with the set of real numbers between 0 and 360 that do not have a 7 in their fifth decimal place, so (on the standard definition of the size of a set) it is false that the former set is smaller than the latter set. But the response we considered in BEACH—i.e., that there is some appropriate finite restriction of the relevant space in which it is strictly true that there are more elements that are instances of the fact type than those that are instances of the foil type—doesn't apply in DART; in DART, we have no further knowledge of the situation (analogous to the information that the number of grains of sand is less than 10^{20}) that can impose such a finite restriction.

Similar points apply to GAS. It is false that there are more spread-out microstates than there are bunched-up microstates; the elements of the two sets can be placed in one-to-one correspondence with each other. And there's no information that we have in virtue of which the set of possible microstates of the gas can be restricted to some finite set. Still, it seems, there is something in the general spirit of the explanations in DART and GAS that succeeds, and for roughly the same reasons that (something in the neighborhood of) the explanation in BEACH succeeds. So, I think that finite restrictions of the relevant spaces in those two cases are red herrings.

The standard mathematical way of accounting for the intuition that one set can be in some sense "bigger" than another set even when they have the same cardinality is to appeal to *measure theory*. A *measure* is a function from certain subsets[10] of a given set X to the extended[11] nonnegative real numbers, and it can be thought of as a generalization of the notion of length (or, in higher dimensions, area and volume); even though the points in a one-inch line can be placed in one-to-one correspondence with the points in a two-inch line (and hence the former set has the same cardinality as the latter set), the two-inch line can still have a *measure* that is twice as large as that of the one-inch line. Indeed, the standard Lebesgue measure has precisely this consequence.[12] So, by appealing to the Lebesgue measure, it seems

---

10. The qualifier "certain" is required because, on the assumption of the Axiom of Choice, some measures are such that not all sets are measurable by that measure. Giuseppe Vitali (1905) first proved the existence of the Vitali set, which is not measurable by the standard Lebesgue measure.

11. The "extended" nonnegative real numbers are obtained from the nonnegative real numbers by adding a single element: $+\infty$.

12. See Tao 2011, Section 1.2.

that we might be able to vindicate the explanations in Dice, Gas, and Dart; the idea would be that the *measure* of the set of states in which the dice sum to 7 is greater than the *measure* of the set of states in which the dice sum to 12, the *measure* of the set of states in which the gas is spread out is greater than the *measure* of the set of states in which the gas is bunched up, and the *measure* of the set of states in which the dart forms an angle that does not have a 7 in the fifth decimal place is greater than the *measure* of the set of states in which it does. We can't *quite* apply this analysis to Beach, since the Lebesgue measure can be defined only in spaces that can be represented as Euclidean *n*-dimensional *real-valued* spaces, and the space of possible numbers of grains of sand is natural-number-valued. The standard mathematical approach here is to appeal to something called an "asymptotic density," which yields the "proportion" of natural numbers up to *n* that have some property, in the limit as *n* approaches ∞.[13] Unsurprisingly, the asymptotic density of natural numbers divisible by 7,296 is lower (indeed, 912 times lower) than the asymptotic density of natural numbers divisible by 8. Asymptotic densities function much like measures for natural numbers; for a discussion of this analogy, see Buck 1946. In order to avoid these complications, I will focus on Dart rather than Beach below.

We will return to the Lebesgue measure in Section 4. But if it is right that an appropriate appeal to the Lebesgue measure can vindicate the explanations in Dice, Gas, and Dart, then it seems as though similar considerations may apply to Something and Material Things; in those cases, it's at least fairly plausible that the *measure* of the set of states in which something exists is larger than the *measure* of the set of states in which nothing exists. This is what I take to be the philosophical core of the Probabilistic Explanation.

3   PROBLEM CASES

However, the explanations in Something and Material Things face a challenge: there are a number of cases that *seem* to be relevantly similar to those cases and yet in which apparently analogous explanations fail. The question, then, is how to distinguish these cases from Dice, Gas, Beach, and Dart, and on which side of the distinction we ought to categorize Something and Material Things.

Here are a few such "problem" cases:

> Case 7: Restroom. You walk up to the airplane restroom, and the sign on the door is broken, so you are wondering whether or not it is occupied. You think to yourself, "There is only one way for the restroom to be

---

13. See Nathanson 2000 and Tenenbaum 1995 for discussions of asymptotic densities.

unoccupied—namely, for nobody to be in the restroom. But there are lots and lots of ways for the restroom to be occupied—Dorit could be in there, or Bernie could be in there, or Mariska could be in there, or Doug and Susan could be in there, etc." So, you continue, it is more likely that this restroom is occupied than that it is unoccupied. You knock on the door and indeed hear a voice yell, "There's someone in here!" You think to yourself, "That makes sense—the fact that there's someone in there is explained by the fact that there are so many more ways for the restroom to be occupied than there are ways for the restroom to be unoccupied."

Case 8: BOMB. Dr. Evil has armed a universe-annihilating bomb and is threatening to detonate it unless his demands are met. The police are pursuing him, but you are unsure of the status of either their pursuit or any efforts to satisfy Dr. Evil's demands. You think to yourself, "There is only one way for the future to go if Dr. Evil detonates his bomb—namely, there will be eternal nothingness. But there are lots of ways for the future to go if Dr. Evil doesn't detonate his bomb—the Red Sox might win the World Series next year, or the Cubs might, or the Yankees might, etc." So, you continue, it is more likely that Dr. Evil will not detonate his bomb than that he will. In fact, Dr. Evil is apprehended later in the day, and his bomb is disarmed. You think to yourself, "That makes sense—the fact that Dr. Evil's bomb didn't detonate is explained by the fact that there are many more ways for the future to go if the bomb didn't detonate than if it did."

Case 9: STRINGS. You hear two string theorists debating about string theory. One of them holds a theory on which spacetime has a total of 10 dimensions, whereas the other holds a theory on which spacetime has 26 dimensions. You think to yourself, "There are a lot more ways for spacetime to be arranged if spacetime has 26 dimensions than if it has 10 dimensions." So, you continue, it is more likely that spacetime would have 26 dimensions than that it would have 10 dimensions. Later, the scientific community comes to agree that the 26-dimension version of string theory is true. You think to yourself, "That makes sense—the fact that there are so many more ways for a 26-dimensional spacetime to be arranged than for a 10-dimensional spacetime to be arranged explains why spacetime is 26-dimensional rather than 10-dimensional."

I hope that you share my intuition that the explanations in RESTROOM, BOMB, and STRINGS are deeply problematic. There are, of course, some distinctions to be drawn among them. BOMB seems to be more like DICE and SOMETHING, where there is only one way for the explanatory foil to be true, while STRINGS seems to be more like GAS, BEACH, and MATERIAL THINGS, where there are multiple ways for the explanatory foil to be true (but where it's intuitive that there are even more ways for the explanatory fact to be true). RESTROOM might seem to be like BOMB, DICE, and SOMETHING, since it might seem that there is only one way for the restroom to be unoccupied; however, just as the claim that there are no material objects leaves unspecified which immaterial objects there are, so too does the claim that the restroom is unoccupied (by humans) leave unspecified whether and how the restroom is occupied by nonhuman objects. Again, I don't think that this difference is the key to understanding the difference between the good explanations we've considered and the bad ones.

Moreover, it is worth noting that if the explanations in RESTROOM and STRINGS were legitimate, that would seem to entail that it was *even more* likely that the restroom would have lots of people in it (after all, there are more ways for there to be lots of people in a restroom than for there to be only one), and that it was *even more* likely that spacetime would be 73-dimensional, or 473-dimensional, than that it would be 26-dimensional (after all, there are more ways for a 473-dimensional spacetime to be arranged than for a 26-dimensional spacetime to be arranged). Similarly, if the explanation of BOMB were legitimate, that would seem to entail that it is *even more* likely that the Universe will continue on for a very, very long time without ever being annihilated by anything, since there are even more ways for a long-running Universe to develop than for a shorter-running Universe to develop. The analogous implication looks to be unproblematic in DICE, GAS, and BEACH; for example, it seems as though it was even more likely that the number of grains of sand on Daytona Beach would turn out to be divisible by 2 (say) than that it would be divisible by 8 (and even less likely that the number would turn out to be divisible by 2,491,237 than that it would be divisible by 7,296). But in RESTROOM, it was *not* more likely that more people would be in the restroom rather than fewer, and in STRINGS, it was *not* more likely that the Universe would turn out to be 473-dimensional rather than 26-dimensional.

4 VAN INWAGEN'S VERSION OF THE PROBABILISTIC EXPLANATION

In his subtle and interesting paper "Why Is There Anything at All?"[14] van Inwagen offers a version of the Probabilistic Explanation.[15] Van Inwagen's explanation has four premises:

(1) There are some beings;
(2) If there is more than one possible world, there are infinitely many;
(3) There is at most one possible world in which there are no beings;
(4) For any two possible worlds, the probability of their being actual is equal.[16]

Van Inwagen's version of the Probabilistic Explanation proceeds as follows:

---

14. Van Inwagen 1996.
15. Van Inwagen credits Robert Nozick (1981: 127–8) with having briefly presented a version of this argument.
16. Van Inwagen 1996: 99.

Now let *Spinozism* be the thesis that there is just one possible world. We proceed by cases.

If Spinozism is true, then, by premise (1), it is a necessary truth that there are some beings, and the probability of there being no beings is 0.

If Spinozism is false, then, by premise (2), logical space comprises infinitely many possible worlds. If logical space comprises infinitely many possible worlds, and if any two worlds are equiprobable—premise (4)—then the probability of every world is 0. If a proposition is true in at most one world, and if the probability of every world is 0, then the probability of that proposition is 0. But then, by premise (3), the probability of there being no beings is 0.

Hence, the probability of there being no beings is 0.[17]

According to van Inwagen, the fact that the probability of there being no beings is 0, then, explains why there are beings rather than no beings.

Van Inwagen is quite explicit that his explanatory goals are limited to the explanation of why there is something rather than nothing and do not extend to the explanation of why there are material things rather than no material things: "The conclusion of the argument is not about the probability of there being no physical beings, but about the probability of there being no beings of any sort."[18] And it's clear that van Inwagen's argument as he presents it can be generalized only to cases in which the explanatory foil is true in only one possible world; this is true in SOMETHING but false in MATERIAL THINGS.

Still, in order to accommodate explanations like those in GAS, BEACH, and DART (as well as DICE, perhaps), and in order to be able to assess the explanation in MATERIAL THINGS, it seems as though we need to extend our discussion beyond cases in which there is only one way for the explanatory foil to be true.

Van Inwagen's central premise (4)—the one that van Inwagen characterizes as "the one that people are going to want to dispute"[19]—is that each possible world has the same probability; on the assumption that there are infinitely many possible worlds, each possible world must therefore have probability 0. If that's right, then (again, assuming infinitely many possible worlds) any proposition that is true in only one possible world (such as the proposition that there are no beings) must have probability 0 too, and hence the negation of any such proposition must have probability 1. Presumably, van Inwagen would be happy to say that any proposition that is true in only a *finite* number of possible worlds also has probability 0 (since any finite sum of 0's is equal to 0) and hence that the negation of any such proposition has probability 1. But in order to extend our discussion to

---

17. Ibid.: 100.
18. Van Inwagen 1996: 100.
19. Ibid.: 101.

cases in which the explanatory foil is true in infinitely many cases, it seems as though we need to appeal to the measure-theoretic strategy introduced in Section 2.

Why does van Inwagen accept premise (4)? He first defines the notion of a *maximal* state of a system: a state x is maximal if it is inconsistent with any state y such that x fails to entail y. Consider a system consisting only of two electrons, A and B, each of which can be in either of two states, spin-up or spin-down. The state x_1 of A and B being in the same spin state is not maximal; x_1 neither entails nor is inconsistent with the state x_2 in which A and B are each in the spin-up state. But x_2 is maximal, since for each possible state y of the system, x_2 either entails y or is inconsistent with it; x_2 entails x_1, for example, and is inconsistent with the state x_3 in which A and B are each in the spin-down state. Van Inwagen then defines a system to be *isolated* with respect to a certain set of its states when "no facts about objects external to the system could in any way have any influence on which of those states the system was in."[20]

Van Inwagen proposes that "for any system of objects (that has maximal states) the maximal states of the system should be regarded as equally probable, provided that the system is isolated."[21] Call this the MAXIMALITY CONSTRAINT. Since possible worlds are maximal states of Reality, and since Reality is isolated, van Inwagen concludes that each possible world must be equally probable. Moreover, according to van Inwagen, we can know a priori that each possible world is equally probable, since we can know a priori both that possible worlds are maximal states of Reality and that Reality is isolated (and, presumably, we can know the MAXIMALITY CONSTRAINT a priori as well); according to van Inwagen, "[w]e do seem to have some capacity for determining *a priori* that some states of some systems are of equal probability."[22]

Clearly, the MAXIMALITY CONSTRAINT will deliver the result that the probability of there being no beings is 0, which is sufficient for van Inwagen's own explanatory purposes. But to extend our discussion to cases where there are infinitely many ways for the explanatory foil to be true, we need some analogous principle that allows us to say that that the measure of possible worlds in which the explanatory facts are true in GAS, BEACH, and DART is larger than the measure of possible worlds in which the explanatory foils are true. As discussed in Section 2, the most natural way to do that is to appeal to a measure (like the Lebesgue measure) that assigns a higher measure to each explanatory fact than to its corresponding explanatory foil.

What is it about the Lebesgue measure in virtue of which it is relevantly analogous to van Inwagen's MAXIMALITY CONSTRAINT? The intuitive idea

20. Van Inwagen 1996: 104.
21. Ibid.
22. Van Inwagen 1996: 103.

behind the Maximality Constraint seems to be that when two propositions p and q are each "maximal" in that they are each true in exactly one possible world, then they must have the same probability (i.e., 0), even if the single possible world in which p is true is different from the single possible world in which q is true. In other words, the "identity" of the world we're considering is irrelevant to its probability; from the standpoint of probability, each maximal possible world is interchangeable with any other one. A natural way, I think, to extend this notion to propositions that are true in infinitely many possible worlds is to say that the "identity" of an *interval* is similarly irrelevant to *its* probability, and thus that any consistent linear translation of an interval will yield an interval with the same probability. Thus, for instance, since the (infinite) set of possible worlds in which some particular gas particle's horizontal location is somewhere in the interval between the left wall of the box and the center of the box can be translated into the (infinite) set of possible worlds in which that particle is somewhere in the interval between the center of the box and the right wall of the box, we conclude that the particle's *probability* of being located in the former interval is the same as its probability of being located in the latter interval. And since the Lebesgue measure has the special property of being *translation-invariant*,[23] it has seemed particularly well suited to grounding probabilities like the ones that appear in Gas.

The Lebesgue measure also has the special property of being *rotation-invariant*; just as with linear translations, any consistent *rotation* of one set will yield a set with the same Lebesgue measure as the original. In Dart, for instance, consider the (nearly) pie-sliced-shaped region that corresponds to a score of 20 points on a standard dartboard, and the (nearly) pie-sliced-shaped region that corresponds to a score of 19 points on a standard dartboard. The former region can be rotated into the latter region; by rotating the whole dartboard 162° counterclockwise, the former region will exactly coincide with the latter region. Thus, the Lebesgue measure of the 20-point region is the same as the Lebesgue measure of the 19-point region; since we want to say that the *probability* that a dart will land in each region of the dartboard is identical, the Lebesgue measure again seems fairly well suited for grounding probabilities in cases like Dart.

Thus, though I want to be quite explicit in acknowledging that van Inwagen never endorses such a principle, it seems to me that van Inwagen's Maximality Constraint is similar in spirit and motivation to the principle that we ought to associate a proposition's probability with its Lebesgue measure in the relevant space. Call this principle Lebesgueism.

However, I have several reservations about the Maximality Constraint and Lebesgueism, as applied to the cases we've been considering. The first problem we have already seen; to the extent that the Maximality Constraint

---

23. See, e.g., Hunter n.d.: 19–20, and Tao 2011: 46–79 for a discussion.

and Lebesgueism vindicate the good explanations in Dice, Gas, Beach, and Dart, they seem to similarly vindicate the bad explanations in Restroom, Bomb, and Strings. After all, exactly analogous reasoning to that in Dice, Gas, and Beach seems to lead to the conclusion that the explanatory facts in Restroom, Bomb, and Strings are more probable than their explanatory foils, which (I'm assuming) is the wrong result. Just as the Lebesgue measure of the set of bunched-up states is lower than the Lebesgue measure of the set of spread-out states in Gas, so too is the Lebesgue measure of the set of unoccupied states lower than the Lebesgue measure of the set of occupied states in Restroom, and similarly for Bomb and Strings. (This is particularly apparent in Bomb because, just as in Something, the set of states in which the explanatory foil is true is a singleton, and the Lebesgue measure assigns a measure of 0 to each singleton set.)

Second, there are well-known paradoxical results that arise from the so-called Principle of Indifference, which seem also to extend to the unrestricted application of Lebesgueism. Bas van Fraassen's famous "cube factory" case[24] (and variations thereon[25]) illustrates the point nicely. If all we know about a "mystery square" is that it is no more than two feet wide, how likely is it that the square is less than one foot wide? If we think of the space of possible *widths* of the square, then Lebesgueism entails that the probability is 1/2, since the Lebesgue measure of the interval (0,1) is half as large as the Lebesgue measure of the interval (0,2). But if we think of the space of possible *areas* of the square, then the probability is 1/4; a square with a width of one foot has an area of one square foot and a square with a width of two feet has an area of four square feet, and the Lebesgue measure of the interval (0,1) is 1/4 the size of the Lebesgue measure of the interval (0,4). The lesson usually drawn from these sorts of cases is that since the same possibilities can be parameterized differently, resulting in different spaces over which the Lebesgue measure can be defined, we can't use the Lebesgue measure to define probabilities. But this, of course, is precisely what Lebesgueism tries to do.

Third, consider an isolated system in which a fair coin is repeatedly flipped until it lands tails, at which point the system self-destructs. There are various maximal states of the system: (1) the coin lands tails on the first flip, at which point the system self-destructs; (2) the coin lands heads on the first flip and tails on the second flip, at which point the system self-destructs; (3) the coin lands heads on the first two flips and tails on the third flip, at which point the system self-destructs, etc. Each of these states is maximal, but I don't see any reason to assign these states equal probability; it seems clear to me that the first state has probability 1/2, that the second state has probability 1/4, that the third state has the probability of 1/8, and so on. This strikes me as a counterexample to the Maximality Constraint.

---

24. See van Fraassen 1989: ch. 12.
25. See, e.g., White 2010.

Fourth, a Carnapian worry: Carnap objected to the equal assignment of probability to each possible "state description" on the grounds that such an assignment would lead to the impossibility of "learning from experience";[26] I think that the MAXIMALITY CONSTRAINT has similar unacceptably skeptical epistemological consequences. For simplicity, consider an isolated system consisting of Ram and an animal in front of him. Ram is having an experience as of a zebra in front of him. But there being a zebra in front of Ram (in such-and-such a position and orientation) and there being a mule cleverly disguised to look like a zebra in front of Ram (in such-and-such a position and orientation) both seem to be maximal states of the isolated system; thus, the MAXIMALITY CONSTRAINT entails that they are equally probable. Since Ram's total evidence (namely, his experience as of a zebra in front of him) doesn't distinguish between these two maximal states of the system, it seems as though Ram should be equally confident that he's looking at a zebra as he is that he is looking at a cleverly disguised mule.[27] Moreover, this point seems to generalize to other skeptical hypotheses; we can always fill in the details of the skeptical state in order to make it maximal, in which case the MAXIMALITY CONSTRAINT will entail that that hypothesis is just as likely as the corresponding maximal antiskeptical hypothesis according to which the subject has the same total evidence as in the skeptical state. So, it seems that me that the only hope of responding to skepticism is to say that some maximal antiskeptical hypotheses are more probable than their corresponding maximal skeptical hypotheses, which requires denying the MAXIMALITY CONSTRAINT.[28]

---

26. See Carnap 1950. Carnap's objection was that Ludwig Wittgenstein's confirmation function $c\dagger$ precludes "learning from experience" because it fails to incorporate relations of inductive relevance. Carnap offered an alternative confirmation function $c*$ that was designed to remedy this defect. For a clear discussion of Carnap, see Salmon 1967: 72.

27. I'm making two assumptions here. First, I'm assuming something in the neighborhood of Lewis's Principal Principle (see Lewis 1980), which plausibly justifies the move from the claim that the zebra hypothesis has the same objective chance as the cleverly-disguised-mule hypothesis to the claim that Ram (who, I'm also supposing, lacks any "inadmissible" information) should "initially" be equally confident in each hypothesis. Second, I'm assuming the principle that if a rational agent initially has the same confidence in two hypotheses, and if his total evidence doesn't support one of these hypotheses over the other, then he should still be equally confident of the two hypotheses after collecting that total evidence. This second assumption is entailed by Conditionalization but doesn't entail it.

28. Of course, even if we do deny the MAXIMALITY CONSTRAINT, it is not as though our antiskeptical work is done; we still need a story about *why* certain maximal antiskeptical hypotheses are more probable than their skeptical cousins. This is not the place to develop that story, and there are several different strategies we might pursue; perhaps certain maximal states are more likely because they are simpler, more unified, or more fit for explanation, or have some other epistemically desirable feature.

5   THE LESSON

The core lesson that I draw from the above is that we should reject van Inwagen's reliance on a priori considerations to calculate the relevant probabilities in cases like SOMETHING and MATERIAL THINGS. On my view, we have no general a priori grounds to think that any two maximal states of an isolated system (or, in particular, any two possible worlds) will have the same probability. Similarly, we have no a priori grounds to think that just because two propositions are identified with sets of possibilities in some space that receive the same Lebesgue measure, those two propositions must be equiprobable.

Rather, at least in many cases—including some that we have been considering—our reasons for assigning probabilities to propositions are at least partly a posteriori in nature. In these cases, it is only when we have good a posteriori reasons to assign equal probabilities to each possible world—or, to assign equal probabilities to sets that receive the same measure in some suitable space—that we are justified in so doing. Of course, none of this is to deny that we can sometimes have good a priori grounds for particular probability assignments. I have good a priori grounds for believing that the proposition that $1 + 1 = 3$ is necessary false, and hence for assigning it a probability of 0; similarly, I have good a priori grounds for believing that the proposition that all dogs are dogs is necessarily true, and hence for assigning it a probability of 1. And we can also have a priori grounds for making comparative probability assignments; my a priori knowledge that the proposition that it will rain tomorrow is logically weaker than the proposition that it will either rain or snow tomorrow grounds my assigning a probability to the latter proposition that is no lower than the probability I assign to the former proposition.

In cases like DICE, GAS, and DART, I think we do have strong a posteriori grounds for thinking that the explanatory facts are likelier than the explanatory foils. Michael Strevens (1998) develops the view that such judgments are often grounded by an appeal to "symmetries in the mechanism of the chance setup in question."[29] Jill North develops a similar view in North (2010).[30] Strevens considers the case of a roulette wheel, which is quite similar in relevant respects to DICE and DART. To simplify a bit, Strevens supposes that ω—the angular speed with which the roulette wheel is initially spun—is the only initial condition of the setup that varies from spin to spin and that affects the probability that the spin will result in the ball landing on a "red" number. According to Strevens:

---

29. Strevens 1998: 238.
30. Whereas Strevens's view appeals only to "microconstancy" (explained below) and the smoothness of the distribution of initial conditions, North appeals to the *uniformity* of the distribution of initial conditions, which is a stronger constraint. However, this difference won't matter for our purposes here.

As a consequence of the assumption of determinism, the laws of nature together with the mechanism of the wheel determine a function $U_E(\omega)$ which is equal to one just in case ω causes a red number to be obtained on the wheel, zero otherwise. . . . "Red" and "black" values of ω form rapidly alternating bands; neighboring bands are of approximately equal size. . . . The equal size of the black and red bands is a consequence of the physical symmetry of the wheel, in particular, of the fact that at any point in any spin, the wheel takes approximately equal time to rotate through a red segment as it does to rotate through a black segment. I will say that such a $U_E(\omega)$ is *microconstant* with ratio 0.5.[31]

In the roulette case, Strevens appropriately emphasizes the "microconstancy" of $U_E(\omega)$, since it is plausible in that case that the narrow "red" bands of $U_E(\omega)$ are of approximately equal size to their neighboring "black" bands. The analogous claim is plausible in DICE; there, too, the "laws of nature together with the mechanism" of the DICE setup induce a microconstant function that takes the initial conditions of the dice roll (the orientation, position, and velocity of each die, say) as inputs and yield outcomes (ordered pairs $\{n, m\}$, where $1 \leq n, m \leq 6$) as outputs. This microconstancy allows us to conclude that each $\{n, m\}$ is equally likely, which allows us to calculate the probability of any particular *sum* by adding up the probabilities of the $\{n, m\}$ pairs that produce that sum; the result, of course, is that a sum of 7 is much more likely than a sum of 12. Similar remarks apply to DART; in that case, the microconstancy of the relevant U_E function will allow us to conclude that "outcomes" involving an angle with a 7 in the fifth decimal place are equiprobable with outcomes involving any other number between 0 and 9 in the fifth decimal place, and hence that the set of outcomes with a number other than 7 in the fifth decimal place is more probable than the set of outcomes with a 7 in the fifth decimal place.

I don't think that microconstancy plays such a starring role in all such cases (nor, I should say, does Strevens commit himself to such a view). If we individuate the outcomes in a dart-throwing case by the region of the dartboard that the dart hits (1-point through 20-points plus the bull's-eye), then I don't think that the relevant U_E function is *micro*constant, since relatively large changes in initial conditions won't affect the result (since the relevant regions of the dartboard are large and connected), and hence the "bands" corresponding to each outcome will be much larger. But this isn't important; perhaps knowledge of microconstancy is just one of many a posteriori grounds for assigning equal probabilities to distinct outcomes. What is important for my purposes is that the grounds are a posteriori in nature rather than a priori; the reason that we are justified in assigning equal probabilities to the relevant outcomes in DICE and DART is that we know empirically that

---

31. Strevens 1998: 239.

the relevant laws and the relevant mechanisms together determine a function that assigns those probabilities.[32,33] Crucially, the reason is *not* merely that we are able to construct a mathematical space of outcomes and *define* a particular measure over that space which assigns equal measures to different regions. If *that* were all there was to it, there would be nothing to prevent the construction of a space of outcomes in DICE that treated the sums as the fundamental outcomes, and hence that licensed the conclusion that an outcome of 12 is equiprobable with an outcome of 7. (This is just another version of van Fraassen's "cube factory" problem from Section 4.)

Of course, none of this is to impugn either measure theory itself or its relevance to the cases we've been considering. But another way of putting the point of this Section is that we need *empirical reasons* to identify a proposition's measure in some space with its probability of obtaining; we can't just construct the space in a mathematically legitimate way and place our faith in the Lebesgue measure. And it's not that there's any problem with the Lebesgue measure in particular; if we have good empirical reasons to identify the probability of a proposition with its Lebesgue measure in a particular space, then I'm all for the Lebesgue measure. We just can't close our eyes in our armchairs and hope.

The above story explains what goes wrong in RESTROOM, BOMB, and STRINGS. In those cases, we lack any empirical reason to assign equal probabilities to the different outcomes—to the outcome in which both Doug and Susan are in the restroom and the outcome in which nobody is in the restroom, to the outcome in which Dr. Evil detonates the bomb and to the outcome in which he doesn't, or to some set of 10-dimensional states of the world and a set of 26-dimensional states of the world that have the same Lebesgue measure. In fact, depending on the case, we often have good empirical reasons not to do that; we might have empirical knowledge, e.g., that the relevant restroom spends more time in its "unoccupied" state than in its "occupied" state, or that the restroom is far less likely to be occupied by

---

32. I think that very similar considerations apply to GAS as well, though a full discussion of that case would require a fuller treatment of statistical mechanics than space allows. See, e.g., Davey 2008; Albert 2000: ch. 3; and Sklar 1993: ch. 2.

33. In DART, there might be some sense in which I've *stipulated* a function that assigns those probabilities; in the description of the case, I said that Keith "has no control over where the dart hits on the dartboard," and perhaps that amounts to the stipulation that the relevant outcomes in DART get assigned equal probabilities. Or, perhaps, there is some background a posteriori knowledge about the science of human throwing behavior that is required in order to conclude that someone with "no control" throws darts that are equally likely to land on any two regions of the dartboard that have equal Lebesgue measures. This issue is subtle, and I can't pursue it thoroughly here, but I don't think that this distinction will matter for any of my purposes in this paper. After all, it seems obviously illegitimate to simply *stipulate* that the various possible maximal states of the universe are equally probable, and this is certainly *not* van Inwagen's strategy; his goal is rather to *argue* for the claim that a priori considerations ground the judgment that the maximal states of any system are equiprobable.

multiple people than it is to be occupied by one person. The putative explanations in these cases attempt to accomplish purely a priori what can in fact be done only a posteriori; without this necessary a posteriori grounding, the explanations fail.

The big question for us, then, is whether we have the necessary a posteriori grounds to endorse the putative explanations in SOMETHING and MATERIAL THINGS—i.e., whether we have good a posteriori grounds to assign an equal probability to an empty universe as to a universe in which there are 17 neutrons (in SOMETHING), or to assign an equal probability to a universe with one God and no material objects as to a universe with one God and one (or two, or three, etc.) material objects (in MATERIAL THINGS). I think it's clear that in SOMETHING and MATERIAL THINGS we are in possession of nothing *remotely* like the grounds for doing this that we have in DICE, GAS, and DART. Unlike in DICE, GAS, and DART, we certainly have no clear idea of the laws or initial conditions that determine the space of possible outcomes in SOMETHING or MATERIAL THINGS (if the notions of law and initial condition even *make sense* in this context). Absent that, I don't think that there's any reason for optimism that SOMETHING and MATERIAL THINGS will turn out to be more like DICE, GAS, and DART than they are like RESTROOM, BOMB, and STRINGS. At the very least, the burden seems to be on the defender of SOMETHING and MATERIAL THINGS to provide us with grounds for thinking that the relevant propositions really are equally probable. As I've argued, van Inwagen hasn't succeeded in doing that, and I'm not aware of anyone else who has fared any better.[34]

REFERENCES

Albert, D. (2000). *Time and Chance*. Cambridge, MA: Harvard University Press.

Buck, R.C. (1946). 'The Measure Theoretic Approach to Density', *American Journal of Mathematics* 68: 560–80.

Carnap, R. (1950). *Logical Foundations of Probability*. Chicago: University of Chicago Press.

Davey, K. (2008). 'The Justification of Probability Measures in Statistical Mechanics', *Philosophy of Science* 75: 28–44.

Dretske, F. (1972). 'Contrastive Statements', *Philosophical Review* 81: 411–37.

Garfinkel, A. (1981). *Forms of Explanation: Rethinking the Questions in Social Theory*. New Haven, CT: Yale University Press.

Hempel, C.G. (1965). 'Aspects of Scientific Explanation', in Hempel, C.G. (ed.). *Aspects of Scientific Explanation and Other Essays in the Philosophy of Science*. New York: Free Press, 331–496.

Humphreys, P. (1989). *The Chances of Explanation*. Princeton, NJ: Princeton University Press.

Hunter, J. (2011). *Notes on Measure Theory*. Manuscript. Available at http://www.math.ucdavis.edu/~hunter/m206/measure_notes.pdf (1/28/2013).

---

34. Thanks to Kenny Easwaran, Tyron Goldschmidt, Marc Lange, and John Roberts for valuable discussion and feedback on the issues raised in this chapter.

Lewis, D. (1980). 'A Subjectivist's Guide to Objective Chance', in Jeffrey, R.C. (ed.). *Studies in Inductive Logic and Probability*, Vol. 2. Berkeley: University of California Press, 263–93.

———. (1986). 'Causal Explanation', in his *Philosophical Papers*, Vol. 2. New York: Oxford University Press, 214–40.

Lipton, P. (1990). 'Contrastive Explanation', in Knowles, D. (ed.). *Explanation and Its Limits*. Cambridge: Cambridge University Press, 247–66.

———. (1991a). 'Contrastive Explanation and Causal Triangulation', *Philosophy of Science* 58: 687–97.

———. (1991b). *Inference to the Best Explanation*. London: Routledge.

———. (1993). 'Making a Difference', *Philosophica* 51: 39–54.

Mellor, D. (1976). 'Probable Explanation', *Australasian Journal of Philosophy* 54: 231–41.

Nathanson, M. (2000). *Elementary Methods in Number Theory*. Graduate Texts in Mathematics. New York: Springer-Verlag.

North, J. (2010). 'An Empirical Approach to Symmetry and Probability', *Studies in History and Philosophy of Modern Physics* 41: 27–40.

Nozick, R. (1981). *Philosophical Explanations*. Cambridge, MA: Harvard University Press.

Potter, M. (2004). *Set Theory and Its Philosophy: A Critical Introduction*. Oxford & New York: Oxford University Press.

Railton, P. (1978). 'A Deductive-Nomological Model of Probabilistic Explanation', *Philosophy of Science* 45: 206–26.

Ruben, D. (1987). 'Explaining Contrastive Facts', *Analysis* 47: 35–7.

Salmon, W. (1967). *The Foundations of Scientific Inference*. Pittsburgh: University of Pittsburgh Press.

———. (1970). 'Statistical Explanation', in Colodny, R.G. (ed.). *The Nature and Function of Scientific Theories*. Pittsburgh: University of Pittsburgh Press, 173–231.

Sklar, L. (1993). *Physics and Chance*. Cambridge: Cambridge University Press.

Strevens, M. (1998). 'Inferring Probabilities From Symmetries', *Nous* 32: 231–46.

———. (2000). 'Do Large Probabilities Explain Better?', *Philosophy of Science* 67: 366–90.

Tao, T. (2011). *An Introduction to Measure Theory*. Providence, RI: American Mathematical Society.

Tenenbaum, G. (1995). *Introduction to Analytic and Probabilistic Number Theory*. Cambridge Studies in Advanced Mathematics. Cambridge: Cambridge University Press.

Van Fraassen, B. (1980). *The Scientific Image*. Oxford: Clarendon Press.

———. (1989). *Laws and Symmetry*. Oxford: Clarendon Press.

Van Inwagen, P. (1996). 'Why Is There Anything at All?', *Proceedings of the Aristotelian Society*, Supp. Vol. 70: 95–110.

Vitali, G. (1905). 'Sul Problema Della Misura Dei Gruppi Di Punti Di Una Retta', *Tipi Gamberini e Parmeggiani* 1905: 231–5.

White, R. (2010). 'Evidential Symmetry and Mushy Credence', in Gendler, T.S. and Hawthorne, J. (eds.). *Oxford Studies in Epistemology*, Vol. 3. Oxford: Oxford University Press, 161–86.

14 Are Some Things Naturally Necessary?

Marc Lange

1 THE DISTINCTNESS PRINCIPLE AND THE ULTIMATE WHY

I read recently about a baby who was trapped during the night of February 26, 2011, in a locked bank vault in Conyers, Georgia. Naturally, I wondered why that had happened. How had the baby managed to get into the vault? More simply, we might ask, "Why was there someone in the bank vault sometime that night (rather than no one in the vault at any time that night)?" The following, even if true, cannot answer this question:

> Smith was in the center of the vault 1 trillionth (10^{-12}) of a second before 3 AM. It is a law of nature that nothing travels faster than the speed of light (3×10^8 meters per second), so in 10^{-12} second, an object can traverse at most 3×10^{-4} meters (0.3 millimeters). The center of the vault is more than 0.3 millimeters from any wall or door. Therefore, considering Smith's initial position and this law, Smith had to be inside the vault at 3 AM. Since 3 AM is at night, it follows that there was someone in the vault sometime that night.

Why is that not an answer?

- *Not* because it depicts the fact being explained (the "explanandum") as explaining itself—since it does not do that. The fact that Smith was in the center of the vault at 10^{-12} of a second before 3 AM is not the same fact as the explanandum: that there was someone in the vault sometime that night.
- *Not* because the purported "explanans" (what's doing the explaining) logically entails the explanandum. Many explanations have this feature (such as explanations that deduce the fact being explained from deterministic laws and initial conditions).
- *Not* because this account leaves us wondering why Smith was in the center of the vault at 10^{-12} of a second before 3 AM. Oftentimes an explanation of G by F will lead us to wonder why F obtains. That the answer to one why question leads us to ask certain other why questions

"is a psychological matter, and the problems thus raised are new explanatory problems" (Hempel 2001: 335); a proposed explanation of *G* by *F* is not rendered incomplete just because it provokes why questions about *F*.

We must look elsewhere to account for the failure of this response to answer our why question.

I suggest that it fails to explain why someone was in the vault that night because it appeals to a fact (that Smith was in the vault at 10^{-12} of a second before 3 AM) that *makes it the case* that the explanandum obtains (that someone was in the vault sometime that night). In other words, Smith's being in the vault at 10^{-12} of a second before 3 AM *constitutes* the explanandum's obtaining. Of course, Smith's being in the vault at 10^{-12} of a second before 3 AM is not the only fact by virtue of which the world qualifies as having someone in the vault sometime that night. Anyone being in the vault anytime that night does just as well. Nevertheless, Smith's being in the vault at 10^{-12} of a second before 3 AM amounts to someone's being in the vault sometime that night.

On this view, the purported explanans is not distinct enough from the explanandum to explain it. The failure of the above response to our why question derives not from the explanandum's figuring in the purported explanans or from the explanans's provoking another why question, but from the explanandum's truth being constituted by the truth of the purported explanans. If *F* suffices (or even helps) to constitute *G*'s truth, then *F* is too close to *G* to help scientifically explain why *G* obtains. Let's call this criterion of adequacy for a scientific explanation "the distinctness principle."[1]

Some scientific explanations might initially appear to violate the distinctness principle. For instance, consider this explanation of why a given gas's pressure rose:

> The gas was heated, so its random molecular motion increased. Therefore, the forces exerted by the gas molecules on the container wall as they collided with it tended to increase. Hence, the pressure increased

---

1. The distinctness principle also accounts for the fact that in a typical context, we cannot use the fact that Smith was in the center of the vault at 10^{-12} second before 3 AM to help explain why Smith was in the vault at 3 AM. That is because in a typical context, when we want to know why Smith was in the vault at 3 AM, we have a particular contrast class in mind: we want to know why Smith was in the vault at 3 AM *rather than not in the vault at any time that night*. To answer this question, we must explain why Smith was in the vault at 3 AM *and* explain why the contrast was not the case, that is, why he was in the vault sometime that night. But by the distinctness principle, that Smith was in the center of the vault at 10^{-12} second before 3 AM cannot explain why Smith was in the vault sometime that night.

since a gas's pressure is the force per unit area in a direction normal to the container wall exerted by the gas molecules colliding with that wall.

A fact about gas pressure is made true by a fact about the normal force exerted by gas molecules colliding with the container wall. Thus, it might appear that we just explained the fact that the gas pressure rose by appealing to a fact that constitutes this pressure fact.

However, the distinctness principle is not violated by this explanation. The facts it uses to explain why the gas's pressure rose are the heating of the gas, various laws relating this heating to the increased force exerted by gas molecules as they collide with the walls, and the fact that the gas pressure just is this normal force per unit area. None of these facts helps to *constitute* the explanandum: that the gas's pressure rose. What the distinctness principle precludes is our using the increase in the per-area normal force exerted by the gas to help explain the increase in the gas's pressure. But our explanation did not do that. It isn't a rise in the force per unit area that explains the rise in pressure. Rather, what explains the rise in the force per unit area also explains the rise in pressure.

A special case of the distinctness principle is that a fact cannot help to explain itself. Trivially, G is what it is about the world by virtue of which G obtains. That a fact cannot help to explain itself might seem uninteresting, but it has subtle consequences. If F entails and explains G, then E can be logically equivalent to F and yet fail to explain G, as when E is ($F\&G$). Since ($F\&G$) suffices to constitute G's truth, ($F\&G$) cannot help to explain G. Scientific explanation is hyperintensional.

The same criteria of adequacy for an explanation of why there is someone in the vault sometime that night (rather than no one in the vault anytime that night) apply to an explanation of why there is something rather than nothing. We violate the distinctness principle if we try to answer the "riddle of existence" by pointing out that there was matter at 10^{-12} of a second before 3 AM, so by the law of matter conservation there had to be matter at 3 AM, and since matter is something, it follows that there is something. That there was matter at 10^{-12} of a second before 3 AM is not the same fact as the explanandum, but it constitutes the explanandum and so is not distinct enough from the explanandum to help explain it. An explanation of why there is something rather than nothing cannot appeal to some thing's existence.

But then what could be an explanans, considering that so many facts involve some thing's existing? There appears to be nothing left available to serve as an explanans. That is the challenge I will try to meet in this paper. I will try to sketch one sort of answer that the "riddle of existence" could receive. I offer no argument that this is the only possible kind of answer; to find one possible kind of answer is challenge enough. I also aim to specify only a certain *kind* of answer rather than to defend a particular answer of this kind. To do that, I would benefit from knowing the fundamental things that exist (a task for science and metaphysics). Until we know that, we may have to settle for knowing the kinds of answer that the riddle of existence might have.

2   SOME SCIENTIFIC EXPLANATIONS ARE NON-CAUSAL

I have taken for granted that in asking why there is something rather than nothing, we are demanding a scientific explanation. If an answer to this question does not have to satisfy the usual criteria of adequacy for a scientific explanation (such as the distinctness principle), then I do not know what it must do. Of course, not all explanations are scientific explanations; there are explanations in mathematics, moral explanations, legal explanations, and even baseball explanations (e.g., for why a given baserunner is entitled to third base). But none of these kinds of explanations is demanded by the riddle of existence. The most straightforward interpretation of the riddle is that it is akin to "Why was there someone in the vault that night?" and so demands a scientific explanation.

Some philosophers who claim to regard the riddle of existence as demanding a scientific explanation may not actually so regard it. Rescher, for instance, suggests that "what is perhaps the most promising prospect" for answering the riddle is that "things exist because 'that's for the best'" (1999: 121). This response does successfully avoid appealing to the existence of another thing. However, Rescher says nothing about how he thinks explanations that use the "best principle" ("Whatever would be for the best is what obtains") coexist alongside scientific explanations that appeal to causes, initial and boundary conditions, mechanisms, symmetry principles, and so forth. Are different why questions to be addressed by different kinds of explanations, and if so, which by which? Is one kind of explanation more fundamental than the other, and what makes it so? What ensures that explanations of the two kinds do not clash? These questions are similar to familiar questions about how explanations appealing to extremum principles (such as the "principle of least action") would have to be coordinated with explanations appealing to efficient causes. More important, there are (as far as I know) no familiar scientific explanations where a fact that involves no values is explained by a fact involving values. Most important, this proposal's most attractive feature for Rescher (apart from its avoiding any appeal to a thing's existence) seems to be that the "best principle" would explain itself (1999: 121–3). But even if the best principle is itself for the best, scientific explanation (as I have already suggested) does not allow self-explanation. The best principle would have to be in force independently of whatever it accounts for. That the best principle endorses itself does not show that it can be responsible for itself. Insofar as Rescher is prepared to flout familiar criteria of adequacy for scientific explanation, he fails to treat the best principle as supplying a scientific explanation.

The riddle of existence must be distinguished from other "ultimate why questions." For instance, let C be logically equivalent to all of the logically contingent facts. Why is it the case that C? This question, I strongly suspect, has no answer. A contingent fact is insufficiently distinct from C to explain it, on pain of violating the distinctness principle. A necessary fact cannot explain C by entailing it, since any logical consequence of necessities must be necessary whereas C is contingent. The only available option is for some necessary fact to explain C without entailing it. But I do not see how that might plausibly be done. (For instance, I do not see what necessary fact might explain C by making C likely or even by giving C some particular, low objective chance.)

Fortunately, the riddle of existence does not ask us to explain all logically contingent facts. It asks us to explain only a particular logically contingent fact: that there is something rather than nothing. I presume that the riddle is not concerned with various things that exist as a matter of broadly logical necessity, such as (arguably) numbers and propositions. Rather, the riddle asks why there exists some contingent thing rather than no such thing. A contingent fact that does not involve the existence of any contingent thing could answer the riddle, and though we could then ask for that fact's explanation, its having none would not undermine its explaining why there is something rather than nothing.

Hempel argues that the riddle of existence cannot have an answer:

> The riddle has been constructed in a manner that makes an answer logically impossible: and scientific explanation can hardly be held to be limited because it cannot satisfy a logically inconsistent requirement. . . . No theory, no conceptual scheme, can explain the existence of anything without assuming the existence of something. (2001: 341)

The riddle of existence poses no mystery, according to Hempel, since it is logically impossible for the riddle to have an answer.

However, Hempel's argument presupposes that the only way for the existence of a (contingent) thing to be explained is by the existence of some other contingent thing. As Rescher (1999: 118) emphasizes, this presupposition does not follow from the notion that the only way for a contingent fact to be explained is by some other contingent fact. On the other hand, it seems to me that Hempel's presupposition derives some support from a popular idea about explanation (though Hempel did not subscribe to it): that any scientific explanation is a *causal* explanation. Consider Lewis's view:

> For an explanation, I think, is an account of etiology: it tells us something about how an event was caused. Or it tells us something general about how some, or many, or all events of a certain kind are caused. Or it explains an existential fact by telling us something about how several

events jointly make that fact true, and then perhaps something about how those truthmaker events were caused. (1986: 73–4)

An explanation qualifies as "causal" if and only if it explains by virtue of describing contextually relevant features of the explanandum's causal history or, more broadly, of the world's network of causal relations. Let's see how Hempel's argument is supported by the view that all scientific explanations are causal explanations.

Admittedly, not every causal explanation has an explanans that appeals to some thing's existence. (For instance, a law of nature might have a causal explanation that describes the causal history that any instance of that law would have, but that explanation does not require that the law ever actually have any instances and so does not posit any thing's existence.) Furthermore, a fact that involves some thing's existence may have a causal explanation that fails to posit any thing's existence. (For instance, a causal explanation of a given body's undergoing zero—rather than nonzero—acceleration may be the body's feeling no forces. Its feeling no forces is an omission, not a cause; it does not posit any thing's existence.) Nevertheless, the explanans in a causal explanation typically involves the existence of some thing, since a cause must involve the existence of some thing and a causal explanation typically describes the explanandum's causes. Therefore, if every scientific explanation is a causal explanation, then there is some reason to think that Hempel is correct in presupposing that to explain the existence of some thing, we must appeal to the existence of some thing, and so the existence of something rather than nothing can have no scientific explanation.

Insofar as this interpretation of Hempel's argument captures its power, it also suggests where the argument may be vulnerable. A scientific explanation that is *not* a causal explanation would not be driven to appeal to some thing's existence by the fact that a cause must involve the existence of some thing. One promising approach for addressing the riddle of existence, then, would be to explore whether the existence of something rather than nothing might have a noncausal scientific explanation.

How can some thing's existence have a noncausal explanation? How does a noncausal scientific explanation work? Let's look at an example. Consider the fact that at every moment that Earth exists, on the equator (or any other great circle on the Earth) there exist two points having the same temperature that are located antipodally (i.e., exactly opposite each other in that the line through them passes through the Earth's center). Why is that? The explanation begins with the fact that temperature is a continuous function. That is, roughly speaking, as you move (let's say) eastward along the equator, temperature changes smoothly rather than jumping discontinuously. Now imagine placing your two index fingers on a globe at two antipodal points on the equator. Take the temperature on Earth at the location x to which your left-hand finger is pointing minus the temperature at the location to which your right-hand finger is pointing. This difference function $D(x)$ must change continuously as you move your two fingers eastward, keeping them at antipodal points on the equator (since a function is continuous if it is the difference between two continuous functions). Suppose without loss of generality that for the two initial points, D is greater than zero (i.e., the left-finger location is warmer than the right). Then, when you have moved your two fingers far enough around the equator that your left finger is now where your right finger began (and vice versa), D must be less than zero. Hence, since D is continuous, there must have been a moment as you were moving your fingers when D went from positive to negative—that is, when $D = 0$. (This step uses the intermediate-value theorem: if f is a real-valued, continuous function on $[a,b]$ and u is a real number between $f(a)$ and $f(b)$, then there is a $c \; \varepsilon \; [a,b]$ such that $f(c) = u$.) At that moment, your fingers were pointing to antipodal points at the same temperature.[2]

This account explains why there is always such a pair of points (rather than no such pair), but it does not explain why two particular antipodal points are at the same temperature (rather than at different temperatures). To explain that fact, we would have to invoke the meteorological conditions at some earlier moment. That would be a causal explanation. In contrast, the explanation that I have just given does not work by tracing the causal histories of the temperatures at certain times at certain antipodal points on Earth. Rather, it works by revealing that there *must* be a pair of antipodal points of equal temperature. Of course, it is not mathematically necessary that Earth exist and have great circles and be characterized at every surface point by a continuous temperature function. But these background conditions are taken for granted in the why question. The question is not why there are at any moment antipodal equatorial points on Earth with the same temperature rather than no Earth or no continuous terrestrial temperature function. Rather, the question is (roughly) why there are at any moment antipodal equatorial points on Earth with the same temperature rather than no such points but still Earth with a continuous surface temperature function. The answer is that the latter is mathematically impossible.[3]

This example is suggestive. First, it suggests that a scientific explanation need not trace a causal history in order to explain. In explaining why at a given moment there exists a pair of antipodal equatorial points at the same temperature, the above argument fails to do what Lewis says a scientific explanation must do. (Recall that according to Lewis, a scientific

---

2. I borrow this sort of example from Colyvan 1998: 321–2, 2001: 49–50, and 2007: 120, though his point is not to give a noncausal explanation. (As given in Colyvan 1998 and 2001, the example is somewhat more complicated: it concerns the fact that there are antipodal points at the same temperature *and pressure*, and so requires the Borsuk-Ulam theorem in place of the intermediate-value theorem.) The example frequently appears in introductory calculus texts (such as Brannan 2006: 145–6).
3. For more examples of such distinctively mathematical scientific explanations along with a fuller account of how they work, see Lange forthcoming.

explanation "explains an existential fact by telling us something about how several events jointly make that fact true, and then perhaps something about how those truthmaker events were caused." On this conception, to explain why there exists such a pair of points at some moment, we would have to say something about which particular antipodal equatorial points are at the same temperature at that moment, and then perhaps something about the causes of their temperatures.) Lewis is mistaken in thinking that all scientific explanations are causal. Perhaps a noncausal explanation of why there is something rather than nothing manages to make no appeal to anything's existence just as the noncausal explanation of the existence of antipodal equatorial points at equal temperature makes no appeal to the causes of the temperatures at any points.

There is a second respect in which this example is suggestive. It reveals one way for a noncausal explanation to work: by revealing that the explanandum is necessary. Such an explanation conforms to the distinctness criterion; that some fact p is necessary entails that p but does not help to constitute p's obtaining. On the contrary, whatever it is that makes p obtain is just the same whether p is necessary or not. (For instance, the fact that no actual knot of a certain kind has ever been untied is constituted no differently whether it is mathematically possible or impossible to untie such a knot.)

There is one important respect in which the antipodal-points example is not suggestive: I do not see any way to argue that the existence of something rather than nothing is *mathematically* necessary in the manner of the existence of antipodal equatorial points of equal temperature.[4] But mathematical necessity is not the only variety of necessity. There is another variety that plays a large role in scientific explanation.

3   WHAT MUST (OF NATURAL NECESSITY) BE, MUST BE

That p must obtain explains why p does in fact obtain. That p is a law of nature explains why p obtains because p's being a law is associated with p's having a variety of necessity: natural (also called physical, nomic, and

---

4. Lewis has an argument that the existence of something rather than nothing is *metaphysically* necessary: what is necessary is what holds in all possible worlds, and a possible world is a maximal mereological sum of objects that are spatiotemporally related, so every possible world has spatiotemporally related objects, so there is no world where there is nothing. But because Lewis is committed to all scientific explanations being causal explanations, he cannot use the metaphysical necessity of something to explain noncausally why there is something. He sees this as a fortunate result; he thinks that it would count against his view if it purported to solve the riddle of existence in this way (Lewis 1986: 73–4). In contrast, I think that the metaphysical necessity that something exist *would* explain why there is something rather than nothing. But I do not accept Lewis's argument for the metaphysical necessity that something exist.

nomological) necessity. For instance, that it is a law that no body travels faster than light speed explains why it is that no actual body exceeds light speed. It is not a coincidence that no body ever exceeds light speed. It is inevitable, unavoidable—necessary. Likewise, that energy must (as a matter of natural necessity) be conserved explains why all of the processes that take place, despite their physical diversity, are alike in conserving energy. Of course, whenever we explain p by appealing to p's natural necessity, we could go on to ask why p is naturally necessary. But an explanation of p's natural necessity is not needed to explain why p obtains; p's natural necessity suffices. (In the same way, the fact that it is mathematically impossible to untie a trefoil knot suffices to explain why no one, however persistent or creative, has ever untied one. This explanation does not need to specify why untying one is mathematically impossible.)

I suggest that the existence of something rather than nothing is naturally necessary, and that is why there is something rather than nothing. The explanans here noncausally explains the explanandum by revealing the explanandum to be necessary. This explanation conforms to the distinctness condition because the explanans does not appeal to a fact that helps to constitute the explanandum; in particular, the explanans (a law of nature's holding) does not involve some thing's existing. That it is a law that p isn't part of what makes it the case that p. As I mentioned in the previous section, what it is that makes p the case is the same whether p holds as a law or as an accident (i.e., as a contingent fact that is not a natural necessity).

The existence of something rather than nothing is naturally necessary because (I suggest further) there is some thing whose existence is required by natural law. Its existence is not logically, metaphysically, or mathematically necessary. Rather, its existence is a contingent fact (since laws of nature generally are contingent facts).[5] Its existence therefore falls within the scope of the question "Why does there exist some contingent thing rather than no such thing?" Any law requiring the existence of a certain contingent thing explains why there is something rather than nothing: because there must be this particular thing, and hence something.[6]

What is an example of a thing that a law of nature says exists? Obviously, no ordinary object's existence is a matter of natural necessity. The world could have proceeded in accordance with the same laws of nature but contained neither you nor me. A thing whose existence is required by law

---

5. The law as a proposition is an abstract object that exists as a matter of broadly logical necessity. But it is not likewise necessary that a given law obtains. Some philosophers have recently argued that laws are metaphysically necessary rather than contingent. The truth of this thesis would in some ways make my task easier, but I do not accept it (see Lange 2009 for further discussion).

6. That there *must be* this particular thing also explains why there *is* this particular thing. That there is this particular thing entails that there is something but fails to explain why there is something, on pain of violating the distinctness principle.

is presumably integral to the world's fundamental structure in a way that ordinary objects are not.

Unfortunately, since we do not yet know the world's fundamental structure, we are in no position to identify or even to offer a plausible candidate for a thing whose existence is required by natural law. However, I think that we can still appreciate what sort of thing's existence might plausibly be required by natural law. Consider classical physics as Newton conceived of it (or, at least, as it is depicted in a typical introductory undergraduate physics textbook)—that is, as equipped with absolute space and absolute time as substances.[7] So interpreted, classical physics would seem best understood as including laws specifying that absolute space and absolute time exist (as well as that space has a certain Euclidean geometry, is three-dimensional, and so forth).[8] That is, if absolute space and absolute time exist (in a world governed by classical physics), then their existence is no accident. If absolute space and absolute time (or, if you prefer, points in space and moments in time) exist as matters of natural law, then the laws require that something exists and thereby explain why there is something rather than nothing.

We can further motivate the thought that in a world governed by classical physics where absolute space and time exist, their existence is required by natural law. Laws of nature are widely recognized as set apart from accidents by their relation to the truth of various subjunctive conditionals. In particular, it has often been suggested that "nomic preservation" (NP) holds:

NP: It is a law that *p* if and only if for any *q* that is logically consistent with the laws, *p* would still have held if *q* had been the case.[9]

For instance, even if you or I had never existed, the laws would still have obtained, though various accidents would not. The existence of space and time seems to have the kind of invariance under counterfactual antecedents that NP says distinguishes matters of law. For example, had you or I never existed, absolute space and time would still have existed. It seems that under any circumstance logically consistent with the laws, there would still have been absolute space and time.

Obviously, however, absolute space would not still have existed, had absolute space not existed! (Arguably, it is not the case that absolute space

---

7. My argument does not require this to be the only way to interpret classical physics. I also do not mean to suggest that Newton himself regarded laws of nature as sufficient to answer the riddle of existence. (See note 14 for a statement of the view Newton expresses.)

8. Heinrich Hertz uses the three-dimensionality of space to explain why various forces decline with the square of the distance. Since the explanandum here is a law, the explanans must be naturally necessary. See Lange 2012.

9. NP requires some details that I shall not elaborate here. I give them (and references to other philosophers who have defended similar principles) in Lange 2009.

would still have existed, had absolute time not existed.) Does this fact show that absolute space lacks the perseverance under counterfactuals that is exhibited by natural necessities? No, this fact accords with NP if the existence of absolute space (and time) is a matter of law—since, in that case, any counterfactual antecedent positing the nonexistence of absolute space (or time) is logically inconsistent with the laws and so falls outside the scope of the counterfactual antecedents under which natural necessities must be preserved. But then we beg the question in using NP to argue that the existence of space and time possesses the invariance under counterfactual antecedents that is characteristic of natural necessities.

We can do better. Take a set of truths that is "logically closed" (i.e., that includes every logical consequence of its members) and is neither the empty set nor the set of all truths. Call such a set *stable* exactly when every member p of the set would still have been true had q been the case, for each of the counterfactual suppositions q that is logically consistent with every member of the set. I suggest that p is a natural necessity exactly when p belongs to a "stable" set.[10] On this view, what makes the laws special is that, taken collectively, they are invariant under as broad a range of counterfactual suppositions as they *could* logically possibly be. *All* of the laws would still have held under *every* counterfactual supposition under which they *could all* still have held. No set containing an accident can make that boast (except for the set of all truths, for which the boast is trivial). Because the laws' logical closure is nontrivially as invariant under counterfactual perturbations as it could be, there is a variety of *necessity* corresponding to it; necessity involves possessing a *maximal* degree of invariance under counterfactual perturbations. No kind of necessity is possessed by an accident, even one that would still have held under many counterfactual suppositions.

The notion of "stability" gives us a way out of the circle that results from using NP to specify the laws as the truths that would still have held under those counterfactual antecedents that are logically consistent with the laws. Accordingly, consider the set containing exactly those facts that are uncontroversially laws of classical physics together with the fact that absolute space and absolute time exist. Plausibly (according to classical physics), this set is stable, and hence the laws require that absolute space and time exist. We no longer need to appeal to the premise that the laws require the existence of space and time in order to argue that the truth of "Had space not existed, then space would not have existed" fails to undermine the claim that space's existence has the invariance under counterfactual suppositions that is characteristic of matters of law. Rather, the definition of "stability" tells us that the given set does not have to be invariant under the

---

10. Again, this proposal requires details that make no difference here. For them (and arguments that the laws form a stable set and that no set containing an accident is stable), see Lange 2009.

counterfactual antecedent "Had space (or time) not existed" in order for the set to qualify as stable.

It is hard to come up with a counterfactual antecedent with which this set is logically consistent but under which this set is not invariant (according to classical physics). Had the Eiffel Tower been taller, the set's members would all still have obtained, and likewise had the Eiffel Tower not existed. What about "Had either the Eiffel Tower been taller or space not existed"? It seems to me very plausible that (according to classical physics) the Eiffel Tower would then have been taller.

Of course, the world is not actually governed by classical physics. But, plausibly, some fundamental things have their existence required by law in the same way as space and time do in the version of classical physics that we have been considering. Perhaps the Higgs field (posited by the Standard Model as responsible for the masses of elementary particles, and whose existence is being tested experimentally as of this writing) is required by the laws—or perhaps the thing required by the laws is something that has not yet even been hypothesized and out of which space and time themselves emerge. In any case, the same considerations I have sketched regarding absolute space and time in classical physics (under one interpretation) plausibly apply to some entity or other, whatever the laws of nature turn out to be.[11] Imagine the set containing exactly the facts that are uncontroversially laws together with the fact that something exists. It is hard to imagine a counterfactual antecedent that is logically consistent with this set under which it would fail to be preserved.[12]

---

11. Rather than some fundamental things having *their existence* required by law, it could instead be that some fundamental things have *some nonzero chance* of their existence required by law. In that case, the laws would again explain the thing's existence noncausally—but statistically rather than deterministically. This is the kind of explanation that Alex Vilenkin (2006) and Lawrence Krauss (2012) give of our spacetime's existence from out of nothing as the product of a quantum tunneling event: "And yet, the state of 'nothing' cannot be identified with *absolute* nothingness. The tunneling is described by the laws of quantum mechanics, and thus 'nothing' should be subjected to these laws. The laws of physics must have existed, even though there was no universe" (Vilenkin 2006: 181).

12. Here is a candidate: Had the Big Bang not occurred. We might well think that there would then have been nothing. On the other hand, perhaps the facts that are uncontroversially laws explain why the Big Bang occurs by entailing that it occurs. Or perhaps the Big Bang's nonoccurrence logically entails that there is nothing, and so this counterfactual antecedent is logically inconsistent with the set consisting of all of the facts that are uncontroversially laws together with the fact that something exists. Or perhaps some feature of the Big Bang's occurrence is a matter of fundamental law. Without more knowledge of the Big Bang, it is difficult to speculate more productively.

4 OBJECTIONS AND REPLIES

It might be objected that this response to the riddle of existence is too easy. There is something, and we want to know why—and to answer "Because there must be something" might seem pretty cheap.

However, it is not cheap. For a thing's existence to be a matter of natural law, a large collection of subjunctive facts must hold, each specifying that the thing would still have existed under certain circumstances, where the range of circumstances represented by these subjunctive antecedents is extremely broad. This is a very steep hurdle that no ordinary thing can pass. (And we would need considerable evidence to justify believing of some thing that it must be.)

It might be objected that no law of nature can posit a particular thing's existence. Rather, a law must take the form "All *F*s are *G*" (which is trivially true if there is nothing).[13] However, I see no good reason why a fact that posits a particular thing's existence cannot function in scientific practice as a law does (e.g., in connection with counterfactuals). That laws cannot dictate some thing's existence is a vestige of a theological view by which science should not be restricted. On that view, a natural law–governed process can bring things into existence only out of other things that already exist; it takes God to bring things into existence without using other things that already exist. This view portrays laws as merely mediating natural processes, any of which requires raw materials. God, in contrast, stands outside of the spacetime framework and so can be responsible for its existence.[14] I see no reason to buy into this picture—not only because of the role it assigns to God, but also because of the role it assigns to laws. I understand laws

---

13. Lewis, for instance, says that the laws are the *generalizations* belonging to the "best system." Many philosophers (such as Hempel and Reichenbach) have held that fundamental laws cannot refer ineliminably to particular times, places, events, or objects on pain of failing to be universal.

    It is perhaps worth noting that on Lewis's "Best System Account" of natural law, it is plausible that the laws require there to be something rather than nothing. For instance, on the Best System Account, there is plausibly a law of the form "At every moment, the total quantity of electric charge is Q." This truth adds great strength at very little cost in simplicity (Lange 2009: 57). (On my own view of laws, of course, this fact is accidental.) So other accounts of law agree that there must be something.

14. Here is one statement of this view: "[S]hould all the present arrangements of our existing natural history be destroyed, there is no power in the laws of our existing natural philosophy to replace them. . . . The laws of nature may keep up the working of the machinery—but they did not and could not set up the machine. . . . For the continuance of the system and of all its operations, we might imagine a sufficiency in the laws of nature; but it is the first construction of the system which so palpably calls for the intervention of an artificer, or demonstrates so powerfully the fiat and finger of a God" (Chalmers 1836: 225).

as standing outside of space and time (as God is supposed to do) and as able to supply noncausal explanations, not merely explanations that describe causal processes; laws can noncausally account for the existence of the things that form the framework (whether space and time or something else) in which all natural processes must operate. Even if the laws include the conservation of matter and so cannot bring matter into existence from a prior state where no matter exists, laws can be responsible for the existence of certain fundamental things that exist at all times or that underwrite time itself. The only motive I can see for saying that laws cannot be responsible for mandating some thing's existence is to leave some work for God to do.

Perhaps the most serious worry faced by my proposal is something along the following lines. If some particular thing exists (and therefore something exists) because some law says that it must, then why does that law hold? If that law is explained by some other law, then why are the laws collectively as they are rather than otherwise? Indeed, why are there any laws of nature at all? Even if a law of nature does not count as a "thing" that "exists" in the sense of "Why is there something rather than nothing?" an appeal to a law still leaves us with a residual why question: why does that law obtain?

I would like to make several brief points in response to this worry. First, as I said earlier, the answer to a given why question is not vitiated by its appealing to facts about which we can ask another why question. If the law specifying the existence of absolute space has no explanation (according to classical physics), then that would not prevent it from explaining (according to classical physics) why there is absolute space. The riddle of existence challenges us to explain why some contingent things exist rather than none at all, and an appeal to a law mandating the existence of some contingent thing can do that. Such a law would be a contingent fact that is not constituted by the existence of any contingent thing, and though we could then ask for that fact's explanation, its having none would not undermine its explaining why there is something rather than nothing.

This brings me to the second point I would like to make in response to the above worry. To explain all of the natural necessities without appealing to any of them is logically impossible in the same way as it seems impossible (according to section 2) to explain all of the contingent facts without appealing to any of them. Accidental facts (i.e., contingent facts that are not naturally necessary) are not modally strong enough to help explain a natural necessity; if a natural necessity depended on an accident, then it would be accidental, too. That is why, in science, laws are explained only by other laws (together with modally stronger facts). Facts possessing a stronger variety of necessity than natural necessity, on the other hand, cannot suffice to explain a naturally necessary fact by entailing it, on pain of the natural necessity's thereby possessing the same stronger necessity as the explanans possesses and so not being contingent (whereas laws are contingent). The only available option is for some fact possessing a variety of necessity stronger than natural necessity to explain all of the laws without entailing any of them. But I do not see how that might plausibly be done. (For instance, I do not see what sort of fact possessing a stronger necessity than natural necessity might explain the laws by making them likely or even by giving them some particular, low objective chance.)

Part of what may be prompting the above worry is that if the explanatory regress that leads to the riddle of existence bottoms out with a fundamental law having no explanation, then seemingly it might just as well have bottomed out one step earlier: with the fact that something exists having no explanation. But it is worth considering what this "just as well" means. It might mean that since a certain itch is not ultimately going to be scratched anyway, we might just as well not have gone to the trouble of invoking fundamental brute laws to explain why there is something rather than nothing; we might just as well have stopped with fundamental brute facts of existence. But my aim is not to scratch an itch; it is to sketch the kinds of explanations there plausibly are. I have tried to identify what it would take for there to be laws specifying that certain things must exist, and it seems to me that the requisite subjunctive conditionals might well be true. If "just as well" is understood not as I just indicated, but instead as meaning "just as plausibly," then I resist the conclusion that the explanatory regress might just as well have bottomed out one step earlier.

Just as a fundamental brute contingent fact may leave some people feeling unsatisfied, so may an infinite explanatory regress. But in the interests of identifying the kinds of explanations there may be, I note that although the natural necessities as a whole may have no explanation, it may be that any given fact p holding with natural necessity has an explanation—though one that appeals to other facts possessing natural necessity. That p must (of natural necessity) obtain explains why p does in fact obtain, and p's natural necessity is associated with various subjunctive facts expressed by conditionals of the form: Were q the case, then p would be the case. Suppose that these subjunctive facts not only are associated with p's natural necessity but also constitute it. In other words, suppose that p's natural necessity just is p's being maximally invariant under counterfactual suppositions in the sense I sketched in the previous section—that is, p's belonging to a "stable" set, where the set's stability consists of various subjunctive facts obtaining.[15] Each of these subjunctive facts may well be naturally necessary in that it may be invariant under exactly the same range of counterfactual

---

15. By this point in the paper, it will come as no surprise to a diligent reader of the footnotes that I offer further details and defense of this proposal in Lange 2009. The subjunctive facts that make p naturally necessary, on this view, are not constituted partly by the fact that p. Rather, they are on an ontological par with the fact that p. Of course, the received view is either that subjunctive conditionals do not express facts at all or that the facts they express obtain by virtue of facts like p. However, among the facts that would seem to be required to make subjunctive facts true are facts about what the laws of nature are. Rather than construe laws as helping to constitute subjunctive facts, I favor the reverse order of ontological priority: that subjunctive facts help to constitute the laws.

antecedents that made p naturally necessary: namely, all of the antecedents that are logically consistent with the laws. For instance, the subjunctive fact that energy would still have been conserved, had we tried to build a "perpetual motion" machine, is one of the subjunctive facts that helps to constitute the natural necessity of energy conservation. This subjunctive fact, in turn, possesses natural necessity by virtue of various other subjunctive facts, such as the fact that had we possessed 23rd-century technology, then energy would have been conserved had we tried to build a perpetual motion machine.

My point is that just as p's natural necessity explains why p in fact obtains, so likewise a given subjunctive fact's natural necessity would explain why that subjunctive fact obtains. Each of the subjunctive facts that (on this picture) helps to constitute p's natural necessity is thereby explained by its natural necessity. Its natural necessity, in turn, is constituted by further subjunctive facts, each of which is explained by its natural necessity, and so on, each successive layer of subjunctive facts being expressed by multiply embedded subjunctive conditionals. With "$q \,\square\!\rightarrow p$" representing "Were it the case that q, then it would have been the case that p," the various layers of facts in this endless explanatory regress take the following form:

$$p$$
$$q \,\square\!\rightarrow p$$
$$r \,\square\!\rightarrow (q \,\square\!\rightarrow p)$$
$$s \,\square\!\rightarrow (r \,\square\!\rightarrow (q \,\square\!\rightarrow p))$$
$$\text{etc.}$$

Each level contains facts that constitute the natural necessity of, and thereby explain, the facts one rung above it. No natural necessity is left unexplained.

Let's summarize. Once we remove all existing things as ineligible to help explain why there is something rather than nothing (since their existence helps to make the explanandum true), nothing seems left available to do the explanatory work. I have tried to meet this challenge by suggesting that some thing's existence may be naturally necessary. In appealing to a natural law, this explanation appeals to a kind of explanans that science already recognizes as true and explanatory. This explanation accords with the conditions of adequacy to which scientific explanations conform. It involves no self-explanation, no violation of the distinctness condition, and no spooks. It is a noncausal explanation and thereby avoids appealing to some cause's existence. A law can explain a thing's existence without itself constituting a thing that exists in the very same way. If the facts that constitute a given fact's natural necessity are subjunctive facts that are themselves naturally necessary, then they may be explained by their natural necessity, leaving none of the naturally necessary facts (or the facts that constitute any fact's natural necessity) without an explanation. This picture constitutes one way for our various desiderata for an answer to the riddle of existence to be satisfied.[16]

REFERENCES

Brannan, D. (2006). *A First Course in Mathematical Analysis*. Cambridge: Cambridge University Press.

Chalmers, T. (1836). *The Works of Thomas Chalmers*, Vol. 1. New York: Leavitt, Lord.

Colyvan, M. (1998). 'Can the Eleatic Principle Be Justified?', *Canadian Journal of Philosophy* 28: 313–36.

———. (2001). *The Indispensability of Mathematics*. New York: Oxford University Press.

———. (2007). 'Mathematical Recreation Versus Mathematical Knowledge' in Leng, M., Pasneau, A., and Potter, M. (eds.). *Mathematical Knowledge*. Oxford: Oxford University Press, 109–22.

Hempel, C.G. (2001). 'Science Unlimited?' in Fetzer, J.H. (ed.). *The Philosophy of Carl G. Hempel: Studies in Science, Explanation, and Rationality*. New York: Oxford University Press, 329–43.

Krauss, L. (2012). *A Universe From Nothing*. New York: Free Press.

Lange, M. (2009). *Laws and Lawmakers*. New York: Oxford University Press.

———. (2012). ' "There Sweep Great General Principles Which All the Laws Seem to Follow" ' in K. Bennett & D. Zimmerman (eds.). *Oxford Studies in Metaphysics*, Vol. 7. Oxford: Oxford University Press., 154-85.

———. (forthcoming). 'What Makes a Scientific Explanation Distinctively Mathematical?', *British Journal for the Philosophy of Science*.

Lewis, D. (1986). *On the Plurality of Worlds*. Oxford: Blackwell.

Rescher, N. (1999). *The Limits of Science*. Pittsburgh: University of Pittsburgh Press.

Vilenkin, A. (2006). *Many Worlds in One*. New York: Hill and Wang.

---

16. Thanks to Matt Kotzen for some helpful (and delightful) discussion.

15 Questioning the Question

Stephen Maitzen

1 INTRODUCTION

The chapters in this volume address the question 'Why is there something rather than nothing?' or else an equivalent version of it such as 'Why is there anything at all?' In honor of G.W. Leibniz, history's most famous champion of the question, let's call it 'Leibniz's Question', or 'LQ' for short. LQ has shown remarkable resilience since Leibniz first posed it more than three hundred years ago (Leibniz 1697). The question just won't go away. Several of the contributors to this volume take LQ very seriously and at face value, and some of them offer elaborate metaphysical answers to it. Some of those answers strike me as merely fanciful; others strike me as truly desperate. For present purposes, however, I needn't name names.

What accounts for this unresolved, centuries-old controversy? Might LQ itself be so apparently intractable—might it invite those truly desperate answers—at least in part because the question itself embodies some confusion? That's exactly my diagnosis of it. I'll argue that LQ as it's often meant by those who ask it—that is, as a question that natural science can't answer even in principle—is *ill-posed* because it rests on false presuppositions, some of which have gone unnoticed. In that sense LQ is a pseudo-question, and it's no wonder then that we can't agree on an answer to it.[1] To put it another way, I aim to 'domesticate' LQ, to deflate its pretensions to being a question that has no naturalistic answer. If LQ has an answer at all, it has a naturalistic answer.

2 NECESSARY OR CONTINGENT? ABSTRACT OR CONCRETE?

For those who accept Platonism about abstract objects, there's a sense in which LQ has a simple and obvious answer: there's something rather than nothing at all because there *couldn't* have been nothing at all. There *had* to

---

1. For a similar diagnosis of the persistent disagreement over Newcomb's problem in rational decision theory, see Maitzen and Wilson 2003.

be something, namely, all of the necessarily existing abstract objects in the Platonic realm, including the real numbers, the empty set and various non-empty sets, and at least some universals. Those objects exist in every possible world, and hence there's no alternative to their existing that could have obtained instead.[2] Some Platonists therefore interpret LQ as a question they can answer by invoking necessarily existing abstract objects, and as a result some of them may regard LQ as resting on a false presupposition, namely, that there *could* have been nothing at all.[3]

In my experience, however, this Platonistic answer rarely satisfies those who take LQ seriously. Non-Platonists see nothing in Platonism to recommend it as an answer, and even Platonists often don't regard it as an answer that gets to the real heart of LQ. Instead, when most people ask LQ, they want to know why there exist any of the visible and often tangible objects they see around them: plants, animals both human and nonhuman, mountains, planets, stars, and so on. It's widely agreed that none of *those* objects had to exist, so why is it the case that any of them do? That question concerns the existence of *contingent* things, and so it misses the point of the question simply to assert the existence of objects that exist necessarily if they exist at all. A satisfactory answer has to cover things that *didn't* have to exist.[4]

But even narrowing our focus to contingent things doesn't go quite far enough. For consider the set whose only member is the planet Mars: the set {Mars}. If {Mars} exists, it exists contingently, because its only member exists contingently and sets owe their identity to their members. But if {Mars} exists, it exists abstractly, and, as I mentioned before, those who ask LQ seem concerned about the existence of concrete objects such as Mars the planet and not, or not primarily, abstract objects such as {Mars} the set. Properly interpreted, then, LQ concerns those things that are contingent (i.e., that didn't have to exist) and concrete (i.e., that exist in spacetime). Why do any of *those* things exist rather than none at all?

Using 'CCT' to abbreviate 'contingent, concrete thing', we can put LQ tersely: 'Why are there any CCTs?' We can omit the traditional coda 'rather than none at all' because, as far as I can see, those five words add rhetorical

---

2. As I explain below in reply to objections, even if it's true that these Platonic entities had to exist, it remains perfectly legitimate to ask *why* they had to exist: you can agree that N exists of necessity and still legitimately ask for an explanation of N's necessity.

3. I'll argue that LQ, as it's typically intended, *does* rest on false presuppositions, but different presuppositions whose falsity is easier to establish. John Heil, 'Contingency' (this volume), challenges the presupposition that there might have been nothing *concrete* at all. I'll argue that LQ rests on false presuppositions even if we *grant* that there might have been nothing concrete at all.

4. Starting with Leibniz himself, philosophers typically interpret LQ as concerning only, or at least primarily, those things that could have failed to exist. See van Inwagen 1996 and O'Connor 2008 among the many recent treatments that interpret LQ this way.

force but not logical content to the question. Notice that LQ doesn't ask, with regard to any particular CCT, 'Why is this thing *contingent*—why doesn't it exist of necessity?' Nor does LQ ask why some particular CCT (some particular table, say) *exists*, a question that shouldn't have struck anyone as profound. Instead, LQ asks why any CCTs at all exist. Leibniz thought, and many have agreed with him, that such a question can't be answered by invoking *only* contingent things and therefore can't be answered by invoking only CCTs. By the same token, and despite the impressive progress of natural science since Leibniz's day, many think that LQ is a question that natural science isn't capable of answering: a question so fundamental and so general that any answer to it must come from *outside* the domain investigated by natural science. I disagree. I think natural science can put the question to bed. If LQ has an answer, there's no good reason to think natural science can't provide it.

3   ANSWERING LQ NATURALISTICALLY

I think LQ has a simple empirical answer. Pick any kind of CCT: penguins, for example. Penguins are CCTs, and if required we can give an empirical explanation of the existence of penguins, an explanation that there's every reason to think will only improve as science continues to progress. Necessarily, if there are penguins there are CCTs, since presumably it's essential to penguins that they be CCTs: in any possible world in which there are penguins, therefore, there are CCTs. Even if it's not *essential* to penguins that they be CCTs, penguins are *in fact* CCTs, or so we assume: in any world in which penguins *are* CCTs there are CCTs, including in the actual world. We often explain some fact F by citing a different fact G whose obtaining is logically sufficient for F. I've therefore explained why there are (some) CCTs (rather than none at all). There are CCTs because there are penguins (among, of course, other CCTs).

How could such an explanation possibly suffice? Stay tuned. The objection that it couldn't possibly suffice stems from one or more of the confusions detailed below. I contend that there's nothing at all defective in my naturalistic answer to LQ: it needn't leave any legitimate question unanswered in principle. In the next section, I'll rebut six objections to the effect that my answer is in some way defective. Examining those objections will reveal that LQ is ill-posed if it's intended or interpreted as a question that natural science can't in principle answer.

4   OBJECTIONS AND REPLIES

Objection A: Penguins aren't the *only* CCTs there are, so your explanation only begins to scratch the surface. By failing to mention any CCTs besides penguins, it falls woefully short of explaining why there exist any of the numerous CCTs and kinds of CCTs that in fact exist.

Reply: It's simply not true that my explanation falls short of explaining why there exist any of the numerous CCTs that exist. For penguins are among the numerous CCTs that exist, and hence the existence of penguins is sufficient for the existence of some of the numerous CCTs that exist. Granted, my explanation doesn't explain the existence of *all* of the numerous CCTs that exist, but it needn't do that in order to explain why there are *any* CCTs, i.e., why there are at least some. Why is there any mud on the carpet? Because the plumber tracked in mud on his shoes, which explains the presence of at least some mud on the carpet even if another culprit, the electrician, tracked in the rest of it.

As for explaining *kinds* of CCTs, my explanation doesn't explain why even *one* kind of CCT exists; it doesn't even try. It asserts the existence of penguins, CCTs that belong to the kind *penguin*, but it doesn't explain why penguins exist, why anything belongs *to* that kind. Answering that question is the job of a different explanation, one there's every reason to think natural science can provide. In citing penguins to explain why there are any CCTs my explanation doesn't thereby explain the existence of any kind of thing at all, a point I'll emphasize in reply to Objection D below.

If the objector complains that my explanation is nevertheless incomplete because it mentions only penguins and not also pens, plums, or protons—the existence of *each* of which suffices for the existence of CCTs—there's of course no reason in principle why my naturalistic explanation couldn't invoke those other CCTs as well. Objection A therefore fails as a principled objection to the project of naturalistically explaining the existence of CCTs: it gives no reason to think that the project can't succeed. Like any project, the project of naturalistically explaining the existence of CCTs has to start somewhere.

Objection B: Your explanation invokes penguins to explain why there are any CCTs at all. But of course penguins *also* need explaining, and whichever CCTs your naturalistic explanation invokes to explain penguins—the evolutionary ancestors of penguins, presumably—will *themselves* need explaining. Your objection fails in principle because it always contains something or other that's unexplained.

Reply: This objection assumes that an explanation falls short if it contains something unexplained. But that assumption misunderstands the concept of explanation that we actually use. If the fire investigator concludes that a short circuit in poorly installed wiring explains why the fire started, we don't regard the explanation as in any way defective because it doesn't also explain why the wiring was poorly installed, why the building materials were combustible, or why enough oxygen was present for combustion to occur. Our concept of explanation allows that an explanation can succeed even if it contains something unexplained.

My point isn't just a pragmatic one about how explanations work in everyday life. Of necessity, *any* noncircular, finite explanation contains something unexplained. In any noncircular explanation, no particular ex-planans appears more than once. Any finite, noncircular explanation con-tains a final explanans, which, because it's not explained by anything else in the explanation, is left unexplained or else explains itself. Of necessity, however, *nothing* explains itself: nothing succeeds as its own explanation.[5] If we rule out the possibility of successful circular explanations, then it fol-lows straightaway that nothing explains itself, since anything's succeeding as its own explanation would be the tightest possible explanatory circle.

But the impossibility of anything's succeeding as its own explanation doesn't depend on the impossibility of successful circular explanations. The impossibility of self-explanation is a logically weaker principle reflecting a basic truth about the concept of explanation, namely, that anything—any fact, event, substance, state of affairs, you name it—is distinct from what-ever (if anything) explains it. It's widely recognized that nothing *contingent* is self-explanatory. But neither is anything else. Suppose that N is necessary rather than contingent, and suppose that E, the explanans for N, is the fact that N *had to* obtain, occur, or exist. Now, E—the fact that N had to obtain, occur, or exist—is one explanation, maybe the strongest possible explana-tion, for why N *does* obtain, occur, or exist. (I hasten to add that this fact about E doesn't make E self-explanatory.) Nevertheless, E must be distinct from N. Even if N and E are both necessary, they remain distinct, for E is a fact *about* N, whereas N *can't* be a fact about N even if N is itself a fact. To repeat: nothing succeeds as its own explanation, so any finite, noncircular explanation contains something unexplained.[6]

One might reply that something can come *close* to explaining itself if the explanation of its existence stems *entirely from its own nature*.[7] But that's not close *enough*: any explanation invoking such a thing as its final explanans leaves something unexplained, namely, why (or how) this thing's existence stems entirely from its own nature and, furthermore, why it *has* a nature of that special sort. If the answer to those questions is 'It couldn't have been otherwise' or even 'It's just analytically true', then of course we're entitled to ask why it couldn't have been otherwise or why it's analytically true. (Asking why something is analytically true differs from asking why something is true *if* it's analytically true, but even that latter, easier ques-tion admits of an answer.) Those questions may seem finicky, but they're perfectly legitimate questions in reply to the assertion that a finite, non-circular explanation might leave *none* of its elements unexplained. What's

---

5. See also Morreall 1980: 210–2, and Wielenberg 2009: 29–30.
6. For structurally similar reasons, nothing could count as an *ultimate purpose*, a 'purpose to end all purposes', a purpose for which it would make no sense to demand an explanation or a justification. See Maitzen 2011.
7. In William Lane Craig's metaphorical phrasing, the ultimate explanation of the existence of CCTs is 'a necessary being ... which *carries within itself* its reason for existence' (Craig 1991: 85, emphasis added).

more, the answers to those legitimate questions—because none of them can be self-explanatory answers—will invite still further legitimate demands for explanation.

Objection C: Because it invokes CCTs at every turn, your naturalistic method of explaining the existence of CCTs is viciously *circular* or else produces a vicious *regress* of explanations.

Reply: I'll reply to each charge in turn. In short, my method of explanation contains no circularity and hence no vicious circularity, and if it produces an endless regress of explanations, the regress isn't vicious.

First, I don't say, 'There are CCTs because there are CCTs', which *would* be circular. I say, 'There are CCTs because there are penguins', and I can add 'and penguins are CCTs' if it's needed to make the implication explicit. Now, the objector might claim to find vicious circularity in my explanation 'There are CCTs because there are penguins and penguins are CCTs' on the grounds that the explanation 'presupposes the existence' of CCTs.[8] But this misguided objection is easily dismissed. *Of course* my explanation of the existence of CCTs presupposes the existence of CCTs: any genuine explanation presupposes the existence of the explanandum that the explanans tries to explain; otherwise, why try to explain it? The explanation 'There's smog because . . .' obviously presupposes the existence of smog. Explanations aren't *arguments*: the point of an explanation isn't to *persuade* its audience that the explanandum exists or obtains, and hence there's no risk that the explanans might 'beg the question' by presupposing the explanandum.[9] On the contrary, the audience already accepts that smog exists and wants to know why it exists. Someone who poses LQ already accepts that CCTs exist and wants to know why they exist. If the objector's charge of circularity were correct, then every genuine explanation would be circular, and the concept of a *circular explanation* would therefore lack the distinctive use that the concept obviously has.[10]

Second, the objector complains that invoking CCTs to explain why there are any CCTs at all produces an endless, and hence vicious, regress

---

8. William F. Vallicella raised this mistaken objection to my explanation in a comment he posted on his blog *Maverick Philosopher*: http://maverickphilosopher.typepad.com/maverick_philosopher/2012/06/the-modified-leibniz-question-the-debate-so-far.html (June 19, 2012, at 7:37 pm).

9. So I find it odd that Richard Gale suggests that an explanation suffers from the defect of being '*pragmatically circular* if the person to whom it is addressed [can't] know some proposition in the explanans without knowing the explanandum' (1991: 268). An explanation might be pragmatically defective because its audience doesn't know enough to *comprehend* the explanans, but that's not the alleged defect Gale defines here.

10. We can distinguish a genuine explanation from a pseudo-explanation. The latter occurs, for instance, when a parent tries to explain to a child why Santa Claus didn't bring her a bicycle for Christmas by saying 'Maybe Santa forgot': the parent isn't really trying to explain an omission on the part of Santa Claus.

of explanations: if CCTs exist because penguins exist, and penguins exist because their evolutionary ancestors existed, and so on, where does it end? But wait: why think it has to end? Why think that an endless regress of explanations would be vicious? On the contrary, given the impossibility of anything's succeeding as its own explanation, an endless regress of explanations is *unavoidable* unless the regress ends with an unexplained fact.

One putative way out of this dilemma would be to allow for the success of a circular explanation, an explanatory account that—unlike an endlessly regressive one—needn't keep adding explanantia because the same explanans occurs more than once. One might say that explanations of this form lack any unexplained or self-explained elements: after all, every element in the circle is allegedly explained by something distinct from it. But one might just as well say, instead, that *none* of the elements in a circular explanation is genuinely explained. For purposes of defending a naturalistic answer to LQ, I needn't resolve this issue: if a circular explanation could succeed, then a naturalistic explanation invoking CCTs to explain the existence of CCTs could go in a circle without thereby failing as an explanation and hence without thereby failing as an answer to LQ. Nevertheless, I'll assume what all sides in the debate seem to hold: circular explanations are inadequate as answers to LQ.

Therefore—to draw the conclusion I asserted earlier in this reply—the only potentially acceptable alternative to an endless regress of explanations is an unexplained fact. As should be clear by now, I don't think the *existence of CCTs* is an unexplained fact. On the contrary, I've offered an explanation of it: there are penguins, and penguins are CCTs, so that's why there are CCTs. But could the explanation of the fact that penguins exist—a fact different from the fact that CCTs exist—itself ultimately rest on a fact that *has* no explanation? Again, for the purpose of answering LQ, for the purpose of explaining why there are CCTs, it doesn't matter: the existence of CCTs can be explained even if what explains it—the existence of penguins—has no explanation. Our concept of explanation allows that A can explain B even if nothing explains A. Exposure to poison gas can explain why Schrödinger's cat dies even if the gas is triggered (as the standard story goes) by the fundamentally indeterministic decay of a radioactive substance. Exposure to poison gas successfully explains the cat's death, and radioactive decay explains the cat's exposure to poison gas, even though (again, according to the standard story) nothing, even in principle, explains why the decay occurred during the cat's time in the box rather than not.

Despite its irrelevance to answering LQ, however, I admit to preferring an endless regress of explanations over a fact that has no explanation. I don't really understand what it could *mean* for there to be no explanation at all for some fact F, for there to be literally no answer to the question 'Why does F obtain?'[11] That's one reason I dislike the standard, indeterministic

---

11. At least where F conceptually *could* have an explanation. I add this qualification because I can think of one fact that *may* have a claim to being an

interpretation of quantum mechanics, which asserts that many facts obtain despite there being no reason at all why they obtain rather than not.[12] (Fortunately for those of us who find that assertion hard to fathom, quantum mechanics faces daunting challenges, including the quantum measurement problem and the difficulty of making quantum mechanics compatible with general relativity.) Indeed, the idea that some contingent facts have no explanation strikes me as no more comprehensible than the idea that there's a smallest nonzero unit of space or time (an idea I can't fathom despite the claim of some in quantum mechanics that space and time are 'quantized' into smallest units). Again, however, this preference of mine doesn't bear on the answer I give to LQ.

One final reason to allow for an endless regress of explanations in answering LQ is the possibility that there's no temporally *first* CCT. If there's no temporally first CCT, and if every CCT is explained in terms of an earlier one, then there's no temporally first explanation and hence there's an endless regress of explanations. As far as I know, nothing in modern cosmology rules out a past that's infinitely long, but an endless regress of explanations doesn't logically require an infinite past. Whether an endless regress of explanations requires an infinite past depends on whether the explanations 'telescope' so that infinitely many of them fit into a finite length of time (much as the infinitely many members of the series $1/2 + 1/4 + 1/8 + 1/16 + \ldots$ never sum to more than 1).

Objection D: Because it invokes CCTs at every turn, your naturalistic method of explanation joins the race in the middle and therefore has no chance of answering LQ. Because it invokes CCTs that already exist, your naturalistic method of explanation has no chance of explaining why there are any CCTs *in the first place*, any CCTs *to begin with*, any CCTs *at all*.

Reply: This objection may get at what Objection C meant in accusing my explanation of 'vicious circularity', an accusation that looked simply confused when assessed in its original wording. In any case, Objection D contains a kernel of truth that's worth examining, but my examination will show that the kernel of truth doesn't in the end support the objection.

I've said that you can explain why there exist any CCTs at all by invoking the existence of penguins. Could you invoke the existence of penguins again

---

inexplicable fact: the fact that the law of noncontradiction holds, the fact that no proposition and its negation are both true. This fact might be too fundamental to be explicable in the sense that putative explanations of it might be *mere reassertions* of it in different language. I trust it's obvious that 'There are penguins' *isn't* a mere reassertion of 'There are CCTs'.

12. To be clear: I'm not claiming that every successful explanation must be a *contrastive* explanation, only that I prefer a view on which there's a contrastive explanation *of* every fact that conceptually could have an explanation at all. Furthermore, given an endless regress of explanations, *modal collapse* (in which all facts obtain of necessity) wouldn't follow from the existence of a contrastive explanation for each fact that's susceptible of explanation.

to explain why there are any *penguins* at all? Clearly not, but what's the difference? I'll explain the difference, and I'll explain why I think Objection D may stem from ignoring the difference.

Why can't you explain the existence of penguins, as such, by invoking only penguins? Because you can't explain why there are any items of a particular kind—in the words of Objection D, why there are any items of that kind in the first place, any to begin with, any at all—by invoking only items belonging *to* that kind, even if your explanation goes on forever. As William L. Rowe puts it, using *man* as the kind in question, 'If *all* we know is that there always have been men and that every man's existence is explained by the causal efficacy of some other man, we do not know *why* there always have been men rather than none at all' (Rowe 1998: 154–5).[13] If you want to explain why there are any items at all belonging to a given kind, you have to invoke something *other* than items of that kind.[14]

To put it more precisely, Objection D seems to rely on the following correct principle governing explanation (with 'substance' used in the metaphysical sense):

(KI)   Where K is any *substantial kind*—i.e., any kind of individual substance—you can't explain why there are any Ks *at all* by invoking only Ks, even if your explanation goes on forever.

The initials 'KI' will remind us that this principle governs the explanation of *kind-instantiation*. KI implies that you can't, for instance, explain why there are any penguins at all by invoking only penguins, even if your explanation goes on forever. That result looks entirely right. But Objection D appears, therefore, to use KI in order to conclude that you can't explain why there are any CCTs at all by invoking only CCTs, even if your explanation goes on forever. That conclusion follows from KI only if 'CCT' denotes a substantial kind, which it doesn't, as I'll argue presently. On this interpretation of it, Objection D starts with the correct principle KI but tries to apply KI outside its range of application; the objection takes a principle stemming from and regulating our practice of explaining *kinds* of things and mistakenly relies on it to block my answer to LQ.

Why does 'penguin' denote a substantial kind, thus bringing penguins within the scope of KI, while 'CCT' doesn't? Since the point is crucial, I'll

---

13. For reasons that should become clear shortly, I take Rowe to be using 'man' as what Wiggins 1967 calls a 'substance sortal' rather than a 'phase sortal'. That is, I read Rowe's use of 'man' as synonymous with 'human being' rather than as a term applicable only during some arbitrarily defined phase in the life of a male human being.
14. Rowe appears to recognize this point when he allows that one *could* explain why men have existed at all by invoking beings of some other kind: in his example, gods (Rowe 1970: 459).

take the time to discuss four ways in which penguins exhibit the characteristic pattern of things forming a substantial kind while CCTs, as such, don't.

First, we can nonarbitrarily *count* penguins but not CCTs. There's a nonarbitrary count of exactly how many penguins occupy a given location—say, the penguin enclosure at the zoo—at a given instant. If CCTs formed a substantial kind, there'd be a nonarbitrary count of exactly how many CCTs occupy a given location at a given instant. To see why there isn't, imagine holding a capped, blue-ink ballpoint pen in your otherwise-empty hand and then trying to count the CCTs you're holding in your hand. Are you supposed to count the pen and its cap as one thing or two? Or consider just the pen-sized CCTs. Are you holding at least eighteen such CCTs: pen; blue-ink pen; ballpoint pen; capped ballpoint pen; blue-ink ballpoint pen; capped, blue-ink pen; capped, blue-ink ballpoint pen; blue-capped pen; blue-capped ballpoint pen; blue-capped, blue-ink ballpoint pen; writing implement; capped writing implement; blue-ink writing implement; capped, blue-ink writing implement; blue-capped writing implement; and blue-capped, blue-ink writing implement? (Whew!) On some ways of counting CCTs, all of the items captured by those eighteen count nouns are distinct CCTs, but on other, no less sensible ways of counting CCTs they're not. Do you also count the pen's barrel shell, ink cartridge, metal tip, and its 'proper parts' such as one-centimeter undetached cross-sections of the barrel shell? Any pen less one of its atoms is (still) a pen-sized CCT; do all of those CCTs count too? The answers to these questions all depend on arbitrary specifications of 'CCT'. There's no nonarbitrary count of the CCTs you're holding.[15]

Second, the proper *parts* of an individual substance don't, at any given time, belong to the same substantial kind as the individual substance itself. By contrast, at any time at which a CCT and its proper parts exist, both the CCT and its proper parts *are* CCTs. At no time is a penguin's beak a penguin, but at any time at which both exist each of them is a CCT. Some examples might seem to cast doubt on my claim about individual substances and their parts, but not if we consider the examples carefully. A rock can break into halves, each of which is then a rock, but the original rock and the two smaller rocks don't coexist. The smaller rocks don't exist before the original rock breaks in half—if the rock has proper parts, those proper parts aren't (yet) *rocks*—and the original rock ceases to exist (or at any rate ceases to be *a rock*) when it breaks in half. If you join two garden hoses by (for example) screwing one into the other, you thereby create a CCT having

---

15. For a somewhat more detailed discussion, see Maitzen 2012, especially 53–5. See Thomasson 2007 for more on the use of a single term such as 'thing' (or in our specific case 'CCT') to 'cover' items belonging to disparate substantial kinds. I should note that even a metaphysically *simple* CCT, assuming such a thing is possible, gives rise to this counting problem. As long as the CCT satisfies some predicate P, there will be a CCT and a P-satisfying CCT in the same location. Is that one CCT or two?

proper parts that are both CCTs and garden hoses. But strictly speaking you don't thereby create a single *garden hose* with proper parts that are garden hoses: instead, you create something you might use as if it *were* a single garden hose. (If the sign at the store says 'Any Garden Hose for $20', you won't have much luck getting the manager to regard two joined hoses as one.) But because 'CCT' doesn't denote a substantial kind, you *can* join the two hoses, each of them a CCT, to create a single CCT.

Third, there's a nonarbitrary answer as to whether a given penguin *persists* from one particular time to another, say, during the year between your visits to the penguin enclosure at the zoo. But the same can't be said for a CCT as such. For 'CCT' might refer to a mereological sum of atoms now, as it happens, arranged 'penguin-wise', a sum whose persistence conditions differ markedly from those of a penguin. If a single atom belonging to that sum undergoes radioactive decay (and is thereby replaced by a numerically different atom), the sum but not the penguin ceases to exist, and the penguin can cease to exist (at a minimum, by postmortem decomposition) even if the atoms belonging to the sum (and thereby the sum) continue to exist. Or 'CCT' might refer to that same sum of atoms *in precisely the shape it now has*, in which case it doesn't persist for more than an instant. Both of those sums are CCTs, but depending on which one of them (or which other thing, such as a penguin) you arbitrarily refer to by 'CCT', the CCT in question persists throughout that year or not.

Fourth, it's conceptually impossible, or at least highly implausible, that two instances of the same substantial kind should *coincide* in space and time, but it's not impossible, or even highly implausible, that two CCTs should coincide in space and time.[16] Even if you insist that (i) a penguin and (ii) that same penguin minus one of the feathers it now has both count as *penguins*— rather than, as I'd insist, one penguin and perhaps one of its proper parts— (i) and (ii) don't now coincide in space; instead, they imperfectly overlap. By contrast, the Venus de Milo and the hunk of marble that wholly constitutes it now coincide perfectly in space despite being, according to some plausible arguments, distinct CCTs. Moreover, the ability of CCTs to coincide in space and time—like the ability of a CCT's proper parts to count as CCTs—only adds to the difficulty of counting CCTs that I discussed above. A particular volume of space in the Louvre Museum contains exactly one statue, exactly one marble statue, exactly one sculpture, and exactly one Venus de Milo, but it's an arbitrary call exactly how many CCTs it contains.

These considerations show, I submit, that 'CCT' doesn't denote a substantial kind. In the phrase coined by David Wiggins (1967: 29), 'CCT' is a *dummy sortal*, a term that functions grammatically like a count noun but doesn't function logically like a count noun (see also Lowe 1989: 11, 25). Other dummy sortals include the nouns 'thing', 'object', 'individual', 'item', 'entity', 'existent', 'being', 'fact', 'event', 'cause', and (in the metaphysical

---

16. See Oderberg 1996 for a thorough defense of these claims.

sense) 'substance'. Because 'CCT' is a dummy sortal rather than a substance sortal, principle KI, even though it's true, *doesn't* rule out invoking only CCTs to explain why there are any CCTs.[17]

Moreover, the other dummy sortals I just listed *also* inevitably fail to denote kinds, even if they're qualified with 'contingent and concrete'. Three of the nouns on that list—'fact', 'event', and 'cause'—wouldn't likely be mistaken for substance sortals, but they share some of the hallmarks of terms that fail to denote kinds, including arbitrariness in counting and in judging persistence. How many facts are there? How many facts are there about penguins? Any answers to those questions are at best arbitrary, and moreover there are Cantorian reasons for thinking that those questions can't *have* correct answers.[18] How many events, and how many causes, occurred in the last hour? How long does a given event, such as the Battle of Hastings, last? When does a given cause stop and its effect begin? The arbitrariness of any answers to those questions suggests that 'fact', 'event', and 'cause' aren't any better than 'CCT' in denoting kinds, and hence it doesn't make any relevant difference if LQ is posed in terms of *those* dummy sortals instead. Finally, I should emphasize, the distinction between grammatical and logical function applies strictly speaking to the *concepts* corresponding to the English terms 'thing', 'object', 'event', and so on (compare Wiggins 1967). Therefore, it makes no relevant difference if LQ is posed in a language using different terms to express those same concepts.

But, one might ask, who cares whether 'CCT' or any other dummy sortal denotes a kind: why think that denoting or failing to denote a kind makes the crucial difference? Notice, however, that denoting or failing to denote a substantial kind makes other important differences, including the differences we just saw with respect to counting, parthood, persistence, and spatiotemporal coincidence. So there's some reason to think it might make a difference to how explanations work as well. Nevertheless, one might try to support Objection D by means of a stronger principle that makes no mention of kinds and *does* rule out invoking only CCTs to answer LQ:

> (PS) Where *F* is any predicate that applies to CCTs only, you can't explain why there are any *F* things *at all* by invoking only things that are *F*, even if your explanation goes on forever.

---

17. Conveniently for my purposes, Rowe commits just such a conflation of a dummy sortal ('dependent being') and a substance sortal ('elephant'): 'The question why there are any dependent beings cannot be answered by noting that there always have been dependent beings, any more than the question why there are any elephants can be answered simply by observing that there always have been elephants' (Rowe 1998: xiv).
18. See Grim 2000: 147–53.

The initials 'PS' will remind us that this principle concerns the explanation of *predicate satisfaction*. Because 'contingent and concrete' is a predicate satisfied by contingent, concrete things only, if PS is true then you can't explain why there are any CCTs at all by invoking only CCTs, even if your explanation goes on forever. But is PS true?

No: PS is too strong. Where the existence of things satisfying predicate G *explains* the existence of things satisfying predicate F, you can invoke G things to explain why there are any F things even if you thereby invoke only things that are (also) F. For example, let F be 'looks red to normal human observers in normal conditions', and let G be 'reflects light of wavelengths roughly in the range 630–740 nm' (the explanandum and the explanans are equally and appropriately vague). 'Because there are G things' is an adequate explanation of why there are any F things. (Again, 'Why are there any G things?' is a *different* question calling for a different answer.) Yet by invoking G things, the explanation thereby invokes only things that are also F. Indeed, scientific explanations such as the one I just gave commonly invoke some microlevel predicate in order to explain why things satisfy some macrolevel predicate, where satisfying the former nomically *necessitates* satisfying the latter. The explanation passes the test of KI because 'looks red to normal human observers in normal conditions' doesn't pick out a substantial kind, for all four of the reasons that 'CCT' didn't either. In any case, PS is false and hence useless as support for Objection D.

Now, one might add a rider to PS to avoid my counterexample:

> (PS*) Where F is any predicate that applies to CCTs only, you can't explain why there are any F things *at all* by invoking only things that are F, even if your explanation goes on forever, *unless* the existence of G things explains the existence of F things and being G implies being F.

Because of its 'unless' clause, PS* avoids my counterexample. But it simply begs the question against me to say that PS* rules out my invoking the existence of penguins to explain the existence of CCTs. For, I've argued, the existence of the former *does* explain the existence of the latter, and it's agreed on all sides that being a penguin implies being a CCT. So if PS* is the correct test after all, my explanation passes it.

In the context of LQ, 'CCT' seems to be what Amie Thomasson (2007: 117) calls a 'covering' term ranging conveniently over heterogeneous items. The term 'CCT' doesn't pick out a category, collection, class, or kind of thing requiring an explanation beyond the explanations available for the items covered by the covering term 'CCT'. However, in demanding an explanation of the existence of CCTs as such, Objection D treats 'CCT' as if it did denote a kind of thing whose instances ought to have *an* explanation appropriate to *things of that kind*. I've tried to show why it's a mistake to treat 'CCT' that way: although the label 'CCT' of course *applies* to every CCT—to every pen, penguin, plum, and so on—CCTs don't form a kind. They don't share a genus. They don't have a common essence.[19]

Again, in rejecting my explanation of the existence of CCTs, Objection D seems to assume that penguins are just *instances* of the kind *contingent, concrete thing*—in which case of course it wouldn't suffice for me to invoke the existence of penguins to explain why that kind *has* any instances. Likewise, if you want to explain why there are any penguins—any instances of that substantial kind at all—it won't suffice to invoke the existence of emperor penguins, which are already instances of the kind *penguin*. 'Because there are emperor penguins' is a bad answer to the question 'Why are there any penguins at all?' (even if it's a sufficient answer to the question 'Why are there any penguins at all left on earth?' in circumstances in which emperor penguins are the only penguins left on earth). But it doesn't follow that 'Because there are penguins' is a bad answer to the very different question 'Why are there any CCTs at all?'

Objection E: Your explanation fails because it isn't a *causal* explanation. You don't show, nor is it true, that the existence of penguins is what causes CCTs in general to exist. Relatedly, your explanation doesn't sustain the required *counterfactual conditional*: it's simply not true that CCTs wouldn't exist if penguins didn't exist.

Reply: True, I don't give a causal explanation. For three reasons, I don't claim that (a) particular penguins or (b) the existence of penguins *causes* (c) the existence of CCTs. First, (b) and (c) are states of affairs, or facts, rather than events or instantaneous physical states, so I think that (b) and (c) can't literally be causes or effects. Second, and more important, I'd never rest my case on an appeal to causation, because the metaphysics of causation is too poorly understood: so poorly, in fact, that anyone demanding a *causal* explanation, in particular, owes us an account of causation that improves on the broader concept of explanation that we employ. No such account exists, to my knowledge.

Fortunately, however, our ability to explain things doesn't await our discovery of an uncontroversial account of causation. Not all good explanations are causal: 'because' differs from 'cause'. To recall my earlier example, (d) things exist that look red because (e) things exist that reflect light of a particular range of wavelengths, but we needn't therefore say that (e) *causes* (d), especially since causation, if it's anything at all, is a relation holding not between abstract states of affairs but between events or between instantaneous physical states.

---

19. Even if all genuine CCTs are instances of kinds, that wouldn't imply that *CCT* is *itself* a kind whose instantiation deserves its own explanation. Each of the items I bought yesterday is an instance of a kind, which doesn't make *item I bought yesterday* a kind unto itself, let alone a kind whose instantiation requires an explanation beyond the explanations available for each item I bought yesterday.

Third, and finally, I don't know how to make sense of the claim that anything causes CCTs *in general* to exist: as I emphasized in reply to Objection D, CCTs don't form a kind whose instantiation ought to have a uniform cause, or a uniform explanation, in the first place. To put it somewhat differently, there isn't *a general way* in which CCTs come into existence: depending on the *kind* of CCT, some (such as tables) are made, some (such as penguins) are born, and some (such as icebergs) simply arise, with naturalistic explanations available in each case.

It's also true that my explanation doesn't sustain the counterfactual conditional 'CCTs wouldn't exist if penguins didn't exist'. But not all good explanations sustain a counterfactual conditional of the form 'If the explanans hadn't existed (or occurred), the explanandum wouldn't have either'. In cases of explanatory overdetermination, such a counterfactual doesn't hold: we can explain the presence of mud on the carpet by blaming the plumber—'There's mud on the carpet because the plumber tracked it in'—even if the electrician would have tracked in mud regardless of the plumber's conduct. The fact that the blame is shared doesn't make either party blameless. Explanatory overdetermination is exactly what occurs in the case of penguins and CCTs: there are CCTs because there are penguins and also because there are pens. (Again, to ask why there are penguins or pens is to make a *different* explanatory demand.) There's of course a counterfactual in the neighborhood that my explanation does sustain: penguins wouldn't exist if CCTs didn't exist. But my explanation's success doesn't depend on its sustaining any counterfactual conditionals.

Objection F: Even if we allow an endless regress of explanations, and even if natural science can explain every CCT *in* that regress, your naturalistic method of explanation can't, even in principle, explain the existence of *the whole regress*. As Hume has Demea say in the *Dialogues*, 'The question is still reasonable, why this particular succession of causes existed from eternity, and not any other succession or no succession at all' (Hume 1779/2007: 64; see also Rowe 1998: 264–5).

Reply: What do the phrases 'the whole regress' and 'this particular succession' even mean? If they refer to the *set* whose members are all and only the CCTs that have ever existed, then the objection simply misfires, for to explain each member of a set *is* to explain the set. Any set's identity is determined wholly by the members it contains. It's therefore confused to ask why, for example, the set {Mars, Saturn} has the members it does rather than having other members (or no members) instead.[20] Likewise, since on this interpretation the

---

20. Rowe acknowledges this confusion in the preface to Rowe 1998. So instead of asking, as he did in Rowe 1970, 'why the set of dependent beings has the members it has, rather than other members or none at all', he asks 'why the property of being a dependent being is exemplified' (Rowe 1998: xix).

objector accepts the existence of sets in general, the question 'Why does the set {Mars, Saturn} exist at all?' reduces to the question 'Why do Mars and Saturn exist at all?' The latter question surely admits of a naturalistic answer.

Barring circular explanations and facts that have no explanation, my naturalistic strategy proposes to account for 'this particular succession' of CCTs by explaining every CCT in terms of other CCTs. Such a strategy produces an infinite regress of explanations, but our discussion of Objection C revealed nothing vicious about that regress. Yes, at every step in the regress we encounter something that didn't have to exist, but that fact doesn't make what we encounter at any step inexplicable. Moreover, we don't *want* an explanation that makes 'this particular succession' of CCTs necessary, or else we lose the contingency of each of the particular CCTs that belong to the succession. Nor does the endlessness of the regress imply that 'the whole regress' is itself unexplained. By analogy, the Peano axioms of arithmetic 'explain' how to generate each positive integer by starting with zero and using the *successor* function; no one, I take it, regards the axioms as insufficient for explaining 'the whole regress' of positive integers just because every positive integer *has* a successor.

If the objector still complains that we fail to explain 'the whole', that we fail to explain 'why there's a succession of CCTs at all rather than none', then I believe Objection F simply restates Objection D by tacitly relying on principle KI: the objector uses 'CCT' as if it denoted a kind whose instantiation can't be explained by invoking what the objector wrongly thinks are instances *of* that kind. To sum it up as a dilemma: Either 'Because there are penguins, and penguins are CCTs' is an adequate answer to 'Why are there any CCTs at all?' or else the question is ill-posed because it demands an explanation for a kind of thing when there's no such kind.

5 VARIANTS OF LQ

Variants of LQ, if they're well-posed questions at all, also admit of naturalistic answers. Take, for example, the question 'Why does the universe exist?' Again, presumably the questioner is asking about contingent and concrete (rather than noncontingent or abstract) aspects or inhabitants of the universe and hence won't be satisfied by a Platonistic answer invoking necessarily existing abstract objects. In that case, then, asking 'Why does the universe exist?' amounts to asking (again) 'Why are there any CCTs at all?', the question I've already answered naturalistically. Or perhaps it's the question 'Why are there *these* CCTs rather than none at all?', which seeks explanations for

---

My answer to the latter question should be easy to predict: 'Because there are penguins, and penguins exemplify that property'. Given that 'dependent being', like 'CCT', fails to denote a substantial kind, my answer doesn't violate principle KI.

particular *kinds* of CCTs (or instances of those kinds): penguins in general (or particular penguins), pens, plums, etc. There's every reason to think such questions have naturalistic answers, and I've diagnosed various confusions behind the insistence that they don't. Or perhaps it amounts to asking 'Why are there these CCTs rather than *other* CCTs?', a somewhat strange question: 'Why are there penguins rather than unicorns?' or maybe 'Why have only *n* penguins actually existed rather than *n* + 1?' Those questions, to the extent to which they make sense, seem to admit of naturalistic answers: there's no reason to think that just any species we can imagine would evolve into existence; we can in principle explain the species that did evolve and the circumstances in which their specimens did or didn't reproduce.[21]

Someone who finds David Lewis's modal realism plausible might try to revive the question 'Why does the universe exist?' as a principled challenge to naturalism by recasting the question as 'Why does the actual world exist?', where the actual world is as Lewis describes it: a concrete object including, or consisting of, everything spatiotemporally related to whoever asks the latter question. According to Lewis, however, the question poses no deep problem: of necessity, *all* possible worlds exist, and 'actual' is only an indexical term referring to the single world inhabited by whoever uses 'actual' on that occasion. On Lewis's view, 'Why is our world actual?' makes no more sense, or at any rate is no harder to answer, than 'Why is here here?' In responding this way, I don't mean to endorse Lewis's controversial ontology of possible worlds, only to show that someone who does accept that ontology has an easy way of dissolving the question 'Why does the actual world exist?'

A different attempt to revive LQ as a challenge to naturalism might be to ask 'Why isn't the actual world a world *without* CCTs?', where the questioner rejects Lewis's indexical analysis and uses 'actual' to designate our world rigidly. In one sense, this question also has an easy answer, or at least it doesn't require the kind of explanation we'd require for a contingent fact, because if 'actual' *rigidly* designates our world, then it's metaphysically necessary that the actual world contains exactly the CCTs that our world contains. World-indexed truths are metaphysically necessary truths. But suppose we waive this objection and agree that the question deserves a less trivial answer. In that case, we can reply as I already have: there are (for instance) penguins, which are CCTs, and hence the actual world contains at least some CCTs. Notice that it would add nothing for the questioner to point out that there didn't *have* to be penguins; no one is claiming there had to be.

Still another attempt to revive LQ as a challenge to naturalism tries to recast it so it falls within the scope of KI, the correct principle of explanation I discussed earlier: 'Why is it that, for at least one substantial kind K, there

21. This assumes, against Kripke 1980: 24, 156–7, that unicorns clearly *could* have existed and, against some systems of modal logic, that there *could* have existed individuals that in fact never exist.

are instances of kind K?'[22] On inspection, however, this question can *also* be answered simply and naturalistically: 'Because there are penguins, and *penguin* is a substantial kind'. One might object that it can't be answered that way, that invoking instances of some substantial kind K can't explain why there are instances of *any* substantial kinds in the first place. But that objection commits essentially the same error we saw in Objection D. Objection D, recall, mistakenly assumed that 'CCT' is like 'penguin' in denoting a substantial kind; again, if that assumption were true, then principle KI *would* rule out invoking only CCTs to explain the existence of CCTs. Similarly, the new objection mistakenly assumes that 'instance of a substantial kind' denotes a substantial kind, i.e., that 'substance' is a substance sortal rather than a dummy sortal. But clearly 'substance' isn't a substance sortal, for all four of the reasons I discussed earlier involving counting, parthood, persistence, and spatiotemporal coincidence.

I don't deny that substantial kinds *exist*; after all, I just appealed to one in answering a variant of LQ. Nor do I deny that we can quantify over both instances and kinds: 'There are instances of the kind *penguin*' and 'Some kinds are instantiated' are both true. None of my answers to LQ imply the contrary. Some may think that no naturalistically acceptable answer can invoke *kinds* as such, on the grounds that kinds (if they're anything) are abstract objects that naturalism can't accommodate. I disagree that naturalism can't accommodate abstract objects.[23] But I can concede the point for now and emphasize, as I did earlier, that my *answer* to the original version of LQ—my answer to 'Why are there any CCTs at all?'—doesn't invoke the existence of kinds; it invokes only the existence of penguins, which are concrete objects if anything is. True, I appealed to kinds in rebutting some confused *objections* to my answer. But I don't compromise the naturalistic character of my answer if I appeal to kinds in rebutting objections that *presuppose* the existence of kinds. In answering the latest variant of LQ, I explicitly invoked the substantial kind *penguin*, but the variant of LQ that I was answering was itself *couched* in terms of kinds, making it appropriate for me to invoke a kind in answering it.

I'll conclude by discussing one last variant of LQ. Michael Burke poses a question that might be thought to refute my claim that explaining each particular CCT suffices to explain why there are any CCTs at all. He asks, 'Why isn't it the case that matter never has existed?' or, more perspicuously, 'Why has matter ever existed?' According to Burke, the law of the conservation of matter can explain why, at any time *t*, matter exists *if* matter has ever existed, but it can't explain why matter has existed in the first place (Burke 1984: 357). Burke's argument for this point isn't entirely clear to me, but it

---

22. I owe a version of this objection to an anonymous referee for Maitzen 2012.
23. Especially if we construe naturalism as the claim that nothing *supernatural* exists—i.e., no nonphysical *minds*, *agents*, or *causes* exist. Abstract objects, being nonsupernatural, are compatible with naturalism thus construed.

looks as if he's tacitly relying on principle KI: invoking the existence of matter at an earlier time may explain matter's existence at all later times, but it doesn't explain why matter has existed rather than not.

Now, if 'matter' denotes a kind of substance, then KI implies that you have to invoke something other than matter in order to explain why matter has existed at all. But there's at least one reason to doubt that 'matter' denotes a kind.[24] Presumably, the parts of any bit of matter are all themselves matter, which sets 'matter' apart from mass nouns that uncontroversially denote kinds, such as 'water' and 'gold'. Not all of the parts of water are themselves water—some are hydrogen atoms, others oxygen atoms—and not all of the parts of even the purest sample of gold are gold—some are protons, others neutrons, and there's no such thing as a gold proton or neutron. But even if, contrary to the reasoning I just gave, 'matter' turns out to denote a kind, it's open to natural science to explain the existence of matter by invoking something other than matter. For example, physicist Lawrence Krauss's book *A Universe From Nothing: Why There Is Something Rather Than Nothing* (Krauss 2012), despite its misleading title, offers to explain the emergence of matter from 'quantum vacuum states' that, while not themselves nothing, are supposed to be something other than matter.[25] Therefore, like LQ and the other variants of it that I've considered, Burke's variant poses no insurmountable challenge to naturalism. Only confusion accounts for thinking otherwise.[26]

REFERENCES

Burke, M.B. (1984). 'Hume and Edwards on "Why Is There Something Rather Than Nothing?"', *Australasian Journal of Philosophy* 62: 355–62.

Craig, W.L. (1991). 'The Existence of God and the Beginning of the Universe', *Truth: A Journal of Modern Thought* 3: 85–96.

Gale, R.M. (1991). *On the Nature and Existence of God*. Cambridge: Cambridge University Press.

Grim, P. (2000). 'The Being That Knew Too Much', *International Journal for Philosophy of Religion* 47: 141–54.

Hume, D. (1779/2007). *Dialogues Concerning Natural Religion*, ed. Dorothy Coleman. Cambridge: Cambridge University Press.

Krauss, L.M. (2012). *A Universe From Nothing: Why There Is Something Rather Than Nothing*. New York: Free Press.

Kripke, S.A. (1980). *Naming and Necessity*. Cambridge, MA: Harvard University Press.

---

24. For further reasons to doubt that it does, see Maitzen 2012: 61.

25. Krauss's explanation invokes gravity in order to explain how the emergence of matter (strictly, mass-energy) from something other than matter nevertheless obeys the conservation laws of physics (Krauss 2012: 99).

26. For helpful comments, I thank John Danaher, David Duffy, Tyron Goldschmidt, Morgan Harrop, Colton Heiberg, Felipe Leon, Rohan Maitzen, and Joshua Rasmussen. I thank Springer Science+Business Media for kind permission to reproduce parts of Maitzen 2012.

Leibniz, G.W.F. (1697). 'The Ultimate Origin of Things'. Translated and edited by Jonathan F. Bennett, http://www.earlymoderntexts.com. Last amended July 2007, accessed June 1, 2012.

Lowe, E.J. (1989). *Kinds of Being*. Oxford: Basil Blackwell.

Maitzen, S. (2011). 'On God and Our Ultimate Purpose', *Free Inquiry* 31, 2 (February/March): 35–7.

———. (2012). 'Stop Asking Why There's Anything', *Erkenntnis* 77: 51–63.

Maitzen, S. and Wilson, G. (2003). 'Newcomb's Hidden Regress', *Theory and Decision* 44: 151–62.

Morreall, J. (1980). 'God as Self-Explanatory', *Philosophical Quarterly* 30: 206–14.

O'Connor, T. (2008). *Theism and Ultimate Explanation: The Necessary Shape of Contingency*. Malden, MA: Blackwell.

Oderberg, D.S. (1996). 'Coincidence Under a Sortal', *Philosophical Review* 105: 145–71.

Rowe, W.L. (1970). 'Two Criticisms of the Cosmological Argument', *The Monist* 54: 441–59.

———. (1998). *The Cosmological Argument*. New York: Fordham University Press.

Thomasson, A.L. (2007). *Ordinary Objects*. New York: Oxford University Press.

Van Inwagen, P. (1996). 'Why Is There Anything at All?', *Proceedings of the Aristotelian Society*, supp. vol. 70: 95–110.

Wielenberg, E.J. (2009). 'In Defense of Non-Natural, Non-Theistic Moral Realism', *Faith and Philosophy* 26: 23–41.

Wiggins, D. (1967). *Identity and Spatio-Temporal Continuity*. Oxford: Basil Blackwell.

16 Ontological Pluralism, the Gradation of Being, and the Question "Why Is There Something Rather Than Nothing?"

Kris McDaniel

1 INTRODUCTORY REMARKS

Ontological pluralism is the view that there are modes of being, ways of existing, or different ways to be something. Ontological pluralism is an intriguing and alluring doctrine, despite its present unpopularity.[1] If it is true, many metaphysical questions must be rethought. One of these is the question of why there is something rather than nothing.

More generally, being wrong about being often leads to being wrong about many ontological questions. Besides denying that there are modes of being, a second, and perhaps even more widespread, mistake made about being is the denial that there are gradations of being, that some things exist more than others or enjoy more being than others. The claim that there are gradations of being also makes more complicated the question of why there is something rather than nothing.

There are both obvious and nonobvious reasons why these doctrines make more complicated the question of why there is something rather than nothing. Let's briefly mention the obvious reasons first. If there are modes of being, that is, different ways *to be*, then either in addition to *or instead of* the question "Why is there something rather than nothing?" we should pursue, for each mode of being, the question of why there is, in that way, something rather than nothing. Similarly, if there are degrees of being, one might wish to ask why something exists to this degree rather than some other degree, rather than simply ask the question of why there is something rather than nothing. As we will see in a bit, on my view, the question of why there is something rather than nothing is not actually a fundamentally important question, and so I would recommend pursuing these other questions *instead of* rather than *in addition to* it. But, as I hope will be clear shortly, on my view the more important questions are *whether* there are things that

---

1. I've defended ontological pluralism in McDaniel (2009), (2010a), (2010b), and (manuscript). Turner (2010) provides a fantastically detailed defense of the view as well.

exist to the fullest degree and, if so, why they exist to that degree rather than to some lesser degree.

In order to better appreciate some of the nonobvious reasons why considerations of modes and degrees of being make more complicated the question of why there is something rather than nothing, some background regarding how I've approached modes and gradations of being will be useful. In the next section, I provide this requisite background.

In order to avoid excessively cumbersome sentences in the pages that follow, I will henceforth use "ontological pluralism" to refer to the doctrine that there are modes of being, "the gradation thesis" to refer to the doctrine that there are gradations or degrees of being, and "the Question" to refer to the question of why there is something rather than nothing.

2 MODES OF BEING AND DEGREES OF BEING

I have found it helpful to think about modes of being and degrees of being in terms that most contemporary metaphysicians are more comfortable with, specifically, by way of the notion of *naturalness* or *structure* as employed by David Lewis (1986), Theodore Sider (2009, 2011), and others. Here I recapitulate the main moves; interested readers are invited to delve more into the details in other published work.[2]

First, we embrace an objective ranking of properties and relations: some properties and relations are *more natural* than others. This objective ranking of properties is *fully comprehensive*: every property or relation appears at some place in the hierarchy. This does not mean that the hierarchy is linearly ordered; it only means that every property or relation bears the *is at least as natural as* relation to some property or relation. But I do accept that the hierarchy terminates at an upper bound: at the top of this hierarchy are the elite, perfectly natural properties and relations, those for which no other property or relation is more natural.

Every property appears in the naturalness hierarchy. Some properties or relations are higher-order properties or relations, that is, are properties or relations *of* other properties or relations. Finally, some of these higher-order properties or relations correspond to quantifiers; we can, if we like, take the semantic value of a quantifier to simply be either a property of properties or a kind of relation between properties; I won't settle this question here. But there is some property or relation that corresponds to the unrestricted existential quantifier of ordinary English, and it appears somewhere in this objective naturalness ranking. Let us call this property *being*.

Being is the "semantic value" of the ordinary unrestricted existential quantifier, the one that is sometimes employed by members of *our* linguistic community. But there could have been other linguistic communities who

---

2. Specifically, see the works described in note 1.

engage in a practice that looks from the outside very similar to the practice of existentially quantifying: such a community would have a primitive expression in their language that functions syntactically and inferentially like the existential quantifier of English. (Perhaps there are even actually such communities, but whether there are—and why there are rather than are not—are not questions that I will pursue here.) Let us call a (possible) expression that functions syntactically and inferentially like an existential quantifier an *e-quantifier*, even when the semantic value of an e-quantifier is not being but some other property. Let us call the semantic values of these e-quantifiers *modes of being*, an expression that is admittedly somewhat infelicitous given that the extensions of some modes of being properly include the extension of being itself. Let us say that a *genuine mode of being* is a mode of being that ranks *at least as high* on the naturalness scale as *being* itself. Let us say that a *fundamental mode of being* is a perfectly natural mode of being. One enjoys a mode of being just in case one falls within the range of the possible e-quantifier that corresponds to this mode. Fundamental entities enjoy fundamental modes of being. In general, let us say that the *degree of being* enjoyed by some entity is proportionate to the naturalness of the *most* natural mode (or modes) of being enjoyed by that entity.

Are there any fundamental entities? I will assume so for the purposes of this paper, though it is certainly worth wondering what kind of argument could be given for the claim that there are fully real entities. One initial, and extremely hazy, thought is that there must be fundamental entities if there are to be any entities at all, since all facts about what there is are ultimately to be accounted for in terms of what fundamental entities there are. In short, there must be fundamental entities because there is something rather than nothing. But it is surprisingly hard to extract a nonhazy thesis from this hazy thought.

Let us turn to the question of whether *being* is itself a fundamental mode of being. In my view, it is not. Elsewhere, I have argued from the fact that shadows, holes, cracks, and other entities that I call "almost nothings" exist to the claim that being itself is not a fundamental mode of being.[3] Here is one thread of this argument. Holes exist, but they are less real than their hosts. An entity's amount of being is proportionate to the naturalness of the most natural possible e-quantifier that ranges over it. So being cannot be a fundamental mode, for if it were, then holes would be as real as their hosts, since both holes and hosts enjoy being. (Recall that, on my system, an entity's degree of being is proportionate to the naturalness of its most natural mode of being.)

So being is not itself a fundamental mode of being. Perhaps this shouldn't be terribly surprising. Natural language did not evolve for the purposes of doing metaphysics or, for that matter, any theoretical inquiry. So it would actually be somewhat surprising if it turned out that we have managed to select

---

3. Specifically, in McDaniel (2010a).

as semantic values for any ordinary locution a property or relation of central importance to metaphysical inquiry. That said, it is an interesting question why being ended up as the semantic value for the ordinary unrestricted English quantifier.

I grant that part of what determines the semantic values of expressions is how high the candidates for being these values rank on the naturalness scale. But how we use these expressions obviously also plays a rather large role, as does the environment we find ourselves in. The latter two components are not always independent—if the only things in our environment were colored black and white, we would have far less of a need for many of our color expressions, and it is likely that if they were used, they would enjoy a different use. But we are finite embodied beings, and I believe essentially so, and this finitude constrains use independently of whatever environment we happen to find ourselves in. In any world possible for creatures like us to be found, there will be perforated objects such that facts about them will not be communicable by creatures like us without them making reference to holes, without counting and hence quantifying over holes, without making comparative qualitative judgments concerning holes and other entities, without ascribing numerical identity to holes across times (and perhaps across possible worlds), and so forth. One can produce "paraphrases" of such talk only if one can construct sentences of infinite length, since, for most sentences about holes, there are infinitely many ways perforated objects could make them true. A god could produce such paraphrases—but not creatures like us. Embodied finite creatures like us are doomed to use e-quantificational expressions in such a way that they are not apt to have as their semantic values fundamental modes of being. So, in my view, being is not a fundamental mode of being, but there is a good explanation for why a more fundamental mode of being was not selected as the semantic value of the unrestricted English quantifier. And this explanation will, of course, generalize to any other natural language spoken by human beings and even, I believe, to any finite and embodied creature.

So I think there are deep reasons why we did not end up selecting a perfectly natural mode of being to serve as the semantic value for ordinary quantificational claims. What is the upshot of these reflections for the Question? The question "Why is there something rather than nothing?" has seemed to some philosophers, perhaps most famously Heidegger, to be an important or deep question to ask. But the notions of something and nothing do not carve nature at the joints. If a necessary condition for a question being metaphysically deep rather than metaphysically shallow is that the concepts used in forming the question must carve nature at the joints, then the Question is a metaphysically shallow question.[4] In this case, there is a more specific reason to think that the Question is a shallow question, which

---

4. Compare with Sider (2011), especially chapters 4 and 12. I am deeply indebted to Sider's work on this topic.

will be discussed in the next section. Whether there is a better question to be asked will be examined in succeeding sections.

3   GLOBAL ABSENCES AND THE QUESTION

It is an interesting question whether there are general patterns to our use of quantificational expressions that can be distilled to and so expressed in the form of explicit conditionals that link whether some situation obtains with whether something exists. It seems to me that there are such patterns, given the strong tendency we have to engage in reification. Here are some illustrative examples of sentences we all endorse. If you and I are both heading north, *there is* a direction that we are both heading in. If you have as many socks as I have guitars, *there is* a number that is the number of your socks and my guitars. If you believe that God exists and I do not, *there is* something that you believe that I reject. And so forth.

As I said, each of these sentences just mentioned is true. In fact, something stronger is the case: each of these sentences is *obviously* true. Moreover, the antecedents of many of these kinds of sentences are clearly true as well. And who would dare to deny *modus ponens*? It is clear and obvious that there are directions, numbers, and contents of beliefs, i.e., propositions. Of course, many clever philosophers have contorted themselves or at least the words they speak by attempting various "paraphrase" strategies for doing away with these entities, but none of these strategies has been successful. In fact, the same sort of reason why finite, embodied beings like ourselves cannot do away with talk of holes also explains why we are not in the position to do away with talk of these other entities.

Does this mean that there really are such entities as directions, numbers, and propositions? Yes, there really are such entities—that is, there are such entities. Often, the word "really" serves mainly as a means to emphasize the point the speaker means to convey, as when one says, "Yes, tax cuts for the extremely wealthy really don't contribute to economic growth." That said, it might be that there is also a *metaphysical* use for the word "really"—when one asks whether there are *really* numbers, what one might have in mind is whether numbers are *fully real*, whether a kind of quantification that encompasses numbers in its domain might be a fundamental kind of quantification. And as I see things, the jury is still out on the question of whether there *really* are directions, numbers, or propositions. That is, in my terminology, it is clear that such entities exist, but it is less clear whether they fully exist.

As mentioned earlier, there is a kind of systematicity to our pattern of reification, that is, our use of quantificational expressions. And this is partly why the semantic value of these quantifier expressions helps ensure that certain bridge principles connect the obtaining of certain situations with the existence of certain entities. Sometimes these bridge principles take the form of biconditionals as well. One of the most celebrated cases of such a biconditional was championed by Frege and states that the number of Fs is equal to the number of Gs if and only if there are exactly as many Fs as there are Gs. The left-hand side of the biconditional is "ontologically committed" to the existence of numbers. But for our purposes here, we will focus on a much more ignominious biconditional, which links the existence of some things to the absence of others.

I suspect that given the way in which we use quantificational expressions and other attendant vocabulary, the following is true: the absence of Fs exists if and only if there are no Fs. In general, we freely and happily traffic in absences. We count them, we dwell on them, we mourn because of them. We even attribute causal relevance to them. Causation by absence must be admitted. Omissions cannot be omitted. Moreover, we treat absences with sufficient seriousness to classify them into kinds: shadows are certain kinds of absences of light, holes are certain kinds of absences of matter, droughts are absences of rain, and so on.[5]

Now, for the purposes of considering the Question, it is important to assess whether or not a full description of our ordinary practices of quantifying over, predicating properties of, and classifying distinct kinds of absences would provide a compelling reason to attribute the biconditional mentioned earlier, namely, that the absence of Fs exists if and only if there are no Fs. For if it does, we have an answer as to why there is something rather than nothing. Even if there were nothing else, the absence of everything else would exist and hence would be something. (Note that these sorts of biconditionals that encapsulate our reificatory practices are not plausibly taken to be merely contingently true. For example, if there are numbers whenever there are equinumerous groups, then it is not a contingent fact that there are numbers whenever there are equinumerous groups.)

Seriously think of how tempting this line of thought has been to generations and generations of teenagers who think about the question of why there is something rather than nothing. This line of thought is often their opening move! Often, they express this line of thought in a way that makes philosophers unhappy. Perhaps they utter the following words, "There must be something, for even if there were nothing, nothing would itself be something." And perhaps philosophers are right to be unhappy, since the standard philosophically regimented use of the phrase "nothing" employs it as a quantifier rather than a name. Of course, expressions can be used in many ways, and even "nothing" can be used as a referring expression if one so desires—and the absence of everything else is as good a thing to be referred to by the word "nothing" as anything else could be. Perhaps the ordinary person thinking about the Question equivocates when she uses the word "nothing"; in its first appearance in the sentence above, it is functioning as a quantifier, but in its second appearance it functions as a referring expression

---

5. On seeing absences, see Sorensen (2008).

for a global absence of everything else. Who knows for sure? But this is one way in which someone could use these words, and this way of using them would certainly fit with what seem to be our conventions governing the vocabulary of absences, namely, to say that an absence of Fs exists when there are no Fs.

Let me be clear: it is not clear that the line of thought mentioned above is correct. But it is also not clearly incorrect. I suspect it is true, but I have no idea how to provide a conclusive argument for the claim that, given what we have ended up meaning by "there is", this abstraction principle expresses a truth. But what I am relatively sure about is that there is little to be said that favors our actual way of using "there is" over this possible way of using "there is", if these two uses do not in fact coincide. If anything, this putative alternative use of "there is" uniformly codifies the relevant abstraction principle and so provides the basis for a principled account of when absences exist rather than the mere hodgepodge we would be left with if this putative alternative use is genuinely an alternative use. So, from a metaphysical perspective, this alternative e-quantifier might be in better shape with respect to naturalnesss than being itself, albeit perhaps only slightly better. It is hard to for me to see how the Question as standardly understood then could be a metaphysically deep question to be asking, since on either way of using expressions such as "there is" the question does not carve nature at the joints.

Of course, none of this shows that absences are *really* real (that is, full existents) or that a scenario in which the only thing that existed would be the absence of everything else is a scenario containing a fully real being. I am certain that absences, even putative global absences, are not fully real beings and that the notions of "something", "there is", and the like are all doing very poorly on the naturalness scale. But nonetheless there are absences. And there is some evidence, which is of course inconclusive, that the notions of something and nothing that we use when asking the question are such that it follows from them that there must be something rather than nothing. But I think that once we see why this might be the case, we also see that we shouldn't be as interested as we once were in the question of why there is something rather than nothing. If *this* is the reason why there must be something, then the question was not a question truly worth pursuing.

Are there better questions to be pursued? This of course remains to be seen. But we should note that many of those who claim to be interested in the question of why there is something rather than nothing are really interested in a narrower question, such as the question of why there are "concrete material things" rather than no "concrete material things". When asking this narrower question, however, one still uses the ordinary quantifier expression, a device not well suited for asking fundamental ontological questions. So I suspect we will be better served if we abandon this device and stipulatively introduce new e-quantifiers that have as their semantic values whatever we take to be the fundamental modes of being. (If it turns out that such modes of being already have a linguistic home in ordinary language, so much the better, but I am doubtful that this is the case.) Then, once we have done this, we can see whether for each such e-quantifier E_n, there is an interesting, well-formed question of why $E_n x\ E_n y\ (x = y)$ rather than $\sim E_n x\ E_n y\ (x = y)$. Call a question of this sort a *Narrow Question*. Of course, it will be very hard to assess whether there are better Narrow Questions without having good evidence as to what the fundamental modes of being are, and acquiring such evidence is an arduous task indeed. And frankly it's not a task that I have completed. Accordingly, what follows will be both highly speculative and provisional. I will focus on ontological schemes that have the following features: first, they enjoy some independent plausibility and are supported by arguments to be found in the contemporary philosophical literature, and, second, they seem to generate potential roadblocks to the possibility of interesting Narrow Questions being formed.

4   POSSIBILITY AND ACTUALITY AS MODES OF BEING

Here we will consider an ontological scheme according to which the merely possible and the actual enjoy different modes of being, both of which are fundamental modes of being. On this view, there are talking donkeys and there are ordinary zebras, but the way in which there are talking donkeys is not the way in which there are zebras. This is a bare-bones statement of the view, but it will be helpful to put some flesh on these bare bones. Behold the meat of modal realism!

The version of modal realism to be discussed is a refinement of Phillip Bricker's modal realism with absolute actuality.[6] On this view, the difference between the merely possible and the actual is not some property that the actual possesses but the merely possible lacks, or vice versa. In fact, possible objects can be qualitative duplicates of actual objects. Just as some actual objects are individuals or substances (rather than sets, properties, or propositions), among the merely possible are individuals or substances. Possible objects can stand in various relations to one another, including the relation of part to whole. Call a relation an *external* relation just in case it does not supervene on the intrinsic properties of the things it relates but does supervene on the intrinsic properties of the whole composed of the things it relates. (Perhaps distance relations are external relations in this sense.) Say that some things are *externally related to each other* just in case they are the relata of some external relation. Perhaps *being related to each other* is a transitive relation, but perhaps not. But in any event the transitive closure of this relation is a transitive relation; call this relation the *C* relation. Say that some things, the *T*s, are *maximally C-related* just in case each of the *T*s

---

6. See Bricker (1996), (2001), and (2006) for articulations and defenses of his version of modal realism with absolute actuality.

is C-related to each of the *Ts*, and none of the *Ts* are C-related to anything that is not one of the *Ts*. Finally, say that a *possible world* is a whole that is composed of maximally C-related things.

Once we have possible worlds in our picture it seems that we can offer a standard account of metaphysical (*de dicto*) possibility in terms of truth at some world and of metaphysical (*de dicto*) necessity in terms of truth at all worlds. But let's note that although one important motivation for embracing possibilism is to provide an analysis of modal notions, it is not the only one. Perhaps it is not even the most important motivation. For the sake of reflection on the Question, and the possibility of interesting variants, we'll consider a version of possibilism that doesn't try to *reduce* metaphysical modality to quantification over possible worlds but still accepts that the biconditionals linking possibility and necessity to truth at a world or all worlds are true.[7] But since we are formulating a version of modal realism in the context of ontological pluralism, we need to be careful when using words like "some" or "all" when stating these biconditionals. There are two fundamental e-quantifiers in play, one of which ranges over the merely possible, and will accordingly be designated by "E_p", and one of which ranges over the actual, and will accordingly be designated by "E_a". Any "unrestricted" quantifier that ranges over the domains of both of these quantifiers is less natural than either quantifier. If one of our projects is to give an account of a modal operator that can preface one of these quantifiers, it is clear that "E_a" is one we want to have prefaced. *But it is not clear that it even makes sense to preface the possibilist quantifier with a modal operator.* This is important, because if it doesn't make sense to preface the possibilist quantifier with a modal operator, then the narrow question of $E_p x\ E_p y$ $(x = y)$ rather than $\sim E_p x\ E_p y\ (x = y)$ is not a legitimate question. That narrow question is a legitimate question only if the presupposition that it makes sense to assert that the alternatives are genuinely possible is correct.

In general, if there is a mode of being such that modal notions do not even apply to it—if, to speak metaphorically, the things enjoying this mode of being are *amodal* rather than denizens of modal space—then the narrow question of why there are things having this mode of being rather than not is an illegitimate and, in fact, ill-formed question.

Let's sharpen the idea that there might be an e-quantifier such that it is in principle not capable of conjoining with a modal operator to form a well-formed sentence. In section 2, I explained the view that there are modes of being—ontological pluralism—by way of there being an objective

---

7. Note that I am focusing on this version of possibilism not because it is the version I find most plausible but because consideration of this version provides a route to seeing how certain ways of replacing the Question with narrower versions of it will not succeed. In the next section, we will discuss the consequences for the Question if modal notions are in some way reduced, and hence are nonfundamental.

naturalness ranking that applies to the metaphysical correlates of quantifier expressions. But if we liked, we could state ontological pluralism as the view that there are possible languages containing semantically primitive quantifiers (e-quantifiers) that are maximally natural expressions and hence are at least as natural as the unrestricted quantifier.[8] This formulation sets aside the question of whether natural expressions need to derive their naturalness from their corresponding semantic values; this is an interesting question, but we won't pursue it here, and it might well be that the two formulations of ontological pluralism are harmlessly interchangeable if the naturalness of an expression must derive from the naturalness of its semantic content. But in any event, for the purposes of this section, it is worth bringing into the forefront the vehicles that carry these semantic values.

Let us call a language that contains only perfectly natural expressions a metaphysically perfect language. Given ontological pluralism, a metaphysically perfect language will contain multiple quantifiers. Given a commitment to multiple fundamental quantifiers, it is natural (but of course not mandatory) to hold that there are distinct sets of variables associated with these quantifiers. That is, the metaphysically perfect language is multisorted.[9] For each set of variables, there will be a maximal set of terms that are their possible substitution instances. These sets will not overlap.

Once we have sorted variables, we need to think about what sorts of predicates are in the metaphysically perfect language. Broadly speaking, it will contain two kinds of predicates, *intracategorial* predicates and *intercategorial* predicates. An intracategorial predicate is such that it can meaningful prefix only terms from exactly one maximal set of terms. An intercategorial predicate can meaningfully prefix terms from more than one maximal set, but for each such predicate, there will be syntactic rules governing how that predicate can combine with these terms. Whether a predicate is an intracategorial predicate or an intercategorial predicate is as much a function of its logical form as whether that predicate is, e.g., a one-place or two-place predicate.

The logical form of the predicate is shown by the range of open sentences one can construct with the predicate. The phrase 'x_1 is to the left of x_2' is an open sentence in which the predicate 'is to the left of' appears, while 'x_1 is to the left of' fails to be an open sentence. On the view under consideration, the *sort* of variables matters as much as the number of variables. One can

---

8. This is the "minimal" version of ontological pluralism; McDaniel (2009, 2010b) also discusses an Aristotelian version of ontological pluralism according to which some semantically primitive quantifiers are *more* natural than the unrestricted quantifier.

9. In my previous work, I did not discuss the possibility of sorting. Turner (2010) explicitly discusses this issue but opts to focus on a version of ontological pluralism that makes use of single-sorted variables. In McDaniel (manuscript-2), I explore in more detail the consequences of multisorted fundamental languages for principles of recombination.

begin with an open sentence, replace a variable of one sort with a variable from another sort, and end with something that fails to be an open sentence.

Now, we've been talking about the logical form of predicates, but in principle there is no barrier to distinguishing sentence operators in a similar way. So, as before, we can distinguish two kinds of operators. Let us call an operator a *broad* operator just in case it can yield a grammatically well-formed sentence when it prefaces any closed sentence, regardless of the kinds of quantifiers, variables, predicates, or names contained within that sentence. Let us call an operator a *narrow* operator just in case it is not broad.[10] Probably purely logical operations such as sentential negation will be broad operators. But *if* there is an operator for metaphysical modality in the perfectly natural language—and it is far from clear that there is—it is still an open question whether it is a broad or a narrow operator.

Now, I haven't given an argument that such an operator would be a narrow operator. But we can now see how it might fail to be intelligible to ask why $E_p x \, E_p y \, (x = y)$ rather than $\sim E_p x \, E_p y \, (x = y)$. Such a question is intelligible only if we can produce a well-formed sentence by prefacing "$E_p x \, E_p y \, (x = y)$" with a modal operator. It might be that we can sensibly ask why $E_a x \, E_a y \, (x = y)$ rather than $\sim E_a x \, E_a y \, (x = y)$, since the "actualist e-quantifier" is one to which a fundamental modal operator can be attached. And certainly, *if* there is such a fundamental operator that can be attached to a perfectly natural e-quantifier, then there is at least one deep question that we can ask instead of the question of why there is something rather than nothing. But we still must be cautious, since there are other modes of being for which the question of why some things enjoy that mode might not even be sensibly asked. The version of possibilism discussed here is one such view. There might be others.

Consider a kind of classical theism, for example, in which God exists in a fundamentally different way from the ways in which all other things are. Perhaps for each nondivine mode of being, expressed by "$E_n x$", it makes sense to ask why $E_n x \, E_n y \, (x = y)$ rather than $\sim E_n x \, E_n y \, (x = y)$. But perhaps with respect to the divine mode of being, "$E_d x$", the question of why $E_d x \, E_d y \, (x = y)$ rather than $\sim E_d x \, E_d y \, (x = y)$ isn't legitimate since claims about the possibility of one of these "alternatives" are not even well formed. On this view, rather than saying "there is no potentiality in God", it really doesn't even make sense, at a fundamental level, to ascribe potentiality to such a being.

In the previous section, I presented a reason to think that the question of why there is something rather than nothing was, from the metaphysical perspective, a surprisingly superficial question. Reflection on why this might be the case prompted us to see whether there were narrower questions than the Question that might be metaphysically deep. It turns out that *being*

---

10. I'm being somewhat lazy here and focusing only on "one-place" sentence operators; more complicated distinctions could and probably should be drawn once we stop being lazy.

itself ain't all it's cracked up to be. So this led us to the hope that we will do better if we focus on the fundamental modes of being rather than being itself. What we've seen in this section is that given ontological pluralism, we need to be cautious in assuming that, for each fundamental mode of being, there is a correspondingly deep question as to why there are things enjoying that mode rather than not. And we will see in the next section that there is a further complication: there might be grounds for thinking that there is no metaphysically fundamental notion of modality at all.

5 NONFUNDAMENTAL MODALITY AND THE PURITY OF THE FULLY REAL

The significance of the Question is also threatened if there is no metaphysically fundamental notion at all. In the previous section, we discussed a version of possibilism, which was a modified version of the form of modal realism defended by Bricker (1996, 2001, 2006) that took seriously the idea that the distinction between the possible and the actual is an existential distinction, i.e., a distinction between modes of being. In that discussion, we provisionally set aside that possibilists of this sort attempt to reduce modal notions to nonmodal ones; a consequence of this sort of reduction is that modal notions are not fundamental or perfectly natural. We will now no longer provisionally set the reductive project aside but take it in full to see its consequences for the Question.

One of the innovative ideas developed by Bricker is that we needn't analyze modal operators in terms of quantifiers over possible worlds. If we like, we can analyze them in terms of *plural* quantifiers over worlds; on this view, a proposition is possible just in case it is true at some world or at some *worlds*. And in this way we can reconcile the possibility of island universes with modal realism: although there is no world consisting of absolutely disconnected concrete chunks of reality, every pair of worlds consists of absolutely disconnected chunks of reality, and so the possibility of there being absolutely disconnected chunks of reality is thereby secured. One alternative proposal offered by Bricker is available for those unfamiliar with or squeamish about plural quantifiers; this proposal is to analyze modal operators in terms of what holds at *sets of worlds* rather than *worlds*: to be possible is to be true at some set of worlds. As before, the possibility of island universes is secured. Moreover, if we like, we can also secure the possibility of there being absolutely nothing at all. We have a choice: we can say that a proposition is metaphysically possible just in case it is true at some nonempty set of worlds, or we can say that a proposition is metaphysically possible just in case it is true at some set of worlds, including the empty set. Let me stress that for the possibilist of this sort, whether the possibilist includes the empty set in the range of the quantifier in terms of which the possibility operator is to be analyzed is a choice that is unconstrained by any "perfectly natural modal properties of propositions", since on this reductionist view there are no such properties. What is *fundamentally* there, for this possibilist, are the actual things, the various possible worlds and sets thereof, and nothing else. So, for this possibilist, the Question is not a deep question. The possibilist can select a meaning for the modal operator according to which the sentence "it is metaphysically possible that there are no actual things at all" expresses a truth, but she can also select a meaning according to which it expresses a falsehood, and *from a metaphysical perspective, neither choice is better than the other*. In this sense, "it is a matter of convention" whether there could be no actual things. It seems to me that the Question is much less exciting if it turns on what is "a matter of convention" in this sense.

And, of course, this version of possibilism is not the only view in modality on which modal notions fail to carve at the joints: there are many varieties of "modal conventionalism", "modal deflationalism", and the like.[11] But for our purposes we will set a detailed discussion of them aside and focus on whether the view that being comes in degrees provides a reason to think that modal notions are not fundamental. I will present an interesting but highly speculative and inconclusive line of thought beginning with the thesis that being comes in degrees and terminating with the thesis that modality is nonfundamental.

I've argued elsewhere that a sufficient condition for being a fully real entity is enjoying a perfectly natural property. This sufficient condition is the contemporary analogy of the medieval principle that beings of reason cannot enjoy real accidents or stand in real relations. Let's take this principle on board not because we are convinced that it is true but rather because we want to see where it leads. Very quickly we get an interesting result: any property shared by fully real entities and less than fully real entities is not a perfectly natural property. Consider *shape properties*, such as being cubical or being pyramid shaped. A beach ball, to which I will provisionally grant the status of a full existent, can enjoy being cubical, but so can a hole, and no hole is a full existent. So being cubical is not a perfectly natural property, given the just mentioned sufficient condition. Perhaps artifacts like pyramids enjoy full reality, but they also enjoy being pyramid shaped, a property that some weirdly situated lumps of trash might come to enjoy, and (so it seems to me) no arbitrary heap is a full existent. So being pyramid shaped is not a perfectly natural property—and so forth for other shape properties. As I mentioned, any property enjoyable by a less than fully real thing is not a perfectly natural property, and *this includes modal properties*. Any modal property enjoyed by a less than fully real thing is not a perfectly natural property, and this includes the property of possibly not existing: holes can be filled, shadows can be eliminated by sufficient illumination, and heaps can be swept away by winds of fate and fortune (or just ordinary wind). These conditions in which nonfundamental objects can go out of existence also indicate conditions under

---

11. See, for example, Cameron (2009) and Sider (2011: ch. 12).

which they never would have come into existence: being a contingent being is a property they enjoy and hence is not a perfectly natural property.

Of course, these are *de re* modal properties, but when we state the Question, the modal presupposition we make is a *de dicto* proposition. It is not that everything that there is is a contingent thing (or every concrete thing, or every actual concrete thing, or whatnot). It is that it is metaphysically possible that there is nothing at all (or nothing concrete, or nothing actual and concrete, or whatnot). The latter claim entails the former, but it is not at all clear whether the former entails the latter. And, more to the point, it is not clear what we should conclude about whether a notion of *de dicto* metaphysical possibility fails to carve at the joints simply because many (or even all) *de re* modal predicates fail to carve at the joints.

There is one way I see for moving from the claim that some entities enjoy less than full reality toward the conclusion that *de dicto* modality also fails to carve at the joints, but it is very contentious, although not without plausibility. First, it requires embracing the claim that linguistic expressions or concepts enjoy their degree of naturalness only derivatively, by standing for, referring to, or representing some entity or entities that enjoy that degree of naturalness directly. For example, one predicate is more natural than another predicate because the corresponding properties are correspondingly ranked. What, then, corresponds to sentence operators, if we wish to ascribe some degree of naturalness to them? Plausibly, if entities must be invoked, then the entities to be invoked are properties of abstracta such as propositions. On this view, the *de dicto* possibility operator corresponds to a property of propositions.

Given the sufficient condition for full reality mentioned earlier, whether this property is perfectly natural then crucially depends on the ontological status of propositions. *Metaphysical possibility carves at the joints only if propositions are fully real entities.* Perhaps propositions are fully real entities, but debating this would take up more space than is available. I find it interesting that the debate about whether the Question is a metaphysically important question could turn on the ontological status of abstracta, and this is so *even if the Question is narrowed to explicitly be about the possibility of there being no concrete entities.* The interesting upshot is this: if there is no fundamental modality, there is no fundamental way to state an alternative to the Question.

REFERENCES

Bricker, P. (1996). 'Isolation and Unification: The Realist Analysis of Possible Worlds', *Philosophical Studies* 84: 225–38.
———. (2001). 'Island Universes and the Analysis of Modality', in Preyer, G., and Siebelt, F. (eds.). *Reality and Humean Supervenience: Essays on the Philosophy of David Lewis.* Lanham: Rowman and Littlefield, 27–55.

———. (2006). 'Absolute Actuality and the Plurality of Worlds', in Hawthorne, J. (ed.). *Philosophical Perspectives*. Oxford: Blackwell, 41–76.

Cameron, R. (2009). 'What's Metaphysical About Metaphysical Necessity?', *Philosophy and Phenomenological Research* 79, 1: 1–16.

Lewis, D.K. (1986). *On the Plurality of Worlds*. Oxford: Blackwell.

McDaniel, K. (2009). 'Ways of Being', in Chalmers, D., Manley, D. and Wasserman, R. (eds.). *Metametaphysics*. Oxford: Oxford University Press, 290–319.

———. (2010a). 'Being and Almost Nothingness', *Nôus* 44, 4: 628–49.

———. (2010b). 'A Return to the Analogy of Being', *Philosophy and Phenomenological Research* 81, 3: 688–717.

———. (n.d.) 'Ontological Categories Are Modes of Being', (unpublished manuscript-2).

———. (n.d.) 'Ways of Being and Time', (unpublished manuscript).

Sider, T. (2009). 'Ontological Realism', in Chalmers, D., Manley, D., and Wasserman, R. (eds.). *Metametaphysics*. Oxford: Oxford University Press, 384–423.

———. (2011). *Writing the Book of the World*. Oxford: Oxford University Press.

Sorensen, R. (2008). *Seeing Dark Things*. Oxford: Oxford University Press.

Turner, J. (2010). 'Ontological Pluralism', *Journal of Philosophy* 107, 1: 5–34.

Contributors

EARL CONEE is professor of philosophy at the University of Rochester. His main areas of research are ethics, epistemology, and philosophy of mind, and he is the coauthor (with Richard Feldman) of *Evidentialism* (Oxford, 2004) and (with Theodore Sider) of *Riddles of Existence* (Oxford, 2005).

DAVID EFIRD is senior lecturer in philosophy at the University of York. He works mainly in metaphysics, philosophy of religion, and philosophical theology and has published articles in various academic journals.

TYRON GOLDSCHMIDT is lecturer in philosophy at the University of Wisconsin at Stevens Point. His research is mainly in metaphysics, philosophy of religion, and philosophy of mind, and he has published in academic journals.

JOHN HEIL is professor of philosophy at Washington University in St. Louis and honorary research associate at Monash University. His books include *The Nature of True Mind* (Cambridge, 1992), *From an Ontological Point of View* (Oxford, 2003), and *The Universe as We Find It* (Oxford, 2012).

CHRISTOPHER HUGHES is reader in philosophy at King's College London. He works in metaphysics, philosophical logic, philosophy of religion, and medieval philosophy, and his books include *Filosofia della Religione* (Laterza, 2005), *Kripke: Names, Necessity and Identity* (Oxford, 2004) and *On a Complex Theory of a Simple God* (Cornell, 1989).

SHIEVA KLEINSCHMIDT is an assistant professor at the University of Southern California, working primarily in metaphysics. She has published articles in *Philosophical Studies*, *Oxford Studies in Philosophy of Religion*, and *Philosophical Perspectives*.

MATTHEW KOTZEN is an assistant professor in philosophy at the University of North Carolina at Chapel Hill. He works mainly in epistemology, philosophy of science, and decision theory and has published in *Nôus*, *Mind*, and the *British Journal for the Philosophy of Science*.

MARC LANGE is Theda Perdue Distinguished Professor and philosophy department chair at the University of North Carolina at Chapel Hill. His books include *Laws and Lawmakers* (Oxford, 2009) and *An Introduction to the Philosophy of Physics* (Blackwell, 2002).

JOHN LESLIE is university professor emeritus at the University of Guelph and a fellow of the Royal Society of Canada. His books include *Value and Existence* (Basil Blackwell, 1979), *Universes* (Routledge, 1989), *The End of the World* (Routledge, 1996), and *Infinite Minds* (Oxford, 2003).

E.J. LOWE is professor of philosophy at Durham University. His books include *The Possibility of Metaphysics* (Oxford, 1998), *The Four-Category Ontology* (Oxford, 2006), *Personal Agency* (Oxford, 2008), *More Kinds of Being* (Wiley-Blackwell, 2009), and *Forms of Thought* (Cambridge, 2013).

STEPHEN MAITZEN is the W.G. Clark Professor of Philosophy at Acadia University in Nova Scotia, Canada. His main areas of interest are metaphysics, epistemology, and philosophy of religion. He has published in various academic journals as well as in some popular venues such as *Free Inquiry* magazine.

KRIS MCDANIEL is associate professor of philosophy at Syracuse University. He works mainly in metaphysics and has published several papers on meta-ontology, composition, persistence through time, and modality.

TIMOTHY O'CONNOR is professor of philosophy at Indiana University Bloomington. He is the author of *Persons and Causes* (Oxford, 2000) and *Theism and Ultimate Explanation* (Blackwell, 2008) and contributing editor of six volumes in philosophy of mind and action theory.

GRAHAM OPPY is professor of philosophy at Monash University. He is the author of *Ontological Arguments and Belief in God* (Cambridge, 1996), *Philosophical Perspectives on Infinity* (Cambridge, 2006), and *Arguing About Gods* (Cambridge, 2006).

GONZALO RODRIGUEZ-PEREYRA is a philosophy tutor at Oriel College and Professor of Metaphysics at the University of Oxford. He is the author of *Resemblance Nominalism* (Oxford, 2002) and several articles on metaphysics and early modern philosophy.

JACOB ROSS is an associate professor at the University of Southern California. He works primarily on ethics, epistemology, and practical reason. His works have appeared in *The Philosophical Review*, *Ethics*, and *The Philosopher's Annual*.

TOM STONEHAM is professor and philosophy department chair at the University of York. He works on philosophy of mind, metaphysics, and the history of philosophy. He is the author of *Berkeley's World* (Oxford, 2002) and various articles in academic journals.

Index